HOLLINS LOCAL HISTORY ROOM

VIRGINIA
ANCESTORS
AND ADVENTURERS

Compiled by

CHARLES HUGHES HAMLIN

Professional Genealogist

Member of
Sons of the American Revolution
Society of Colonial Wars
The Huguenot Society
The Jamestowne Society
Founders and Patriots of America
Virginia Genealogical Society
National Genealogical Society
American Legion
Veterans of Foreign Wars

929.1

H

Three Volumes in One

GENEALOGICAL PUBLISHING CO., INC.
BALTIMORE   1975

'75-05493

Originally Published
Richmond, Virginia

Volume 1—1967
Volume 2—1969
Volume 3—1973

Reprinted
Three Volumes in One
Genealogical Publishing Co., Inc.
Baltimore, 1975

Library of Congress Cataloging in Publication Data
Hamlin, Charles Hughes, 1907-
 Virginia ancestors and adventurers.
 1. Virginia—Genealogy. I. Title.
F225.H2252   929'.1'09755   74-18046
ISBN 0-8063-0642-4

Made in the United States of America

VIRGINIA
ANCESTORS
AND ADVENTURERS

Volume 1

VIRGINIA

ANCESTORS AND ADVENTURERS

TABLE OF CONTENTS

Dedication i

Preface ii

Foreword iii

SECTION ONE

Revolutionary War Size Rolls 1

Powhatan Courthouse 3
Carter's Ferry 7
Albemarle Courthouse 8
Cumberland Courthouse 16
Winchester Barracks 19

SECTION TWO

Proof of Importations 21

Abstracts of Original Court Records............... 25

Extracts from the Virginia Gazette 67

Census Records 75

SECTION THREE

Contributions by others 88

SECTION FOUR

INDEX

(1) Revolutionary War Size Rolls 105

(2) General 113

DEDICATION

To the young in spirit, who find excitement in the pursuit of truth,

And to the unsure, who are seldom quite positive when they have found it,

And to the perplexed, who wonder what to do with it afterwards,

And to the curious, but with some reservations in regard to meddling,

And to the debonair, who can take the bitter with the sweet, but who prefer the sweet,

And to the well-intentioned, provided they give us fair warning,

And to those who will allow us a little pride without asking what we are proud of, a difficult question at best,

And to all those nice people whose niceness is apparent without documentary proof,

To all of these this book is warm-heartedly dedicated.

--Anon.

PREFACE

My first words shall be for our ancestors; for it is both just to them, and seemly, that on occasions such as this that our tribute of memory should be paid them. For, dwelling always in this country, they have handed it down to us free by their exertions. So, they are worthy of our praises. While it is we, ourselves, who consolidated our power and secured independence, both in war and in peace.

Remember that this greatness was won by men with courage, with knowledge of their duty. So they gave their bodies to the commonwealth and received, each for his own memory, praise that will never die, and with it the grandest of all sepulchres. Not that in which their mortal bones are laid but a home in the minds of men, where their glory remains fresh to stir to speech or action as the occasion comes by. For the whole earth is the sepulchre of famous men; and their story is not graven only on stone over their native earth, but lives on far away, without visible symbol, woven into the stuff of other men's lives.

--Pericles of Athens
[c495-429 BC]

FOREWORD

"Oh, who will shoe yer foot, my dear?
And who will glove yer hand?
And who will kiss yer red rose lips,
When I'm gone to the Kentuck land?"

                              --Frontier Song

   I find the title, "Ancestors and Adventurers," intriguing and
fascinating, especially in combination and alliance with "Virginia".

   There is a certain 'joie de vivre' and pleasure in a happy combination of words. I am therefore a little proud that the three
volumes of "They Went Thataway" which have preceeded this compilation,
secured interest and favor by its title first and then by the nature
and type of material within its contents.

   Needless to say, it is sincerely hoped that this new series, of
like material, will enjoy equal success and be of equal benefit to
those interested in Virginia genealogy and the migration of their
ancestors.

   Ancestor is a good word and an interesting one to most of us. The
dictionary very coldly explains that it is derived from the Latin of
'ante' [before] plus 'cedo' [go] and that it means forefather; pro-
genitor; one from whom descent is derived. This is very satisfactory
for the dictionary.

   But, let us put the word ancestor in combination with the word
Virginia and immediately there is flashed upon the mind a much more
virile and vibrant image. An image of gentility, honor, chivalry,
character, bravery, etc.

   Sad to relate, sometimes ancestors, Virginia or otherwise, are
proclaimed by the ignorant, the jealous, and the small-minded, as
images of snobbery. We are not in the least concerned with these or
of their opinions.

   We are concerned with the historical fact that our ancestors
came to an alien and savage shore, found a nameless and hostile

continent, where they seated and maintained themselves upon their
individual plots of land. Never think that their land was a gift.
They worked for it, fought for it, and died for it. In the process
they built a nation. Thus, Virginia and the nation has a rich and
wonderful heritage which is now all too often taken for granted or
forgotten in our mad and frantic rat race of everyday living in
these so called days of progress.

Now then, when we add the word 'Adventurers' to the words,
!Virginia' and 'Ancestors' we conjure in our minds, as if by magic,
a truly proud and heroic image. We visualize a Virginia gentleman
ancestor who undertook ventures involving danger and risk. He was
necessarily bold, brave, and daring, of good breeding and education,
[sometimes imprudent and reckless]. In fact he had the qualities
and characteristics which we secretly desire in our own selves.

He was of that hardy breed which poured into Virginia from
England, Scotland, Ireland, Wales, France, and the Colonies to the
northwards and whose immediate descendants, in their turn,
"adventured" to the south and west to claim and settle new lands
and to endure and prevail against fantastic and excessive handicaps
and hardships.

The descendants of our adventuresome Virginia ancestors now
number in the millions and are scattered throughout the whole world.
I therefore 'venture' to suggest that it is not only our duty but
our very proud privilege to seek them out and by their sometimes all
too few records to know of them.

May our own efforts, in our own all too short time, be worthy,
and the dreams of our ancestors continue to be fulfilled by our
descendants.

> "So, take my hand and walk
> this golden land with me."

> --current song

May 1, 1967

Charles Hughes Hamlin
P. O. Box 3525
Richmond, Virginia   23234

VIRGINIA
ANCESTORS AND ADVENTURERS

SECTION 1

REVOLUTIONARY WAR SIZE ROLLS:

Location

   The Virginia State Library, Richmond 19, Virginia.

TITLE

   Revolutionary Army, Volume 1 - Register [Accession #24296]

SOURCE AND DESCRIPTION

   A Register and Description of Non-Commissioned Officers and
Privates at

                     Chesterfield Courthouse
                     Powhatan Courthouse
                     Carter's Ferry
                     Albemarle Courthouse
                     Cumberland Courthouse
                     Winchester Barracks

   These records are stated to have been removed from a collection of
miscellaneous military records which had been gathered together in one
bound volume entitled, "Papers Concerning the Army of The Revolution,
Volume 1" from which this material was extracted, restored and bound as
a separate item. The original "Papers....." are an Archives Collection
of long standing and there is, seemingly, no record of how it was acquired
or when.

COMMENT:

   The Chesterfield Courthouse "Size Roll" [generally designated as
the "Chesterfield Supplement"] is not included within this compilation
as portions of it appeared in "They Went Thataway, Vol. 3" [1966] by this
writer. All of the names of the soldiers of the other five rolls cited
above are included herein [total 802].

   In addition to the names of the soldiers on these rolls we have extracted the information as to the age given; his trade; place of residence
or enlistment; and place born.

   The original rolls include further information on each soldier as to
his size; color of hair, eyes, and complexion; status; date of enlistment;
former service; date sized; and remarks. If this additional information is

2

desired on a specific soldier, it may be obtained by writing the Archives Section of the Virginia State Library, Richmond, Virginia.

Some of the descriptions of the various soldiers are very interesting and contain such items as: well made - slim made - tender made - well set, etc. Some are noted as being bald - greyhaired - white beards - freckled - full faced - one white eye, etc. The complexions were generally noted as being yellow - fair - dark - red - pale - or fresh.

It should be noted that most of these names [some were left out] appear in Virginia Soldiers of the Revolution (1912 Supplement) by H. J. Eckenrode, Archivist. His list only includes the name, reference to source and place of enlistment. Many of these names on the original rolls were very dim or faint and some were almost illegible. In such cases a comparison of the name was attempted with the name as it was indexed by Mr. Eckenrode, who had access to the records more than 55 years ago. In most such instances his reading was accepted as being correct.

--Charles H. Hamlin

Noncommissioned officers and privates at

POWHATAN COURTHOUSE

Name	Age	Trade	Residence	Born
Nicholas Baker	26	butcher	Virginia	Culpeper
Bowling Bettisworth	19	planter	King George	Westmoreland
Elijah Barber	17	farmer	Stafford	Stafford
Hilbert Burch	21	blacksmith	Goochland	Goochland
John Banton	19	cabinet-maker	Powhatan	Powhatan
Robert Bradshaw	20	farmer	Goochland	Goochland
William C. Bailey	23	farmer	Fairfax	Fairfax
Robert Boxell	18	planter	Frederick	Westmoreland
Martin Biry	26	founderer	Frederick	Cork, Ireland
Thomas Bates	21	B.Smith	Fauquier	Fauquier
Andrew Barns	18	planter	Frederick	Virginia
Joseph Boxell	22	planter	Frederick	Virginia
John Brent	29	blacksmith	Berkeley	England
John Broomfield	39	Stocking weaver	Shenandoah	England
John Bradford	25	farmer	Shenandoah	Maryland
John Bowen	16	weaver	Berkeley	Virginia
John Brown	15	planter	Prince William	Prince William
Richard Barrett	19	planter	Westmoreland	Westmoreland
Thomas Brown	18	planter	Prince William	Prince William
Barnes Burns	28	carpenter	Spotsylvania	Leinster, Ireland
Richard B_____	23	planter	Westmoreland	Westmoreland
James Byas	20	shoemaker	Louisa	Louisa
Elijah Bluford	30	shoemaker	Northumberland	Northumberland
George Buford	17	planter	Northumberland	Northumberland
Samuel Barksdale	22	planter	Albemarle	Albemarle
Enoch Cox	19	planter	Culpeper	King George
Benjamin Cave	18	planter	Culpeper	Culpeper
John Campbell	26	planter	Culpeper	King William
George Coffer	22	planter	Culpeper	Culpeper
Charles Corbin	21	planter	Culpeper	Culpeper
David Canard	22	planter	Culpeper	Culpeper
Medley Chilton	19	planter	Middlesex	Culpeper
William Corder	23	planter	Fauquier	Fauquier
John Clark	32	planter	Orange	Canterbury, England
John Coopper [sic]	25	waggoner	Albemarle	Albemarle
Julius Chancillor	17	farmer	Goochalnd	Goochland
Peter Creek*	26	sadler	Stafford	"on sea"

*(former service 5 years 9th Pennsy Regt.)

Name	Age	Trade	Residence	Born
Charles Croucher	30	planter	Orange	Middlesex
Benjamin Collins	45	carpenter	Orange	Caroline
William Crause	30	turner	Pittsburg	England
James Canter	18	planter	Frederick	Virginia
John Canter	19	planter	Fauquier	Virginia
Thomas Coyl	21	planter	Frederick	Virginia
John Cook	26	planter	Shenandoah	England
Mathew Clay	35	planter	Shenandoah	England
Jeremiah Carnine	18	planter	Berkeley	Jerseys

4

Name	Age	Trade	Residence	Born
John Cross	20	planter	Berkeley	Maryland
Joseph Connor	20	blacksmith	Berkeley	Ireland·
Hugh Coffell	21	?	Prince William	Ireland
Solomon Garrell	25	planter	Orange	Prince George Co., Maryland
William Gipson	19	carpenter	Orange	Norfolk, Va.
William Garton	36	planter	Orange	Spotsylvania
John Glover	35	planter	Frederick	Ireland
Richard Gee	21	planter	Shenandoah	Shenandoah
Metcalf Gill	19	sailor	Northumberland	Northumberland
Joshua Gowin	22	carpenter	Louisa	Louisa
Ollivir Griffen	34	Indian-sailor	Northampton	Northampton
John Gunter	37	planter	Louisa	Lancaster (Va.)
Brumma Gee	23	tailor	Fairfax	Austalia [sic]*
James Grant	23	S.maker	Loudoun	Kilkany, Ireland
Thomas Giles	24	sailor	Northumberland	Crocican [sic] France
Thomas Goosebury	18	planter	Berkeley	Berkeley
Sherrod Griffin	20	planter	Amherst	Amherst
Jeremiah Greggory	20	planter	Amherst	Louisa
Alex. Gardner	34	planter	Augusta	Baltimore, Maryland
Thomas Goodman	17	planter	Berkeley	Baltimore, Maryland
Robert Grayson	19	planter	Spotsylvania	Caroline
Henry Gatteswood	29	planter	Spotsylvania	Spotsylvania
John Giles	39	carpenter	Bedford	Virginia
William Galley	21	planter	Loudoun	Dublin, Ireland
John Gentry	19	planter	Hanover	Hanover
Carter Garrett	16	planter	Louisa	Spotsylvania
John Gooddens	22	blacksmith	Charlotte	Halifax
Michael Guffie	22	?	Albemarle	Ireland
Richard Grinah	33	_____	Prince Wm.	Middlesex
Benjamin Hutson	19	planter	Culpeper	Culpeper
Joel Harvy	17	planter	Culpeper	Culpeper
William Hundren	36	weaver	Richmond Co.	Richmond Co.
William Haynie	25	planter	Culpeper	Culpeper
Richard Hudling (?)	17	planter	Fauquier	Fauquier
Isaac Howell	29	warter	Goochland	Powhatan
William Hix	37	cooper	Goochland	Hanover
Ralph Hughes	21	farmer	Stafford	Stafford
Thomas Horton	30	shoemaker	King George	Stafford
Morris Hassie	18	cooper	Fairfax	Waterford, Ireland
Jesse Humphrey	18	farmer	Caroline	King George
Benjamin Henson	20	planter	Amherst	Amherst
William Harrison	24	butcher	Fauquier	Chester, England
Zachariah Holladay	18	planter	Orange	Orange
Samuel Horton	17	planter	Albemarle	Nansemond
Josiah Harper	18	planter	Berkeley	Maryland
John Harper	22	planter	Berkeley	Maryland
Leonard Helm	21	planter	Frederick	Pennsylvania
Henry Howard	18	farmer	Berkeley	Virginia

---

*There is something wrong here as the first European settlement of Australia was not until 1788. Could this mean Austria?

Name	Age	Trade	Residence	Born
Thomas Howard	19	planter	Berkeley	Virginia
John Harper	19	planter	Berkeley	Pennsylvania
Richard Hill	20	cooper	Berkeley	Ireland
Edmond Harris	30	planter	Augusta	Ireland
William Hall	19	planter	Berkeley	Virginia
(?) Humphress	18	planter	Stafford	Northumberland
Patrick McNeel	18	Silversmith	Orange	Orange
Alexander McKinsey	23	hatter	Albemarle	Albemarle
Jacob Millar	19	blacksmith	Frederick	Pennsylvania
John Miller	45	planter	Berkeley	Ireland
Henry Myre	35	blacksmith	Berkeley	Holland
Daniel Martin	29	planter	Stafford	Stafford
William McMullion	23	sailor	Spotsylvania	Ireland
Spencer McDonald	22	planter	Fauquier	Fauquier
John Malery	21	planter	Louisa	Louisa
Moses Mott	23	planter	Northumberland	Northumberland
John McCray	32	planter	Louisa	Scotland
Benjamin McDanold	13	planter	Hanover	Caroline
John Martin	16	planter	Fluvanna	Fluvanna
Nathaniel Mitchum	50	bulletcaster	Dinwiddie	Sussex
Benjamin Man	31	planter	Louisa	King William
William Mullin	17	planter	Stafford	Caroline
Daniel McCartey	26	barber	Spotsylvania	Dublin, Ireland
Thomas Martin	19	farmer	Stafford	Pennsylvania
John McNeal	19	farmer	Loudoun	Fairfax
James Morton	20	tailor	Loudoun	Boston, Mass.
James McMullin	23	weaver	Loudoun	Cork, Ireland
Henry Mander	21	planter	Loudoun	Somerset, England
Ignatus Stevenson	30	carpenter	Culpeper	Middlesex
Frederick Shaw	32	planter	Frederick-Town, Md.	Germany
William Shepperd	19	farmer	Henrico	Henrico
John Sanders	16	farmer	Henrico	Hanover
Littleberry Scott	18	farmer	Henrico	Charles City
John Salmon	18	farmer	Goochland	Goochland
John Shaver	16	farmer	Fauquier	Pennsylvania
George Shaver	19	farmer	Fauquier	Pennsylvania
Paul Swaney	20	planter	King George	Stafford
John Smith	26	sailor	Fauquier	Jaimaca [sic]
Joseph Smith*	34	planter	Frederick	Frederick
*(former service 3 years 8th Penn. Regt)				
George Sheynar	35	tanner	Berkeley	Germany
David Spong	18	planter	Berkeley	Maryland
David Steel	24	planter	Shenandoah	Pennsylvania
James Shepherd	18	planter	Shenandoah	Virginia
George Shierman	22	planter	Shenandoah	Virginia
Jacob Seabourn	17	planter	Berkeley	Jersey
William Shope	19	sadler	Berkeley	Pennsylvania
Benjamin Steel	21	planter	Westmoreland	Westmoreland
William Sperling	18	planter	Westmoreland	Westmoreland
Mathew Stewart	34	carpenter	Caroline	Kingston, Jamaica
Richard Sto__?__	30	butcher	Prince Wm.	Middlesex, England
James Sprowse	40	planter	Fluvanna	Fluvanna

Name	Age	Trade	Residence	Born
William Sullins	19	planter	King William	King William
Archey Toney	19	planter	Goochland	Goochland
Manlove Tarrant	43	planter	Loudoun	Kent, Delaware
Thomas Tarrant	20	tailor	Amherst	Sussex, Jerseys
Joshua Tuggle	23	planter	Amherst	Goochland
William Taylor	32	planter	Essex	Richmond
William Taylor	23	planter	Berkeley	Pennsylvania
William Townshend	16	planter	Shenandoah	Frederick
John Taylor	—	planter	Hampshire	Baltimore, Maryland
Thomas Thomson	23	schoolmaster	Fairfax	Norfolk, England
Frances Tugger	28	farmer	King George	Virginia
Samuel Taylor	31	wagon Mstr.	Shenandoah	Jersey
Miles Travvis	28	planter	enlisted Berkeley	Ireland
John Thomas #1	30	S.maker	Caroline	Prince George
Byas Tomasson	24	planter	Louisa	Louisa
Spencer Thomas	24	planter	Northumberland	Northumberland
Rodham Trussell	24	wheelright	Northumberland	"
Job Thomas	30	planter	Northumberland	"
John Thomas #2	31	planter	Northumberland	"
Presley Terrill	18	planter	Orange	Frederick, Maryland
Henry Thomas	19	planter	Cumberland	Amherst
John Thomas #3	27	shoemaker	Northumberland	Northumberland
William Troop	19	planter	Westmoreland	Westmoreland
Rolin Williams	17	cooper	Henrico	Henrico
William Woodrum	18	farmer	Goochland	Goochland
Edward Whelor	23	joiner	Fairfax	Fairfax
Samuel Wright	19	farmer	Stafford	Caroline
Bailey Willis	15	farmer	Stafford	Stafford
Lewis Willies	16	planter	Stafford	Stafford
James Wright	27	B.layer	Albemarle	Repannie, Pennsylvania
James Williamson	19	S.Carpenter	Fairfax	Northumberland, England
Levy Williams	15	farmer	Fairfax	England
William Wilkerson	18	farmer	King George	England
John White	20	joiner	King George	England
Benjamin Wilkerson	20	planter	King George	England
Benjamin Woods	21	harness maker	Philadelphia	New York
Benjamin Wine	39	planter	Fauquier	Stafford
Gabriel Waren	32	carpenter	Orange	Spotsylvania
David Wright	19	fuller (?)	Frederick	Virginia
Thomas Warters	25	tanner	Frederick	England
John Wiseley	18	planter	Frederick	Pennsylvania
Stephen Weeks	19	cooper	Berkeley	Virginia
Philip Woolf	45	carpenter	Berkeley	Pennsylvania
Joseph Wigley	22	planter	Westmoreland	Westmoreland
Martin Walls (?)	37	tanner	Prince William	Jersey
William Willis	—	planter	Westmoreland	Suffolk, Va.
John Waley	19	turner	Caroline	Caroline
Clark Williams	16	planter	Northumberland	Northumberland
Thomas Waddy	19	planter	Northumberland	Northumberland

* * *

7

Noncommissioned officers and privates at

CARTER'S FERRY - 1781

Name	Age	Trade	Residence	Born
William Hughs	33	shoemaker	Caroline	Caroline
Charles Hoff	26	planter	Prince William	Hampton Jerseys
William Hail	21	planter	Westmoreland	Westmoreland
John Harper	18	planter	Berkeley	Philadelphia, Pennsylvania
Caleb Hipenstall	19	planter	Fluvanna	King George
Julius Holland	18	planter	Buckingham	Cumberland
Richard Henson	46	carpenter	Louisa	Westmoreland
Linth Helms	20	farmer	Frederick	Frederick
John Hendrick	26	planter	Louisa	Louisa
Rodham Harcum	23	sailor	Northumberland	Northumberland
Richard Hambey	24	planter	Loudoun	Lizleston, England
Thomas Hall	19	planter	Fairfax	Fairfax
William Higgins	25	butcher	Loudoun	London, England
Jasper Hover	48	planter	Loudoun	Germany
Zebedee Hall	24	planter	Fairfax	Fairfax
John Hinwood	25	joiner	Loudoun	London, England
Ruben Hoofman	23	cooper	Culpeper	Culpeper
George Holt	26	planter	Loudoun	Harford, England
John Hilliar	28	S.maker	Loudoun	London, England
Jacob Hall	23	planter	Fairfax	Fairfax
Thomas Hughs	21	planter	Stafford	Stafford
Joseph Howard	28	planter	Berkeley	England
James Hawkins	22	farmer	Frederick	Frederick
Joseph Horton	24	planter	Loudoun	Harford, England
James Pursell	38	carpenter	Prince William	Prince William
William Pettett	49	planter	Louisa	Ireland
William Pitman	18	planter	Northumberland	Northumberland
John Pettett	27	S.Maker	Fairfax	Fairfax
Charles Pearpoint	18	Indian	Loudoun	Frederick, Maryland
John Plod	28	planter	Amherst	Bremen, Germany
Everad Pullin	24	weaver	_____	_____
George Pigg	23	joiner	King & Queen	_____
John Plunckett	18	farmer	Berkeley	York Co., Penn.
William Pruett	25	planter	Bedford	Pittsylvania
Thomas Pruett	21	planter	Bedford	Pittsylvania
John Payne	19	planter	Spotsylvania	Spotsylvania
John Price	16	carpenter	Shenandoah	Shenandoah
Grief Peauman	16	_____	Charles City	Charles City
James Peace	16	_____	Rockingham	Virginia
William Price	20	shoemaker	Stafford	King George
John Pickett	23	sailor	Accomack	England
George Philby	34	_____	Accomack	North Carolina
Constant Plane	32	_____	Northampton	Hamburg
John Plumline	23	barber	Hampton	Germany
Benjamin Powel	20	_____	Accomack	Virginia
Obediah Plumley	20	_____	New Kent	New Kent
John Potter	19	_____	Fluvanna	Goochland
Benjamin Payne	20	_____	Buckingham	Buckingham

Name	Age	Trade	Residence	Born
____?____ Phillips	20	planter	Stafford	Stafford
Lewis Peyten	20	planter	Amherst	Amherst
Daniel White	23	carpenter	Brunswick	Brunswick
William Woolley	20	barber	Prince William	Westershire, England
David Wright	19	fuller	Frederick	Frederick
John Walker	28	farmer	Northumberland	Northumberland
Samuel Wright	20	shoemaker	Stafford	Caroline
Stephen Weeks	19	cooper	Berkeley	Berkeley
Joseph Watson	19	planter	Loudoun	Loudoun
Jesse Warton	19	planter	Loudoun	Loudoun
Thomas Wells	19	planter	Fauquier	King George
Benjamin Williams	21	S.maker	Henrico	Henrico
Job Worford	20	b.smith	Loudoun	Kingwood, Jerseys
Joseph Wilson	24	planter	Fauquier	Cork, Ireland
Joshua Wosham	36	planter	Chesterfield	Chesterfield
Michael Wilkerson	25	planter	Loudoun	St. Mary's, Maryland
John Whitman	28	weaver	Hampshire	Augusta
Jacob Westfall	29	farmer	Hampshire	Sussex, Jerseys
Lewis Wells	42	brewer	Frederick	Elur (?),Germany
Thomas Williams	60	planter	Berkeley	London, England
Samuel Weeks	16	planter	Hampshire	Virginia
John Williams	29	planter	Hampshire	Dublin, Ireland
Joseph Whipple	18	Wheelright	Frederick	New York
Jeremiah Walker	19	sadler	Amherst	Stafford
James Ware	19	planter	King & Queen	_____
___?___ ___?___	27	tailor	Pittsylvania	Chester, England

* * *

Noncommissioned officers and privates at

ALBEMARLE COURTHOUSE

Name	Age	Trade	Residence	Born
John Axline	21	planter	Hampshire	Bucks, Pennsylvania
Thomas Able	22	planter	Shenandoah	Shenandoah
Daniel Allen	19	planter	Amherst	Amherst
Reubin Alderson	26	planter	_____	_____
Issac(?) Alloway	41	planter		
Samuel Allen	18	planter	King & Queen	_____
Moses Allen	15	farmer	Hampshire	(?) Jersey
Elijah Abbott	19	planter	Stafford	Stafford
William Arnold	23	joiner	Spotsylvania	Spotsylvania
Masny Arrasmith	18	planter	Stafford	Westmoreland
Jesse Armstrong	19	planter	King George	King George
Jacob Anderson	22	planter	Hampshire	Prince William
Thomas Atkinson	17	planter	Caroline	Ireland)
Arthur Adison	17	_____	Northampton	Northampton
John Angel	22	cooper	Berkeley	Baltimore, Maryland
John Alford	27	tailor	Rockingham	Monaghon Ireland

Name	Age	Trade	Residence	Born
Christopher Baker	53	stiller	Hampshire	Germany
David Buffington	18	planter	Hampshire	Hampshire
Samuel Britman	27	planter	Berkeley	Bedfordshire, England
George Booker	19	weaver	Frederick	Frederick
John Bazill	17	S.maker	Berkeley	Baltimore, Maryland
Philip Bitgood	32	(?)	Augusta	Exeter England
John Brown	22	planter	culpeper	Spotsylvania
John Biggs, Jr.	27	farmer	Amherst	Baltimore, Maryland
Richard Bean	30	tailor	Amherst	Lancaster
Richard Burwell	17	planter	King & Queen	_____
James Bray	18	planter	King & Queen	_____
Philip Bowers	22	_____	King & Queen	_____
John Burcher	16	planter	Berkeley	Frederick, Maryland
Henry Brown	20	planter	Spotsylvania	King George
Benjamin Bowling	20	shoemaker	Spotsylvania	Prince William
Alexander Bonnell	44	shoemaker	Spotsylvania	Cork, Ireland
McD. Burnett	27	G.polisher	Greenbrier	Dublin, Ireland
Canada Bradshaw	17	planter	Bedford	Bedford
(?)ason Brown	20	planter	(?)	Cumberland
Jeumes Bears	21	planter	Cumberland	Loudoun
John Brunt	19	Blacksmith	Cumberland	Prince Edward
Robert Brown	16	planter	Goochland	King & Queen
John Brookens	27	planter	Culpeper	Orange
Griffis W. Beckham	20	shoemaker	Northumberland	Northumberland
James Bowser	19	_____	Nansemond	Nansemond
Southy Bayly	20	farmer	Accomack	Accomack
Zadock Bayly	16	farmer	Accomack	Accomack
John Bush	30	_____	Culpeper	Stafford
Cornelius Bybee	18	planter	Fluvanna	Fluvanna
Luke Brown	27	sailor	Fairfax	Kildeer, Ireland
James Bates	19	planter	Louisa	King George
Lott Bearcraft	15	planter	Northumberland	Northumberland
William Barnes	25	planter	Northumberland	Northumberland
John Bond	22	planter	Louisa	Louisa
Peter Bowls	23	planter	King & Queen	Gloucester
William C. Bugg	19	planter	Bedford	Fluvanna
Martin Bruton	23	s.maker	King William	Dublin, Ireland
Jeremiah Burns	18	wagoner	Stafford	Kilkaney, Ireland
John Beevers	20	planter	Loudoun	Hundredun, New Jerseys
Robert Briant	36	planter	Loudoun	Woster [sic] England
Henry Burns	32	planter	Loudoun	Waterford, Ireland
Frederick Burgit	21	planter	Hampshire	Maryland
Robert Brown	24	planter	Hampshire	Cumberland, Pennsylvania
Cornelius Batcheldor	23	wagoner	Loudoun	New York
Elias Barbee	18	planter	Culpeper	Culpeper

Name	Age	Trade	Residence	Born
Charles Biles	26	planter	Halifax	Fairfax
James Byrne	26	planter	Loudoun	Kilkaney, Ireland
George Barns	33	planter	Stafford	Stafford
Henry Brent	41	tailor	Fairfax	Fairfax
John Bolinger	21	s.maker	Berkeley	Bucks Co., Pennsylvania
James Berry	40	sailor	Hampshire	Limbrick, Ireland
Nicholas Best	16	farmer	Hampshire	Lancaster Co., Pennsylvania
Carfield Brown	19	planter	Culpeper	Culpeper
Sydner Cosby	18	planter	Louisa	Louisa
George Clutton	18	planter	Lancaster	Lancaster
William Cole	20	planter	Northumberland	Northumberland
John Crow	20	planter	Fluvanna	Ireland
Joshua Cockrill	19	sailor	Northumberland	Northumberland
Thomas Conley	31	b. smith	Albemarle	Fairfax
John Carrill	25	baker	Colechester, Connecticut	Colechester, Connecticut
Patrick Coleman	22	planter	Fairfax	Ireland
John Chubb	23	planter	Montgomery, Maryland	Montgomery Maryland
William Coleman	22	planter	Fairfax	Cork, Ireland
Sanford Carder	19	planter	Hampshire	Culpeper
Jesse Carter	18	planter	Hampshire	Prince William
Robert Collins	17	planter	Hampshire	Hampshire
Arthur Clay	25	planter	Shenandoah	England
Robert Corderrey	22	planter	Botetourt	Middlesex, England
Olliver Crafford	26	s.maker	Culpeper	Culpeper
Travis Chambers	25	cabinet joiner	Goochland	Amherst
William Coalter	26	b.smith	Albemarle	Lancaster, Pennsylvania
Rodham Clark*	28	planter	_____	_____
*(Drafted in Richmond County)				
Griffin Crush*	26	planter	_____	_____
*(Drafted in Richmond County)				
John Cotes*	24	planter	_____	_____
*(Drafted in Richmond County)				
Benjamin Carrell	27	s.maker	King & Queen	_____
John Conery	23	planter	Mecklenburg	Munster, Ireland
Robert Collins	24	planter	Berkeley	Cumberland, Pennsylvania
John Croucher	19	planter	Spotsylvania	Spotsylvania
William Cruse	32	planter	Westmoreland	Somersetshire, England
(?) ___ (?)	40	_____	Frederick	Armagh, Ireland
Thomas Dowell	37	planter	Prince William	Prince William
Henry W. Davies	22	carpenter	Fluvanna	Hanover
Ancill Davies	19	planter	Fluvanna	Cumberland
Samuel Decker	24	farmer	Hampshire	Hampshire
Peter Dunn	20	s.maker	Berkeley	Germany

Name	Age	Trade	Residence	Born
Alexander Dinney	30	planter	Frederick	Ireland
William Dyson	24	planter	Hampshire	London, England
Charles Dockerdy	54	planter	Lancaster, Pa.	N.Gall, Ireland
Robert Dobey	22	planter	Augusta	South Carolina
John Depriest	17	planter	Amherst	Amherst
David Davies	21	planter	Botetourt	Groten, Rhole Island
Thomas Duglass	21	planter	Northumberland	Northumberland
Alman Dunstan	19	planter	Glouster	_____
Thomas Davies	24	B.layer	Augusta	?
John Durham	18	planter	King & Queen	King & Queen
John Dayley	17	planter	Berkeley	Pennsylvania
Samuel Dobbins	50	planter	Bedford	Richmond Co.
William Donald	48	joiner	Fauquier	Chester, Pa.
William Davies	22	_____	Botetourt	Backenridge, New Jersey
Bartholomew Drake	20	b.smith	Bedford	Powhatan
Aquilla Davies	25	planter	Culpeper	Charles Co., Maryland
Thomas Donoho	19	planter	Cumberland	Essex
Edward Davies	21	____	Culpeper	Charles Co., Maryland
Benjamin Duvall	22	planter	Loudoun	Loudoun
John Foster	17	___	Prince William	Prince William
Edward Farr	23	weaver	Louisa	London, England
Eppa Fielding	25	sadler	Northumberland	Northumberland
John Fleming	23	sailor	Louisa	Louisa
John Franklin	20	carpenter	King William	Limbrick, Ireland
Patrick Francis	18	planter	Fluvanna	Fluvanna
Benjamin Fisher	17	planter	Essex	Essex
John Finix	22	planter	Northumberland	St.Mary's Co. Maryland
Nicholas Francis	23	s.maker	Loudoun	Burks Co., Pa.
John Fortune	18	farmer	Amherst	Amherst
John Fields	48	farmer	Amherst	Charles City
Edward Fathorn	30	b.smith	Amherst	London, England
James Fitzpatrick	30	planter	Hampshire	Pennsylvania
Samuel Fortune	32	planter	Powhatan	Caroline
Hezekiah Freeman	20	joiner	Culpeper	Gloucester
John Ford	27	planter	Culpeper	Culpeper
George Feegins	14	_____	Westmoreland	Westmoreland
George Francis	28	gardner	Lower Carolina	South Carolina
John Farrell	24	carpenter	Prince William	Prince William
Thomas Fisher	30	_____	Accomack	_____
John Francis	29	____	Gloucester	Ireland
Shadrack Fortune	24	____	Accomack	Accomack
William Foster	24	fuller	Elizabeth City	Warminster, England
William Floyd	18	farmer	Alexandria	Alexandria
George Fibbay	35	farmer	Accomack	Washington, North Carolina
John Finch	16	farmer	Prince William	Prince William
James Hagarty	25	planter	Hampshire	Tiroan, Ireland
Walter Hooper	20	planter	Frederick	Frederick
Joseph Hughs	30	planter	Hampshire	Frederick, Maryland
Henry Hatter	23	joiner	Buckingham	Wiltshire, England

Name	Age	Trade	Residence	Born
Bartholomew Homes	23	joiner	King William	James City
Zephaniah Harris	18	farmer	Louisa	Amherst
John Hughes	29	farmer	Loudoun	Frederick, Maryland
William Harris	40	planter	Prince William	England
William Houston	31	sadler	Spotsylvania	King George
Thomas Hagarty	23	ditcher	Spotsylvania	Ireland
Julias Holland (transferred) enlisted at Bedford Co.				
Charles Hardy	24	planter	Amherst	Albemarle
Bennet Hancock	18	shoemaker	Chesterfield	Chesterfield
Thomas Hall	22	_____	Chesterfield	England
William Holdaby	30	carpenter	King & Queen	King & Queen
William Haverd	17	planter	Loudoun	London, England
Joseph Hughs	31	planter	Culpeper	Newcastle, Pa.
John Henley	19	planter	King & Queen	King & Queen
William Habon	32	planter	Richmond	Westmoreland
Abraham Harrell	20	planter	Montgomery	Frederick
John Harrell	20	planter	Montgomery	Frederick
Phillip Hoil (?)	16	planter	Hampshire	Pennsylvania
Charles Holidy	41	planter	Culpeper	Culpeper
James Hagerty	25	planter	Hampshire	Ireland
Richard Hill	48	planter	Loudoun	England
Henry Jerdone	20	tailor	King & Queen	_____
Thomas Jackson	23	weaver	Bedford	London, England
John Jones	25	planter	Fauquier	Fauquier
James Johnson	15	planter	Chesterfield	Goochland
Richard Jones	18	planter	Charlotte	Charlotte
Charles Jenkins	17	planter	King William	Gloucester
William Johnson	25	Bricklayer	Goochland	Brunswick
Isaac James	21	planter	Northumberland	Northumberland
William Jones	25	planter	Accomack	Northumberland
John Joynes	24	____	Accomack	Accomack
Edward Joines	16	_____	Accomack	Accomack
William Johnson	19	_____	Accomack	Accomack
James Jackson	18	_____	Shenandoah	Culpeper
Zachariah Johnson	20	planter	Louisa	Northampton (North) Carolina
Jacob Johnson	21	weaver	Loudoun	Somerset, Jerseys
William Jacobs	21	planter	Frederick	King George
Joseph Jones	19	tailor	Fairfax	Prince George, Maryland
Benjamin Johnson	21	planter	Prince George, Maryland	Charles Co. Maryland
William Jackson	20	planter	Amherst	Albemarle
John Jones	33	S.maker	Greenbrier	(?)
John Jones	43	farmer	Rockingham	Shropshire, England
John Irwin	20	farmer	Rockbridge	Dublin, Ireland
Philip Johnston	27	farmer	Frederick	Caroline Co.,Va.
Thomas Jones	19	farmer	Calvert, Maryland	Calvert, Maryland
John Keen	18	wheelright	Spotsylvania	Spotsylvania
James Kirk	17	farmer	Stafford	Stafford
John King	22	farmer	Stafford	London, England

Name	Age	Trade	Residence	Born
Thomas Lind	35	stiller	Hampshire	Staffordshire, England
George Lower	50	carpenter	Hampshire	Philadelphia, Pa.
Richard Litteral	18	farmer	Amherst	Westmoreland
Mathias Long	21	Blksmith	Rockingham	Rockingham
William Lockward	20	planter	Amherst	Albemarle
Joseph Lewis	21	farmer	Berkeley	England
James Lines	50	planter	Cumberland	Charles City
James Lindsay	26	cop.smith	Spotsylvania	Philadelphia, Pa.
Andrew Leech	19	planter	Stafford	Spotsylvania
Phillip Lockart	15	planter	Amherst	Albemarle
John Rocke	25	planter	Augusta	Guonni (?) Whale(s) [sic]
Daniel Long	19	planter	Culpeper	Culpeper
Benjamin Loden	16	_____	Cumberland	_____
Joseph Lucas	21	_____	Powhatan	Powhatan
Nicholas Lambert	40	planter	Culpeper	Pennsylvania
Henry Linck	16	planter	Cumberland	Cumberland
Henry Lors	19	Silversmith	Frederick	Frederick, Md.
Francis Lucas	26	_____	Culpeper	Culpeper
Dennis Laughlin	28	turner	Northampton	Ireland
Lewis Linton	16	_____	Northampton	Accomack
Hubbert Lewis	22	planter	Dinwiddie	Dinwiddie
John Leonard	21	barber	Shenandoah	Germany
Robert Leonard	27	butcher	Augusta	Ireland
Joseph Lucas	19	planter	Montgomery	Henry [sic]
James Love	30	shoemaker	Lancaster	England
Manuel Lucas	17	farmer	Montgomery	Henry [sic]
Deddrick Leman	30	shoemaker	York	Germany
John Link	25	farmer	Shenandoah	Pennsylvania
Lewis Linton	19	farmer	Accomack	Accomack
Michael LaRues	35	glazier	Portsmouth	France
James McGraw	28	s.maker	Hampshire	Cork, Ireland
James McArthur, Sr.	50	weaver	Hampshire	Glasgow, Scotland
James McArthur, Jr.	16	weaver	Hampshire	Burlington,Jerseys
Thomas Mathews	21	draftsman	Frederick	Dublin, Ireland
Thomas Miller	33	planter	Essex	Amherst
Richard McCary	20	planter	Amherst	Amherst
George Mitchell	18	planter	_____	_____
(substitute - enlisted Richmond Co.)				
James Muir	21	joiner	King & Queen	_____
James Morris	20	waterman	King & Queen	_____
John McGuire	34	planter	Woster, New England	Ireland
Thomas May	27	_____	Berkeley	Cornwall, England
Henry Morris	34	planter	Hampshire	Bedford
Joseph McAfee	21	tanner	Caroline	_____
William McQuiddy	17	planter	Spotsylvania	Spotsylvania
Andrew Mitchell	51	s.maker	Rockingham	N.Castle (?)
Shadrack Munk	22	planter	Bedford	Halifax Co., North Carolina
Thomas McClanham	18	planter	Botetourt	Botetourt
James Murray	20	planter	Augusta	Cork, Ireland
John Massey	18	planter	Fluvanna	Buckingham

Name	Age	Trade	Residence	Born
William Morris	21	planter	Botetourt	Plymouth, England
Robert Melton	19	planter	Bedford	Albemarle
Thomas Morris	23	weaver	Augusta	England
John McKenny	49	weaver	Augusta	Scotland
Peter Moore	15	_____	Louisa	Orange
James Mason	27	_____	Hampshire	London, England
James McDonahou	50	_____	Richmond	Ireland
Richard Neal	22	carpenter	Fauquier	Queens Co., Ireland
Miles Northam	19	_____	Accomack	Accomack
Major Northam	25	_____	Accomack	Accomack
Richard Nicholas	23	_____	Northampton	Northampton
Jeremiah Neil	18	_____	Hampshire	Hampshire
John Quin	33	shoemaker	Amherst	London, England
Michael Reggers	21	planter	Loudoun	Maidenhead, Jerseys
John Ringo	18	planter	Loudoun	Amiwell, Jerseys
John Russell	21	planter	Loudoun	Loudoun
Phillip Richards	33	planter	King & Queen	_____
Thomas Rosewater	33	planter	Bedford	King William
Hugh Roak	40	planter	Amelia	Arma, Ireland
James Ross	47	planter	Spotsylvania	Hanover
Richard Rose	20	planter	Spotsylvania	King & Queen
Bartholomew Reason	20	planter	Culpeper	England
Cunrod Roller	29	planter	Loudoun	Bucks Co., Pa.
John Roller	22	planter	Loudoun	Bucks Co., Pa.
John Robertson	25	tailor	Loudoun	London, England
David Roach	24	planter	Rockingham	Orange
John Robertson	25	tailor	Loudoun	England
Thomas Rutter	19	____	Nansemond	Nansemond
Edward Riely	33	planter	Fauquier	Ireland
John Riley	45	planter	Fauquier	Ireland
John Rolls	48	planter	Caroline	_____
Jacob Riggs	15	B.smith	North Carolina	Accomack
Preeson Richards	19	_____	Accomack	Accomack
William Richards	16	_____	Northampton	Accomack
John Roberts	30	_____	Accomack	Accomack
Peter Redlock	40	planter	Dinwiddie	Dinwiddie
John Robertson	30	s.maker	Frederick	England
Charles Read	39	schoolmaster	Albemarle	Ireland
Frederick Ripl(?)	34	miller	Augusta	Germany
David Ray	17	planter	Amherst	Amherst
Alexander Roberts	16	planter	Amherst	Amherst
Samuel Swift	18	planter	Northumberland	Northumberland
Edward Sandford	24	planter	Westmoreland	Westmoreland
Anthony Surrough	20	sailor	Westmoreland	France
William Sneed	17	farmer	Hanover	Hanover
John Stowers	19	farmer	Loudoun	Market Harbour, England
John Speak	17	farmer	Fairfax	Fairfax
Frederick Sisson	18	planter	Loudoun	Northampton

Name	Age	Trade	Residence	Born
Cornelius Slacht	28	weaver	Loudoun	Maidenhead, Jerseys
Paul Shrye	17	planter	Loudoun	Pennsylvania
Daniel Simkins	63	planter	Frederick	Westchester, New York
George Sherman	20	planter	Shenandoah	Shenandoah
Ambrose Smith	23	planter	King & Queen	_____
Thomas Shackelford	20	planter	King & Queen	_____
Lewis Stoneberger	27	joiner	Shenandoah	Philadelphia, Pa.
Mathias Sheets	23	planter	Shenandoah	Lancaster Co., Pennsylvania
James Stephens	21	tailor	Spotsylvania	Spotsylvania
Patrick Swayney	20	planter	Loudoun	Ireland
John Smith	20	planter	Brunswick	Brunswick
Benjamin Smith	25	planter	Buckingham	Chesterfield
William Smothers	19	planter	Powhatan	Albemarle
Francis Scott	33	cooper	Scotland	_____
Allen Stubbs	15	planter	Prince William	Prince William
Midley Shelton	21	planter	Culpeper	Culpeper
Thomas Slape	19	_____	Albemarle	England
Thomas Toney	46	_____	Bedford	Hanover
William Tinsley	14	_____	Hanover	Hanover
Benjamin Slack	45	planter	Louisa	Stafford
Moses Self	20	planter	Northumberland	Northumberland
Benjamin Whiley	21	turner	King & Queen	King & Queen
Joseph Walden	21	planter	Henry	Cumberland
Aaron Woosley	21	planter	Henry	Cumberland
John Warren	23	planter	Spotsylvania	Spotsylvania
William Wall	19	planter	Culpeper	Culpeper
* Robert Wilcox	28	weaver	Loudoun	London, England
Henry Williams	18	_____	Botetourt	Bedford, Pa.
Godfrey Woolf	19	planter	Culpeper	Washington, Maryland
* Robert Wilcox	28	weaver	Loudoun	Ireland
* (note: may be the same soldier)				
William Walker	21	_____	Queen Ann, Maryland	Queen Ann, Maryland
John Weaver (negro)	25	planter	Richmond	Lancaster
Balsom Williams	22	_____	Bedford	Lancaster, Pa.
James B. Woodrum	17	planter	Goochland	Goochland
Robert Wooten	21	planter	Henry	Halifax
Clark Wise	22	planter	Culpeper	Culpeper
John Warren	14	planter	Chesterfield	Chesterfield
William Wash	26	planter	Louisa	Louisa
John Wavers	18	planter	Shenandoah	Pennsylvania
Alexr Whisler	20	planter	Middlesex	Middlesex
Benjamin Wine	40	planter	Stafford	Stafford
Clark Williams	15	planter	Northumberland	Northumberland
Roger Williams	17	planter	Northumberland	Northumberland
Argyle Wilkins	19	planter	Northampton	Northumberland
Peter Wall	20	planter	Dinwiddie	Dinwiddie
Robert Walden	18	planter	Dinwiddie	Dinwiddie
Edward White	66	distiller	Botetourt	England
Abraham Warwick	30	_____	Frederick	Loudoun
Thomas Wade	16	_____	Hanover	Louisa

Noncommissioned officers and privates at

CUMBERLAND COURTHOUSE

Name	Age	Trade	Residence	Born
Shadrack Battle	26	planter	Louisa	Albemarle
John Brown	34	saddler	Washington	England
Reuben Bussiplin	23	_____	Essex	Essex
Tarpley Bailey	21	sailor	Westmoreland	Fairfax
Jacob Borah	19	planter	Hampshire	Augusta
Thomas Bates	22	planter	Fauquier	Frederick
Jonathan Boswell	15	planter	Fairfax	South Carolina
William Bedingt [sic]	24	shoemaker	Frederick	Dublin, Ireland
Zadock Bailey	15	_____	Accomack	Accomack
William Bunting	19	_____	Accomack	Accomack
George Benston	26	_____	Accomack	Maryland
Robert Boyd	19	Latter	Chesterfield	Chester, Pa.
Southey Bailey	18	_____	Chesterfield	Chester [sic], Virginia
Jesse Blades	47	cooper	Chesterfield	Somerset, Md.
William Blake	45	_____	Chesterfield	Accomack
Smith Beesley	28	_____	Chesterfield	Accomack
William Bennett	20	_____	Chesterfield	Accomack
James Brown	19	planter	Dinwiddie	Dinwiddie
William Brabston	32	_____	Frederick	Ireland
Robert Bryson	31	coppersmith	Frederick	Scotland
Michael Barnett	19	planter	Augusta	Augusta
Thomas Barnett	30	planter	Rockingham	Rockingham
Isaac Burton	43	(?)	Winchester	England
Joseph Bottomley	23	_____	Berkeley	Scotland
Jacob Bowyer	24	butcher	Berkeley (?)	Pennsylvania
Larkin Brown	18	planter	Amherst	Amherst
Samuel Bybie	17	planter	Amherst	Amherst
John Bott	27	farmer	Frederick	England
Isaac Bustead	22	carpenter	Rockbridge	New York
John Brown	22	_____	Berkeley	Scotland
Aaron Crofford	17	planter	Culpeper	Culpeper
William Carney	27	weaver	Loudoun	Ireland
Charles Charity	26	planter	Cumberland	Surry
James Couzens (negro)	23	planter	Goochland	Goochland
James Cross	21	planter	Dinwiddie	Dinwiddie
Bartholomew Crews	18	planter	Chesterfield	Chesterfield
William Canonbrig	20	planter	Bedford	Fluvanna
John Custason	18	planter	Hampshire	Fauquier
William Cabell	18	_____	Northampton	Northampton
Parker Copes	18	planter	Northampton	Accomack
Thomas Crew	24	_____	Northampton	Hispaniola *
George Colony	26	_____	Accomack	Hispaniola *
Jesse Christian	21	planter	Dinwiddie	Prince Edward
John Curtis	14	planter	Dinwiddie	Dinwiddie

---

*Hispaniola is a large island in the Caribbean sea. We can speculate that these two soldiers arrived in Virginia originally as sailors.

Name	Age	Trade	Residence	Born
Presley Cockrell	21	_____	Lancaster	Northumberland
Elijah Coplin	18	_____	Prince George	Amelia
Andrew Chadoin	21	_____	Buckingham	Chesterfield
John Church	35	_____	Augusta	Ireland
Charles Coffin	19	planter	Goochland	Hanover
James Carney	24	planter	Washington	Ireland
James Cooley	37	carpenter	Frederick	Scotland
Samuel Carbin	16	farmer	Berkeley	Maryland (?)
___?___ Connor	32	shoemaker	Amherst	England (?)
John Copage	29	b.smith	Fauquier	Fauquier
William Cook (Sr.?)	25	_____	Fauquier	Dublin, Ireland
James Coleman	25	butcher	Richmond	Galloway
Patrick Cumberford	24	farmer	Rockingham	Kings County
William Capell	19	farmer	Northampton	Northampton
William Dixon	18	farmer	Berkeley	England
John Dean	30	shoemaker	Middlesex	Middlesex
Francis Dawson	23	_____	New Kent	Williamsburg
Edward Dickerson	22	blacksmith	Accomack	Northampton
Selby Delistatious	18	_____	Accomack	Northampton
John Dafter	19	_____	Accomack	England
Littleton Dolby	21	_____	Northampton	Northampton
James Delany	27	_____	Accomack	Ireland
Charles Dobbins	20	planter	Dinwiddie	Prince Edward
Severn Delastatious	22	planter	Accomack	Accomack
Henry Denny	26	planter	Frederick	Frederick
Westbrooke Day	48	breeches-maker	Augusta	England
Christopher Dunkin	21	weaver	Fauquier	North Jersey
Edward Demastres	20	planter	Amherst	Amherst
James Demastres	21	planter	Amherst	Amherst
William Dinsmore	16	planter	Amherst	Amherst
Spilsby Davis	30	planter	Caroline	Caroline
John Deahan	23	joiner	_____	Germany
John Dugmore	29	planter	Winchester	Kent, England
John Day	22	planter	Culpeper	Fauquier
Henry Griffith	23	planter	Northumberland	Northumberland
John Gladen	21	farmer	Accomack	Accomack
Hugh Gilling	34	shoemaker	Accomack	Ireland
John Gunter	23	farmer	Accomack	Accomack
John Gleeson	18	tailor	Northampton	Virginia
Taliaferro Grigsby	19	_____	Fauquier	Stafford
John Gottlip	26	miller	Hanover	Germany
Evan Gettans [or Gettaus]	43	tailor	Rockbridge	Shrewsbury, England
Josias Greene	21	carpenter	Hanover	Henrico
John Grissel	31	shoemaker	(enlisted at Hampton)	Germany
Anthony Haden	16	tailor	Hanover	Hanover
William Henchin	18	planter	Stafford	Stafford
Ephraim Howlet	30	tailor	Northumberland	Northumberland
Thomas Hastings	21	farmer	Accomack	_____
John Hall	27	saddle maker	(enlisted at Accomack)	Ireland

Name	Age	Trade	Residence	Born
Alexander Harrison	19	_____	(enlisted at Accomack)	Accomack
Ezekiel Hickman	24	_____	Accomack	Accomack
William Hill	21	_____	Accomack	Accomack
Smith Hazleep	21	_____	Accomack	Accomack
William Hale	19	_____	Augusta	West Jersey
John Harris	21	_____	Dinwiddie	Prince George
Abraham Hope	22	_____	Shenandoah	Germany
John Henderson	32	planter	Albemarle	Scotland (?)
Jacob Hout (or Howl)	20	farmer	Berkeley	?
John Hambleton	37	farmer	Botetourt	?
Samuel Hueston	36	farmer	Augusta	Ireland (?)
Thomas Hudnell	22	Blksmith	Fauquier	Fauquier
Griffith Haines	22	farmer	Hanover	Hanover
William Hooker	22	farmer	Fairfax	?
John Holdbrook	17	farmer	Goochland	Louisa
Christopher Heatherlin	36	wheelright	Frederick	Chester, [torn]
Elisha Maddox	39	_____	Accomack	Delaware
George More	40	mason	Amherst	N. Jersey
Francis Miller	20	sadler	Amherst	Germany
Jonas Morgan	37	farmer	Shenandoah	Culpeper
Daniel Murray	53	weaver	Fauquier	Dublin, Ireland
Christopher McCannon	29	joiner	Fauquier	Dublin, Ireland
William Moseby	28	joiner	Powhatan	Powhatan
William Macky	18	farmer	Goochland	Goochland
John Maddox	16	shoemaker	Amherst	Amherst
Edwin Marsh	20	planter	Northumberland	Northumberland
Joseph Mash	18	planter	Northumberland	Northumberland
Ezekiel Mosses	19	silversmith	Northumberland	Northumberland
Nicholas Moore	28	_____	Accomack	Ireland
Donald McDonald	48	planter	Dinwiddie	Scotland
John Milikin	38	blacksmith	Frederick	Chester, Pa.
Littleberry McKinney	16	_____	Sussex	Sussex
James Mattonly	20	planter	Fairfax	Fairfax
John McKinney	27	farmer	Frederick	Chester, Pa.
Michael Moreland	22	farmer	Berkeley	Ireland
Edward McGlauchling	18	farmer	Augusta	Pennsylvania
John Smaw	27	_____	Accomack	Accomack
John Shepherd	39	_____	Accomack	Accomack
William Scott	23	shoemaker	Accomack	Accomack
Richard Simpson	25	_____	Accomack	Accomack
William Simpson	25	_____	Accomack	Accomack
Edward Stewart	23	planter	Dinwiddie	Chesterfield
Lewis Smith	22	planter	Dinwiddie	Prince George
Joseph Smith	25	planter	Dinwiddie	Prince George
John Stewart	24	planter	Dinwiddie	Prince George
William Smith	29	tailor	Augusta	England
James Sprouce	48	planter	Louisa	Fluvanna
John Spong	19	tailor	Montgomery	Reading, Pa.
John Smith	30	carpenter	North (?)	Ireland
John Smith	30	b.smith	Augusta	England
William Stark	17	farmer	Buckingham	Fauquier

Name	Age	Trade	Residence	Born
George Summerson	22	farmer	Caroline	York
Edward Smith	30(?)	_____	Lancaster, Pa.	Ireland
William Smith	19	Latter	Loudoun	Halifax
William Sommers	29	farmer	Dumfries	Charles County, Maryland
James Stewart	17	farmer	Cumberland	Prince Edward
___?___ Stephens	38	farmer	Frederick	Frederick
___?___ Smith	33	gunsmith	Frederick	Lancaster, Pa.
___?___ Salisbury	19	shoemaker	Prin. Anne	Smithfield, Va.
John Summerskill	35	farmer	Frederick	Yorkshire, England
John Stewart	24	(furnished a substitute)		
Richard Thorn	17	_____	Accomack	___?___
Nevit Taylor	23	_____	Accomack	Accomack
Selby Taylor	22	_____	Northampton	Accomack
Jonathan Tharp	20	_____	Accomack	Accomack
Major Topping	28	_____	Accomack	Accomack
Eyres Taylor	24	_____	Accomack	Accomack
John Taylor	25	_____	Accomack	Accomack
Samuel Terpin	25	_____	Dinwiddie	Virginia
Berry Thompson	22	_____	Halifax	Virginia
William Thurmond	16	_____	Amherst	Amherst
John Tucker	18	_____	Amherst	Amherst
Henry Townsen	22	_____	Rockingham	Frederick
Richard Thorns	19	planter	Accomack	Accomack
Robert Tule(?)	18	Shoemaker	Hanover	Louisa
John Taylor	15	planter	Hampshire	Ann Arundel, Maryland

* * *

Noncommissioned officers and privates at

WINCHESTER BARRACKS

Name	Age	Trade	Residence	Born
Francis Peyton	28	tailor	_____	Germany
James Pollard	15	farmer	_____	Culpeper
Francis Pierce	19	negro	_____	Caroline
John Plagge	31	farmer	_____	Germany
Joseph Ridley	26		Frederick	Germany
John Ross	55	brewer	Caroline	Scotland
Robert Roach	19	_____	Fauquier	Fauquier
Thomas Reed	38	farmer	Fairfax	England
Ephraim Russell	19	tailor	Botetourt	Augusta
John Rogers	24	tailor	Augusta	Cork, Ireland
Robert Roach	18	farmer	Fauquier	Fauquier
David Wellson	25	farmer	Rockingham	Scotland
Edward Wright	18	farmer	Botetourt	England
William Woster	32	farmer	York	England
Benjamin Whitmore	19	baker (mulatto)	Alexandria	Fairfax

Name	Age	Trade	Residence	Born
Charles Whitson	14	(mulatto)	Stafford	Stafford
Bayly Willis	17	farmer	Stafford	Stafford
Jesse Whitt	17	farmer	Goochland	Goochland
Stith Wilkinson	18	carpenter	Powhatan	Powhatan
Thomas Williams	17	farmer	Botetourt	Bedford, Pa.
Thomas Wade	17	farmer	Hanover	Hanover

* * *

SECTION TWO

PROOF OF IMPORTATIONS

PROOF OF IMPORTATIONS

Brunswick County, Va. Court Order Book 1, page 241 -

3 May 1739 - John Scott, Gent., came into court and made oath that it is now
three years since his importation from Great Britain [thus 1736] and that he
never before now has received the benefit of the Act of Assembly which allows
fifty acres of land for every person imported from Great Britain aforesaid,
which is ordered to be certified.

Ibid. Thomas Avent makes oath likewise and states it is now thirty-eight
years since his importation [thus he arrived circa 1701].

Ibid. Michael Cadet Young makes oath likewise and states it has been seventeen years since his importation from Great Britain [thus he arrived ca 1722].

Ibid. Also Cornelius Keith makes oath likewise and states it is now thirty
years since his importation [thus he arrived ca 1709].

Ibid. Marmaduke Johnson from Ireland makes oath likewise and states it has
been twenty years since his importation [thus 1719].

Ibid, page 242 - John Hopkins came into court and made oath likewise and
states it has been six years since his importation from Great Britain. [thus
he arrived ca 1733].

Ibid. Patrick Dempsey makes oath likewise and states it has been eighteen
years since his importation from Ireland [thus ca 1721].

Ibid. John Jackson made oath likewise and stated it has been three years
since his importation from Great Britain [thus ca 1736].

Brunswick County, Va. Court Order Book 5, page 255 -

July Court 1754 - John Hillton made oath that he imported himself direct
from the Kingdom of Great Britain into this Colony about thirty-three years
since (1721) and that this is the first time of his proving such importation.

Brunswick County, Va. Court Order Book 6, page 45 -

March Court 1750 - Richard Burnett made oath (as above) and stated he imported himself directly from the Kingdom of Great Britain some years past.

Ibid, page 46 - Richard Branscomb made oath he imported himself from Great
Britain into the Province of Maryland about 14 or 15 years ago and from
thence into this colony where he served a part of his servitude, etc.

Henrico County, Virginia, Order Book (1707-09), page 4 -

1 November 1707 - Upon the petition of John Jones, this is to certify that
there is due unto him 200 acres of land for the importation of himself,
Anne, his wife, and Isaac and John (Jones) his children under age, the same
being legally proved in open court.

Ibid, page 11 - 1 December 1707 - Upon petition of John Thomas - certification that there is due unto him 100 acres of land for the importation of
himself and Mary, his wife, into the colony.

Ibid, page 18 - 2 February 1707/08 - Upon petition of Simon Jeffreys -
certification that there is due him 50 acres of land for the importation
of his own person into this colony.

Ibid, page 105 - 1 November 1708 - Upon petition of John Martin - certification that there is due unto him 200 acres of land for the importation of
himself, his wife, Esther, with Margaretta and Mary, his children, into this
colony.

* * *

ABSTRACTS OF ORIGINAL COURT RECORDS

D I C K E N

MADISON COUNTY, VIRGINIA - ORIGINAL RECORDS

Note by CHH: Madison County was formed 1792-3 from Culpeper County.

Deed Book 6, page 236 -

WHEREAS: JOEL DICKEN OF THE COUNTY OF BOONE, STATE OF KENTUCKY, by a
Power of Attorney dated 22 October 1817 authorized JAMES DICKEN to sell and
convey his right, title and interest in a tract of land in Madison County,
Virginia, which upon the death of HENRY LEWIS, late of the county of
Madison, descended from him, the said Henry (Lewis) to his heirs at law, of
whom the said JOEL DICKEN was one, in right of his mother, MARTHA DICKEN,
LATE MARTHA LEWIS, and WHEREAS: RICHARD DICKEN AND WILLIAM DICKEN, OF THE
SAID COUNTY OF BOONE, KENTUCKY by a Power of Attorney dated 31 October 1817,
who are also sons of MARTHA DICKEN, LATE MARTHA LEWIS, and heirs of the
said HENRY LEWIS, authorized the said JAMES DICKEN to sell their shares,
etc.   Therefore, the said JAMES DICKEN sells to Thomas and Zachariah Shurley
of the County of Madison - for $160.00 - two lots of land containing 24
acres and 34 acres, etc. - reference to a suit by Thomas Kirtley and others
versus William Lewis and others on 23 November 1804 and to a report dated
20th June 1805, etc.   JAMES DICKEN also, in this deed sells his own right
and share in the above property, etc.   Recorded 1818.

NOTE: Boone County, Ky. was formed 1798 from Campbell County.

Deed Book 6, page 238 -

8 November 1817 - WHEREAS: I, DAVID CONNER OF THE COUNTY OF FRANKLIN,
STATE OF INDIANA, Who intermarried with BETSEY DICKEN, who is one of the
children and legal heirs of RICHARD DICKEN AND MARTHA, HIS WIFE, LATE OF
BOONE COUNTY, KENTUCKY, each of whom are now deceased, which said MARTHA
DICKEN was one of the children and legal heirs of HENRY LEWIS, DECEASED,
late of the County of Madison, in Virginia -

Now therefore, I, DANIEL CONNER, appoint my trusty friend and BROTHER
IN LAW, JAMES DICKEN, OF THE COUNTY OF BOONE, IN KENTUCKY, my true and
lawful attorney to recover from Thomas Bohannon of the County of Madison,
all such sums of money, etc., in his hands and due me from the estate of
HENRY LEWIS, DECEASED and also to sell and convey my undivided interest
or portion of a tract of land to which I am entitled to as an heir of the
said HENRY LEWIS and in the DOWER OF CATHARINE LEWIS at her death, etc. -
certified by WILLIS GRAVES, Notary Public of Boone County, Ky., the same
date as above.   Recorded 15 January 1818.

NOTE: Franklin County, Indiana was formed 1811 from Wayne and Ripley.
Wayne was formed 1810 from Indian Lands.

Madison County, Virginia, Deed Book 6, page 240 -

31 October 1817 - WHEREAS: JOHN CONNER OF THE COUNTY OF FRANKLIN, STATE OF INDIANA, intermarried with POLLY DICKEN, one of the children and heirs of RICHARD DICKEN AND MARTHA, HIS WIFE, LATE OF THE COUNTY OF BOONE, KENTUCKY, who are both now deceased, the said MARTHA DICKEN being one of the children of HENRY LEWIS, DECEASED, LATE OF THE COUNTY OF MADISON, IN VIRGINIA, and WHEREAS: GEORGE CARN (OR CORN ?) of the County of BOONE, KENTUCKY having intermarried with NANCY YAGER, LATE NANCY DICKEN, one of the children and heirs of the aforesaid RICHARD DICKEN and MARTHA DICKEN, now deceased, and also, WHEREAS: RICHARD DICKEN AND WILLIAM DICKEN, both of the County of Boone, Kentucky, each of whom are likewise children of the aforesaid RICHARD AND MARTHA DICKEN, and entitled to a portion of the estate of the aforesaid HENRY LEWIS, DECEASED, - do appoint our trusty friend and BROTHER, JAMES DICKEN·OF THE COUNTY OF BOONE, KY., our true and lawful attorney to recover from Thomas Bohannon of Madison County, Va., etc., - Certified by WILLIS GRAVES, Notary Public of Boone County, Ky. Recorded 15 January 1818.

Deed Book 7, page 92 -

4 November 1820 - WHEREAS: LONDON SNELL AND JUDITH, HIS WIFE, FORMERLY JUDITH DICKEN, who is an heir of MARTHA DICKEN; and HENRY DICKEN, who is also an heir of the said MARTHA DICKEN, and as such are entitled to an equal child's part of two lots of land which descended to the said MARTHA DICKEN, LATE MARTHA LEWIS, as an heir of HENRY LEWIS, DECEASED, late of Madison County, in Virginia, etc., -

This Indenture by SIMEON KIRTLEY, attorney for the said LONDON SNELL AND JUDITH, HIS WIFE, and for HENRY DICKEN OF THE COUNTY OF SCOTT, STATE OF KENTUCKY, of one part, sell to Anthony Bohannon of the County of Madison, Va., - for $80.00 - all their right, title, claim, and interest, etc. Recorded 23 November 1820.

NOTE: Scott County, Ky., was formed 1792 from Woodford County.

COMMENT: The Power of Attorney cited above, is recorded id ref p.98 and reveals that London Snell and Judith, his wife, and Henry Dickens were all of the County of Scott, Ky., and that their attorney, Simeon Kirtley, was of the County of Harrison, Ky.

Richard Dickens who married Martha Lewis, daughter of Henry Lewis, is thought by this compiler to have been the son of CAPTAIN CHRISTOPHER DICKENS OF CULPEPER COUNTY, VA. who made his will 21st August 1778 in that County (WB "B" p 273) and among 15 children named his son, RICHARD DICKENS.

Will Book 2, page 18 -

27 December 1804 - Thomas Bohannon, with Henry Price his security, gives a $3,000.00 bond as Guardian of JAMES DICKEN, ELIZABETH DICKEN, RICHARD DICKEN, JULIA DICKEN, and WILLIAM DICKEN, children of RICHARD DICKEN who intermarried with MARTHA LEWIS, now deceased, all of whom are under lawful age, etc. Recorded same date.

Madison County, Virginia Deed Book 2, page 328 -

7th October 1811 - Settlement of the estate of Henry Lewis, deceased:

Heirs and Legatees: Catharine Lewis (widow and relict)
                         MARTHA DICKEN
                         Thomas Kirtley
                         John Lewis
                         Henry Lewis
                         William Lewis
                         Thomas Lewis
                         James Lewis
                         Erasmus Chapman
                         Abraham Lewis
                         Frances Harrison
                         John Kirtley
                         Simeon Lewis
Recorded 24 October 1811

* * *

B U L L

BRUNSWICK COUNTY, VIRGINIA - RECORDS

Order Book 4, page 182 -

May Term 1752 - THOMAS BULL, of this County, came into Court and made oath that he imported himself into this Colony of Virginia, directly FROM THE KINGDOM OF GREAT BRITAIN, about 31 years since (thus about 1721) and that this was the first time of his proving such importation. Ordered by the Court to be certified.

COMMENT: If he was about 21 years when he arrived in Virginia then he was born circa 1700 or thereabouts.

Deed Book 5, page 456 -

26 September 1753 - DEED OF GIFT FROM THOMAS BULL OF BRUNSWICK COUNTY IN VIRGINIA - for love and affection for his well beloved son, ROBERT BULL OF SAID COUNTY, a tract of land containing 150 acres on the Reedy Creek in said county, adjoining lands of Edward Robertson - land of the said THOMAS BULL, etc. Witnesses: Edward Goodrich, James Cook, Stephen Sisson. Recorded same date.

NOTE BY CHH: Robert Bull and Rachell, his wife, sold the above land 27 December 1757 (£45) to Ambrose Harwell of Brunswick Co., stating therein that the land was his by deed from his father, Thomas Bull and which was part of a patent granted said Thomas Bull January 12, 1746.

Brunswick County, Virginia, Deed Book 6, page 223 -

27 December 1757 - THOMAS BULL AND SUSANNA, HIS WIFE, of the County of Brunswick sell 99 acres of land to Lemuel Harwell, being the land he lives on, etc.

Deed Book 8, page 376 -

22 September 1766 - THOMAS BULL OF THE COUNTY OF HALIFAX, IN THE PROVINCE OF NORTH CAROLINA sells to Swan Prichard of the County of Brunswick in the Province [sic] of Virginia - for £10 - 46 acres of land in the County of Brunswick, adjoining lands of Thomas Jackson, etc. Recorded 23 September 1766.

Virginia State Library (original) Payroll of Capt. Brisco's Co. of Militia on the Expedition under General Clark against the Shoneys [Shawnees] 1780, July 20.

Captain Parmenas Briscoe
Lieut. Magil
Ens. Buskirk
    36 privates - among them,

            THOMAS BULL - entered July 20, 1780.
            Discharged Aug. 21, 1780. Time of
            Service 33 days. Sum due £2.4.0

Two of the men of this unit were listed as killed on August 8th (1780)

            on Reverse,

March 25, 1783 - Capt. Parmenas Briscoe came before me, one of the magistrates for LINCOLN CO., and made oath that the within pay roll is just and true. Signed, Hugh McGary.

Frederick County, Virginia, Superior Court Deed Book 2, page 512 -

20 day of 4th mo 1796 - Roger Barton and Margt his wife, of County of Frederick sell to ROBERT BULL OF COUNTY OF BERKELEY £65 - a tract of land in County of Berkeley, which land was conveyed to said Barton by Arthur Watson and Lydia his wife 15th of 6th mo. 1789, near the foot of the North Mtn., adjoining other lands of said Bull - land of Thos. Mattocks - David Gerrard, containing 63 acres. Recorded 20 April 1796.

Ibid, Deed Book 24B, page 461 -

5 November 1793 - John Crumley and Hannah his wife of Newberry County, District of Ninety-Six, State of South Carolina - sell to ROBERT BULL of County of Berkeley, in Virginia [now West Virginia] for £293, a tract of land in County of Frederick, State of Virginia, being part of Kings Patent granted to Giles Chapman who conveyed the same to James Crumley and part of two other tracts of land granted to said James Crumley - and the said James

Crumley in his last will devised the same to Samuel Crumley and became the property of the said John Crumley by being heir at law to the said Samuel Crumley and the said John sold the premises to Henry Crumley 30 October 1787 and the said Henry assigned bond to Robert Bull, etc. Proved by witness 3 December 1793. Recorded 3 May 1796.

Ibid, Deed Book 28, page 341

27 March 1804, Robert Bull and Sarah his wife, of County of Berkeley sell to William Linn of County of Frederick for £845 a certain tract of land in County of Frederick (same land and same wording as above deed) Recorded 3 April 1804.

* * *

Cumberland Parish, Lunenburg County by L. C. Bell, page 315 -

Refers to the marriage of REBECCA CROSS TO PETER EPES on February 15, 1798. She was the daughter of JOHN CROSS AND ELIZABETH, HIS WIFE, of Lunenburg County.

Lunenburg County, Will Book 3, page 390 -

JOHN CROSS dated his Will 13th (?) November 1790 which was probated 13 January 1791 and named therein the following legatees:

Beloved wife, Elizabeth Cross (of whom more later) -
Son, William Cross
Daughters:
1. Mary, wife of Ashley Davis
2. Jeane, wife of Peter Lamkin Jr.
3. Martha, wife of John Chappell
4. Elizabeth Cross (more later)
5. Rebecca Cross (more later)

Grandchildren:
1. Ashley Davis
2. Polly Davis
3. unborn child (Davis) - other records: her name was Elizabeth.

This Will was very remarkable in that he left so many slaves (all of them named) that I could not count them with any accuracy. In addition to his other lands he left 1,000 acres IN THE COUNTY OF DAVIDSON IN THE WESTERN PART OF NORTH CAROLINA to his two sons in law, Peter Lamkin Jr. and John Chappell.

JOHN CROSS married in 1765 ELIZABETH COCKE, a daughter of ABRAHAM COCKE (died testate 1760) and his wife, MARY BATTE (daughter of William Batte). Elizabeth (Cocke) Cross married secondly, Sydnor of Nottoway County and died testate 1815.

Elizabeth Cross, daughter of John Cross and Elizabeth Cocke, married her first cousin, THOMAS HAMLIN, son of Charles Hamlin and his wife, AGNES COCKE.

Rebecca Cross, as cited above, married PETER EPES and died testate in Lunenburg County in 1847 (WB 13, page 64).

Culpeper County, Deed Book UU, page 455 -

20 October 1828 - Deed of Gift - John W. Marshall of the County of Culpeper to William Augustine Calbert and James Livingstone Calbert - children of William I. Calbert and Harriet, his wife - WHEREAS the said William I. Colbert, with his family, is about to move to the STATE OF TENNESSEE and the said John W. Marshall being desirous to aid and assist the said Colbert and his family and to secure to the said W. A. and J. L. Colbert (children as aforesaid) and in consideration of his attachment and friendship for the said children - grants to the said William I. Colbert, as Trustee for the said children, the following property - one light wagon - two horses and gear - bed, furniture, two trunks - one gun - etc. Witnesses: Jeremiah Strother, Rawl B. Green - Recorded 20 October 1828.

COMMENT: The above names are spelled variously as indicated. The name is also spelled COLVERT in the Will of SAMUEL COLVERT (Will Book I, page 93) dated 12 April 1823 Culpeper County whose heirs were named therein as: sons, Joseph, John, William I. (he, executor) and the heirs of his deceased son, Eliakim, and a legacy to his daughter, Nancy Daniel. The Will was probated ten days later on 22 April 1823. (Culpeper Marriage Register 1781-1853, page 30 - (blank date) William I. Colvert to Harriett Weeden. F. String-fellow, Minister.

Virginia State Library Accession #21943 -

16 November 1790 - Indenture in which Vivion Daniel and Elizabeth, his wife, of the County of Fayette (KENTUCKY) - William Quarles and Frances, his wife, of the County of Spotsylvania (Va.) - Thacker Vivion, of the STATE OF GEORGIA - Rhodes Thomson and Salley, his wife, of the COUNTY OF WOODFORD (Ky.) - Charles Vivion of the STATE OF NORTH CAROLINA - William Farguson and Margarett (sic) his wife, of the County of Spotsylvania (Va.) - Jackey Vivion - Thacker Smith Vivion - Milton Vivion - Thomas Vivion - Harvey Vivion - Flavel Vivion - Sons of John Vivion, deceased, of the COUNTY OF FAYETTE (Ky.) - Austin Webb - John Vivon Webb - William Webb, Jr. - Garland Webb - Thacker Webb - Charles Webb - Wyatt Webb, children of William and Jane Webb, the said Jane being a daughter of John Vivion, deceased, Reuben Sanford and Frances Vivion Sanford, his wife, the said Frances being a daughter of William and Jane Webb, of the one part - sell to Isaac Graves of the County of [obliterated] of the other part - for £342 - a tract of land containing 380 acres in the County of Orange, being part of a larger tract belonging to the late John Vivion, deceased, (adjoining land of the said (Isaac) Graves, etc. [Note by CHH: each heir specified to own 47½ acres as their share or portion]. Witnesses: Henry Tandy, Vincent Vass, Jr., John Groom, William Bledford

Nottoway Co. Deed Book 3, page 169 -

12th day of December 1805 - Indenture in which Stephen Cocke of COUNTY OF WASHINGTON, STATE OF KENTUCKY sells to John Cocke of the County of Nottoway, State of Virginia for 950 pds current money of Virginia, a tract

of land in the County of Nottoway containing 254½ acres, being a part of the
land devised to the said Stephen Cocke by his late father, Stephen Cocke,
deceased, of the said County of Nottoway by his last Will and Testament,
purchased of Anthony Walke, executor of Anthony Walke, deceased, beginning
at Hamlin's corner, on Cocke's road, along Hamlin's line - to Nottoway River,
etc. Witnesses: Edward Bland, Spencer Boyd, Stith Hardaway. Recorded
June 5, 1806.

Note by CHH: Stephen Cocke sells the same day, 350 acres of land in Nottoway
County to Stith Hardaway (ibid, page 174).

Ibid, page 328 -

4 November 1806 - Indenture in which Amey Cocke of the COUNTY OF WASH-
INGTON, STATE OF KENTUCKY and formerly of the County of Nottoway, in Virginia - sells to Stith Hardaway and John Cocke, both of said County of
Nottoway - Whereas, Stephen Cocke, the elder, did by his last will devise to
the aforesaid Amey Cocke, during her life, the use and right of the lands
devised by him to his sons, Thomas Cocke and Stephen Cocke, and whereas,
Stephen Cocke, the younger, did on the 12 day of December 1805 convey to
said Stith Hardaway and John Cocke the title to the lands devised him by
Stephen Cocke, the elder, and whereas the said Stephen Cocke, the younger,
hath this day conveyed by deed to the said Amey Cocke 360 acres on Cartright
Creek in COUNTY OF WASHINGTON, KENTUCKY, during her natural life - for her
full interest in the land conveyed to the said Stith Hardaway and John Cocke,
etc. Certified by John Reed, Clerk of Washington Co., Ky. Court on Liber C,
page 221. Recorded Nottoway Co. Court Dec. 3, 1807.

Ibid, page 424 -

2 June 1808 - Power of Attorney from Amey Cocke, widow of Stephen Cocke,
formerly of Nottoway County in Virginia, but now of Grainger County, State
of Tennessee - appointing my son, Thomas S. Cocke, my true and lawful attorney,
etc. Certified by James Moore and John Cocke, Justices of Granger County,
Tennessee, same date. Recorded Nottoway County, Sept. 1, 1808.

Fauquier Co., Deed Book 17, page 246 -

Indenture dated 2 May 1808 in which Jacob Faubin and Diana, his wife,
late Diana Rector, of COCKE COUNTY, STATE OF TENNESSEE, and late of Fauquier
County, State of Virginia, of one part, sell to George Glascock of Fauquier
County, of the other part - witnesseth that whereas Henry Rector, deceased,
of Fauquier Co., in and by his last will dated the 8th January 1799, devised
his estate to his then wife, Nancey, for her life, and then to be equally
divided among his Representatives, and whereas after the death of the said
Nancey, Administration of said estate was granted the said George Glascock,
who sold a tract of land containing 150 acres for 450 pds. Virginia money,
and whereas Jacob Faubin and Diana his wife being heirs and devisees aforesaid and having received their proportionable share of said money, do sell
their part and claim, etc. Witnesses, W. Garrett, Ezekiel Campbell, Coleman
Smith. Certified by Justices of Cocke County, Tennessee, same date as above.
Recorded Fauquier Co., Va. 26 September 1808.

York County Record Book 4, page 151 -

October 23, 1666 - John Petit, a Frenchman by birth but an ancient in-
habitant of this country, whereof his marriage, children, long abode, many
services, and approved fidelity have justly made him reputed a member, hath
petition that he might be admitted into a stricter tie of obedience to his
Sacred Majecty by being made denizen to this country. It is by the Governor,
Council and Burgesses of this Grand Assembly (at James City) granted and
ordered.

NOTE BY CHH: (ibid page 287) is a record of the last will and testament of
John Petit, Chirurgin (surgeon) of York County and Parish, dated 1 December
1669; probated 26 April 1670.

Stafford County, Court Records (1664-1668) page 121 -

December 10, 1690 - David Lindsey made humble petition to this court
that he being 64 years of age (thus born ca 1626) and having served in the
wars under King Charles II, BOTH IN ENGLAND AND IN FOREIGN COUNTRIES, and
having served the full time of four years in this county [sic] with Thomas
Gregg - to exempt him from (tax levies) and county duties. Petition granted.

Henrico Co. Wills and Deeds (1714-1718) page 219 -

Last Will and Testament of Charles Perault dated 24 March 1716/17,
Recorded 2 December 1717.

I, Charles Perault, LATE OF BORDEAUX, PROVINCE OF GUIENNE, IN FRANCE,
at present in the Parish of King William, in Henrico County, in Virginia, etc
To my dear and beloved wife, Margaret Perault, the plantation where I
live, for her lifetime, after her death, to my son, Daniel Perault. My wife
executrix.
Witnesses: Abra: Salle, Chastaine, Isaac Lafort.

Certification, 26 August 1717 by Abraham Salle that he had translated
the above will from the original in French.

NOTE BY CHH: (Douglas Register page 372) In a general list of French
Protestant refugees in King William Parish of Henrico County (in the period
ca 1714) is listed Charles Perault, his wife, one son, three daughters
(total six) - Proven descendants are eligible for membership in the Huguenot
Society of Manakin Town.

York Co. Orders, Wills, etc. #16 (1720-1729) page 524 -

Last Will and Testament of James Falconer, dated 1 February 1727/8,
probated May 20, 1728.

My whole estate to be equally divided between my well beloved wife and
my daughter (neither are named) but if my daughter die without issue, her
part to my brothers and sisters in the COUNTY OF MURRAY IN SCOTLAND. My
executors to be my daughter's grandfather, Colonel George Newton of Norfolk
County and Captain Edward Tabb of York County.

Witnesses: Joshua Curle, Plany Ward, Richard Hurst, James Faison.

NOTE BY CHH: He is referred to a Reverend Mr. James Falconer in the Inventory of his estate, which inventory is signed by Elizabeth Falconer (ibid pp. 531-2)

Henrico Co. Miscl. Records Vol. 4 (1738-1746) page 1123 -

23 April 1740 - Indenture in which Philip Smith of Bertie Co. (Province) of North Carolina sells to Frances Wilkinson, widow, of the other part - for £30.0.1, a tract of land in County of Henrico, Colony of Virginia, containing 400 acres, being patented by Samuel Good 28 September 1731 and by him sold to the said Philip Smith 10 September 1731 [sic] etc. Witnesses: Thomas Cheatham, John Hamlin, Charles Cheatham, Thomas Hamlin.

Campbell Co., Deed Book 13, page 3-

20 October 1820 - Indenture in which James Hines and Caroline B., his wife - Thomas Lawton and Elizabeth Ann, his wife - William Taylor and Amelia C. his wife, and Kelly Hines and Lucy K., his wife - of WARREN CO., STATE OF KENTUCKY, of one part - sell to German Jordan of Campbell Co., State of Virginia - for $120.00, all the estate right, title, interest, property and claim which they have into and upon a parcel of land in Campbell Courthouse, Virginia, being a lot and tenement of which Booker Ramsey died seized and which we, as heirs, inherit and sell the same containing 2 acres more or less.

NOTE: All parites sign and acknowledge before the Justices of WARREN COUNTY, KENTUCKY, who certify same. Rec. Campbell Co., Va. January 8, 1821.

Campbell County, Virginia, Marriage Register #1, page 96 -

Dec. 27, 1806 - Thomas Lawton to Elizabeth A. B. Ramsey

ibid, page 77 - Sept. 28, 1805 - James Hines to Caroline B. Ramsey
ibid, page 77 - Sept. 26, 1816 - Kelly Hines to Lucy Ramsey.

Amelia County, Virginia, Marriages by Williams, page 89 -

11 September 1786 - Booker Ramsey to Ann Elizabeth Munford with consent of John Munford, guardian of Elizabeth.

Augusta Co. Deed Book 33, page 410 -

18 June 1806 - Indenture in which John Summers, Sr. of County of Augusta, State of Virginia, and Andrew Summers of sd County and State, etc.... Whereas, the said John Summers did serve as a private soldier for the term of 7 years in the 47th Regiment of Foot Commanded by Lt.Gen. Peregrine LaSellis reference to which being had to a certificate of Discharge dated at Quebec 6 Sept. 1763, signed by James Spilac (?), Major of the sd Regiment and whereas the said John Summers inconsequence of his services as aforesaid is entitled to a certain quantity of land under the Proclamation of the King of England. Now, the said John Summers for the sum of £5 doth grant, etc. unto the said Andrew Summers all the land to which he is entitled, etc. etc.

Louisa County, Deed Book C, page 86 -

 7 August 1760 - Indenture in which Peter Copeland and Elizabeth, his wife,
of the COUNTY OF CHOWAN, PROVINCE OF NORTH CAROLINA, sells to James Isbell
of Orange County [does not specify whether N.C. or Va.] - for £95, a tract
of land in the County of Louisa, Colony of Virginia, containing 400 acres -
on the county line, etc. Witnesses: George Taylor, James Madison, Andrew
Shepherd. Recorded 28 July 1761.

COMMENT: Orange Co., Virginia Will Book 1, page 72, shows a Henry Isbell was
bequeathed 300 acres of land in Orange County, Va. by James Cox in his will
dated 16 December 1738 which indicates James Isbell of Orange Co. was probably
of Virginia, rather than North Carolina.

Halifax County, Will Book 3, page 206 -

 Will of Daniel Malone, dated 3 November 1795 and prob. 20 December 1795.
daughter, Mary Irvin, slave
  "   Elizabeth Tranum, slave, "living in STATE OF GEORGIA at my plantation"
son,   Thomas
  "   Nathaniel
daughter, Becky Andrews
son,   Drury Malone, 100 acres of land in GEORGIA, being part of the land
               whereon he now lives.
son,   John, balance of said tract
son,   Jameson -
son,   Banister -
son,   Daniel -

Executors: James Irvine, Clement Tranum, and John Andrews.

Codicil: To my daughter, Polly Harding, one shilling. To my daughter,
         Susanna Raynolds, dec'd, one shilling. To my son, Peter Malone,
         one shilling.

Southampton Co. Deed Book 4, page 265 -

 22 January 1770 - William Westbrook of DOBBS COUNTY, NORTH CAROLINA,
sells to Samuel Westbrook of County of Southampton of Virginia, for £40 -
a tract of land in said County of Southampton, on the north side of Meherrin
River, containing 110 acres being one-third of the manor plantation of John
Westbrook deceased, and father of the said William Westbrook, who bequeathed
the said one-third or 110 acres unto his said son, William, by his last will
and Testament - adjoining the land of his brother, John Westbrook, etc.
Witnesses: Joshua Nicholson, Joshua Claud, Jr., Samuel Westbrooke, Jr.
Recorded 10 May 1770.

COMMENT: A John Westbrook of Isle of Wight Co. dated his will Feb. 13, 1719
probated July 23, 1733 (WB 3 page 357) and named therein his sons: John,
Thomas, William, and James; and daughters, Ann and Sarah. He mentioned his
wife but did not name her. [See next deed following.]

Southampton Co., Deed Book 4, page 272 -

22 January 1770 - John Westbrook of DOBBS COUNTY, NORTH CAROLINA sells
to Samuel Westbrooke of County of Southampton in Virginia for £35, a tract
of land in sd county on Northside of Meherrin River containing 110 acres,
it being one-third of the manor plantation of John Westbrooke, deceased,
father of the said John Westbrook, bequeathed to him in the last will of his
sd father, adjoining the land of the widow of the said decedent which she
holds during her widowhood (or life) - and the land of his brother, William
Westbrook - which land was formerly granted by patent to James Ramsey about
the year 1725, etc. Witnesses: Joshua Nicholson, Joshua Claud, Jr., Samuel
Westbrooke, Jr. Recorded 10 May 1770.

Lunenburg Co. Deed Book 21, page 31A -

6 October 1806 - We, the undersigned, being of the STATE OF KENTUCKY and
COUNTY OF MADISON, have appointed Thomas Townsend and William Townsend, of
the same county and state, our true and lawful attorneys, to recover and receive that part of the estate coming to us as legatees of Richard Stone,
decd. of Lunenburg Co., Virginia.

                        Signed: George Miller, Lovina (?) Townsend,
                                 Daniel Richardson, Elen Estes, Andrew
                                 Estes, Jacob Williams, Ren Braminett (?)

Acknowledged and certified before and by Justices of Madison Co., Ky., same
date, Recorded Lunenburg Co., Va. 8 January 1807.

Ibid, Deed Book 22, page 52A-

11 August 1807 - Power of Attorney from Peter Townsend of County of
Lunenburg to his friends Joseph Townsend and William Townsend of same county -
to commence suit to recover on a bond left in their possession by Thomas
Townsend of Kentucky, Edmund Winn, Minor Wilkes, Sr. of County of Lunenburg
and John Wilkes of Co. of Franklin (va.), dated 12 January 1807, etc.
Recorded the same date.

Pittsylvania Co., Deed Book 33, page 276 -

16 April 1832 - Power of Attorney by Austin Townsend, Maria A. Townsend
and Susan J. Townsend of Pittsylvania County to Granville Jordan of County
of Campbell, Va., to receive for them all property devised them by their
brother Clement Townsend, deceased, of the COUNTY OF [blank] and STATE OF
MISSISSIPPI. Recorded same date.

Ibid, page 352 -

16 July 1832 - (Power of Attorney)... Whereas Clement Townsend lately
departed this life IN THE STATE OF MISSISSIPPI, and probably in WILKINSON
COUNTY, unmarried, and without a child, possessed of real and personal
estate - Now, know ye that we, Richard Townsend, the father of said Clement

Townsend, decd, and Austin Townsend, Wilcher J. Townsend, Mariah Townsend, and Susan J. Townsend, brothers and sisters of said Clement Townsend, decd, all of the County of Pittsylvania, State of Virginia and do ordain and appoint Anthony Minter (?(of County of Pittsylvania our true and lawful attorney, etc. Recorded same date.

Ibid, page 354 -

14 March 1832 - James Dunnica, Justice of County of Cole, STATE OF MISSOURI certifies he performed the marriage ceremony between Waller Bolton and Mary Lansdoun and 'at the same time and place I did solemnize the rites of matrimony between William Bolton and Sarah Lansdoun." Dated 21 March 1832. Recorded Pittsylvania Co., Va. 21 May 1832.

Ibid, page 355 -

The above marriage certifications were accompanied by a Power of Attorney from Waller Bolton, Mary his wife, and William Bolton and Sarah, his wife, to secure for them property belonging to estate of Johnson Lansdown, deceased, late of Pittsylvania Co., Va. as being his lawful heirs, etc. 26 March 1832. Recorded Pittsylvania Co., Va. 21 May 1832.

Ibid, Deed Book 34, page 104 -

17 September 1832 - Power of Attorney from Richard Townsend and Frances Townsend of County of Pittsylvania, Va. to Anthony Minter of sd county and state to secure a $2,000.00 legacy left to his mother, Frances Townsend by the last will and testament of Clement Townsend, decd, late of the county of WILKINSON, STATE OF MISSISSIPPI, etc. Recorded 17 September 1832.

Mecklenburg County, Deed Book 22, page 98 -

13 May 1826 - Indenture in which William Newton and Martha his wife - Daniel Sizemore and Elizabeth his wife of the County of Mecklenburg in Virginia and John Townsend and Anna, his wife, of the COUNTY OF PERSON IN NORTH CAROLINA - all legatees of John Sizemore, deceased, of the one part, sell to Morgan Puryear of the County of Mecklenburg in Virginia for $407 100 acres of land in said county of Mecklenburg, on southside of Dan River (all parties signed before a J.P. in Mecklenburg County which was certified.) Recorded 15 May 1826.

Halifax Co. Deed Book 7, page 444 -

16 October 1769 - Indenture in which William Owen of the COUNTY OF ROW ANN [sic] PROVINCE OF NORTH CAROLINA sells to John Epps of the County of Halifax, Colony of Virginia, for £50, a tract of land containing 114 acres in the said county of Halifax on the south side of Banister River, adjoining land of Richard Echol, being part of a tract granted to Robert Barrott by patent dated March 1, 1754, etc. Witnesses: Edward Tuck, Davis Powell, Mark Powell. Recorded 16 November 1769.

Halifax Co. Deed Book 16, page 128 -

6 September 1793 - Indenture in which Nathaniel Epps, Moses Epps, David Powell, Sr., John Comer, Edy Epps, Temperance Epps, of the county of Halifax; Ambrose Gresham of the County of Lunenburg; and George Reaves of the COUNTY OF WILKES IN NORTH CAROLINA - parties of one part - sell to William Epps of the aforesaid County of Halifax of the other part - parties being legatees of John Epps, deceased, sell to William Epps for £100 a certain tract of land in Halifax County, on the south side of Banister River containing 40 acres, etc. Witnesses: Moses Dunkley, John Dunkley, Henry Dunkley, Moore Comer. Recorded 24 February 1794.

Ibid, Deed Book 47, page 315 -

30 December 1841 - William Baird and Lucy Ann, his wife, of the COUNTY OF PERSON, STATE OF NORTH CAROLINA sell to William Epps of County of Halifax, State of Virginia, for $2960.00, a tract of land in County of Halifax, Virginia, on the State line, east of Mayo Creek, adjoining Baird's own line, containing 592 acres, etc. Certified before Justices of Person Co., N.C. and Lucy Ann Baird relinquishes her dower right. Recorded January 25, 1842.

NOTE: A following record reveals William Epps has a wife named Nancy. He and Nancy sell 100 acres of this land to Barton Link 30 November 1850 (Deed Book 54, page 270.)

Lunenburg County Deed Book 35, page 106 -

21 September 1850 - Edmund P. Taylor, Thomas Taylor, John W. Irby and Martha, his wife, Waller Taylor, Edward B. Hicks, attorney for Charles T. Nelson and Louisa, his wife, John C. Epes, attorney for William H. Taylor and Sarah, his wife, and Lew Jones, attorney for Lewis S. Taylor and Martha his wife, of one part, sell Thomas W. Winn of second part -$174.25 - 85 acres of land in County of Lunenburg, being part of the land belonging to the late W. M. H. Taylor, dec'd bought of Col. Edmond F. Taylor and Mrs. Davis etc.

Affidavit by Clinton Fitzgerald of COUNTY OF PANOLA, STATE OF MISSISSIPPI that John W. Irby signed the foregoing writing before him (carried to p.239) - another affidavit in Panola Co., Miss. that Martha Irby, wife of John W. Irby appeared and signed her name.

Affidavit by Justice, that E. B. Hicks, attorney for Charles T. Nelson and Louisa, his wife, signed the foregoing writing in Brunswick Co., Va. Lew Jones, attorney for Lewis S. Taylor and John C. Epes, attorney for William H. Taylor, both signed in Lunenburg Co., Va.

Ibid, Deed Book 35, page 175 -

16 April 1851 - Osborne J. Moore and Rebecca N., his wife of COUNTY OF CARROLL, STATE OF MISSISSIPPI sell to John H. McKinney and Richard Jones of County of Lunenburg, State of Virginia, for $400.00 - their individual interest in a tract of land in County of Lunenburg, Va. on Crooked and Beaver Pond Creeks, the said interest being one-fifth, it being the land devised to

the said Rebecca N. Moore by her father and mother, Benjamin Gee and Bridget
N. Gee, etc. Recorded 8 September 1851.

Lunenburg Co. Deed Book 35, page 514 -

16 June 1854 - Doctor A. Grant, OF THE COUNTY OF ALEXANDER, STATE OF
ILLINOIS, guardian of Matilda C. Cole and Mary E. Grant, appoints John H.
Brown of said County of Alexander (Illinois) his true and lawful attorney for
estate due his said wards in State of Virginia, as heirs at law of John T.
Cole and Mary B. Cole, deceased, etc. Certified by presiding Judge of Court
of County of Alexander, State of Illinois. Recorded Lunenburg Co., Va.
19 July 1854.

Ibid, Deed Book 37, page 110 -

24 September 1853 - Deed in which Richard J. Epes of the COUNTY OF
SUMPTER, STATE OF ALABAMA, sells to Jane Tisdale of the County of Lunenburg,
State of Virginia, for $400.00, all his estate, right, title and interest
in a tract of land in the County of Lunenburg, State of Virginia, containing
125½ acres, known as the old Courthouse tract, etc. Certified signature of
Richard J. [or I.] Epes by Thomas J. George, Justice of Peace of Sumpter Co.,
Alabama. Recorded 11 November 1862.

Ibid, page 111 -

4 April 1861 - Daniel Townsend and Nancy S. Townsend, his wife, OF
JACKSON COUNTY, ALABAMA, sell to James Smith of Lunenburg Co., Va. - for
$60.00 - a tract of land containing 18¼ acres in County of Lunenburg, Va.,
etc. Certified by Justice of Jackson Co., Alabama. Recorded 10 November
1862.

Montgomery Co. Deed Book C, page 33 -

7 April 1797 - Elisha Bowman of the COUNTY OF SURRY, STATE OF NORTH
CAROLINA - sells to John Harrison of County of Montgomery, State of Virginia,
for £100, a tract of land containing 70 acres in the County of Montomery,
etc. Recorded May Court 1797.

NOTE BY CHH: Ref. to marriages of Montgomery and Fincastle Counties, Va.
by Ann L. Worrell, page 10 - March 14, 1791, Elisha Bowman to Rebecca
Lorton, Israel Lorton, Surety.

Isle of Wight Co., Deed Book 9, page 182 -

20 January 1753 - Thomas Bullock of NORTH CAROLINA, COUNTY OF
PERQUIMANS, sells to John Lawrence of County of Isle of Wight in Virginia
for £5.10, 50 acres of land in Isle of Wight County purchased by sd
Thomas Bullock from Samuel Bosman 25 November 1728, etc. Recorded
6 September 1753.

Isle of Wight Co. Deed Book 13, page 325 -

24 December 1775 - John Bullock and Sarah, his wife, of COUNTY OF
PERQUIMENS, PROVINCE OF NORTH CAROLINA, sell to Thomas Newby, Jr. of County
of Isle of Wight Colony of Virginia, for £52.10, 170 acres of land in County
of Isle of Wight near the head of the Western Branch of Nansemond River -
which land was given and devised by Roger Nevil to his daughter Rachel Nevill
who intermarried with William Bullock, father of the aforementioned John
Bullock, and who being the only male descendant of the sd William Bullock and
Rachel, his wife, etc. Recorded 4 January 1776.

Rockbridge Co. Deed Book B, page 547 -

9 July 1793 - Indenture in which William Blain and Mary, his wife,
OF THE COUNTY OF GREENBRIER [now West Virginia] and William Anderson and
Catherine, his wife, late Catherine Blain, OF THE COUNTY OF FAYETTE, STATE
OF KENTUCKY, heirs of William Blain, deceased, sell to James Caruthers of the
County of Rockbridge, State of Virginia, Lot #22 in the Town of Lexington,
the said William Blain having departed this life, intestate, and having sold
said lot but had not made a legal conveyance - said parties of first part
sell to said James Caruthers, for £500, said Lot #22, etc. Certified by
Justice of Fayette Co., Ky. that William Anderson acknowledged the indenture
as his act and Deed and Catharine, his wife, relinquished her right of dower.
Recorded Rockbridge Co., Va. Dec. 23, 1793.

NOTE BY CHH: In Deed Book c, page 8 - dated 31 July 1793 - a duplicate of
the above Deed of Sale of Lot #22 is written up as by William and Mary BLAIR
of Greenbrier Co., heirs of William BLAIR, deceased, etc.

Nottoway Co. Will Book 6, page 438 -

Last Will and Testament of Theodorick Jones, of MADISON COUNTY, STATE
OF ALABAMA, dated 23 March 1820. Certified before a Special Term of the
Orphan's Court of MORGAN COUNTY, ALABAMA 5th March 1824. Recorded Nottoway
County, Va. 6th February 1834.

Names a brother as Littleberry H. Jones. Legacies to loving wife, Ann
[Jones], daughter, Susannah S. H. Cunliffe, daughter Frances L. Jones, and
son William A. M. Jones. Wife, Ann, executrix. Witnesses: John M. Leake,
John R. B. Eldridge. Wiley Russell.

Nottoway Co. Deed Book 1, page 412 -

16 August 1794 - John Winn OF MASON COUNTY, STATE OF KENTUCKY and John
Tabb of County of Amelia in Virginia, of one part, sell to Freeman Epes of
Nottoway Co., Va. for 53,910 lbs. of tobacco a tract of land containing 246
acres, 1 rood, 32 poles, in County of Nottoway on the east side of Lazaretta
Creek, etc. Witnesses: Murdock Cooper, John Gooch, Susanna Duke Gooch,
William Harper, W. Worsham, Wm. Cabaniss, Edw. Bland, Jr., Wm. Piles. Recorded
5 December 1794.

42

Nottoway Co. Deed Book 1, page 554

6 May 1796 - William Chalmers of FORTS CREEK IN THE COUNTY OF WARREN, STATE OF GEORGIA, appoints Richard Warthen of Little Ogechee IN THE COUNTY OF HANCOCK, STATE OF GEORGIA, his true and lawful attorney, to apprehend a certain negro man named Anthony, my property, who has eloped from my service.

NOTE BY CHH: Richard Warthen tracked down the escaped slave and found him in jail in Nottoway Co., Va., committed there as a runaway, who called himself Tom and said that he belonged to John Hubbard of THE STATE OF GEORGIA, purchased by him lately of William Chambers [sic] of the STATE OF GEORGIA. Recorded 7 July 1796.

Prince George Co. Deeds, etc. (1713-1728) page 216

8 December 1717 - Indenture in which William Lowe OF THE PROVINCE OF NORTH CAROLINA sells to George Pace of the Colony of Virginia in Prince George Co., a tract of land in Bristol Parish, County of Prince George, containing 150 acres, being the plantation whereon the said George Pace now dwells - for the sum of £10, etc. Witnesses: Robert Munford, Buller Herbert, George Tillman. Recorded 11 March 1717/8.

Ibid, page 545 -

24 October 1721 - Power of Attorney from Hugh Hall of the Island of Barbados, Esquire, eldest brother of Captain John Hall, lately deceased in Virginia, appointing Major George Braxton of Yorke River, in Virginia, his true and lawful attorney to recover from ___[blank]___ Jackson, Administrator his, the estate of his said brother [Capt. John Hall] etc. Witnesses: John Epes, William Epes, Walter Vernon, Jr. Recorded Prince George Co. 12 June 1722.

Ibid, page 581 -

6 November 1722 - Power of Attorney by James Minge, OF NORTH CAROLINA, Gent. appointing his trusty and well beloved friend, Captain Edward Wyatt of the County of Prince George in the Colony of Virginia, his true and lawful attorney to rent or lease his lands in Martin Brandon Parish, not to exceed ten years, etc. Witnesses: Edward Johnson, Thomas Hooper. Recorded 12 February 1722/3.

NOTE BY CHH: In the Quit Rents of 1704, James Minge, Sr. is listed with 500 acres in Prince George Co. and James Minge with 1086 acres in Charles City Co.

Ibid, page 592 -

14 February 1722/3 - Power of Attorney from Nathaniel Woodward, of BOSTON, IN THE COUNTY OF SUFFOLK, BLOCKMAKER, son and heir of Samuel Woodward, late of Boston, aforesaid, marriner, deceased, appointing his friend Mr. Thomas Eldridge of Surry County in Virginia, Gent., his attorney, to recover possession of a certain tract of land, containing 600 acres in the County of Prince George, upon Appomattox River, in the Colony of Virginia, which

land was granted unto Christopher Woodward, father of the aforesaid Samuel Woodward by patent dated 24 August 1637, under whom I claim, etc. Witnesses: Thomas Lathropp, Elias Cotting, Thomas Lothropp, Jr. Recorded 9 April 1723.

NOTE BY CHH: In the recordation, Boston is further identified as being in NEW ENGLAND. See next item.

Prince George Co. Deeds, etc. (1713-1728) page 593 –

Depositions - 13 August 1722:

Jonathan Dows of Charlestown, IN NEW ENGLAND, Esquire, testifies that Samuel Woodward, who married in New England, at Boston, to one of Mr. Francis Hudson's daughters, was reported to be the proprietor or owner of a plantation lying on Appomattox River in Virginia, and that he, the deponent, was employed to buy part of the said plantation for Col. William Randolph, and what he did in that affair was approved of as lawful and the said Woodward's claim to the said estate was accounted lawful, etc.

Also certifications by his Excellency, Samuel Shute, Esq., Captain General and Governor-in-chief of his Majestys Province of Massachusetts Bay in New England, and by -

Captain Thomas Ruck, Marriner, and Francis Hudson, Shipwright, both of Boston, in the County of Suffolk, in New England, being of full age, testify that Nathaniel Woodward of Boston, blockmaker, was the reputed son and heir of Samuel Woodward, heretofore of Virginia and late of Boston, aforesaid and Elizabeth (Hudson) his wife, both deceased, etc. Recorded Prince George Co., Va. 9 April 1723.

NOTE BY CHH: In the Quit Rents of 1704 Samuel Woodward is listed with 600 acres in Prince George County and 350 acres in James City County. In the muster of the Inhabitants of Virginia 1624-1625 is Christopher Woodward, age 30 (thus born ca 1595) who came over in the Tryall 1620.

Ibid, page 594 -

9 April 1723 - Buller Herbert, Gent. of the County of Prince George, Colony of Virginia, gives bond in the sum of 120 pds sterling money of Great Britain unto Nathaniel Woodward of Boston in the County of SUFFOLK, PROVINCE OF MASSACHUSETTS BAY in NEW ENGLAND, to pay unto the said Nathaniel Woodward 60 pds sterling within 1000 days, being in full for 600 acres of land in the said County of Prince George and lately sold to the said Herbert by the said Woodward, without fraud or further delay, etc. Witnesses: Richard Kennon, Elias Cotting, Thomas Lottropp, Jr. Recorded same date.

Ibid, page 719 -

2 September 1723 - Power of Attorney from John Clay of THE PROVINCE OF NORTH CAROLINA, appointing Major Robert Munford of Prince George County, his true and lawful attorney to acknowledge in open court his deed of sale of land in Prince George County to Henry Thweatte of Prince George Co., etc.

44

Witnesses: James Thweatte, Miles Thweatte, John Ellis, Jr. Recorded 9 June 1724.

NOTE BY CHH: This record is followed by the above cited deed, bearing same date, containing 70 acres, being one half of that moiety formerly belonging to John Clay, deceased, etc. The Quit Rents of 1704 lists John Clay with 350 acres and Thomas Clay with 70 acres, both tracts in Prince George Co.

Prince George Co. Deeds, etc. (1713-1728) page 959 -

7 October 1726 - Power of Attorney from Elizabeth Cart, of London, widow and William Smith, of London, merchant - Whereas William Smith, late of the CITY OF BRISTOL, merchant, deceased, did, in his last will dated 27 September 1704 (amongst other devises and bequests therein contained) did give, devise, and bequeath the remaining part of his plantation and land in Virginia, being 2,000 acres, all stock, etc. to his son, Joseph Smith, for his natural life, and after his decease unto the children of the said Joseph Smith, that were then born, or that should be born on the body of his then wife, and for default of such children, then to his right heirs, as in and by the said will duly proved in the Preogative Court of Canterbury, by the said Joseph Smith, the sole executor therein named, may appear. Now know ye, that we, the said Elizabeth Cart and William Smith, the only surviving children of the said Joseph Smith and Hester, his wife (the person intended in and by the said will) etc. appoint Robert Hall and David Wallace, both of Martins Brandon, on James River in Virginia, our lawful attorney, for us, to our use and behoof [sic] immediately from and after the decease of our said father, the said Joseph Smith, to take possession of the said plantation, which lyeth and extendeth near Mattapony, by York River in Virginia aforesaid and is now in the occupation of the said Joseph Smith, etc. Witnesses: John Posford, Jonathan Evendon. Recorded 14 February 1726/7.

Ibid, page 986 -

2 November 1725 - Power of Attorney from Elizabeth Taylor of the ISLAND OF BARBADOS, PARISH OF ST. MICHAEL, wife to Richard Taylor, late of this Island, merchant, but now of the KINGDOM OF GREAT BRITAIN, whereas the said Richard Taylor by his certain Letter of Attorney dated 11 May 1724, did appoint me, Elizabeth Taylor, his dear and loveing wife, his lawful attorney, and did impower me to substitute one or more attorneys, etc., I do appoint my good friend, (Capt.) Charles Fisher, Master of the Ship, Mary Galley, my true and lawful substitute attorney to demand, sue, etc. Richard Moseley of Virginia, by virtue of a Bond by him, the said Richard Moseley duly executed 24 April 1724, etc. Witnesses: Enoch Jenkins, Edward Hormon. Recorded 9 May 1727.

Ibid, page 1029 -

Last Will and Testament of Robert Jones Junior dated NORTH CAROLINA April 6, 1727, probated 8 August 1727.
States that he is of BARTTE [sic] PRECINCT (probably Bertie County) Legacy to his father, Robert Jones Senior of 100 acres of land in Prince

George Co. in Virginia, for his natural life and with reversion to my eldest son, Thomas Jones, and also his other land in aforesaid county of Prince George to my said son, Thomas. Executor, his father Robert Jones Senior, whom he further instructs to sell his land in this precinct [i.e., Bertie, N.C.] and his other stock, etc. and divide the money equally between his wife and children. Witnesses: William Dennis, Abraham Burton, Henry Jones,Jr.

NOTE BY CHH: In the Quit Rents of 1704 a Robert Jones has 241 acres in Prince George County.

Prince George Co. Deeds, etc. (1713-1728) page 1037 -

5 October 1727 - Indenture in which John Lowe, William Lowe, and George Pace, OF CAROLINA, of one part, sell to William Short of the County of Surry, in Virginia - (lease and release) a certain tract of land in Prince George County containing 674 acres, more or less, on the southside of Appomattox River, etc. Recorded 10 October 1727. Sarah, wife of John Lowe, relinquished her right of dower.

Norfolk Co. Will Book 2, page 17 -

Last Will and Testament of Frederick Bracegirdle, late of the CITY OF LONDON, but now in the County of Norfolk, Province of Virginia, dated 3 May 1773, proved July Court 1773.

My worthy friend, John Runsberg, resident in the Borough of Norfolk, Province of Virginia, my whole and sole heir to all money that have, shall, or may come to me out of the arrears due in DONAGHEADY PARISH IN THE COUNTY OF TYRONE IN IRELAND amounting to upwards of 2,000 pds. sterling, the collec- tion of which Mrs. Trusty Cary was agent chosen by my late father, The Reverand George Bracegirdle, Rector of the above Parish of Donagheady, etc. After the death of the said John Runsberg, it is my will that his wife, Rebecca, shall enjoy the same estate - aforesaid John Runsberg my whole and sole executor. Witnesses: William McGrath, John Fudge, John William Gilbert Voltaneier (?).

Patrick Co. Deed Book 7, page 218 -

29 November 1828 - Power of Attorney from Abram Penn and Wilson Penn, heretofore residenters [sic] of the County of Patrick, State of Virginia and removing our residence to the westward and leaving our business un- settled, etc. authorize and empower Edmund Penn of the County of Patrick aforesaid our lawful attorney, etc. Recorded February Court 1829.

NOTE BY CHH: The above Abram Penn (Jr.) wife, Sally Critz, was a brother of Edmund Penn and both were sons of Colonel Abram Penn Sr. (died June 26, 1801).

Ibid, page 391 -

4 January 1830 - Thomas Penn, Attorney in fact for Abram Penn of CHRISTIAN COUNTY, KENTUCKY, wells to James Kennedy, John W. Kennedy, and

Joseph Kennedy, Jr. of Patrick Co., Va. - for $332.00 - 332 acres of land
(by survey) in County of Patrick, Va. on a branch of Spoon Creek, etc.
Recorded September Court 1830.

NOTE BY CHH: Captain Thomas Penn was another brother of Abram Penn, Jr.

Patrick Co. Deed Book 7, page 397 -

    Power of Attorney from Abram Penn and Sally, his wife, now of Todd
County, STATE OF KENTUCKY, to Thomas Penn of the County of Patrick, State
of Virginia - Whereas: Sally Penn, formerly Sally Critz of Patrick Co., Va.
has inherited from her father, Hamon Critz, a landed estate in the State of
Virginia and County of Patrick, together with other property consisting of
negroes and chattels lately in the possession of the said Hamon (Critz)
and whereas Abram Penn has intermarried with the said Sally and have issue
born by her - Now Know Ye, etc. dated 10 January 1829 and certified by the
clerk of court and Justices of TODD Co., KY. Recorded in Patrick Co., Va.
September Court 1830.

(handwritten: CRITZ, VA (used to go up here to pick apples w/ Grandma!)

Ibid, Deed Book 6, page 293 -

    13 April 1824 - Thomas Penn, of Patrick Co., Va., Attorney in fact for
George Penn of LOUISIANNA, sells 198 acres of land in Patrick Co. to
Claiborne Shelton for $300, etc. Recorded April Court 1824.

NOTE BY CHH: George Penn was another son of Col. Abraham Penn, Sr.
(d.1801). Other records indicate George Penn (1770-1828) married Sally
Gordon.

Ibid, Deed Book 2, page 335 -

    14 April 1802 - William Fulcher and John Mills of the City of Richmond
and State of Virginia, sell to Major John Martin of STOKES COUNTY AND STATE
OF NORTH CAROLINA, two negro girls named Darkes (about 18) and Eavy (about
3 years) now in the hands of Abraham Martin of Stokes Co., N. C. for 100 pds.
Va. currency, etc. Witnesses: Abraham Penn, William Bell. Recorded April
Court 1804.

Ibid, Deed Book 7, page 384 -

    25 June 1830 - Indenture in which William Carter, Senior, of Patrick
Co., Va. makes a deed of gift for love and affection for his grandchildren:
Susan Martin, Anne Martin, Ruth Martin, and John Martin, children of James
Martin OF THE COUNTY OF SURRY, STATE OF NORTH CAROLINA, a Negro woman, Zelpha,
and her two children, Matilda and Jean, and a Negro boy named Clark, etc.
Recorded August Court 1830.

Nelson Co. Deed Book 1, page 119 -

    23 October 1809 - Indenture in which Thomas Jopling and Molly his wife,
of Nelson County, Virginia, sell to:

Ralph Jopling
John Jopling
Nancy West, wife of Bransford West
Sarah Ball, widow of William Ball, dec'd
Katharine Thurmond, widow of Gutheridge Thurmond, dec'd
Jane Jopling
All of the County of Nelson, Va., and to:

William Jopling OF NORTH CAROLINA [Caswell Co.]
Benjamin Jopling OF NORTH CAROLINA [Person Co.]
Daniel Jopling of Albemarle Co., Va.
Patsey Thomas, wife of Michael Thomas of Albemarle Co.

And to:

Michael Thomas, Ralph Thomas and Betsey Farguson, wife of
Daniel Ferguson, who are the children of Mary Thomas, dec'd,
late the wife of Ralph Thomas and formerly Mary Jopling, of
the County of Nelson - all parties of the other part -

Whereas, the lands hereafter described and conveyed were purchased by Ralph
Jopling, late of the County of Amherst, Va. deceased, father of the parties
aforesaid, except the children of Mary Thomas, dec'd, of whom he was the
grandfather, and whereas the said lands were conveyed and assured to the said
Thomas Jopling, agent of the said Ralph Jopling, last named by Colbert Blair
of the County OF BURKE IN STATE OF NORTH CAROLINA (by deed) dated 8th October
1789 and whereas the said Ralph Jopling by his last Will dated 28 June 1791
recorded in the County of Amherst did devise the said lands equally to his
sons Ralph and James, who since departed this life, intestate and without
issue, leaving all the aforesaid parties his heirs, etc. Parties of the first
part now sell, grant, and convey to parties of the second part wo tracts of
land (except one-twelfth part) in the COUNTY OF BURKE, N.C. (1) containing
323 acres and (2) adjoining the first tract and contains 150 acres, etc.

<u>Amherst Co. Will Book 3, page 195</u> -

Will of Ralph Jopling dated 28 June 1791 and proved 5 September 1791.

Wife, Catharine

Sons:
Ralph - land in BURKE CO.,N.C.
James - land in BURKE CO.,N.C.
Thomas
William (see Note)
Daniel
John
Ben

Daughters:
Sarah Jopling
Jane Jopling
Ann Jopling
Catharine Thurmond
Martha Thomas
Mary Thomas (deed)
(her children, Michael, Ralph,
and Betsy)

Executors: Wife, Catharine; son, James; Thomas Farrar, and Richard Farrar.
Witnesses: Sherod Griffin, John Snider, Jas. Eric, Jas. Trail.

Note: Legacy to son William Jopling, a negro boy named Squire. Executors
Bond - £3,000.

Amherst Co. Deed Book I, page 329 -

23 December 1801 - James Jopling and Martha, his wife; Edmund Powell and Lucy, his wife; Pleasant Martin and Rebeckah, his wife; Hannah Allen; Ann Childress; and John Griffin, of one part sell to Edward and Holeman Jopling, of the other part, for $10.00, 1,813½ acres of land in KANAHAWA COUNTY [WEST VIRGINIA] on the right hand fork of the Thirteen Mile Creek, which is a branch of the Great Kenhawa [sic], which land was patented to Thomas Jopling, etc. Witnesses: William Lee Harris, Benjamin Childress, Richard C. Pollard, Jesse Jopling, William Dixon. (No date of acknowledgment or of recording.)

NOTE BY CHH: The parties of the first part are named as children and heirs in the last Will and Testament of Thomas Jopling of Amherst Co., Va. dated August 10, 1789, probated September 7, 1789. (See W.B. 3, page 116.)

Bedford Co. Deed Book 25, page 312 -

22 March 1836 - "I, Lewis Turner, of the COUNTY OF MURRY, IN THE STATE OF TENNESSEE having heretofore relinquished, many years since, all the claim which I might have in the Estate of Elisha Hurt or Mildred Hurt, his widow, in right of my wife, Mildred, deceased, the daughter of the said Elisha and Mildred Hurt, do now confirm the same and do forever quit-claim, surrender, give up, etc. all my right, title, claim, interest, etc. in the consideration that I had no heirs by my said wife and that I, therefore, ought not in justice to claim it, etc. ..." Certified before Justices of Murry Co., Tenn. Recorded Bedford Co., Va. 27 June 1836.

NOTE BY CHH: Lewis Turner married Milly Hurt Dec. 24, 1805, Elisha Hurt bondsman, (Bedford Co. marriages). I don't see a Murry Co. Tenn. listed. It may be meant for Maury Co.

Bedford Co. Deed Book 21, page 481 -

30 June 1829 - Power of Attorney from John H. Meador of the COUNTY OF ALLEN, STATE OF KENTUCKY to John Turner of the County of Bedford in Va. - to sell for him 2 tracts of land in Virginia, one in Bedford Co. and the other in Franklin Co. in which he holds an undivided interest in right of his late grandfather, Joseph Wright, etc. Certified before the justices of Allen Co., Ky. Recorded Bedford Co., Va. 26 October 1829.

Ibid -

19 November 1827 - Power of Attorney from John Meador and Jinny, his wife; Joseph Meador and Nancy, his wife; Jubal W. Meador; Bennett Meador and Judith, his wife - of the COUNTY OF SUMNER, STATE OF TENNESSEE to John Turner of the County of Bedford, State of Virginia, their lawful attorney, to sell two tracts of land in Virginia in the counties of Bedford and Franklin, etc. Certified before the justices of Sumner Co., Tenn, etc. Recorded Bedford Co., Va. 26 October 1829.

NOTE BY CHH: (ibid, page 482) 11 April 1829 - John Turner of Bedford Co.,

49

Va., by virtue of the above powers of attorney sold to Jonas Minter 139 acres in the County of Bedford, formerly owned by Nancy Meador, deceased.

Bedford Co. Deed Book 21, page 484 -

28 August 1829 - Power of Attorney from Elizabeth Caldwell OF THE COUNTY OF SIMPSON, STATE OF KENTUCKY, appointing her father, Henry Caldwell of the same county and state, her lawful attorney to receive of and from Benjamin Turner, of Bedford Co., Va., who was executor of Solomon Hardy, deceased what is her due from the estate of the said Solomon Hardy as the daughter and heir of "my deceased mother, Mornin Caldwell, late Mornin Hardy" etc. Certified before the Justices of Simpson County, Kentucky and recorded at Bedford Co., Va. 26 October 1829.

Shenandoah Co. Deed Book G, page 467 -

8 February 1790 - Zachariah McKay of the COUNTY OF SULLIVAN, STATE OF NORTH CAROLINA, gives power of attorney to Jeremiah McKay and Sinnett Young of the County of Shenandoah, in Virginia, etc. [Note: James McKay is one of the witnesses] Recorded 29 April 1790.

Ibid, Deed Book H, page 2 -

30 September 1790 - James McKay of County of Shenandoah gives power of attorney to Isaac McCarty in the COUNTY OF NELSON, STATE OF KENTUCKY, respecting a"certain piece of land located by Richard Parker for me", etc. [Note: Jeremiah McKay is one of the witnesses.] Acknowledged and recorded 1 October 1790.

Ibid, page 29 -

28 December 1790 - Jeremiah McCay [sic] of the County of Shenandoah gives his power of attorney to David Job in the COUNTY OF WASHINGTON and to Abraham McKay [sic] of GREENE COUNTY, BOTH IN NORTH CAROLINA STATE, to receive his wife's portion of the estate of Joseph Whitson, deceased, etc. Recorded 30 December 1790.

Ibid, Deed Book S, page 64 -

18 Nov. 1809 - James McKay, Moses McKay, Zachariah McKay and Sally, his wife, and Robert McKay, who are four of the children of James McKay, Junior, dec'd and devisees in the Will of the said James McKay the elder, of Shenandoah Co. sell to Joseph Stover and Philip Spengler of said County for 400 pds - four undivided eighth parts of the undivided whole of two tracts of land, being the same tracts devised to the children and widow of James McKay Junior [sic] deceased by the Will of James McKay the elder - and which said James McKay, the younger, deceased, left nine children of whom the said James, Moses Zachariah and Robert are four - and will inherit on death of their mother, Mary, widow of James McKay the younger, dec'd. Recorded 7 January 1811.

50

Shenandoah Co. Deed Book S, page 65 -

18 November 1809 - Mary McKay, widow and relict of James McKay, Jr., decd., and Leah McKay, Abraham McKay, Nancy McKay and Thomas Vaughan and Polly his wife (late Polly McKay) children of the said James McKay, Jr., decd - all devisees in the Will of James McKay the elder, deceased and all of THE COUNTY OF DEARBORUN [sic] IN THE INDIANA TERRITORY, by James McKay, their attorney, sell to Joseph Stover and Philip Spengler of County of Shenandoah, the life interest of the said Mary McKay and the 1/8th undivided interest of each of the above named children of James McKay, Jr., dec'd of two tracts of land in Shenandoah Co., Va. etc. Recorded 7 May 1810.

NOTE BY CHH: James Mc Cay (McKay) Junior died in 1788 as is proven by an Administrator's bond dated 30 October 1788 by Mary McKay, Robert McCay and James Leith, with James McCay, their security (W.B. B, page 502.) James McKay Senior survived until 1797 and died testate, mentioning among others the children of his deceased son, James. (W.B. E, page 105).

Amelia Co. Will Book 2X, page 10 -

Last Will and Testament of Hans Hinrick Stegar dated 6 March 1761, probated 27 November 1761.

"To my loved wife, Tralucia Steegar [sic] 100 acres of land, being part of the tract I live on, [several other bequests to her] and also, to her, one half of my houses in St. Ann's Lane IN YE PARRISH OF ST. JOHNS ZACCHARY, IN THE CITY OF LONDON; also one-half of the two houses in Snowe's Field in THE PARRISH OF ST. GEORGE, SOUTHWARTH, with seventeen shares of my PENNSYLVANIA lands,"etc.

Legacy to his daughter, Tralucia Greensword "the whole remaining part of my estate to my son, Hans William Steeger"[sic]

Executors: wife, Tralucia; daughter Tralucia Greensword, and son, Hans William Steger [sic]. Witnesses: Gower Dennis, Matthew Ormsby, William Carr.

NOTE BY CHH: The name of the daughter, Tralucia "Greensword", is written in the Will with this spelling and also as "Greenswoard". In my opinion it should have been transcribed or deciphered as "Greenswood". Amelia County marriages by K. B. Williams (p.92) exhibits a marriage bond dated 1st April 1762 in which Henry Robertson marries Tralucia Greenwood, widow. Ambrose Estes, bondsman.

Ibid, Deed Book 7, page 585 -

20 April 1762 - Indenture in which Tralucia Steger, the wife of Hans Hendrick Steger, sugar refiner, of the bank side Southwark in the County of Surry, but late of the Parish of Nottoway and County of Amelia, deceased, and daughter of William Ginn of St. Ann's Lane in the PARISH OF ST. JOHN'S ZACHERY IN THE CITY OF LONDON, deceased - gives to Henry Robertson - for love and affection unto the said Henry Robertson and Tralucia, his wife, "daughter of me," Tralucia Steger, one half of all my estate, right, title,

etc. of my PENNSYLVANIA LAND shares and one half of my right of all that can
be got and recovered by a schedule of deeds, papers, and writings, belonging
to the aforesaid Hans Steger and deposited in the hands of William Barclay,
merchant, in London, April 24, 1754, etc. "my freeholds, rents, and profits
in London," etc. Recorded 22 April 1762.

Amelia Co. Deed Book 7, page 586 -

24 April 1754 - A schedule of Deeds, papers, etc. belonging to Mr. Hans
Steger of Bank side, Southwark [Parish] Surry Co., sugar refiner, and now on
a voyage to Virginia, left and deposited in the hands of Mr. William Barclay,
of London, merchant, for safe keeping and secure custody:

(1) Indenture tripartite bearing date 9 January 1707 [sic] made between
    Elizabeth Walton - William Ginnes - James Freeman and Edward Loyd.

(2) Letters of Administration dated 14 April 1750 out of the Prerogative of
    Canterbury granted to Tralucia Stegar of the goods of William Ginne, her
    late father.

(3) An assignment of a lease from Richard Palmer to Hans Steger dated
    9 April 1750.

(4) An Indenture (In Trust) dated 27 March 1754 between Hans Steger and
    Tralucia, his wife, to Christian Fraley.

(5) A memorandum and certificate as follows (to wit) A77 - This is to cer-
    tify that William Ginn of St. Ann's Lane hath had 34 share of the lands,
    stocks, and profits of and belonging to the Pennsylvania Land Company,
    in co-partnership in London and all improvements of the same, hemp, flax,
    etc. transferred to him in the said company's books number 116, page 39,
    this 11 day of May 1721, etc.
                        Signed by William Barclay -
Recorded Amelia Co. 22 April 1762.

Virginia Taxpayers - By Fothergill, p. 118 -

Dinwiddie Co. 1782:
                William Stegar 1 - 1
                Stegar & Co.   0 - 1

State Enumerations of Virginia, p. 12: -

The estate of Henry Robertson, deceased, is recorded in Amelia
County Personal Property Tax list of 1782 - 8 whites 16 blacks.

Shenandoah Co. Book A, page 148 -

24 November 1772 - Jacob Borden and Mary, his wife, of County of
Frederick sell to George Adam Bowman of the COUNTY OF LANCASTER, IN PENNSYL-
VANIA, adjoining land of John Boughman, containing 180 acres. Recorded
County Court of Dunmore Nov. 24, 1772. NOTE: His Will can be found in
Shenandoah Co. WB E, page 144 (1797).

Shenandoah Co. Deed Book G, page 200 -

    ? January 1789 - Abraham Bowman, of the COUNTY OF FAYETTE, DISTRICT OF
KENTUCKY and State of Virginia, appoints his trusty friend and brother, Isaac
Bowman, of the County of Shenandoah, in Virginia, his true and lawful attorney
to conduct his business in the Counties of Shenandoah and Frederick, to rent
his plantation in the County of Frederick; to prosecute a suit in chancery
brought by him in the County Court of Frederick against Jacob Bowman, heir-at-
law of Jacob Bowman, deceased, to compel him to make a title to certain lands
bequeathed by the last Will of George Bowman, deceased, to George Bowman,
Abraham Bowman, Joseph Bowman, and Isaac Bowman, etc. Recorded 29 January
1789.

Ibid, page 238 -

    6 April 1789 - Jacob Bowman, of Laurance (sic) County in District of 96,
Commonwealth (sic) of South Carolina, eldest son and heir at law of Jacob
Bowman, late of the same place but now deceased, who was eldest son and heir
at law of George Bowman, the elder, sometime of Cedar Creek in the County of
Frederick, in Virginia, now deceased - of one part, to Isaac Bowman, of
Shenandoah Co., Va. one of the sons of the said deceased George Bowman, of
the other part - Whereas the said George Bowman by his Will dated 3 November
1764, of record in Court of Frederick did direct his plantation on Cedar
Creek containing 720 acres, should be divided in four parts among his sons:
George (since dead), Isaac Abraham, and Joseph, each part to contain 180
acres, and whereas the said deceased Jacob Bowman, of one part, and his
brothers, Abraham, Joseph, and Isaac Bowman, all then of the County of
Frederick, Va., sons of the said deceased George Bowman, have since discovered that through the ignorance of the person who drew the Will that the
said Abraham, Isaac and Joseph Bowman only took an estate for life in the
lands devised and not a fee simple, as was intended, and the reversion, after
their deaths, descended to him, the said deceased Jacob Bowman, as then
elder brother and heir at law of their father, and well knowing how much he
would deviate from the character of an honest man should he take advantage
of the unskillfullness [sic] of a clerk and thereby destroy the just designs
of his father in making a proper provision for his children, etc. etc. relinquishes and quit-claims his right, title, claim, etc. Acknowledged and
recorded 30 April 1789.

Ibid, Deed Book H, page 195 -

    9 March 1791 - Jacob Baughman, of the COUNTY OF GREEN, STATE OF NORTH
CAROLINA, appoints his brother, Abraham Baughman, of the County of Shenandoah,
Va., his true and lawful attorney to secure the rents for his land due from
Daniel Coffman and title to land purchased of Martin Garver, etc. Proved by
the affirmation of Samuel Carver, a witness, and recorded 29th September 1791.

Ibid, Deed Book L, page 65 -

    15 August 1797 - Jacob Bowman and Elizabeth, his wife, eldest son and
heir of Jacob Bowman, dec'd, late of the County of Shenandoah, Va., but now
of GREEN COUNTY TERRITORY, southside of the Ohio, or STATE OF TENNESSEE sell

to David Jordan of Shenandoah Co. - for £1000 - two tracts of land in County
of Shenandoah, adjoining each other (1) containing 200 acres and (2) containing 36 acres, etc. [Note: Elizabeth Bowman relinquishes her dower rights,
certified by Justices of Green Co., Tenn.]

Shenandoah Co. Deed Book N, page 198 -

21 December 1791 - Jacob Boughman of the Territory of the United States,
south of the Ohio, of one part, to his son, Henry Boughman, of the County of
Shenandoah in Va., conveys two tracts of land in the said County of Shenandoah,
one tract being the same on which he formerly lived and got with his wife by
the last Will and Testament of his father in law, Doctor John Henry Neff containing 200 acres and the other granted by patent to him containing 235 acres
dated 10 January 1787, on Mill Creek, etc. (signed in German script) Certified
by Clerk of the County of Sevier, State of Tennessee. Recorded 7 March 1803.

Ibid, Deed Book W, page 449 -

[Date blank] - Daniel Boughman and Darcus, his wife, of the County of
Lincoln, STATE OF TENNESSEE (he being heir and devissee of John Boughman,
dec'd) sell to Abraham Boughman of the County of Shenandoah, in Va., for
$350.00 - one undivided eighth part in four tracts of land left to him in the
will of his deceased father, John Boughman, which land contains about 202
acres and 72 poles, about one mile below New Market, etc. Certified by Clerk
of Lincoln Co., Tennessee 9 February 1816. Recorded Shenandoah Co., Va.
9 April 1816.

Ibid, Deed Book N, page 521 -

Will of Isaac Bowman, dated 20 June 1824, proved 15 November 1826.

Mentions a valuable tract of land he has already given his eldest son,
Philip, in County of Shenandoah, and land in the STATE OF INDIANA he has
given his sons, Abraham, Joseph, and John Bowman, as their respective portions
of his real estate. Also, slaves he has given to each of the above sons.
Legacy to daughter Susannah, wife of Wm. H. Richardson, now resident in STATE
OF OHIO, of 500 acres, being lot #232 ILLINOIS MILITARY GRANT in STATE OF
INDIANA. "To my Daughter, Eliza B., wife of Joseph M. Fauntleroy of the
County of Frederick, 500 acres in STATE OF INDIANA." To beloved wife, Mary,
land in Shenandoah County and Frederick County including land "I lately
purchased of my son Philip." Legacies to six younger children (all underage)
namely, Isaac, George, Robert, Washington, Mary, and Rebecca - "the
families and slaves I acquired by intermarriage with my wife, Mary." Names
his friend and nephew, George Brinker. Mentions fact of his first wife and
their children by her. Mentions his several lots of land in TOWN OF
JEFFERSON IN STATE OF INDIANA. His ferry across the Ohio River, and tracts
of land in the Illinois Grant. A tract of 1400 acres in STATE OF KENTUCKY
on waters of Green River and Delaware Creek and about 1100 acres in Counties
of Shenandoah and Frederick. Executors, wife, Mary, and nephew, George
Brinker, and four sons, Isaac, George, Robert, and Washington (as they arrive
at lawful age). CODICIL - Mentions he was appointed guardian of his four
eldest children - Philip, Abraham, Catharine, and Susannah, to receive their
portions of their mother who was one of the daughters of Philip Gatewood,
dec'd.

Fauquier Co. Deed Book 33, page 51 -

10 May 1832 - Spencer Glasscock of the COUNTY OF RALLS, STATE OF
MISSOURI sells to Alfred Rector of County of Fauquier, State of Virginia,
for $325, 230 acres of land in said County of Fauquier, on Goose Creek, being
the same land on which Jesse Glasscock lived at the time of his decease and
being the same tract which George Glasscock by his last Will devised to the
said Jesse Glasscock and his heirs, etc."all my right and title in said land
which includes my interest in my deceased brother, Levin Glasscock's portion
together with all my interest in my father, Jesse Glasscock's negroes."
Certified before Stephen Glasscock and James Carson, two Justices of Ralls
County, Mo. Affidavit by Charles Glasscock, Clerk of County Court of Ralls
County, Mo. Recorded Fauquier Co., Va. 27 August 1832.

NOTE BY CHH: (ibid, page 256) 26 Sept. 1832 - Stephen Glasscock of the
County of Ralls, Missouri sells John Glascock of County of Fauquier, Va. the
undivided third part of 164 acres in Fauquier County which formerly belonged
to Hezekiah Glasscock, dec'd.

Fauquier Co. Deed Book 20, page 284 -

March 12, 1811 - Gregory Glascock and Jemima, his wife, of County of
Fauquier, sell to William Glascock, Sr. of County of Frederick, Va. for
$50.00 all their right and title in a tract of land in County of NELSON,
STATE OF KENTUCKY, containing 1063 acres reserving to themselves 200 acres
from above survey, said land being part of 4687½ acres granted to said Gregory
Glascock by Treasury Warrant #19310 and entered 29 March 1784 signed by James
(Garrard ?) then Governor of Kentucky, etc. - John Glascock, Sr., Wm. Gore,
Moses Hays, witnesses.

Bedford Co. Will Book 1, page 309 -

Will of John Brander dated 27 March 1777 and prob. 28 July 1778.

To nephew, John Brander, of Bedford Co., all "my estate, real and personal."
[and he executor, with John Fitzpatrick and Wm. Austin, Sr., both of Bedford.]

To nephews, James and Andrew Shaws, of SHIRE OF ELGIN IN NORTH BRITAIN, 100 pds.
sterling.

To "my niece, Elspeth Carmichael, daughter of my sister, Margaret, 50 pds.
sterling, and to Wm. Carmichael, my nephew, 50 pds. - and to my nephew,
Alexander Shaw, joiner, in EDINBURGH, 50 pds. sterling, and he, said John
Brander, to pay my sister, Margery Brander, 5 pds. annually as long as she
lives." Witnesses: Guy Smith, Wm. Smith, James McMurray.

Mecklenburg Co. Deed Book 14, page 51 -

30 November 1808 - Richard Hutcheson of the County of FRANKLIN, STATE
OF GEORGIA - John Turner of the COUNTY OF GREEN, STATE OF GEORGIA of one
part, sell to Jacob Shelor of Mecklenburg Co. for 200 pds., a tract of land
in County of Mecklenburg, it being the same tract devised to be sold by the

last Will of Mathew Turner, dec'd containing 127 acres including the Mill known by the name of Crabtree, etc. Witnesses: Samuel Simmons, John Hutcheson (son of Charles), Edwin H. Peete, Cavel Jackson. Recorded 12 December 1808.

Lunenburg Co. Deed Book 28, page 416 -

18 September 1829 - Power of Attorney by Edward Epps of County of Lunenburg appointing Benjamin J. White, NEAR FLORENCE, ALABAMA to recover from Charles O. Hudson STATE OF ALABAMA debt due him, etc. Recorded same day.

Accomack Co. Deed Book 1692-1715, page 473 (Transcript) -

26 December 1701 - Anderson Parker of Sussex County, PROVINCE OF PENNSYLVANIA gives Power of Attorney to his well beloved brother, John Parker, of the County of Accomack, in Virginia, to receive from Mr. Francis Mackemie of Accomack County who is executor of the Will of Mr. Edmund Custis, Gent. dec'd., a legacy by the said Custis to Margaret Robins,"now wife to me"(Anderson Parker) etc. Teste: Edward Parker, Charles Parker, John Barnes, Jr. Recorded Feb. 11, 1701/2.

Pittsylvania Co. Deed Book 40, page 142 -

17 May 1837 - Indenture in which John Mustain, of the COUNTY OF MONROE and STATE OF MISSISSIPPI, sells to James Hines of County of Pittsylvania, State of Virginia - by his lawful attorney, Avery Mustain, for $100.00, a tract of land containing 122 acres in the County of Pittsylvania; adjoining the land of Avery Mustain, Martha Mustain, and others, it being the land the said John Mustain derived from his father (not named) etc. Recorded 19 June 1837.

NOTE: The power of attorney from John Mustain is annexed to the above deed and recorded on page 144 (ibid, ref. p. 145) same date (17 May 1837) Avary Mustain and Frances Mustain, his wife, sell 134 acres of land in Pittsylvania County to James Hines.

Ibid, Deed Book 38, page 310 -

31 December 1835 - Indenture in which Shadrack Mustain and Margaret, his wife, of BEDFORD COUNTY, STATE OF TENNESSEE, sell to Joel Mustain of Pittsylvania County, State of Virginia - for $175.00 all right, title, interest, and claim in a certain tract of land in the said county of Pittsylvania, Va. which was willed to the said Shadrack Mustain by his father, Avery Mustain; at the death of his mother, Mary Mustain, etc. Certified by Justices of Bedford Co., Tenn. same date and Recorded Pittsylvania Co. 18 April 1836.

NOTE BY CHH: Shadrack Mustain married Margaret Devin, daughter of Joseph Devin and his wife, Elizabeth Nowling [Pittsylvania marriage Register]. Shadrack was named son and legatee (among others) in the Will of Avery Mustain. (Rev. War soldier) (deed 1833) (Pittsylvania W.B. 1, page 242)

Amelia Co. Deed Book 4, page 217 -

22 November 1751 - Indenture in which Samuel Bumpass of the PROVINCE OF NORTH CAROLINA, of one part, sells to David Zachary, of the County of Orange, of the other part - for 50 pds. current money of Virginia - a tract of land in County of Amelia (Colony of Virginia) containing 400 acres, on the south side of Little Nottoway River and bounded as mentioned in a patent granted to Robert Bumpass (father of the said Samuel Bumpass) bearing date 15 December 1749, etc. Witness: William Watson, Bartholomew Zachary, Saml. Yarbrough. Recorded 28 November 1751.

COMMENT: Samuel, Robert, and John Bumpass are listed as heads of households in a tax list of Orange Co., N.C. in the year 1755. [North Caroliman Magazine, Vol. 1, page 107.]

Ibid, Deed Book 7, page 434 -

25 December 1760 - Indenture in which Edward Munford OF NORTH CAROLINA & COUNTY OF HALIFAX, sells to Robert Munford of Amelia County, Va. for £600, 620 acres of land in Amelia County on North side of Deep Creek, bounded by lands of the said Robert Munford. Mr. John Hall and James Hudson, etc. Witnesses: John Hall, Robert Stark, Robert Hall, John Hall, Jr., Joseph Hardaway, etc. Recorded 22 January 1761.

Isle of Wight Co. Deed Book 8, page 265 -

2 August 1749 - Thomas Bullock of COUNTY OF PERQUIMMON, PROVINCE OF N NORTH CAROLINA, blacksmith, sells to John Baldwin of County of Gloucester in Virginia, planter, £28 that tract of land on which he, Thomas Bullock lately dwelt, in County of Isle of Wight on the western Branch of Nansemond River, in Newport Parish, containing 257 acres, which land he purchased of John Pope and his son John Pope 22 December 1729, etc. William Bullock is a witness. Recorded Aug. 3, 1749.

Brunswick Co. Deed Book 34, page 381 -

25 November 1846 - Whereas by descent from Gray F. Dunn, dec'd - Mary M. Dunn and Frances Jane Dunn, Children of said Gray F. Dunn, title to certain lands in State of Virginia now hold equal and undivided in sd. lands so derived, and whereas, George W. Smith has intermarried with said M. Dunn and Richard S. Epes has intermarried with said Frances Jane Dunn - now for $500.00 paid said George W. and Mary M. Smith by said Richard S. Epes - convey right, title and interest, etc. in sd lands lying in Counties of Brunswick and Lunenburg, etc.

Certification of above, as their act and deed, received from COUNTY OF SHELBY, STATE OF TENNESSE, of George W. and Mary M. Smith, to the Clerks of Brunswick and Lunenburg Counties, Va. dated 27 November 1846. Recorded Brunswick Co., Va. April 5, 1847.

Brunswick County Marriages by Fothergill, page 35: 10 Nov. 1843 - Richard Epes to Frances Jane Dunn.

Amelia Co. Deed Book 9, page 137 -

26 December 1766 - Indenture in which Henry Blanchet of PROVINCE OF
NORTH CAROLINA (tho late of the County of Amelia, Va.) sells to Reuben
Palmer of County of Amelia - for 60 pds - a tract of land in said County of
Amelia containing 90 acres, adjoining land of John Blanchet, brother of said
Henry Blanchet and others (named) etc. Witnesses: Humphrey Beckley, John
Belcher, Holdcroft Norvell. Recorded 28 May 1767.

Ibid, page 198 -

5 January 1767 - Reuben Palmer of County of Amelia, Colony of Virginia,
for 50 pds - (Deed of Trust) to Henry Blanchet, OF THE PROVINCE OF NORTH
CAROLINA, to secure purchase of 90 acres of land and also a negro man named
Richmond - said 50 pds. to be paid 1st January 1769, etc. (Note: Assigned
by Henry Blanchet, all his rights of within mortgage to Joel Mann.

Middlesex Co. Deed Book (1754-67), page 11 -

7 November 1753 - Indenture in which William Upshaw Davis of THE COUNTY
OF EDGECOMBE, PROVINCE OF NORTH CAROLINA, sells to John Kidd of the County
of Middlesex, Colony of Virginia - for £65 - that tract of land in said
County of Middlesex where on the said John Kidd now lives - on White Oak Run,
Williamson's Spring Branch - containing 140 acres, being part of 670 acres
the said Davis hath lately purchased of Thomas Kidd 25 September last (1753)
Recorded 7 May 1754.

Norfolk Co. Wills and Deeds E (1666-1675), page 5 -

14 July 1666 - Whereas John Ward agreed with Captain hand for his and
his wife's passage FOR ENGLAND FROM JAMAICA, etc.... Wherefore it is ordered
that the said Land doe find the said Ward and his wife sufficient allowance
of diet aboard or ashore during his stay aboard ship, etc.

COMMENT: I think Capt. (Henry) Land got his ship from Jamaica to Virginia
and could not continue the journey to England and John Ward had him in
court for his board, etc.)

Wythe Co. Deed Book 12, page 156 -

17 February 1831 - Robert H. Bogle and Mary, his wife, of COUNTY OF
WASHINGTON, STATE OF INDIANA, sell to Mark Bogle, son of said Robert H.
Bogle, of the County of Wythe, in Virginia - for $1.00 - and for natural
love and affection - a tract of land in said County of Wythe on Walker's
Creek containing 51 acres, etc. Witnesses: Henry W. Hackett, Margaret
Hackett, (Judges of Washington Co., Indiana)- Recorded Wythe Co.
13 Feb. 1832.

NOTE BY CHH: Mark Bogle sold this same land to Dunn Bogle 20 January 1832.
Robert H. Bogle was named as son in Will of' Ralph Bogle (d.1841 - W.B. 5,
page 395.)

58

Wythe Co. Deed Book 12, page 446-448 -

1 October 1832 - Deed of Gift from Robert H. Bogle and Mary, his wife,
of WASHINGTON COUNTY, INDIANA for natural love and affection for Dunn Bogle,
son of the said Robert H. Bogle - a tract of land in Wythe County on Walker
Creek containing 86 acres. Recorded 14 October 1833. (Sam date, same parties
to Dun Bogle - 6 tracts of land containing 726 acres. Recorded 14 October
1833.

Brunswick Co. Deed Book 20, page 525 -

6 February 1809 - John Epps and Elizabeth, his wife, of Newbury District,
STATE OF SOUTH CAROLINA, and William Cureton and Martha, his wife, of JACKSON
COUNTY, STATE OF GEORGIA (by their Power of Attorney to John Epps, aforesaid)
sell to Hugh Love of County of Brunswick, State of Virginia - for 460 pds.
8 sh. one half of a tract of land in County of Brunswick, being the land
William Baugh died possessed of and the above parties claim and sell as heirs
and legatees of said William Baugh, dec'd, containing 704 acres, of which one-
half is 352 acres. Recorded September 25, 1809.

Brunswick Co. Deed Book 29, page 141 -

15 October 1831 - Power of Attorney from Francis Epps of Brunswick County
to George Stainback of said county to receive a sum of money due him as executor
of Eaton P. Vaughan IN GRANVILLE COUNTY, NORTH CAROLINA, from the estate of
Mary A. Vaughan, dec'd. Recorded same date.

Norfolk Co. Deed Book 47, page 206 -

5 May 1817 - George S. Wise, at present of BROOKLYN IN COUNTY OF KINGS,
STATE OF NEW YORK, gives a Power of Attorney to George D. Wise of Norfolk,
State of Virginia, to sell and dispose of his share, title, and interest in
a tract of land in County of Norfolk, Virginia, known as Craney Island, etc.
Certified by Charles J. Doughty, Notary Public of Brooklyn, N.Y. Recorded
Norfolk Co., Va. Aug. 19, 1817.

Ibid, page 327 -

14 July 1818 - Bill of sale from George A. Albertee, Jr. OF DORSET
COUNTY, MARYLAND who sells to Lemuel Reams of AMITE COUNTY, STATE OF MISSISSIPI
for $750.00, a negro woman slave named Betsey, age 30 years and her two children
named Maria (age 6 or 7) and Sarah (18 mo.). Witnesses: James F. Lee and
William Rogers. Recorded Aug. 17, 1818, Norfolk County, Va.

Nottoway Co. Deed Book 2, page 19 -

5 April 1798 - Power of Attorney from Abraham Hatchett of Nottoway Co.,
Va., administrator of Daniel Parham, deceased, late of Amelia Co., Va. to his
trusty friend, Joseph Farley of aforesaid County, Gent., to receive all
monies due the said deceased IN THE STATE OF GEORGIA, and to sell all personal

property of said Daniel Parham dec'd that is not practicable to remove to
the State of Virginia, but to take possession of the negroes of sd dec'd and
remove them to Virginia, etc. Recorded 5 April 1798.

NOTE: Other records name Mary as wife of Abraham Hatchett.

Nottoway Co. Deed Book 3, page 244: 5 Feb. 1807 - Deed of Gift from
Abraham Hatchett and Mary his wife to Wm. Hatchett their son for natural
love and affection of - 194½ acres in said county. Recorded same date.

Nottoway Co. Will Book 4, page 17 -

Last Will and Testament of Chastain Roberts of THE COUNTY OF ROCKING-
HAM, STATE OF NORTH CAROLINA dated 30 July 1816 - probated August Sessions
1816.

To beloved wife, Polly, 4 slaves and all my property, real and personal,
in this State and in Virginia - my executors, my wife Polly Roberts, and
William Bethell. Witnesses: Andrew Foster, James Wall, Anderson Handson.
Certified by Clerk of Court of Rockingham Co., N. C., and recorded Nottoway
Co., 8 November 1816.

1850 Census, Nottoway Co.

127/127 - Thomas W. Epes on land of Lewellin Jones, age 42, Tavern Keeper,
```
                        b. Nottoway      $3000.
        Emily G.,       34  b. Lunenburg
        Algernon S.,    13  b. Nottoway
        Thomas W., Jr., 10  b.  "
        William Taylor, 22  b. VERMONT        teacher
        R.H.L.Burke,    25  b. Prince Edward  M.D.
        John H. Osborne 34  b. IRELAND        Engineer
        Emile Shevalis  28  b. FRANCE         Engineer
        Wm. B. McMurry  25  b. IRELAND        Engineer
```

Montgomery Co. Deed Book K, page 129 -

5 April 1828 - Deed of Gift from Sebastian Wygle, County of Montgomery
to his son William Wygle of sd County for natural love and affection - 300
acres of land in said county. Recorded 14 April 1828. (See record below.)

Montgomery Co. Deed Book M, page 267 -

15 July 1831 - Indenture in which William Wygal OF THE COUNTY OF LEWIS,
STATE OF MISSOURI sells to John Wygal, Jr. of the County of Montgomery, State
of Virginia - for $31.87 - all the right, title, interest or claim the said
William Wygal hath in a tract of land in the County of Montgomery in Va.,
containing 2¼ acres and a grist mill which was conveyed by Philip Cecil
9 August 1827 to Sebastian Wygal, Sr., James Wygal, and John Wygal, Jr.
which part is 1/9th part of 1/3rd of said land which accrued to the said
William Wygal by the death of his father, Sebastian Wygal Senior, etc.

Certified by Justices of LEWIS COUNTY, MISSOURI. Recorded September Court
1837. (Note by CHH: The same day, 15 July 1831, William Wygal, son and co-
heir of Sebastian Wygal, Sr. dec'd of COUNTY OF LEWIS, STATE OF MISSOURI
sells James Wygal, who is also a co-heir of the said Sebastian Wygle, Sr.,
his part of a 400 acre tract in Montgomery Co., Va. which is undivided, etc.
Recorded September Court 1837.

Montgomery Co. Court Order Book 16, page 155 -

August Court 1808 - On the motion of John Wygle who proved to the
satisfaction of the court that he intermarried with Sally HEVNER, daughter
of Phillip Hevner, now deceased, who formerly resided in the STATE OF
PENNSYLVANIA, the same is ordered to be certified.

Montgomery Co. Court Order Book 24, page 180 -

September 1828 - A copy of the last Will and Testament of John Harrison,
deceased was presented in court with the certificate from the Court of Pleas
and Quarter Sessions of JEFFERSON COUNTY, IN THE STATE OF TENNESSEE, ordered
to be recorded. William Elliott, with Philip Kinser and Abijah Whitt, Jr.
his securities gave bond for $800.00 as Administrator of the estate of the
said deceased.

NOTE BY CHH: Montgomery County records by Worrell (p.49) states this Will
was probated June 1828 in FRANKLIN CO., TENN. and in which he named a daughter,
"Feebe" Hankins and grandsons, Jafaniah and David Harrison.

Montgomery Co. Will Book 4, page 412 -

STATE OF TENNESSEE, COUNTY OF JEFFERSON, at the Courthouse in Dandridge
2nd Monday, December 1827, Edward Hankins presented last Will and Testament
of John Harrison dec'd and David Harrison, one of the heirs of the testator
opposed the same, etc. whereupon at March Session 1828 came the parties, by
their attorneys and a jury, etc. (Jury found the paper purporting to be said
last Will and Testament is his last Will, etc.) and the same be admitted to
record. David Harrison to pay costs.

The Will of Jno. Harrison of COUNTY OF JEFFERSON, TENNESSEE, dated
3 January 1826:

To my worthy daughter Feebe Hankins a negro girl - And other items.
to Edward and Feebe Hankins. Zefaniah Harrison has received one negro boy
by name of Jes, being share of his father's estate and David Harrison has
received 165.75 worth of land and one negro woman named Jenny and $10.00,
one sorrel horse and one black mare and saddle, being his share of his father's
estate. My executor, Edward Hankins.

Certified by Clerk of Court of Jefferson Co., Tenn. 18 March 1828.
Recorded Montgomery County Court, Va. September 1828. William Elliott
appointed administrator.

Montgomery Co. Deed Book C, page 33 -

Elisha Bowman of COUNTY OF SURRY, STATE OF NORTH CAROLINA, sells to
John Harrison of County of Montgomery, State of Virginia for £100 - 70
acres in County of Montgomery, etc. Recorded May Court 1797.

Ibid, page 507 -

12 August 1801 - Barbary Wigle, widow and relict of John Wygle, dec'd
of the COUNTY OF JEFFERSON AND STATE OF KENTUCKY, sells to John Crow of
County of Montgomery, State of Virginia, for $20.00 her right of dower, as
widow to said John Wigle, dec'd in a tract of land in Montgomery County
which the said John Wigle died seized - adjoining land of said John Crow,
etc. (Deed acknowledged by Barbary Wygle and certified by Clerk of
Jefferson Co., Ky.) Recorded March Court 1802.

Ibid, Deed Book D, page 44 -

9 September 1803, David Harrison and Ann, his wife, of COUNTY OF
JEFFERSON, STATE OF TENNESSEE, sell to Thomas McHenry of County of
Montgomery, State of Virginia for £100, a tract of land containing 65 acres
in County of Montgomery on Minsers branch waters of Meadow Creek, etc.
Recorded December Court 1803.

NOTE BY CHH: Montgomery Co marriages; Jan. 11, 1791, David Harrison to
Anna Chase. John Chase, Security.

Norfolk Co. Will Book 2, page 17 -

Last Will and Testament of Robert Steed, dated 2 December 1769 and
proved July Court 1773.

"I, Robert Steed, LATE OF BERMUDA, but at present of the Borough of
Norfolk, in Virginia, shipmaster ...

"...To my loving sister, Elizabeth Steed of BERMUDA - £30.

"...To my loving brothers John and Richard, all my wearing apparel.

"...To my loving wife, Hannah Steed, all the residue of my estate,
both real and personal."

Culpeper Co. Deed Book W, page 439 -

18 October 1802 - Power of Attorney from Mary Strother, widow, and
relict of John Strother, deceased of Culpeper County, Va. to her trusty
friends, James Slaughter and Susanna, his wife, of Anson County IN THE
STATE OF NORTH CAROLINA to recover from the Administrators of her brother,
James Wade, deceased, property belonging to his estate, etc. Witnesses:
Joseph Browning, Charles Browning, William Crawford. Recorded same day.
NOTE BY CHH: (ibid page 440) - The deed following the above, is a deed of

Gift from Mary Strother to her loving son in law, James Slaughter, and
Susanna, his wife, of ANSON COUNTY, NORTH CAROLINA, of all her right, title,
and interest of her part of her deceased brother, James Wade's estate.
(dated and recorded same day).

Culpeper Co. Deed Book HH, page 392 -

7 October 1816 - William F. Thompson and Elizabeth, his wife, of the
CITY OF WASHINGTON, sell to French Strother of the County of Cylpeper for
$1,000 - all their interest, claim, title, or demand in and to the lands of
the late Captain John Strother, decd possessed except so much thereof as is
allotted to Mrs. Helen Strother for her dower, etc. Recorded 17 Feb. 1817.

Rappahannock Co. Deed Book K, page 148 -

4 May 1857 - Henry St.G. Strother and Mary E., his wife, French Strother,Jr.
and Susana, his wife, and Charles O. Strother OF THE COUNTY OF CALLOWAY, STATE
OF MISSOURI, of one part, sell to John A. Browning of County of Rappahannock,
in Virginia, of the other part - for $225.00 - 10 acres of land in County of
Rappahannock, conveyed to the said Henry St.G. Strother, Charles O. Strother,
and French Strother, Jr. by their father, French Strother by deed dated
3 May 1844 (DB E, p. 513) etc. Certified the same day by all three parties
of the first part by Thomas Patton, a Justice of the Peace for Calloway Co.,
Missouri. Other certifications by the same Justice, the same date that the
various wives of each had been examined privately apart and relinquished
their right of dower, etc. Recorded Rappahannock Co. 15 June 1857.

Culpeper Co. Deed Book O, page 446 -

1 November 1788 - Power of Attorney from John Strother of County of
Culpeper, State of Virginia, Administrator and heir at law of John Strother,
seaman, son of Francis Strother, late of said County near the head of the
Rappahannock River, deceased, to William Anderson, merchant, of London, to
be my treu and lawful attorney, to recover from Captain Briton, who commanded
the ship on which John Strother, dec'd served on, etc. Recorded 17 November
1788.

NOTE BY CHH: Virginians in the Revolution by Gwathmey, page 95, lists a John
Brittain, Master, Navy - Served on the Patriot. Francis Strother died testate
1777 and named his wife Ann (who was a duaghter of Samuel and Ann Fargeson)
his brother, John and sons: John, Francis, Samuel, and George.

Fauquier Co. Will Book 8, page 410 -

Will of George Glascock dated 10 February 1815 - no date of probate.

"Mansion and plant I bought of John Rector and Thos. Nord to my wife,
Hannah [also to her, slaves] for her natural life and at her decease to be
sold, etc." Proceeds to Son, Moses - merchant and grist mill; to Son,
Thomas, land where he now resides. Mentions boundaries of land to Moses to
be set and estate by Henry Glascock and Jesse Glascock. To daughter, Mary
Jackson, wife of Vincent Jackson, all that land I own in GREEN CO., TENN.

and to son John Glascock to be equally divided between them. "To my son, Hezekiah Glascock, land where he now resides which was purchased by me from Barnett Hough and John Rector, for his natural life and if his present wife Eda, formerly Eda Bishop, should survive the longest, then to her and 1/3 the lands for her natural life."

"To son, Jesse Glascock, land on which he now resides which I purchased of Henry Rector's heirs."

"To son, Acquila, land I purchased of John Withers (275 acres) and a slave boy Henry" -

To daughter, Sarah Crosby, wife of George Crosby $1000 -
To daughter Winifred Brown, wife of Robert Brown, land where Joseph Neal
     now resides and a negro boy Beny.
"My LAND IN KENTUCKY to be sold and proceeds equally divided." Executors: sons, Moses, Jesse and Acquilla. Witnesses: Elisha Dowell, Henry Glasscock, Thos. Rector, Jr.,and Joseph Rector. Recorded 25 April 1826. (Exors Bond $10,000.)

Fauquier Co. Will Book 15, page 193 -

     Will of Thomas J. Glascock of RALLS COUNTY, MISSOURI, 18 July 1836 -

To sister, Sally Balthorpe -
Brother Joseph, lots of land in ? , Virginia and my land in SHELBY COUNTY, MISSOURI (120 acres) - To brother Aaron - 480 (acres ?) in SHELBY COUNTY, MO. To brother David O. Glascock, debts due me, slaves, etc. Legacies to wife of Aaron B. and wife of David O. David O. Glascock, executor. Witnesses: Francis Jett and Wm. H. Peake. Certified before Harrison Glascock, Clerk of Court for RALLS COUNTY, MO. by the witnesses 4 August 1836. Recorded RALLS COUNTY, MO. in NEW LONDON 15 March 1837. Recorded Fauquier Co., Va. 28 June 1837. Administration granted to Eli Crupper who qualified.

Amelia Co. Deed Book 2, page 342 -

     10 September 1745 - Isham Epes and Amy, his wife, of Bath Parish, in Prince George County sell to Thomas Bowrey, late of the ISLAND OF ST. CHRISTOPHERS, for £200 - all that tract of land containing 1993 acres in the County of Amelia, on the north side of Little Nottoway River and on both sides of the Main Sellar fork of Deep Creek, adjoining land of Francis Eppes, Thomas Chappel, John Taylor, John Willis, John Nance, and Anderson's line - 150 acres part thereof being granted to the said Isham Eppes by patent dated 3 October 1734 - 400 acres granted said Isham Eppes by patent dated 21st November 1734 and 1443 acres residue granted to said Isham Eppes by double letters pantent dated 10 July 1745, etc. Witnesses: John Ornsbey, George Currie, John Dabney, and Hugh Miller. Recorded 17 January 1745.

Amelia Co. Deed Book 5, page 453 -

     9 April 1756 - Isham Epes and Amey his wife, of Bath Parish in Dinwiddie County sell to Thomas Bowrey of the Isle of St. Christopher for £200 - 1993 acres in County of Amelia on north side of Little Nottoway River, etc.

COMMENT: This deed is almost an exact copy of the deed of 10 September 1745 and concerns the same parties and the same land. The only difference I can see is that Isham Epes is now of Dinwiddie County instead of Prince George County. The witnesses to the two deeds are entirely different. It is also noted that Amey Eppes signed both records in jointure with her husband Isham Eppes.

Amelia Co. Deed Book 8, page 529 -

25 April 1764 - Thomas Bowrey the Elder, lately OF THE ISLAND OF ST. CHRISTOPHER, now of the Dominion of Virginia, Gentleman, gives his Power of Attorney to Jacob Morgan, Robert Munford, Joseph Carruthers, and Francis Epes, Gentlemen, etc. Witnesses: John Baird, Peter R. Bland, Neill Buchanan, Sr. Jacob Phillips Morgan. Recorded 28 March 1765.

NOTE: Torrence Wills lists a will of Mary Bowry in Charles City County in 1773.

Amelia Co. Deed Book K, page 495 -

14 August 1772 - Thomas Bowry the Elder of the ISLAND OF ST. CHRISTOPHER sells to Francis Eppes of the County of Amelia - for £250.3 - 397 acres of land in the Parish of Nottoway, County of Amelia, adjoining land of said Francis Epes, Peter Epes' new line-- on Cellar Creek, etc. Thomas Bowry, Jr. is one of the witnesses. Recorded September 24, 1772.

Ibid, page 497 -

14 August 1772 - Thomas Bowry the elder sells to Peter Epes of the County of Prince George - for £355.10 - 474 acres of land in Amelia County, parish of Nottoway, adjoining land of Francis Epes, Hamlin's line - Cellar Creek. Recorded 24 Weptember 1772.

Ibid, page 499 -

14 August 1772 - Thomas Bowry the Elder of ISLAND OF ST. CHRISTOPHER sells to Francis Epes of County of Amelia for £1,089 - 1452 acres in County of Amelia on north side of Little Nottoway River - on Cellars Creek - adjoining land of Peter Epes, Morgan, Boyd, Allen or Crenshaw, etc. Recorded 24 September 1772.

NOTE: These transactions were completed by virtue of a Power of Attorney from Thomas Bowry, Sr. of ISLE OF ST. CHRISTOPHER, to his son Thomas Bowery,Jr. (ibid p. 502.)

Amelia Co. Deed Book 23, page 429 -

Bedford County, STATE OF TENNESSEE, Power of Attorney dated 14 October 1811 by John Eppes and Martha Eppes to their trusty and loving friend, William Allen, to receive all such sums and property as may belong to them from the estate of their father, Daniel Allen, deceased, in Amelia County, State of Virginia, giving him full power and authority, etc. Acknowledged before and certified by the Clerk of Court of BEDFORD COUNTY, TENNESSEE, same date. Recorded Amelia Co., Va. 28 Nov. 1811.

NOTE BY CHH: (ibid, page 514): 3rd March 1812 John Epps and Martha, his wife, of Bedford Co., Tennessee, sell John Allen of County of Amelia, Va., for $612.00 - 153 acres of land in County of Amelia, etc. Recorded 28 Aug.1812.

Amelia Co. Deed Book 24, page 227 -

Power of Attorney dated 22 March 1814 from Paul M. Cunningham, Administrator of Estate of John Eppes, deceased, of Bedford Co., STATE OF TENNESSEE to Abner Chappell as his attorney within the boundaries of the State of Virginia, etc. Certified by Clerk of Circuit Court of Bedford Co., Tenn. Recorded Amelia Co., Va. April 25, 1815.

Sussex Co. Deed Book P, page 148 -

13 August 1827 - Susan Parham of the County of LIMESTONE, STATE OF ALABAMA, gives her Power of Attorney to Francis Eppes of the same county and State to transact all her business in the State of Virginia, etc. Acknowledged before and certified by the Justices of Limestone County, Alabama, the same day and recorded in Sussex County, Va. Court 6 September 1827.

NOTE BY CHH: This Francis Eppes (Jr.) who removed from Sussex Co., Va. to Limestone Co., Alabama was the son of Thomas Eppes and his first wife, Sally (Sarah) Winfield, who was the son of Francis and Phoebe Eppes. The aforesaid Francis Eppes, Jr. married 17 January 1820 Elizabeth Ogburn, daughter of Augustine Ogburn and his wife, Elizabeth Massenburg (all of which records and proof are in my files.)

Ibid, page 461 -

Whereas John R. Davies of County of Sussex, State of Virginia, by indenture dated 8 August 1817 sold to William Sterling of the COUNTY OF MERCER, STATE OF KENTUCKY, 200 acres and a water grist mill, reserving to him the said Davis a life interest in said property and at his death to the said Wm. Sterling or his heirs and whereas the heirs of the said William Sterling are desirous to dispose of their several interests in the said land, do herewith constitute and appoint Samuel Sterling of the County OF LOGAN, STATE OF KENTUCKY, their attorney to sell and convey said land, etc. said Samuel M. Sterling M. Sterling of County of Logan, Kentucky sells to Henry W. Eppes of Sussex Co., Va. their reversionary right in the tract of land on which the said John R. Davies now resides - 200 acres - for $800.00 - as attorney for himself and for Thomas Sterling, William Sterling, Lyne Sterling, Edmund Sterling, Ann Holloway (formerly Sterling), Lucy McDowell (formerly Sterling), Elias Davidson and Jane, his wife, (formerly Sterling), William Sullivant, Michael Sullivant, and Joseph Sullivant, etc. Recorded Sussex County Court 3 December 1829.

Sussex Co. Deed Book R, page 102 -

Henry W. Eppes, Acting only as Attorney in a special manner for Thomas Malone of THE STATE OF ALABAMA, sells to Mary Malone, for $642.00, all the reversionary right of the said Thomas Malone in the tract of land on which the said Mary Malone now lives, in County of Sussex, on Sapony Creek, containing 214 acres, etc. Recorded 4 December 1834.

Sussex Co. Deed.Book R, page 172 -

23 March 1835 - Benjamin Hill of the County of CLEMENT, STATE OF OHIO, sells to Sarah W. Eppes of the County of Sussex, State of Virginia, for $45.31 all the equal, undivided half of a tract of land in the County of Sussex containing 18½ acres, ádjoining lands of Charles Hill, Thomas J. Eppes, Henry S. Hardaway, Robert Wills, etc. Witnesses: John McKain, Owen T. Fishback. Certified by two Justices of Clement Co., Ohio. Recorded Sussex Co. Va. court 6 August 1835.

Ibid, page 258 -

23 September 1834 - Power of Attorney from Thomas Malone, Jr. of County of Limestone, STATE OF ALABAMA, appointing Henry W. Eppes of Sussex Co., Va. his true and lawful attorney to sell a tract of land in County of Sussex, on Sapony Creek containing 225 acres, etc. Recorded 3 March 1836.

Sussex Co. Deed Book T, page 216 -

BEDFORD COUNTY, STATE OF TENNESSEE - 6 February 1843 - Dennis Wheelhouse appoints Henry W. Eppes of Sussex County, Virginia, his true and lawful attorney to receive and/or prosecute his claims in County of Sussex, Virginia or elsewhere, etc. Certified by Officers of Bedford County, Tenn. Recorded Sussex Co., Va. 2 March 1843.

Sussex Co. Deed Book V, page 13 -

22 February 1851 - Robert W. Smith and Dorothy Ann, his wife, of SHELBY COUNTY, STATE OF TENNESSEE, sell to Susan O. Eppes, of County of Sussex, in Virginia, for $275.00, a certain mill and 3½ acres óf land attached thereto in County of Sussex on Sapony Creek, adjoining lands of Henry W. Eppes, dec'd (and others) etc. Acknowledged before and certified by Justices of Shelby Co., Tenn., 27 Feb. 1851. Recorded Sussex Co. Court 3 April 1851.

* * *

EXTRACTS FROM THE FILES OF

THE VIRGINIA GAZETTE

    (a) 1766

    (b) 1767

    (c) 1771

    (d) 1774

EXTRACTS FROM THE FILES OF THE VIRGINIA GAZETTE

Files of 1766: JONATHAN PROSSER, Tailor, from LONDON,
Humbly begs leave to inform Gentlemen, and others, that he has lately opened
Shop near Mr. Thompson's Store in Williamsburg. All Gentlemen that will
favour him with their Custom may depend upon being expeditiously served,
their Clothes well made, and that he will do every thing in his Power to
merit a Continuance of their Favours.

N.B. Ladies riding Habits, and Gentlemens hussar Dresses, neatly made.

Files of 1766: If Samuel Fleming, or the lawful Representative of
_____Fleming, who married a Sister of Margaret Wethers's of East
Grinstead, SUSSEX COUNTY, in ENGLAND, will apply to Benjamin Johnston in
Spotsylvania County, something to Advantage may be heard of. No further
Notice will be given.

Files of 1766:   Hanover, July 10, 1766

I intend leaving the Colony soon, unless I meet with better Business than
I have any View of at Present.

                        --John Hook

Files of 1766:   I intend for the WEST INDIES very soon.

                        --Joseph Lyell

Files of 1766:   Smithfield, April 1, 1766

I intend to leave the colony soon for GREAT BRITAIN.

                        -- Henry Hodsden

Files of 1766:   To be Sold at the Subscriber's Shop below the Capitol,
                      Williamsburg, for ready Money, or such Credit
                      as shall be agreed upon,
Tables, Chairs, Desks, Cupboards, and a large Beaufet with glass Doors.
Two new riding Chairs, the one a double, fixed on Braces, with Harness for
two Horses; the other a single Italian, with Harness. Also several other
things. The riding Chairs will be finished in about a Fortnight, and the other
Articles as fast as sold. A more than common Allowance will be given for
ready Money; and if Credit, Notes of Hands, with Security, if required.

As I intend for WILMINGTON IN NORTH CAROLINA, I hope those indebted to me
will settle and pay, or give their Notes as above, that I may be able to
satisfy my Crediture before my Departure.

                        -- John Ormeston

70

<u>Files of 1766:</u>   William Coakley, from the WEST INDIES, now residing in the town of Norfolk,

Undertakes to cure the following Disorders, viz. Cancers, Cankers, Mortifications Fistulas, Polypusses, Ringworms of all Kinds, the Gravel, Dropsy, Dry Grips, &c. He also practices in every Branch of Surgery, Mid-wifery, and Physick,N.B. The Terms on the above Disorders is "No Purchase no Pay."

Neither does the Practioner make use of Incision in the Cure of any of the above.

<u>Files of 1766:</u>   Alexander, Fairfax County, May 26
                                    Five Pounds Reward

Run away, on the 20th instant, four convict servant men (ENGLISHMEN) from the subscribers, Viz. Francis Wingali, about 25 years of age, a stout able fellow, and about 5 feet 10 inches high; had on when he went away a gray coat and jacket, a pair of black plush breeches, a pair of white thread stockings, has short brown hair, felt hat, and is by trade a shoemaker.

STEPHEN DEVOUX, by trade a baker, about 20 years of age, about 5 feet 9 inches high, is a grim looking lusty fellow, and much pitted with smallpox; had on when he went away a green lapelled jacket, double milled drab coloured broadcloth breeches bound with worsted binding, osnabrug shirt and trousers, brown hair lately cut short and felt hat.

JAMES TRUMP, about 26 years of age, about 5 feet 5 inches high by trade a baker, of a thin yellow complexion, has a remarkable scabbed head, and wears on it a stripped worsted cap and felt hat; had on when he went a short gray jacket, blue breeches, and osnabrug shirt and trousers.

JOHN HENES, by trade a sawyer, about 25 years of age, 5 feet 7 inches high, has hair lately cut short, and wears a check shirt, osnabrug shirt and trousers, blue broadcloth breeches, walks very lame, occasioned by one leg being much shorter than the other, and the heel of the shoe on the short leg is about two inches and a half thick. They took with them that night a small boat painted red and blue, and are supposed to have gone down the Potowmack river. Whoever takes up and brings the said servants to the subscribers shall have the above reward or 20 s. for each servant. They may probably change their names.
                              --Robert Adam
                              Peter Wise

<u>Files of 1766:</u>   The Subscriber intends for ENGLAND soon. He has about 2000 bushels of Liverpool Salt, which he will sell very reasonable for ready money.
                              --Robert Dickens

<u>Files of 1766:</u>   The Subscribed intends for SCOTLAND in a few weeks.

                              --Thomas Mitchell

Files of 1766:   Williamsburg, December 18, 1766

    The Subscriber intends to leave this Colony soon. All who have any
demands against him are desired to apply to Jerman Baker and William Biers.

                            -- Thomas Knox

Files of 1766:   Richmond, September 12, 1766

    As I intend for Britain immediately after next General Court, I must
beg the favour of those indebted to me to discharge their balances, as it
is not convenient to give further indulgence. I have put my affairs under
the management of Mr. David Ross of GOOCHLAND County, with full power to
transact every matter for me in this country. Those who have any demands
against me are desired to bring in their accounts, and receive payment.

                        --Alexander Baine

Files of Oct. 17, 1766:   The Subscriber, from LONDON, begs leave to inform the public that he still continues near the Market street in Norfolk,
to make and repair all sorts of plain, repeating and horizontal watches,
and all kinds of repeating and musical clocks. Those Gentlemen who will
please to favour him with their commands, may depend upon the utmost
despatch and care, from
                        Their obliged humble servant,
                        William Skinner.
N.B. Neat enamel dial plates put to watches.

Files of 1766:   Petersburg, December 10.

    I intend to leave the Colony soon.

                        -- Walter Robertson

Files of November 1766:   STEPHEN BUCK,
                             Tailor from London,
    BEGS leave to inform his Customers, and others that he has removed
from the Red Lyon to a house adjoining Mr. Attorney's; where he continues t
to carry on his business with the greatest expedition. Gentlemen and
others, who please to favour him with their custom, may depend upon being
well served, with the genteelest taste and newest fashions, and no pains
spared to merit a continuance of their favours.

    N.B. Ladies Riding Habits neatly made, and five per cent discount
for ready money.

Files of 1767:   The Subscriber gives this publick notice that he intends
to go for ENGLAND with Capt. Lilly.

                        --Edward Moir

72

York, Dec. 30, 1767

   The Subscriber, being desirous to return to ENGLAND, would be willing
to sell off his stock in trade, his storehouse, with all its appurtenances.

                        -- George Wilson

Files of 1767:   Run away from the subscriber in King William County, on
the 3rd of March 1767, an indented servant man named James Leaker, an
ENGLISHMAN, born in POWLET, in the county of Somersetshire, yeoman, about
23 years of age, has dark brown hair, and sandy complexion; had on when he
went away a blue close bodied coat, buckshkin breeches, Newmarket coat, and
other apparel, and has a remarkable fore leg. As he may endeavour to get
on board some ship, all masters of vessels are cautioned from carrying him
off. Whoever apprehends the said servant, and conveys him to me, shall
have 50 s. reward, and if out of the colony, 5 l.

                        --Samuel Garlick

Files of 1767:   The subscriber's affairs requiring his attendance in
GREAT BRITAIN as soon as possible, he desires his several debtors to make
immediate payment of their respective balances, to enable him to embark in
a short time. He will let the house lately in the occupation of Mr. Francis
Riddlehurst, in the town of Hampton, known by the sign of the Bunch of
Grapes, being the best accustomed house in the said town. Also to be sold,
several kinds of very good furniture, belonging to the said house. For terms
apply to the subscriber, on the premises.

                        -- Nathaniel Elby

Files of 1771:   As I intend for ENGLAND in a short Time, for the
Recovery of my Health, and being desirous, before my Departure, to have my
Affairs settled, I hereby desire all Persons to whom I am indebted to apply
for Payment, and those who have Accounts on my Books to settle them, by Bonds
or otherwise, between this and the first of April next.

                        -- George Jackson

Files of 1771:   The Subscriber's Affairs requiring his Attendance in
GREAT BRITAIN as soon as possible, he desires his several Debtors to make
immediate Payment of their respective Balances, to enable him to embark in
a short Time. He will let the House lately in the Occupation of Mr.
Francis Riddleburg, in the Town of Hampton, known by the Sign of the Bunch
of Grapes, being the best accustomed House in the said Town. Also to be
sold, several Kinds of very good Furniture, belonging to the said House.
For terms apply to the Subscriber, on the Premises.

                        -- William Kenyon

Files of 1771:   John and Anthony Craggs intend for ENGLAND soon.

<u>Files of 1774</u>:   William Ashburn, Cutler from LONDON, has opened Shop near the Capitol in Williamsburg, and makes and sells all Sorts of Knives, Razors, Scissors, Surgeons Instruments, and Box and Spring Fleams on a new Construction, which are much approved by the most eminent Farriers in GREAT BRITAIN; also grinds and repairs all Sorts of Edge Tools in the above Branch, cleans Fire Arms, and makes Springs and Screws. All such as please to favour him with their Custom may depend on the utmost Punctuality and reasonable Charges, and Commissions from the Country duly executed.

<u>Files of 1774</u>:   If Elizabeth Lothian, Daughter of Baillie John Lothian of Burntisland in NORTH BRITAIN, who has been in this Country about nine Years, will send to the Post Office, she will receive a Letter from a Relation of hers, who does not know in what Part of the Country she lives. She must acquaint the Printer, it seems, what was her Grandmother's Name by the Mother's Side.

<u>Files of 1774</u>:   As I intend to leave the Colony soon, those who are indebted to me are requested to make an immediate Settlement, and those who have any Demands against me to bring in their Accounts.

--Ephraim Ross

<u>Files of 1774</u>:   The Subscriber intends for LONDON this Summer, where he purposes to carry on his Business and would be glad to furnish some of his old Customers with Suits of Clothes; and as he intends to deal in Cloth &c. he presumes he can afford to serve them on the best Terms. Those who are indebted to him need expect no indulgence after the July Meeting; and all persons having Demands against him are desired to bring in their Accounts, that they may be adjusted. Letters directed to Mess. Norton and Son, Merchants in Gould Square, LONDON, will be duly attended to.

--John Conrad Gunther

<u>Files of 1774</u>:   Intending to return to ENGLAND as soon as I can settle my Affairs in Virginia, I offer for Sale, or on Annuity for Life, as may best suit a Purchaser, my HOUSE, FURNITURE, SERVANTS, &c in this Town. The pleasant Situation of the House needs no Panegyrick; and the Servants, I will venture to say, are as good as any in the Colony. Should any Gentleman of the Faculty be inclined to purchase, I have this Year imported a fresh Assortment of Medicines for private Practice.

--Matthew Pope

<u>Files of 1774</u>:   As soon as the Subscriber can dispose of his Effects and settle his Affairs, he proposes to leave this Colony. A valuable Collection of Books in English, Latin, Greek, Mathematicks, Philosophy, and other Subjects, with Book Case, Desk, Tables, and other Furniture, are for Sale.

--Charles Mac Iver

74

<u>Files of 1774:</u>   To be Sold, on Thursday next, if fair, otherwise next
                         fair Day, at Westbury, in Charles City,
All the Personal Estate of Littlebury Cocke, deceased, consisting of Horses,
Cattle, Sheep, and Hogs, also Household and Kitchen Furniture. Six Months
Credit will be allowed, the Purchasers giving Bond, with approved Security,
to
                    Rebecca Hubbard Cocke, Executrix
                    NEWPORT (RHODE ISLAND)

                         * * *

CENSUS RECORDS

Highland Co, Va.

Warwick Co., Va.

Tyrrell Co., N. C.

Pittsylvania Co., Va.

1850 Census of Highland Co., Virginia

		Age		Birthplace
22-22	Jacob C. Doil	48	Farmer	Hagerstown, Md.
	Margaret	47		Pendleton Co.
	Mary A.	22		"
	William	21	Farmer	"
	John	21	Farmer	"
	Olive	17		"
	George	19		"
	Jacob	15		"
	Elizabeth	13		"
	Nancy J.	11		"
	Theodarus (male)	9		Bath Co.
33-33	Thomas Moore	40	Stone mason	Ireland
	(living in household of John Wade, Sr.)			
48-48	Samuel Ruckman	66		Somerset Co., N.J.
	Margaret	60		Bath Co.
	Asa	20		"
	David V.	16		"
	Rhoda Watson	20		"
70-70	Elizabeth Bodkin	72	Farming	Pennsylvania
	(living alone)			
76-76	John Casy	33		Ireland
	Matilda	24		Pendleton Co.
	Mary A.	6		"
	Elbee	4		"
	John	1		Highland Co.
	Edward Rorick	58		Ireland
78-78	John Burk	48	Farmer	Ireland
	Sarah	53		Pendleton Co.
89-89	Thomas Brown	35		D. C.
	Margaret L.	9		Pendleton Co.
	(living in household of Wm. Bodkin)			
90-90	Thomas Brown	73	Farmer	Italy
	Elizabeth	64		Maryland
	James	28		D. C.
	Sally	22		Pendleton Co.
92-92	Debora Ervine	63	Farmer	Pennsylvania
	Jared	20		Pendleton Co.
	Alzina	16		"
	Hannah M. Church	10		"
	William Brown	11		"
	Henry Tharp	6		"

102-102	Samuel Hoover	57	Pendleton Co.
	Margaret	66	Pennsylvania
	Rufus	28	Pendleton Co.
	Barbara	24	"
121-121	Benjamin Grove	77 Miller	Pennsylvania
	Hannah	70	"
	David	26	Rockingham Co.
143-143	Frederick Bird	72 Farmer	Augusta Co.
	William High	47	Pennsylvania
	Jane	24	Bath Co.
	James	9	Harrison Co.
	John	8	"
	Mary E.	3	"
	Sarah E.	5/12	Highland Co.
148-148	Isaac Briscoe	74 Farmer	North Carolina
	Druscilla	73	Wood Co.
	Nancy	33	Bath Co.
	Priscilla	27	"
158-158	John Man	52	South Carolina
	Mary C.	46	Bath Co.
	Robert E.	21	"
	(living in household of Isaac Gunn)		
166-166	David Gwin	47	Bath Co.
	Martha	26	New York
	Elizabeth R.	7	Bath Co.
	Laura M.	5	"
	Mary V.	2	Highland Co.
178-178	Charity Mullenax	64	Pennsylvania
	(living with William and Margaret Mullenax and their seven children)		
183-183	Elizabeth Bird	79	Maryland
	(living in household of John Bird)		
193-193	James Davis	67 Farmer	Pennsylvania
	Phebe	60	Pendleton Co.
	Martha	91	Pennsylvania
	Harvey S.	23	Bath Co.
	Phebe J.	14	"
219-219	Edward Curby	67	Great Britain
	Ann	57	New York
	Hytrometus	17 (male)	"
	John	14	"

198-198	John Sharp	78	Farmer	Pennsylvania
	Elizabeth	77		"
	John Hilly	18		Bath Co.
	William	17		"
	Harriet	27		"
	Mary	11		"
	Martha	10		"
	Jackson	7		Highland Co.
	Henry	3		Bath Co.
	Polly	33		"
	James	14		"
239-239	Michael Doil	72		Ireland
	Ann	50		Bath Co.
	Sally	15		"
	Esther	12		"
	Amanda	10		"
	Elizabeth	5		"
	Bridget Houdishell	20		"
	John H. "	21		Augusta Co.
	Michael D. "	3/12		Highland Co.
	Samuel Sprowl	56		Bath Co.
	William "	44		"
243-243	William Green	47		Ireland
	Mary	26		"
	Ellen	6		Bath Co.
	Margaret J.	5		"
	Mary A.	3		Highland Co.
	William	6/12		"
244-244	John Pray	60	Farmer	New York
	Elizabeth	58		"
	Nelson	26	Teacher	"
	Mary E.	24		Pendleton Co.
	Phebe A.	18		"
246-246	James Gwin	33	Farmer	Bath Co.
	Mahala	29		New York
256-256	Thomas Marin	23		Ireland
274-274	Henry Flesher	73		Pendleton Co.
	Christena	72		North Carolina
	Henry	29		Pendleton Co.
	Barbara	21		"
	Hannah	2		Highland Co.
	John H.	1		"
	Christena Motes	27		Pendleton Co.

80

293-293	Conrad Cremer	33		Germany
	Elizabeth	35		"
	(Can't give it in English)	10 (female)		Shenandoah Co.
	Adam	8		"
	Philip	6		Pendleton Co.
	Henry	4		"
	Anthony	3		Highland Co.
296-296	A. Hanson Camble	37		Bath Co.
	Isabella S.	26		Missouri
	Charles L.	9		Pendleton Co.
	Mary L.	6		"
	William A.	2		Highland Co.
316-316	James M. Clark	43	Preacher	Maryland
	Mary H.	43		Pennsylvania
	Asberry J.	8		Pendleton Co.
	Martha J.	6		Greenbrier Co.
	Mary F.	3		Botetourt Co.
	Margaret C.	2		Pocahontas Co.
329-329	Joshua Mily	40		Switzerland
	Salomeny	26		Pendleton Co.
	John	10/12		Highland Co.
338-338	Joseph E. Gray	52	Saddler	Albemarle Co.
	Sarah	53		Maryland
	Robert C.	29	Teacher	Rockingham Co.
	Joseph A.	16		Pendleton Co.
	Sarah V.	13		"
360-360	Jacob Seybert	74	Farmer	Maryland
	Mary	74		Rockingham Co.
	Jacob	35	Farmer	Pendleton Co.
	Catharine	30		"
	Sarah	12		"
	Mary E.	5		"
362-362	John Peck	80	Farmer	Pennsylvania
	Elizabeth	70		Pendleton Co.
	Jacob	16		"
	Wm. Halterman	32		"
	Elizabeth "	29		"
	Sarah "	10		"
	Louisa "	5		"
	Andrew J. "	2		Highland Co.

[Note by CHH: Next door (#363-363) are living Abraham and Susan Peck and their three children.]

397-397	Ellener Wimer	91	London

(living with Philip and Ann Wimer and their five children)

414-414	Edward Caton	31	Farmer	Ireland
	Mahala	20		Pendleton Co.
	Mary E.	8/12		Highland Co.
432-432	Augustus Shoemate	46	Tailor	Maryland
	Elizabeth	38		Rockingham Co.
	Louisa J.	19		"
	Frances C.	17		"
	Margaret	13		"
	Jacob	10		"
	William	6		"
	Elizabeth	4		"
	Albert	6/12		Highland Co.
441-441	William W. Flemming	38	Farmer	Nova Scotia
	Margaret L.	36		Bath Co.
	Mary J.	9		"
	Clara	6		Missouri
	Robert H.	4		Pendleton Co.
	Isabella V.	6/12		Highland Co.
448-448	John T. Tabler	39	Preacher	Maryland
	Elizabeth	41		Frederick Co.
	Mosheim	9	(male)	Wythe Co.
	Jasper	8		Hardy Co.
	Andromache	6	(female)	"
	Sarah E.	4		"
	Hugh	2		Highland Co.
	Thomas Wright	25		Bath Co.
454-454	Joseph Jones	64	Farmer	New Jersey
	Sarah	63		Augusta Co.
	Margaret	26		Pendleton Co.
	Joseph	23		"
	Sarah	18		"
459-459	Daniel Waybright	63	Farmer	Pennsylvania
	Rachel	60		Pendleton Co.
	Nathan	23		"
	Henry	6		"
	Harrison	10		"
470-470	Luther Emmerson	39	Preacher	Massachusetts
	Catharine	34		Albemarle Co.
	Ann	5		Pendleton Co.
	Ellen	2		Highland Co.
	John	6/12		"
	Nancy	42		None given
472-472	John McDonal	40	Stonemason	Scotland

(living in household of William & Barbara Hevener)

475-475	Anton Mily	30 Cabinet maker	Switzerland
	Amandam	28	Augusta Co.
	William E.	5	"
	Anton B.	3	Highland Co.
	Mary J.	9/12	"

524-524	Benjamin F. Jackson	31 Farmer	North Carolina
	Ruth	25	Pendleton Co.
	John	7	"
	Virginia J.	6	"
	Hannah E.	3	Highland Co.
	Indiana	3/12	"
	Samuel Wilson	16	Pendleton Co.

| 535-535 | John O. Cain | 52 Weaver | Ireland |
| | Martha | 60 | Louisa Co. |

537-537	Isabella Wilson	12	Ohio
	Sarah H.	7	Pendleton Co.
	(living in household of Sally Hicklin, age 68)		

627-627	John Murphy	35	Ireland
	Polly	34	Bath Co.
	John	7	"
	Elizabeth	5	"

* * *

1850 CENSUS OF WARWICK CO., VIRGINIA

| 19-21 | Nathaniel Seburn | 64 Merchant | North Carolina |
| | (living alone) | | |

| 56-62 | Miranda Walls | 39 (male) Farmer | Maryland |
| | Sarah R. | 25 | Elizabeth City Co. |

69-75	Joshua P. Fitchett	52 Farmer	South Carolina
	Martha F.	34	Warwick Co.
	Mary F.	14	"
	Margaret M.	11	"
	John T.	10	"
	Charles	8	Elizabeth City Co.
	James P.	5	"
	Margaret S.	3	"
	Georgia	1	"

[Note by CHH: The family of John E. Fitchett (age 32) and Mary J., his wife, are listed next door (#70-76) with their three children.]

| 81-87 | Thomas Turner | 43 Painter | England |
| | (living in household of John Smelt) | | |

105-112   William S. Hamilton   45   Boston, Mass.
          (living in household of John Gambol)

118-125	Jeremiah Evans	36	Farmer	Dorchester Co., Md.
	Charlotte	36		Northampton Co.
	John W.	3		Warwick Co.

* * *

1850 CENSUS OF TYRRELL CO., NORTH CAROLINA

1	Joseph Holsey	60		New Jersey
	Mary "	53		N.C.
	Joseph H. Wynne	4		Virginia
	Mary L. Sutton	15		N. C.
	Eliza Etheridge	24		N. C.
11	William Reynold Jr.	38		England
	Emily	38		N. C.
	Mary E.	15		"
	James W.	10		"
	Benjamin	7		"
	Rhoda C.	5		"
	William P.	3		"
17	William Reynold Sr.	61		England
	Matilda	16 (?)		England
66	Benjamin Francis	57	Teacher	Virginia
	(living with family of James & Nancy Dunbar)			
113	Franklin Liverman [Note 1]*	30		N. C.
	Letta	25		"
	Mary P.	11/12		"
	Sarah Penner	55		Delaware
	John "	16		N. C.
	James "	19		"
115	William B. Vickery [Note 2]*	27		Rhode Island
	Sarah	25		N. C.
	Charlotte Powers	18		"
122	John Frances	50		N. C.
	Ann	34		Delaware
	Thomas	11		N. C.
	Mariah	8		"
	John	4		"
	Sady E.	11/12		"

*[See Tyrrell County, North Carolina Marriages, page 86]

149	Luther Babbet	34	Mass.
	Martha	23	N. C.
	Charles M.	3	"
	Martha E.	1	"
216	Romulus Knight [Note 3]*	30	Virginia
	Matilda	30	Maryland
	Mary E.	4	N. C.
	Charles A.	1	"
	Mary Jones	21	"
270	Joseph D. Hufton [Note 4]*	53	Virginia
	Joannah	50	N. C.
	Joseph H.	8	"
	Mary	5	"
	Eliza A. Swain	18	"
282	Benjamin Abbot	64	Ireland
	Sarah	52	Delaware
	Sarah E.	20	Maryland
	Isaac Harrington	20	N. C.

285	Charles C. Hopkins	25	Virginia

(living with family of William R. Palmer)

296	George Mason	72 Tailor	Virginia

(living with family of Zachariah & Susan Routon)

316	James Cosgrove	32 Farmer	Virginia
	Elizabeth	44	N. C.
	Henry A. Pledger	18 Student	"
	Elizabeth Melson	13	"
	William	10	"
	Mary C.	8	"
	Eliza Garret	26	"
370	James Crane	28	Virginia
	Mary	30	Virginia
	William	7	Virginia
	Frances	6	N. C.
	James H.	4	"
	Patsy R.	1	"
	Mirium Allcock	20	"
	William J. "	3/12	"

[Living next door to James Crane (age 52) and family (#369). See Note 5.]

376	Thomas Curlin	25	Virginia
	Sarah	30	N. C.
	Virginia	6	"
	Mary I.	4	"
	Irena C.	1	"

* See Tyrrell County, N.C. Marriages, page 86.

401	John Mateland	50 Teacher	New York
	Emaline	25	N. C.
417	James Forbes	66	Penn.
	Elizabeth	61	N. C.
	John W. Tarkinton	28	"
477	Truman Willouby	50	Penn.
	Isabella	32	N. C.
500	Hugh Chisholm	48 Shoemaker	Scotland
	Charles Fitzgerald	23 Carpenter	N. C.
538	William Dunn	47 Miller	Maryland
	Ellen	42	"
	Samuel J.	22	"
	Martha	18	N. C.
	Franklin Swain	24	"
	William C. Sawyer	4	"
	Ferribbee Bryan	28 (Female)	"
541	William B. Etheridge	28	Virginia
	Elizabeth M.	29	N. C.
	David E. Leigh	11	"
546	Benjamin F. Miles	30	New York
	Mary M.	26	N. C.
	Ann M.	6	New York
	Franklin	3	New York
	Reuben	2	N. C.
	Edward	11/12	"
564	Lemuel S. Rice	43 Teacher	Maine
	Sack E.	34	N. C.
	John W.	7	"
	William C.	5	"
	Henretta	2	"
	Caroline Chesson	22	"
589	William Yeates	23	Virginia
	Mary	15	N. C.
590	Frederick Overton [Note 6]*	24	N. C.
	Eliza "	19	"
	Henry Drew [Note 6]*	28 Sailor	England
	Mary J. "	21	N. C.
592	William Hardison	50	Virginia
	Hestor	49	N. C.
	William S.	10	"
	Matilda E.	7	"
609	Jarvis McGowan	20 Teacher	Vermont
	(living in household of Mathias Owens. Note 7)*		

* See Tyrrell County, N.C. Marriages, page 86.

86

NOTES

TYRELL COUNTY, NORTH CAROLINA - MARRIAGES

Note 1 -

    4 Nov. 1847 - Franklin Liverman to Lettice Tricett
    28 Dec. 1852 - James H. Pinner to Sarah Baswight
    29 Feb. 1858 - James H. Pinner to Mary A. Creef
    22 Apr. 1861 - John B. Pinner to Sarah M. Mann

Note 2 -

    13 May 1849 - Benjamin Vickory to Sarah Powers
    (This is very probably William B. Vickery, and Charlotte Powers
    would be his sister-in-law)

Note 3 -

    23 Dec. 1844 - Romulos B. Knight to Matilda Dunn

Note 4 -

    20 May 1836 - Joseph Hufton to Joanna Swain

Note 5 -

    14 April 1817 - James Crain to Elizabeth Gibson
    28 July 1817 - James Crain to Olla Owens

Note 6 -

    29 Jan. 1850 - Frederick Overton to Eliza Davis
    1 May 1849 - Henry Drew to Mary J. Davenport

Note 7 -

    11 Feb. 1829 - Mathais Owens to Patsey Davenport

* * *

87

1850 CENSUS PITTSYLVANIA CO., VIRGINIA

9-9	Ann Benedict	51	Teacher	Massachusetts
	Christina "	16		"
	Mary E.	13		"
10-10	Jordan M. Bell	26	Tailor	Virginia
	Eveline Stott	18		N. C.
	Mary J. Bell	18		"
	Samuel A. Douglas	74	Tailor	Va.
	Mary A. Douglas	56		"
	Martha A. Douglas	27		"
	Susan R. Douglas	26		"
	William Morreen	31	Tailor	"
13-13	George W. Dame	37	Episcopal Clergyman	Mass.
	Mary M.	36		Va.
	J. Cushing	13		"
	Lucy	9		"
	Wm. M.	4		"
	Ellen S.	6 mo.		"
14-14	James Lawrence	42		Penn.
	Ann	36		"
	Margaret	14		"
	John	12		"
	Mary	10		"
	William	8		"
	James	5		"
17-17	Allen G. Stokes	31	Merchant	N. C.
	Margaret M.	29		Va.
	Charles P.	2		"
	Eugene Carrington	11	(female)	"
	William Lindsey	21	Clerk	"
18-18	Samuel Pike	30	Tailor	N. Y.
19-19	Henry Fitzgerald	20	Clerk	N. C.
25-25	Walter Fitzgerald	70		Maryland
	Mary C.	71		Virginia
	Thomas Barber	11		"
26-26	Moses Levi	28	Sadler	Germany
	Aron Myers	23	Sadler	"

* * *

SECTION THREE

Contributions by others

CONTRIBUTIONS BY OTHERS

The following received from Mrs. Anne Fitzgerald, Kentucky Historical Society, Frankfort, Kentucky. Thank you very much, Mrs. Fitzgerald.

Deed Book A, Burlington, Boone County, Kentucky, pages 5-12, December 13, 1797:

INDENTURE between AUGUSTINE JAQUELINE SMITH and SUSANNAH, his wife, of the County of Fairfax [Va.] and PETER TAFF of Middlesex County [Va.], WILLIAM TAFF of Essex County [Va.]

    The said AUGUSTINE JACQUELINE SMITH and SUSANNAH, his wife, in consideration of a Deed bearing even date with these present by said PETER TAFF and WILLIAM TAFF releasing and confirming unto the said AUGUSTINE JACQUELINE SMITH in fee simple all this right title and Interest in and to a certain tract of Land containing eight hundred acres more or less in the county of Fairfax which the said William Taff claimed as devisee of Thomas Taff who was heir at law of John Woodbridge as also in consideration of one dollar to him the said Augustine J. Smith in hand paid by the said Peter Taff and William Taff. The receipt whereof is hereby Acknowledged have given granted, bargained and sold and by these present do and each of them doth give grant bargain and sell unto the said Peter Taff and William Taff their heirs and Assigns a Certain Tract or parcel of Land Granted by Pattent under the hands of Isaac Shelby, Governor of the Commonwealth of Kentucky with the Seal of the said State thereunto annexed unto JESSE TAYLOR containing two thousand Acres by Survey bearing the date the thirteenth day of October one thousand seven hundred and eighty six lying and being in Fayette County in Kentucky on the waters of Big Bone Lick Creek and bounded as following to Wit:- .... etc.

Aug. J. Smith (seal)
Susannah Smith (seal)

Signed sealed & delivered
in the presence of - The Words
"Given & Granted give and
Grant in Fayette County
in Kentucky" being first interlined.

Jno Moss   )
John Lovell)
Jos Corter)

Boone County, Kentucky, Deed Book A, pages 30-31, October 23, 1799:

INDENTURE between JOHN GAY of Rockbridge County, Virginia and JOSEPH BRANN of Boone County, Kentucky - 234 Acres on Eagle Creek in Boone County, Kentucky for £100. Property adjoins lands of: [no names listed]

[Signed] John Gay (Seal)

Sealed and delivered in presence of
Alex^r Lowry   Joseph Miers
Wm. Junkins   Nath'l McClure

Recorded February 4th 1800. Proved by oath of Alex^r Lowry, Wm. Junkins and Nathaniel McClure.

Cave Johnson   CBC

The following received from Mrs. Robert P. Moore, Box 496, Lexington, N. C.
Thank you very much, Mrs. Moore.

CEMETERY RECORDS

Lafayette County, Miss.

Buckner - Craig - Isom Cemetery:

Sarah G. Craig
Wife of John J. Craig &
dau. of Jones & Mary Isom
b. Maury Co., Tenn.
Jan. 1, 1812
married Jan. 25, 1831
d. Jan. 25, 1856
aged 44 years 21 days

David Craig
son of David & Ellen Craig
b. Orange Co., N. C.
Aug. 15, 1783
Imigrated to Maury Co., Tenn.,
June 1805. Thence to Lafayette Co.
Miss., 1836
d. Sept. 4, 1849
aged 66 years 21 days

E. P. Craig
b. March 1822
d. Feb. 1840

Robert Isom
son of Mary & Jones Isom
b. Maury Co., Tenn.
26 April 1821
d. Nov. 1832

John J. Craig
son of David & Agnes Craig
b. Williamson Co., Tenn.
Jan. 30, 1806
Imigrated to Lafayette Co., Miss. 1834
died Dec. 29, 1865

Mrs. Mary Craig
daughter of Joseph & Sarah Gale
b. Chesterfield Co., Va.
April 1, 1791
d. Jan. 7, 1851
aged 59 years 8 months 23 days

Jones Isom
son of George & Ellen Isom
b. 4 Nov. 1818 - d. April 1840
In 22nd year of life

College Hill Presbyterian Church
4 miles from Oxford:

Ephraim E. Davidson
who was born in Burke Co., N.C.
May 12, 1785
died Sept. 22, 1850
aged 65 years 4 months 5 days

J. O. Davidson
born June 28, 1791
died Dec. 12, 1856
aged 65 years 5 months 14 days

Willie Thornwell
son of E. G. & S. B. Davidson
born Dec. 28, 1862
died Aug. 1863

John Neelly
b. Botetourt Co., Virginia
Jan. 14, 1800
d. Nov. 22, 1851

Mary Brank, wife of E. E. Davidson
born Dec. 25, 1789
died Dec. 25, 1864

R. R., consort of J. O. Davidson
born Nov. 18, 1793
died June 16, 1870
aged 78 years 6 months 28 days

(This church was organized
in 1836)

* * *

Lafayette Co., Mississippi, Deed Book B, p. 315

This indenture made and entered 31 March 1840 - German Baker & Mary his wife
of County of Marshall, Mississippi -- to Jordan Branch of the town of
Petersburg and State of Virginia -- 160 acres for $480 -- land lying in
Lafayette County, Mississippi -- known as the north east quarter of section
twenty-five, etc. No witnesses. Recorded April 2, 1840.

REVOLUTIONARY WAR PENSION APPLICATIONS

File # S 30974   Philip Crowder

Declaration made State of Illinois, Sangamon Co. 9 October 1832
Philip Crowder appeared in court - resident of above state and County,
aged 72 - said he was b. 7 April 1760 in Amelia Co., Va. and removed
when about 5 years of age to the County of "Macklinburg," Va. where he
said he resided when called into service - in 1785 removed to "Weatherford"
Co. (Rutherford) North Carolina where he said he remained until 1791 in which
year he removed to Green Co., "Kenticky"- in 1830 removed to Sangamon Co.,
Ill. where he said he had since resided. The only record of my age is upon
the leaf of a Testament given to me by my father and now in my possession -
purpoting to be a register of the births and deaths in my father's family.

In Aug. 1776 - I was enrolled at Macklinburg Co. [sic] as a substitute for
my brother WILLIAM in a company of militia commanded by Capt. Richard
Swepston - from Macklinburg we marched with another company of militia commanded by Capt. Petty through Brunswick and Dunwoodie Counties, by Peters-
borough, Cobham and Suffolk Town to Portsmouth were attached to a reg. commanded by Col. Fred Macklin & Major James Anderson. All the militia stationed
at Portsmouth - were as I understand at the time commanded by Gen. Scott who
joined us at Portsmouth Town a few days before our discharge. At this time
I served three months as orderly sergeant - During the 3 months that we were
in or near Portsmouth, we were employed in protecting the country against
the Tories who were embodied in small companies in the Dismal Swamp. etc. etc.

About the first of Jan. 1781, in Macklinburg Co. [sic] Va. I was enrolled as
a drafted man in a Co. of militia commanded by Capt. Jesse Sanders. Abt. the
tenth of the month we marched to Brunswick Co. --- marched then through Cobham
and Cabin Point to Suffolk Town. Here we organized and our Co. was attached
to a regiment (I think the seventeenth) commanded by Col. Alexander Dick and
Major Long, both regular officers - Gen. Mulenburg commanded all the militia
at this place. From Suffolk Town we marched to the Wet Camp where we were
joined by Genl. Steuben, who aided in drilling the troops. The object for
which the militia was called out at this time - was to counteract the
operation of Benedict Arnold - who then had possession of Portsmouth Town -
and prevent this --- into the country etc. etc.

The same year 1781 I was enrolled at Macklinburg Co., Va. as a drafted man
in a Co. commanded by Capt. Richard Eperson & Lieut. Jno. Clay --- marched
thru Prince Edwards Co. to Yorktown to the seige of York where I remained
until the surrender of Cornwallis ---

James Haggard, a clergyman and William Miller residing in sd. County (Sangamon)
certified -- well acquainted with Philip Crowder, etc. Mr. Miller had known
applicant for 30 years.

File # S 10496   Sterling Crowder

Schedule - District of Kentucky JJ   Jessamine County Court -

On this 17th day of Jan. 1831 appeared open Ct. etc. Sterling Crowder aged
74 yrs. & a resident of Jessamine Co. --- makes declaration in order to obtain
the provisions made by the Acts of Congress of the 18th March 1818 & 1st of
May 1820 -- that he the sd. Sterling Crowder enlisted for the term of 3 years
in the Reg. commanded by Col. Lewis & Major Abner Buford on the line of the
State of Virginia on the Continental establishment -- served out his term of
enlistment & was honourably discharged in 1776 by sd. Buford & he is inscribed
on the pension list of the U. S. Kentucky Agency 11th Feb. 1819 but has not
drawn for several years because of owning a small tract of land ---
(this involves a controversy he was having with his son over some property
son's name was Currency -- also mentions that Currency owed Samuel Crowder
some money.)

William Crowder-(Lucy)
File # R2540; BLWt 36280-160-55

State of North Carolina - Cleveland Co.

On 25 April 1854, personally appeared etc. Garret Crowder aged 69 years and
declares that he is the son of William Crowder deceased, who formerly resided in Mecklenburg Co., Va. in the time of the Revolutionary War - that
some time in the year 95 he the aforesd. William Crowder, removed to this
County and State and lived until the 10th Nov. 1840 and died.

That this deponent (Garret Crowder) has frequently and repeatedly heard his
father say he served in the Revolutionary war while living in the County of
Mecklenburg and State of Virginia --- about 3 or 4 months --- that he was
drafted and served under Capt. Robert Smith -- service done in 1781, sometime near the close of the war --- deponent believes his father and mother
were married in 1771 or 1772 --- signed JARRET CROWDER

State of N. C. Cleveland Co.

3 May 1855 Lucy Crowder aged 70 years or upwards - resident of above Co.
appeared --- widow of William Crowder --- said her husband lived in
Mecklenburg Co., Va. - believes he was drafted for the term of 6 mos. and
continued in actual service for about 3 months at which time he got a
parole to go home and then she understands he got a substitute to go in his
place who served out the said term --- states she married the aforesd.
William Crowder Sept. 1825 or the year 1826 --- her name before she married
was Lucy Thompson that her husband died 9 November 1839.

[Marriage bond is dated 15 Sept. 1825-- have done a great deal of work on
this family as I am descended from this William Crowder --- he and his
brother Philip (see above) removed to Rutherford Co. and lived in that part
of the County that later became Cleveland County -- my notes on the Crowder
family and families too extensive to include here --Mrs.Robert P. Moore]

File # R7662   Boling Nicholson

State of Kentucky - Spencer Co.

21 July 1835 -- appeared Boling Nicholson aged 75 years --- that he was
drafted for a tour of three months a private in the army of the Revolution
(but the year not recollected) -- drafted in Edgecomb Co., North Carolina
and served in Capt. Thomas Barrow Co. of Infantry in Col. Benj. Sowel's
Reg. Wm. Brinkel was a field officer and under the command of Gen. Sumner
and marched from Edgecomb Co. to South Carolina and served the most of the
sd. tour about the sand hills and a creek named Drounding Crk. then was
marched back through N. C. crossing Broad River then to Salisbury and thence
to Shallow Ford on the Yadkin and crossed here and was soon after discharged
in weighting by the aforesd. Col. Sowel --- states that after he returned
home to Edgecomb Co., N. C. he was again drafted for three months but from
age and infirmity etc. etc. he cannot state names of the officers ---
recollects he was marched to Hallifax on Roan Crk. where he was employed
the whole of his time at hard labour entrenching and was honourably discharged --- knows of no person who can prove his service and that he was
born NEAR WILLIAMSBURG in VIRGINIA in the year 1759 and that he has a
record of his age, and that he was living in Edgecomb Co., N. C. when called
into service and after the Revolution he moved into South Carolina where he
married and moved to Kentucky Pulasky Co. ---

[This man was living in Greenville Co., South Carolina in 1790 - appears
in census - then appears in 1800 census Pendleton District, S. C. - have
seen other references in some Kentucky abstracts pertaining to him.]

                                James Nickleston
File # S 8918;
BLWt 7295-160-55

State of North Carolina - Stokes Co.

On 5 October 1844 appeared James Nickleston a resident of Stokes Co.--
aged 82 years -- that he entered the service of the U. S. as a volunteer and
served as herein after stated viz: he was a resident of the County of
Surry, (now Stokes, N.C.) He left his home with his father Isaac who was a
reg. soldier in the service of the U. S., at home on furlough as well as he
can now recollect about the year 1781, and went with the sd. Isaac to Duplin
Court House, N. C. where the army was then stationed. I there joined the
troops as a volunteer, the Captain's name that I was enrolled with I do not
now recollect, though a man by the name of Tayford was our Major, the -- or
name of the -- I cannot recollect. And after staying there some time the army
was divided and my father was sent somewhere near Charleston, South Carolina
and I still remained at Duplin Court House. And afterwards was taken by our
Major Rayford as a servant, as a trainee of our horses, and frequently cooked
and sometimes washed for our mess. From that time until the close of the
War, which was as well as I now recollect 15 months from the time I joined
the army, at which time my father being discharged came by after me when we
returned home together, to Surry, now Stokes, where I now live and have ever
since. The officers who I was under and those of our mess was Major Rayford,
Captains Hadley, Hill and Lambe. Our Cols. name as well as I can recollect
was Tirpin McRea. I was not in any engagements--- marched from Duplin Ct.
House to a little village by the name of Elizabeth Town where I was taken
sick --- said he was born in the COUNTY OF ALBEMARLE, VIRGINIA - the year
he did not recollect.

File # S 38263   Robert Nicholson

District of Virginia
Isle of Wight Co.

On this 5th day of Feb. 1828, personally appeared in open Ct. at this Feb.
term of sd. county of Isle of Wight it being a Court of Record by Legislative
enactment, Robert Nicholson aged 64 years, resident in Southampton Co. in
the State of Virginia aforesd. --- declares he served in Rev. -- entered as
lieutenant in Capt. Isaac Moores Co. 19th Apr. 1777 in the 10th North
Carolina Reg. commanded by Col. Abram Shepard and sometimes in the same
year was transferred to the first South Carolina Reg. commanded by Col.
Thomas Clark, that he made his original declaration the 2nd June 1818 and
the number of his pension certificate is 5918 and moreover, etc. etc. ---
declarant is at this time occupied in teaching two or three small children
and resides in the family of Mr. John Urquhart -- his eye sight fails him
very much and that he cannot keep much longer to produce his present em-
ployment and that he has none of his family with him, but a dau. in dis-
tress --- declared under oath that he entered into the service of the U. S.
19th April 1777 in the County of Perquimans, in the State of North Carolina.

File # S 21912   Joshua Palmer

Union District, South Carolina

3 Oct. 1832 appeared in Court Joshua Palmer resident of sd. District aged
82 years --- entered service in October 1775 as a volunteer in Capt.
Brandon's Co. in the Reg. commanded by Col. John Thomas and Maj. Henderson
and served in the tour known by the name of "Snow Camp" about 4 months -
In May 1776 was drafted and joined the Co. commanded by Capt. Jolly in Col.
Thomas' Reg. and marched to Prince's Fort --- pursued the Indians, etc. and
having destroyed them returned to the Seneca (?) Fort etc. etc. - discharged
in October by Col. Thomas --- In March 1778 entered the service as a Captain
in the Militia in Col. Thomas' Reg. and marched to Augusta and thence to
Florida served three months --- In March 1779 again took command of a Co.
in the Reg. commanded by 'Col. Wafford and marched to Augusta and thence to
Bacon's Ridge, when the Reg. was divided and I fell under the command of
Col. Brandon and then marched to Quaquaw Swamp - and then to Battle of Stone---
discharged--- In Feb. 1780 again took command of a Co.˙and joined Col. Purvis
near Augusta at Cubbert Crk. served three months and was discharged - in July
following resigned commission --- no more regular tours but was actively employed in the neighborhood in different capacity until Battle of Cowpens in
which was Adjutant to Col. Brandon Reg. and then continued in an irregular
scouting service until the entire cessation of hostility --- was born in
AMELIA CO., VA. 12 March 1750 as have been told but no record of age ---
lived in Union District, South Carolina when entered service and lived there
ever since.

Jan. 1856 South Carolina - Union District
Know all men by these presents that I Purmesion (?) Palmer of State and
District aforesd. do constitute and appoint A. S. Wallace etc. etc. to
prosecute the claim of my father Capt. Joshua Palmer for an increase for
cavalry service Capt. Palmore was Pensioner Act. 7 June 1832 and died
Dec. 1, 1835.

File # W 8552   Amos Richardson

State of Tennessee - Campbell Co., September Term of Court 1832

11th Sept. 1832 appeared Amos Richardson a resident of sd. Co. of Campbell in
State aforesd. aged 70 years --- that he entered the service of the U. S.
under the following named officers and served as herein states --- one three
months tour in the Militia of Burk Co. in the State of North Carolina in Capt.
Shokys company in the reg. commanded by Col. Lock - and was discharged
26 Jan. 1781 as will appear by reference to the discharge hereunto annexed
marked A - also a tour of duty in 1782 for 3 months and 6 weeks as will
appear, etc. etc. Marked B signed by Capt. Alexander Gordon - in the Reg.
commanded by Col. Isaacs - that his 1st discharge for 3 mos. was signed at
Salisbury by Lt. Maurice Rowe. He states that he was a volunteer in every
tour of duty he performed - was mustered into service the 1st tour of duty
he performed upon the Catawba River below Charlotte joined Genl. Washington
and Genl. Green, Col. Washington commanded the horse - from there we marched
to the Cheraws - from there a detachment was sent to Salisbury to guard the
prisoners at which place I received my first discharge - On the second tour
of duty we rendevoused upon the waters of the Yadkin River near Hamlin's
store where Col. Isaacs commanded - from there we marched down through
Chatham, Guilford and Randolph in pursuit of Col. Fannon. Was at the taking
of --- and Still two of Col. Fannon's men who were condemned and shot as
tories. ---

                                                        his
Test: William Cary   Clk.   Amos   x   Richardson
                                                        mark

James Hickey Sen. a clergyman and Rollings James certified were well acquainted with Amos, etc.

Interrogatory 1st by the court where and in what year were you born - Ans.
I was b. in 1762 in Bedford Co., Va. 2nd any record of age? Ans. I have
at home. 3rd. Where living when called into service - where have you lived
since the Rev. War, and where do you live now? Ans. When first I entered
the service I lived upon the Catawba River where I lived until the war. I
then moved to this Country before this was a state. --- State the names of
the Regular officers who were with the troops where you served, etc. ---
Genl. Morgan lay on one side of the swamp and we on the other. Genl.
Washington, Col. Washington, Col. Fifer, Maj. Read lay on the same side of
the swamp we did --- this is in reference to the first tour of duty --- the
next tour under the command of Col. Isaacs. We were not with the regular
troops. State the names of persons to whom you are known in your present
neighborhood, etc. Ans. James Hickey Senr. - Rollings James - Joshua
Craven - John Cooper - Edward Williams.

Court of Quorum: Caleb M. David, Eamon - Gross, Enoch Rice

State of Tennessee
Campbell Co.

Be it known that before me John Murray a J.P. for the Co. aforesd. personally appeared Amos Richardson aged 92 years --- states he is the
identical Amos Richardson who was a Rev. Soldier or Pensioner of the State
of North Carolina and that he now resides in the State of Tennessee,

Campbell Co. and has resided there for near 40 years past and draws a pension
etc.   By these presents, constitute, appt. and fully empower and authorises
etc. F. E. Hasslen of Washington, D. C. as my true attorney, etc.

signed, Amos Richardson

Witnesses: Lindsey Wilson
            Thomas Richardson   18 April 1852

State of Tennessee
Campbell Co.

3 Jan. 1854 appeared Mrs. Fanny Richardson aged 65 years --- that she is
the widow of Amos Richardson, deceased --- that she was married to Amos
17 Dec. 1840 - that her said husband died 2 May 1853 - that she was not
married to him prior to the 2nd day of January 1800, but at the time
stated that there is a public record of her marriage.

Copy of marriage bond included dated 11 Dec. 1840 and signed by Amos
Richardson and Thomas Richardson.

State of Tennessee
Anderson Co.

To any regular minister of the Gospel having care of souls or any Justice
of the Peace for sd. Co. Greetings - I, William Gross of the County Court
of Anderson aforesd. by virtue of the power in me vested by law to
license you or either of you to celebrate the Rites of Matrimony between
Amos Richardson and Fanny Farmer by uniting them as husband and wife.
Given at Office in Clinton the 11th day of Dec. 1840.

This executed on the 17th Dec. 1840 by celebrating the rites of matrimony
between Amos Richardson and Fanny Farmer and uniting them together as
husband and wife, etc.

John Key - J.P.

File # S 31932   Amos Richardson

State of Georgia
Elbert Co.

19 Sept. 1832 - appeared Amos Richardson in Ct.--- that he entered the
service of the U. S. under Capt. George Russell commanded by Col. Campbell,
Col. John Sevier, and Major Isaac Lane, as a volunteer private soldier of
the 1st of Sept. 1780, and left the same about the last of November 1780,
making three months - that when he entered the service he resided on the
Waters of the Holston River then in the State of North Carolina, now
Tennessee, and that he joined his detachment at Tolbert's Mills on Doe
River in the State of N. C., now Tenn. from thence marched over Yellow
Mountain to Kings Mountain, and was in that Battle fought there against
the British and Tories, the American forces was commanded by Col. Campbell,
Col. Shelby, Col. Sevier and Col. Cleveland, the exact date he does not
recollect. That he also entered the service of the U. S. under the follow-
ing named officers and served as herein stated - under Capt. Samuel Alexander

commanded by Col. Elijah Clark, Col. Dunn, and Maj. Shelby, as a volunteer, private soldier on the 4th of Feb. 1781 making a little more than ten months service, that when he entered this service he lived on the Waters of the Holston River then in the State of N. C., now Tenn. and that he joined his detachment at David Millers on the waters of Green River, N. C. and marched from thence to Augusta in the State of Georgia, and beseiged the enemy for about nine weeks, who surrendered the Fort on 5 June 1781, from Augusta marched to the mouth of Broad River at a place called Clarks Fort then in Wilkes Co., now Lincoln, State of Ga., and at that place was discharged.

Says that he was born in LOUDOUN COUNTY in the State of Virginia, on 18 Sept. 1764 --- says that he has no record of his age. When called into service he lived on the Waters of Holston R., then N.C., now Tenn. lived in Bedford Co., Virginia for one year then removed to Union District in South Carolina where he lived 5 years or thereabouts, from there he removed to Elbert Co., in the State of Georgia, where he has lived ever since ---

Names of persons to whom I am known in my present neighborhood - William Dooly, Esq., Benjamin Bobo Esq., Lewis McMullan, Lewis Stevens, Senr. and Wiley Thompson.

[From other evidence this man appears to have lived in Greenville Co. and Pendleton Co., S.C. 1790 & 1800. However, he clearly stated "Union Dist., S.C. which was a part of Ninety-Six Dist. at one time as were the others.]

File # S 30680   Jesse Richardson

State of Kentucky - Pulaski Co.

21 August 1835 - appeared Court Jesse Richardson aged about 75 years - that he entered the service of the U.S. while a resident of BOTTETOURT CO., VA. sometime in the latter part of the spring or first of the summer in 1778 - volunteered for a 6-months tour in the Co. of Capt. James Newell, Jesse Evans Lt. - he belonged to the Reg. of Col. Preston --- received no written discharge - afterwards in the fall of the year 1779 he removed to the west what is now Kentucky and sometime in the summer of 1780 he volunteered to serve under Capt. George Adams, Wm. Moore, Lt., Joseph Kennedy, Ensign ÷ belonged to the Reg. of Col. Benjamin Logan --- received no written discharge - afterwards in the summer of 1782 while living in what is now Lincoln Co., Ky. volunteered to serve in the Co. of Capt. John Snoddy belonged to the Reg. of Col. Benjamin Logan--- can prove by William Owen a Rev. pensioner a part of his service -- known to Martin Owens a clergyman of Pulaski Co. and to Joseph Porter Esq. --- was born in the early part of the year 1760 in the COUNTY OF LOUDEN in State of Virginia - no record of his age and never saw one - his father died while he was very young and he states his age from what one of his brothers told him and does not know the day or month in which he was born --- since the Rev. war he lived sometime of what is now Garrard Co., Ky. and then moved back to and lived in Lincoln Co. a few years and then moved to what is now Pulaski Co., Ky. in which he has lived ever since its establishment except three or four years he lived a part of his time below the mouth of the Tennessee - he owns land in Pulaski now and considers this county his residence at this time.

                                                    --Jesse Richardson

The sd. William Owens aged about 85 years --- states he does of his own
personal knowledge know that the above named J. R. in the year 1778 while
a resident of the State of Virginia volunteered --- that he belonged to the
same company --- defending the frontiers of Virginia from the Indians.

-- William x Owens Senr.

State of Kentucky - Wayne Co.

Joseph Chrisman verified Jesse Richardson's statements as to his tours of
duty 28 July 1835.

The statement of Joseph Kennedy of Madison Co., Ky. aged 79 years on the
28th day of August last in relation to the application of Jesse Richardson,
now of McCracken Co., Ky. but lately of Pulaski Co., Ky. says he was acquainted with Jesse Richardson in the fall of 1779 when sd. Richardson
moved to English's station. In the summer of 1780 I think there was a
campaign commenced against the Shawnee Indians, etc. -- Sept. 1839

-- Jo Kennedy

Treasury Dept. - Second Comptroller's Office - July ? 1841

Under the act of April 1838, entitled "An act directing the transfer of
money remaining unclaimed by certain Pensioners, and authorizing the payment
of the same at the Treasury of the United States" The widow of Jesse
Richardson a Pensioner on the Roll of the Kentucky Agency, at the rate of
twenty three dollars and 33 cents per annum, under the law of the 7th June
1832, has been paid at this Dept. from the 4th of March 1831 to the 17th Dec.
1839.

File # W18810   Joseph Richardson

Pension Application (widow)

No. 4331 North Carolina - Sally Richardson, widow of Joseph Richardson, who
died on the --- about 22 years since of Stokes in the State of N. C. who was
a private in the company commanded by Captain Morgan of the Regt. commanded
by Col. McClannahan in the Virginia line for 9 months Va.

Inscribed on the Roll of N. Carolina at the rate of 30 Dollars per annum to
commence on the 4th day March 1831.

Know all men by these presents that we Joseph Richardson and Francis
Peyton Gentlemen are held and firmly bound unto our Sovereign Lord George
the Third by the Grace of God of Great Britain France and Ireland King
Defender of the Faith - in fifty pounds Current Money to be paid to our said
Lord the King his Heirs and Successors to the which payment will and truly to
be made We bind ourselves, our Heirs, Executors and admrs. jointly and severally
by these presents, Sealed with our Seals and dated this 12th day of January
in the Seventh year of his Majesty's Reign -

Whereas there is a marriage suddenly intended to be solemnized between the
above named Joseph Richardson and Sally Compton spinster:- The condition of

this obligation is such that if there be no lawful cause to obstruct the same then this obligaztion to be void else to remain in full force and virtue.

--Joseph Richardson (Seal)
Francis Peyton (Seal)

State of Virginia Loudoun County to wit -

I, Charles G. Eskridge Clerk of the County Court of Loudoun in the State aforesaid do hereby certify that the foregoing is a true transcript from the original Marriage bond filed in my office.

In testimony whereof I have hereunto set my hand and affixed my seal of Office this 12th day of February 1845 and in the 69th year of the common-wealth

-- Eskridge

(Certificate of Pension issued the 2nd day of March 1846 and sent to Hon. ? S. Reid, H. R.)

(Arrears to the 4th of March, $450.00
(Semi-annual allowances ending 11th $15.00 -- $465.00)

State of North Carolina
County of Stokes
        Be it known that on this first day of July 1839 personally appeared before me Charles Banner (Bonner?) a Justice of the Peace for the Court of Pleas and Quarter Sessions for said County. Sally Richardson a Resident near the Rockingham County line in North Carolina twenty five miles from Stokes Court House, aged Eighty Seven years next August who being duly Sworn accord-ing to law doth on her oath make the following Declaration in order to obtain the benefit of the provision made by the Act of Congress passed July 4th 1836, and the Act Explanatory of said Act passed the 3rd March 1837, that she married to Joseph Richardson when she was only 17 years of age by a parson Anders or Andrews in the County of Loudoun and Commonwealth of Virginia in the year 1769 or 1770 that her maiden name was Sally Compton but from the loss of memory and infirmities of old age, she being totally blind for the span of upwards twenty years past, she cannot remember the many services that her husband Joseph Richardson actually served, but remembers that he served under a Capt. Morgan when they resided in Lowden County, Virginia against the Indians six months and other services against the Indians towards Red Stone and across the Allegany Mountains to the Cherokee tribe in 1776. She thinks under the Command of a General or Col. Christa five months service and the last he went as a Sargeant under a Capt. Pawlin from Bottetourt County, Virginia, and was gone six months at least in which he stated he had been in the Battle of Guilford, North Carolina. She hopes reference being had to the Rolls of the Militia of Virginia Revolutionary Soldiers will now plainly show the services rendered by her husband aforesaid for which she claims a pension. She further states that she was married as above state, by Parson Anders in Lowden County, Virginia to the said Joseph Richardson in the year seventeen hundred & sixty nine or seventy and that her husband died in Rockingham County, N. Carolina twenty two years past and that she has remained a widow ever since that period as reference to the proof hereunot -- will now fully appear, tho she has no family record of the ages of her children. But her first born was William Richardson is now seventy years old if living. Next was Nancy would be now

sixty eight years & the remainder of her children was born in succession until
we had twelve in all only two living & our youngest is now forty seven years
old - Sworn to & Subscribed the truth of which I am fully satisfied before me.

? Bonner (Banner?)

her
Sally x Richardson
mark

I do hereby certify that the above Sally Richardson from Bodily infirmity &
Blindness is not able to travel to our Court House by any means without a very
great risque ----

State of North Carolina
Stokes County

I Reuben D. Golding Clerk of the Court of Pleas & Quarter Sessions for
Stokes County aforesaid do hereby certify that Charles Bonner (Banner?) a
Magistrate as above and that the foregoing signature ----

Know all men by these presents that I Dotia Martin of the County of Rockingham
and State of North Carolina am one of the children & legal representatives of
Joseph Richardson a Revolutionary War soldier and Sally Richardson his wife
who is now deceased do hereby irrevocably constitute and appoint L. B. True
of Washington, D. C. my true and lawful attorney for me and in my name to
examine into & present any claim that may be due or found to be due the
children & legal representatives of Joseph Richardson in virtue of the services
of the said Joseph Richardson in the Revolutionary War and the several acts of
Congress in relation thereto and that might have accrued to either of the said
parties and drawn in their life time and now due their legal representatives -
I hereby authorize my said agent to do all things that I might and could do if
personally present and I hereby ratify all that my said attorney may do in ---
to be legally --- in the -----. I --- any authority I may have given to any
other person ------

Wm. Martin
Samuel Henry

her
Dotia x Martin
mark

State of North Carolina
County of Rockingham

On this 4th day of May 1832 personally appeared before me Dotia Martin and
acknowledged the foregoing power of attorney to be her acknowledgment and I
certify that I well know the said Dotia Martin and that she is the person now
present and who executed the foregoing power of attorney.

J. W. Martin   JP

Honl. Commissioner of Pension
Washington, D. C.

Mt. Vernon Rockcastle
County, Dy.   26 Dec. 1855

Dear Sir,

Mrs. Francis Gann of Wayne County, Kentucky was qualified to her declaration for a pension in June last, as the Daughter & heir at law of Sarah

Richardson (deceased), widow of Joseph Richardson (deceased) due on account of his services as Lieutenant in the North Carolina Line for three years or near it from 1776 or 1777 - that Sarah Richardson was married to her husband Joseph Richardson in Lowden Co., Va. in the year 1763 or 4 or near that date - served under Capt. Rice & Col. Murfrie & states her name was Sarah Compton before marriage - to make sure I am right - in July last I addressed a letter to Andrew Martin of Rockingham County, North Carolina to prove the dates the old people died there, and that his widow never drew a pension - Stating at the same time the probable value of the claim, he being one of the heirs. Martin handed my letter to Mr. Dillard of Rockingham Co. in N. C. - to answer it, in which he replies that it was said - Joseph Richardson was a sergeant in Capt. Paulins Compy. in the Va. Line and that Sarah Richardson his widow applied for and received a pension of $450.00 before she died - his statement being so very different from the statement of Mrs. Gann in her declaration, and knowing the marriage was before the Revolution, if Richardson was a Seargeant and he died in 1817 - and his widow - 1846 - the pension was greatly more than $450 if the widow was pensioned at all - as Andrew Martin was one of the heirs - I concluded Dillard & him wanted to deter Mrs. Gann the daughter heir of Richardson from prosecuting the claim, - Dillards letter was dated in August last - I then addressed you a note to assertain the fact - certainly whether Sarah Richardson widow of Joseph Richardson of North Carolina had ever applied for or obtained a pension in her lifetime.

I received your letter dated Oct. 17, 1855 stating it does not appear that Sarah Richardson widow of Joseph Richardson of North Carolina was ever pensioned or Eaven made application for a pension. Your letter fully satisfied me that - Andrew Martin and Mr. Dillard of N. C. was trying to deceive me and deter me from prosecuting the claim, as proof has to be had in N. C. as to the date the old people died, I have been trying ever since to get proof the date they died, and have in consequence thereof I have not sent the papers off - now today I have received another letter written by Andrew Martin one of the heirs, of Rockingham Co., N. C. dated 8th Dec. 1855 in which he states. - Mr. Dillard had written as to the pension officer and had received a letter - that the claim made by Sarah Richardson widow of Joseph Richardson applied for a pension in her lifetime from Patrick County in the State of Virginia, that she aledged Joseph Richardson was a private & that her pension was allowed after she died to her son in law Thomas Martin.

I am as yet still of the opinion that Andrew Martin, one of the heirs of Rockingham Co., N. C. and his friend Mr. Dillard is in parternship in the claim & write to me misrepresenting the case --- and prevent me from going on with the claim here for Mrs. Gann the daughter of Sarah Richardson - Dillard's letter to me said Richardson was a sergeant - and Andrew Martin one of the heirs in his letter now states Richardson was a private soldier - I am still sure they are misrepresenting the case to me to get to attend to the business in N. C. and I write now to know the fact whether or not Sarah Richardson ever applied for a pension as the widow of Joseph Richardson from Patrick County in the State of Virginia and when you are looking at the papers... look careful as she alledged her name was Sarah Compton before marriage and where and when the marriage was made - and the kind of service alledged.

May be other widow of the name of Sarah Richardson widow of Joseph Richardson may be applied from Patrick County, Virginia, but if the widows name was not Sarah Compton I know the application refused to is not the parties I am attending to for - if her name is alledged to be Sarah Compton before

marriage I am dun with the case if not I will still stand by the interest of
Mrs. Gann one of the heirs and a more respectable Lady than she is don't live
in Kentucky. Consequently I have such confidence in this claim.

You may think I have written much - but this cause which I want to know
I am right, certinlly before I proceed further - & this I must know. The
claim is worth notice & I have full confidence in it - nevertheless the
letters now before me --- to from North Carolina and you are the only one
can satisfy me that I am mistaken in the case. Please look up the papers if
ever filed by the widow and let me know the contents thereof the dates it is
also alledged she died and the dates her claim and all the particulars and
when it appears she did die, I do not want nor intend to be mistaken in this
case - I do not want the fellows to defraud me out of the claim - you will
confer on me as well as Mrs. Gann a great favor to let me know all the information can be derived from the record in your office relative to this
claim --- So I may know what course to take.

                                I am Dear Sir
                                Verry Truly
                                Alfred Smith

These Gentlemen writes to me big in letters - I know nothing about their
reputation - I do not wish to misrepresent the--- the records at the department will tell whether they are writing to me the truth or not.

                                A. Smith

                        * * *

INDEX TO SECTION ONE

REVOLUTIONARY WAR SIZE ROLLS

Abbott, Elijah	8	Beesley, Smith	16
Able, Thomas	8	Beevers, John	9
Adison, Arthur	8	Bennett, William	16
Alderson, Reuben	8	Benston, George	16
Alford, John	8	Berry, James	10
Allen, Daniel	8	Best, Nickolas	10
Moses	8	Bettisworth, Bowling	3
Samuel	8	Biggs, John Jr.	9
Alloway, Isaac	8	Biles, Charles	10
Anderson, Jacob	8	Biry, Martin	3
Angel, John	8	Bitgood, Philip	9
Armstrong, Jesse	8	Blades, Jesse	16
Arnold, William	8	Blake, William	16
Arrasmith, Masny	8	Bluford, Elijah	3
Atkinson, Thomas	8	Bolinger, John	10
Axline, John	8	Bond, John	9
		Bonnell, Alexander	9
B_____, Richard	3	Booker, George	9
Bailey, Southey	16	Borah, Jacob	16
Tarpley	16	Boswell, Jonathan	16
William C.	3	Bott, John	16
Zadock	16	Bottomley, Joseph	16
Baker, Christopher	9	Bowen, John	3
Nicholas	3	Bowers, Phillip	9
Banton, John	3	Bowling, Benjamin	9
Barbee, Elias	9	Bowls, Peter	9
Barber, Elijah	3	Bowser, James	9
Barksdale, Samuel	3	Bowyer, Jacob	16
Barnes, William	9	Boxell, Joseph	3
Barnett, Michael	16	Robert	3
Thomas	16	Boyd, Robert	16
Barns, Andrew	3	Brabston, William	16
George	10	Bradford, John	3
Barrett, Richard	3	Bradshaw, Canada	9
Batcheldor, Cornelius	9	Robert	3
Bates, James	9	Bray, James	9
Thomas	3,16	Brent, Henry	10
Battle, Shadrack	16	John	3
Bayly, Southy	9	Briant, Robert	9
Zadock	9	Britman, Samuel	9
Bazill, John	9	Brookens, John	9
Bean, Richard	9	Broomfield, John	3
Bearcraft, Lott	9	Brown, Carfield	10
Bears, Jeumes	9	Henry	9
Beckham, Griffis, W.	9	James	16
Bedingt, William	16	John	$3,9,16^2$

Brown, Larkin	16
Luke	9
(?)ason	9
Robert	9^2
Thomas	3
Brunt, John	9
Bruton, Martin	9
Bryson, Robert	16
Buffington, David	9
Buford, George	3
Bugg, William C.	9
Bunting, William	16
Burch, Hilbert	3
Burcher, John	9
Burgit, Frederick	9
Burnett, McD.	9
Burns, Barnes	3
Henry	9
Jeremiah	9
Burton, Isaac	16
Burwell, Richard	9
Bush, John	9
Bussiplin, Reubin	16
Bustead, Isaac	16
Byas, James	3
Bybee, Cornelius	9
Bybie, Samuel	16
Byrne, James	10
C__?__,__?__	10
Cabell, William	16
Campbell, John	3
Canard, David	3
Canter, James	3
John	3
Canonbrig, William	16
Capell, William	17
Carbin, Samuel	17
Carder, Sanford	10
Carney, James	17
William	16
Carnine, Jeremiah	3
Carrill, Benjamin	10
John	10
Carter, Jesse	10
Cave, Benjamin	3
Chadoin, Andrew	17
Chambers, Travis	10
Chancillor, Julius	3
Charity, Charles	16
Chilton, Medley	3
Christian, Jesse	16
Chubb, John	10
Church, John	17
Clark, John	3
Rodham	10
Clay, Arthur	10
Mathew	3

Cluttin, George	10
Coalter, William	10
Cockrell, Joshua	10
Presley	17
Coffell, Hugh	4
Coffer, George	3
Coffin, Charles	17
Cole, William	10
Coleman, James	17
Patrick	10
William	10
Collins, Benjamin	3
Robert	10^2
Colony, George	16
Conery, John	10
Conley, Thomas	10
Connor, (?)	17
Joseph	4
Cook, John	3
William	17
Cooley, James	17
Coopper, John	3
Copage, John	17
Copes, Parker	16
Coplin, Elijah	17
Corbin, Charles	3
Corder, William	3
Corderrey, Robert	10
Cosby, Sydner	10
Cotes, John	10
Couzens, James	16
Cox, Enoch	3
Coyl, Thomas	3
Crafford, Oliver	10
Crause, William	3
Creek, Peter	3
Crew(s), Bartholomew	16
Thomas	16
Croffard, Aaron	16
Cross, James	16
John	4
Croucher, Charles	3
John	10
Crow, John	10
Cruse, William	10
Crush, Griffin	10
Cumberford, Patrick	17
Curtis, John	16
Custason, John	16
Dafter, John	17
Davies, Ancell	10
Aquilla	11
David	11
Edward	11
Henry W.	10
Thomas	11
William	11

Davis, Spilsby	17	Foster, John	11
Dawson, Francis	17	William	11
Day, John	17	Francis, George	11
Westbrooke	17	John	11
Dayley, John	11	Nicholas	11
Deahan, John	17	Patrick	11
Dean, John	17	Franklin, John	11
Decker, Samuel	10	Freeman, Hezekiah	11
Delany, James	17		
Delistatious, Selby	17	Galley, William	4
Severn	17	Gardner, Alex	4
Demastres, Edward	17	Garrell, Solomon	4
James	17	Garrett, Carter	4
Denny, Alexander	11	Garton, William	4
Henry	17	Gatteswood, Henry	4
Depriest, John	11	Gee, Brumma	4
Dickerson, Edward	17	Richard	4
Dinsmore, William	17	Gentry, John	4
Dixon, William	17	Gettans, Evans	17
Dobey, Robert	11	Giles, John	4
Dobbins, Charles	17	Thomas	4
Samuel	11	Gill, Metcalf	4
Dockerdy, Charles	11	Gilling, Hugh	17
Dolby, Littleton	17	Gipson, William	4
Donald, William	11	Gladen, John	17
Donoho, Thomas	11	Gleeson, John	17
Dowell, Thomas	10	Glover, John	4
Drake, Bartholomew	11	Gooddens, John	4
Duglass, Thomas	11	Goodman, Thomas	4
Dugmore, John	17	Goosebury, Thomas	4
Dunken, Christopher	17	Gottlip, John	17
Dunn, Peter	10	Gowin, Joshua	4
Dunstan, Alman	11	Grant, James	4
Durham, John	11	Grayson, Robert	4
Duvall, Benjamin	11	Greene, Josias	17
Dyson, William	11	Griffen, Oliver	4
		Sherrod	4
Farr, Edward	11	Griffith, Henry	17
Farrell, John	11	Griggory, Jeremiah	4
Fathorn, Edward	11	Grigsby, Taliaferro	17
Feegens, George	11	Grinah, Richard	4
Fibbay, George	11	Grissel, John	17
Fielding, Eppa	11	Guffie, Michael	4
Fields, John	11	Gunter, John	4,17
Finch, John	11		
Finix, John	11	Habon, William	12
Fisher, Benjamin	11	Haden, Anthony	17
Thomas	11	Hagarty, James	11,12
Fitzpatrick, James	11	Thomas	12
Fleming, John	11	Hail, William	7
Floyd, William	11	Haines, Griffith	18
Ford, John	11	Hale, William	18
Fortune, John	11	Hall, Jacob	7
Samuel	11	John	17
Shadrack	11	Thomas	7,12

Hall, Thomas	7,12	Hope, Abraham	18
William	5	Horton, Joseph	7
Zebedee	7	Samuel	4
Hambey, Richard	7	Thomas	4
Hambleton, John	18	Houston, William	12
Hancock, Bennet	12	Hout, Jacob	18
Harcum, Rodham	7	Hover, Jasper	7
Hardy, Charles	12	Howard, Henry	4
Harper, John	4,5,7	Joseph	7
Josiah	4	Thomas	5
Harrell, Abraham	12	Howell, Isaac	4
John	12	Howlet, Ephraim	17
Harris, Edmond	5	Hudling, Richard	4
John	18	Hudnell, Thomas	18
William	12	Hueston, Samuel	18
Zephaniah	12	Hughes, John	12
Harrison, Alexander	18	Ralph	4
William	4	Hughs, Joseph	11,12
Harvy, Joel	4	Thomas	7
Hassie, Morris	4	William	7
Hastings, Thomas	17	Humphress, (?)	5
Hatter, Henry	11	Humphrey, Jesse	4
Haverd, Williams	12	Hundren, William	4
Hawkins, James	7	Hutson, Benjamin	4
Haynie, William	4		
Hazleep, Smith	18	Irwin, John	12
Heatherlin, Christopher	18		
Helms(s), Leonard	4	Jackson, James	12
Linth	7	Thomas	12
Henchin, William	17	William	12
Henderson, John	18	Jacobs, William	12
Hendrick, John	7	James, Isaac	12
Henley, John	12	Jenkins, Charles	12
Hickman, Ezkiel	18	Jerdone, Henry	12
Higgins, William	7	Johnson, Benjamin	12
Hill, Richard	5,12	Jacob	12
William	18	James	12
Hilliar, John	7	William	12^2
Hinson, Benjamin	4	Zachariah	12
Richard	7	Johnston, Philip	12
Hinwood, John	7	Joines, Edward	12
Hipenstall, Caleb	7	Jonen, John	12^3
Hix, William	4	Joseph	12
Hoff, Charles	7	Richard	12
Hoil, Phillip	12	Thomas	12
Holdaby, William	12	William	12
Holdbrook, John	18	Joynes, John	12
Holidy, Charles	12		
Holladay, Zachariah	4	Keen, John	12
Holland, Julias	7,12	King, John	12
Holt, George	7	Kirk, James	12
Homes, Bartholomew	12		
Hoofman, Rubin	7	Lambert, Nicholas	13
Hooker, William	18	LaRues, Michael	13
Hooper, Walter	11	Laughlin, Dennis	13
		Leech, Andrew	13

Leman, Deddrick	13	Martin, Daniel	5
Leonard, John	13	John	5
Robert	13	Thomas	5
Lewis, Hubbert	13	Mason, James	14
Joseph	13	Mash, Joseph	18
Linck, Henry	13	Massey, John	13
Lind, Thomas	13	Mathews, Thomas	13
Lindsay, James	13	Mattonly, James	18
Lines, James	13	May, Thomas	13
Link, John	13	Melton, Robert	14
Linton, Lewis	13²	Milikin, John	18
Litteral, Richard	13	Miller, Francis	18
Lockart, Philip	13	Jacob	5
Lockward, William	13	John	5
Loden, Benjamin	13	Thomas	13
Long, Daniel	13	Mitchell, Andrew	13
Mathias	13	George	13
Lors, Henry	13	Mitchum, Nathaniel	5
Love, James	13	Moore, Nicholas	18
Lower, George	13	Peter	14
Lucas, Francis	13	More, George	18
Joseph	13²	Moreland, Michael	18
Manuel	13	Morgan, Jonas	18
		Morris, Henry	13
McAfee, Joseph	13	James	13
McArthur, James, Sr.	13	Thomas	14
James, Jr.	13	William	14
McCannon, Christopher	18	Morton, James	5
McCary, Richard	13	Moseby, William	18
McCartey, Daniel	5	Mosses, Ezekiel	18
McClanham, Thomas	13	Mott, Moses	5
McCray, John	5	Muir, James	13
McDonahow, James	14	Mullin, William	5
McDonald, Benjamin	5	Munk, Shadrack	13
Donald	18	Murray, Daniel	18
Spencer	5	James	13
McGlauchling, Edward	18	Myre, Henry	5
McGraw, James	13		
McGuire, John	13	Neal, Richard	14
McKinney, John	14,18	Neil, Jeremiah	14
Littleberry	18	Nicholas, Richard	14
McKinsey, Alexander	5	Northam, Major	14
McMullin, James	5	Miles	14
McMullion, William	5		
McNeal, John	5	Payne, Benjamin	7
McNeel, Patrick	5	John	7
McQuiddy, William	13	Peace, James	7
		Pearpoint, Charles	7
Macky, William	18	Peauman, Grief	7
Maddox, Elisha	18	Pettett, John	7
John	18	William	7
Malery, John	5	Peyton, Francis	19
Man, Benjamin	5	Lewis	8
Manders, Henry	5	Philby, George	7
Marsh, Edwin	18	Phillips, (?)	8

Pickett, John	7	Sanders, John	5
Pierce, Francis	19	Sandford, Edward	14
Pigg, George	7	Salisbury, (?)	19
Pitmam, William	7	Salmon, John	5
Plagge, John	19	Scott, Francis	15
Plane, Constant	7	Littlebury	5
Plod, John	7	William	18
Plumley, Obediah	7	Seabourn, Jacob	5
Plumline, John	7	Self, Moses	15
Plunckett, John	7	Shackelford, Thomas	15
Pollard, James	19	Shaver, George	5
Potter, John	7	John	5
Powel, Benjamin	7	Shaw, Frederick	5
Price, John	7	Sheets, Mathias	15
William	7	Shelton, Midley	15
Pruett, Thomas	7	Shepherd, James	5
William	7	John	18
Pullin, Everad	7	Shepperd, William	5
Pursell, James	7	Sherman, George	15
		Sheynar, George	5
Quin, John	14	Shierman, George	5
		Shope, William	5
Ray, David	14	Shrye, Paul	15
Read, Charles	14	Simkins, Daniel	15
Reason, Bartholomew	14	Simpson, Richard	18
Redlock, Peter	14	William	18
Reed, Thomas	19	Sisson, Frederick	14
Reggers, Michael	14	Slack, Benjamin	15
Richards, Phillip	14	Slacht, Cornelius	15
Preeson	14	Slape, Thomas	15
William	14	Smaw, John	18
Ridley, Joseph	19	Smith, (?)	19
Riely, Edward	14	Ambrose	15
Riggs, Jacob	14	Benjamin	15
Riley, John	14	Edward	19
Ringo, John	14	Joseph	5,18
Ripl(?), Frederick	14	John	$5,15,18^2$
Roach, David	14	Lewis	18
Robert	19^2	William	18,19
Roak, Hugh	14	Smothers, William	15
Roberts, Alexander	14	Sneed, William	14
John	14	Sommers, William	19
Robertson, John	14^3	Speak, John	14
Rocke, John	13	Sperling, William	5
Rogers, John	19	Spong, David	5
Roller, Cunrod	14	John	18
John	14	Sprouce, James	18
Rolls, John	14	Sprowse, James	5
Rose, Richard	14	Stark, William	18
Rosewater, Thomas	14	Steel, Benjamin	5
Ross, James	14	David	5
John	19	Stephens, (?)	19
Russell, Ephraim	19	James	15
John	14	Stevenson, Ignatius	5
Rutter, Thomas	14	Stewart, Edward	18

Stewart, James	19	Walker, Jeremiah	8
John	18,19	John	8
Mathew	5	William	15
Sto_____(?), Richard	5	Wall(s), Martin	6
Stoneberger, Lewis	15	Peter	15
Stowers, John	14	William	15
Stubbs, Allen	15	Ware, James	8
Sullins, William	6	Warton, Jesse	8
Summerskill, John	19	Warwick, Abraham	15
Summerson, George	19	Watson, Joseph	8
Surrough, Anthony	14	Wavers, John	15
Swaney, Paul	5	Waren, Gabriel	6
Swayney, Patrick	15	Warren, John	15^2
Swift, Samuel	14	Warters, Thomas	6
		Weaver, John	15
Tarrant, Manlove	6	Weeks, Samuel	8
Thomas	6	Stephen	6,8
Taylor, Eyres	19	Wells, Thomas	8
John	$6,19^2$	Westfall, Jacob	8
Nevit	19	Whelor, Edward	6
Samuel	6	Whiley, Benjamin	15
Selby	19	Whipple, Joseph	8
William	6^2	Whisler, Alexander	15
Terpin, Samuel	19	White, Daniel	8
Terrill, Presley	6	Edward	15
Tharp, Jonathan	19	John	6
Thomas, Henry	6	Whitman, John	8
Job	6	Whitmore, Benjamin	19
John	6^3	Whitson, Charles	20
Spencer	6	Whitt, Jesse	20
Thompson, Berry	19	Wigley, Joseph	6
Thomson, Thomas	6	Wilcox, Robert	15^2
Thorn(s), Richard	19^2	Wilkerson, Benjamin	6
Thurmond, William	19	Michael	8
Tinsley, William	15	William	6
Tomasson, Byas	6	Wilkins, Argyle	15
Toney, Archey	6	Wilkinson, Stith	20
Thomas	15	Williams, Balsom	15
Topping, Major	19	Benjamin	8
Townsen, Henry	19	Clark	6,15
Townshend, William	6	Henry	15
Travvis, Miles	6	John	8
Troop, William	6	Levy	6
Trussell, Rodham	6	Roger	15
Tucker, John	19	Rolin	6
Tugger, Francis	6	Thomas	8,20
Tuggle, Joshua	6	Williamson, James	6
Tule (?), Robert	19	Willies, Lewis	6
		Willis, Bailey	6,20
W____(?), ____(?)	8	William	6
Wade, Thomas	15,20	Wills, Lewis	8
Waddy, Thomas	6	Willson, David	19
Walden, Joseph	15	Wilson, Joseph	8
Robert	15	Wine, Benjamin	6,15
Waley, John	6	Wise, Clark	15

Wiseley, John	6
Woodrum, James B.	15
William	6
Woods, Benjamin	6
Woolf, Godfrey	15
Philip	6
Woolley, William	8
Woosley, Aaron	15
Wooten, Robert	15
Worford, Job	8
Wosham, Joshua	8
Woster, William	19
Wright, David	6,8
Edward	19
James	6
Samuel	6,8

GENERAL INDEX

SECTIONS TWO and THREE

Abbot, Benjamin	84
Sarah	84
Sarah E.	84
Adam(s), Capt. George	98
Robert	70
Albertee, George A. Jr.	58
Alexander, Capt. Samuel	97
Allcock, Mirium	84
William J.	84
Allen, _____	64
Daniel	64
Hannah	48
John	65
Martha	64
William	64
Anderson, _____	63
Catherine (Blain)	41
Major James	92
William	41,62
Andrews, Becky	36
John	36
"Parson"	100
Arnold, Benedict	92
Ashburn, William	73
Austin, William Sr.	54
Avent, Thomas	23
Babbet, Charles M.	84
Luther	84
Martha	84
Martha E.	84
Baine, Alexander	71
Baird, John	64
Lucy Ann	39
William	39
Baker, German	92
Jerman	71
Mary	92
Baldwin, John	56
Ball, Sarah (Jopling)	47
William	47
Balthorpe, Sally	63
Banner, Charles	100,101
Barber, Thomas	87
Barclay, William	51
Barnes, John Jr.	55
Barrott, Robert	38

Barrow, Capt. Thos.	94
Barton, Margaret	30
Roger	30
Baswight, Sarah	86
Batte, Mary	31
William	31
Baugh, William	58
Baughman (See Boughman)	
Abraham	52
Jacob	52
Beckley, Humphrey	57
Belcher, John	57
Bell, Jordan M.	87
Mary J.	87
William	46
Benedict, Ann	87
Christina	87
Mary E.	87
Bethell, William	59
Biers, William	71
Bird, Elizabeth	78
Frederick	78
John	78
Bishop, Eda	63
Blain, Catherine	41
Mary	41
William	41
William (Jr.)	41
Blair (See Blain)	
Colbert	47
Mary	41
William	41
Blanchet, Henry	57
John	57
Bland, Edward	33
Edward Jr.	41
Peter R.	64
Bledford, William	32
Bobo, Benjamin	98
Bodkin, Elizabeth	77
William	77
Bogle, Dunn	57,58
Mark	57
Mary	57, 58
Ralph	57
Robert H.	57,58
Bohannon, Anthony	28
Thomas	27,28

Bolton, Mary (Lansdown)   38
    Sarah   38
    Waller   38
    William   38
Borden, Jacob   51
    Mary   51
Bosman, Samuel   40
Boughman (Bowman)
    Abraham   53
    Daniel   53
    Darcus   53
    Henry   53
    Jacob   53
    John   51,53
Bowman (Boughman)
    Abraham   52,53
    Catherine   53
    Elisha   40,61
    Eliza B.   53
    Elizabeth   52,53
    (?)(Gatewood)   53
    George   52,53
    George (Jr.)   52
    George Adam   51
    Isaac   52,53
    Jacob, Sr.   52
    Jacob (Jr.)   52
    John   53
    Joseph   52,53
    Mary   53
    Philip   53
    Rebecca   53
    Rebecca (Lorton)   40
    Robert   53
    Susannah   53
    Washington   53
Bowrey, Mary   64
    Thomas   63,64
    Thomas (Jr.)   64
Boyd, _____   64
    Spencer   33
Bracegirdle, Frederick   45
    Rev. George   45
Braminett, Ren   37
Branch, Jordan   92
Brander, John   54
    John (Jr.)   54
    Margaret   54
    Margery   54
Brandon, Capt.   95
    Col.   95
Brann, Joseph   90
Branscomb, Richard   24
Braxton, Maj. Geo.   42
Brinkel, William   94

Brinker, George   53
Briscoe, Druscilla   78
    Isaac   78
    Nancy   78
    Capt. Parmenas   30
    Priscilla   78
Briton, Capt.   62
Brittain, John   62
Brown, Elizabeth   77
    James   77
    John H.   40
    Margaret L.   77
    Robert   63
    Sally   77
    Thomas[2]   77
    William   77
    Winifred (Glascock)   77
Browning, Charles   61
    Joseph   61
Bryan, Ferribee   85
Buchanan, Neill Sr.   64
Buck, Stephen   71
Buford, Maj. Abner   93
Bull, Rachel   29
    Robert   29,30,31
    Sarah   31
    Susanna   30
    Thomas   29,30
Bullock, John   41
    Rachel (Nevill)   41
    Sarah   41
    Thomas   40,56
    William   41,56
Bumpass, John   56
    Robert   56
    Samuel   56
Burk(e), John   77
    R. H. L.   59
    Sarah   77
Burnett, Richard   24
Burton, Abraham   45
Buskirk, Ensign   30

Cabaniss, William   41
Cain, John O.   82
    Martha   82
Calbert (Colbert) (Colvert)
    Harriet   32
    James Livingston   32
    William Augustine   32
    William I.   32
Caldwell, Elizabeth   49
    Henry   49
    Mornin   49

Campbell, Col.	97	Clay, John	43,44
Ezekiel	33	Lt. John	92
Carmichael, Elspeth	54	Thomas	44
Margaret (Brander)	54	Cleveland, Col.	97
William	54	Coakley, William	70
Carn (Corn ?)		Cocke, Abraham	31
George	28	Agnes	31
Nancy (Dicken)	28	Amey	33
Nancy (Yager)	28	Elizabeth	31
Carr, William	50	John	32,33
Carrington, Eugene	87	Littlebury	73
Carruthers, Joseph	64	Mary (Batte)	31
Carson, James	54	Rebecca Hubbard	73
Cart, Elizabeth (Smith)	44	Stephen (Sr.)	33
Carter, William Sr.	46	Stephen (Jr.)	32,33
Caruthers, James	41	Thomas	33
Cary, Mrs. Trusty	45	Thomas S.	33
William	96	Coffman, Daniel	52
Casy, Elbee	77	Colbert (See Colvert-Calbert)	
John	77	J. L.	32
John (Jr.)	77	W. A.	32
Mary A.	77	William I.	32
Matilda	77	Cole, John T.	40
Caton, Edward	81	Mary B.	40
Mahala	81	Matilda C.	40
Mary E.	81	Colvert (See Colbert-Calbert)	
Chalmers, William	42	Eliakim	32
Chapman, Erasmus	29	Harriet (Weeden)	32
Giles	30	John	32
Chappell, Abner	65	Joseph	32
John	31	Nancy	32
Martha (Cross)	31	William I.	32
Thomas	63	Comer, Moore	39
Chase, Anna	61	Compton, Sally	99,100,102
John	61	Conner, Betsy (Dicken)	27
Chastaine, _____	34	Daniel	27
Cheatham, Charles	35	David	27
Thomas	35	John	28
Chesson, Caroline	85	Polly (Dicken)	28
Childress, Ann	48	Cook, James	29
Benjamin	48	Cooper, John	96
Chisholm, Hugh	85	Murdock	41
Chrisman, Joseph	99	Copeland, Elizabeth	36
Christa, Col.	100	Peter	36
Church, Hannah M.	77	Cornwallis (Lord)	92
Clark, Asberry J.	80	Corter, Joseph	90
Col. Elijah	98	Cosgrove, Elizabeth	84
General	30	James	84
James M.	80	Cotting, Elias	43
Margaret C.	80	Cox, James	36
Martha J.	80	Craggs, Anthony	72
Mary F.	80	John	72
Mary H.	80	Craig, Agnes	91
Col. Thomas	95	David	91
Claud, Joshua Jr.	36,37	David (Jr.)	91
		(Continued)	

Craig, Ellen 91
  E. P. 91
  John J. 91
  Mrs. Mary 91
  Sarah G. 91
Crane, Elizabeth 86
  Frances 84
  James 84,86
  James Sr. 84
  James H. 84
  Mary 84
  Olla 86
  Patsy R. 84
  William 84
Craven, Joshua 96
Crawford, William 61
Creef, Mary A. 86
Cremer, Adam 80
  Anthony 80
  Conrad 80
  Elizabeth 80
  Henry 80
  Philip 80
Crenshaw, _____ 64
Critz, Hamon 46
  Sally 45,46
Crosby, George 63
  Sarah (Glascock) 63
Cross, Elizabeth (Cocke) 31
  Jeane 31
  John 31
  Martha 31
  Mary 31
  Rebecca 31
  William 31
Crow, John 61
Crowder, Currency 93
  Garret 93
  Jarret 93
  Lucy (Thompson) 93
  Philip 92,93
  Samuel 93
  Sterling 93
  William 92,93
Crumley, Hannah 30
  Henry 31
  James 30,31
  John 30,31
  Samuel 31
Crupper, Eli 63
Cunliffe, Susannah S. H. 41
Cunningham, Paul M. 65
Curby, Ann 78
  Edward 78
  Hytrometus 78
  John 78

Cureton, Martha 58
  William 58
Curle, Joshua 35
Curlin, Irena C. 84
  Mary I. 84
  Sarah 84
  Thomas 84
  Virginia 84
Currie, George 63
Cushing, Ellen S. 87
  J. 87
  Lucy 87
  William M. 87
Custis, Edmund 55

Dabney, John 63
Dame, Rev. Geo. W. 87
  Mary M. 87
Daniel, Elizabeth 32
  Nancy (Colvert) 32
  Vivian 32
Davenport, Mary J. 86
  Patsey 86
David, Caleb M. 96
Davidson, E. G. 91
  Elias 65
  Ephraim 91
  Jane (Sterling) 91
  J. O. 91
  Mary (Brank) 91
  R. R. 91
  S. B. 91
  Willie Thornwell 91
Davies, John R. 65
Davis, Mrs. 39
  Ashley 31
  Ashley (Jr. 31
  Elizabeth 31
  Eliza 86
  Harvey S. 78
  James 78
  Martha 78
  Mary (Cross) 31
  Phebe 78
  Phebe J. 78
  Polly 31
  William Upshaw 57
Dempsey, Patrick 23
Dennis, Gower 50
  William 45
Devin, Elizabeth (Nowling) 55
  Joseph 55
  Margaret 55
Devoux, Stephen 70
Dick, Col. Alexander 92
Dicken, Betsy 27
  (Continued)

Dicken, Capt. Christopher 28
   Elizabeth 28
   Henry 28
   James 27,28
   Joel 27
   Judith 28
   Julia 28
   Martha 27,28
   Martha (Lewis) 27,28,29
   Nancy 28
   Polly 28
   Richard 27,28
   Richard (Jr.) 28
   Robert 70
   William 27,28
Dillard, Mr. 102
Dixon, William 48
Doil, Amanda 79
   Ann 79
   Elizabeth 77,79
   Esther 79
   George 77
   Jacob 77
   Jacob C. 77
   John 77
   Margaret 77
   Mary A. 77
   Michael 79
   Nancy J. 77
   Olive 77
   Sally 79
   Theodarus 77
   William 77
Dooly, William 98
Doughty, Charles J. 58
Douglas, Martha A. 87
   Mary A. 87
   Samuel A. 87
   Susan R. 87
Dowell, Elisha 63
Dows, Jonathan 43
Drew, Henry 85,86
   Mary J. 85,86
Dunbar, James 83
   Nancy 83
Dunkley, Henry 39
   John 39
   Moses 39
Dunn, Ellen 85
   Frances Jane 56
   Gray F. 56
   Martha 85
   Mary M. 56
   Matilda 86
   Samuel J. 85
   William 85

Dunnica, James 38

Echol, Richard 38
Elby, Nathaniel 72
Eldridge, John R. B. 41
   Thomas 42
Elliott, William 60
Ellis, John Jr. 44
Emmerson, Ann 81
   Catharine 81
   Ellen 81
   John 81
   Luther 81
   Nancy 81
Eperson, Capt. Richard 92
Epes (See Eppes, Epps)
   Algernon S. 59
   Amy 63,64
   Emily G. 59
   Frances (Dunn) 56
   Francis 63,64
   Freeman 41
   Isham 63,64
   John 42
   Peter 31,32,64
   Rebecca (Cross) 31,32
   Richard J. 40
   Richard S. 56
   Thomas W. 59
   Thomas W. Jr. 59
   William 42
Eppes (See Epes, Epps)
   Elizabeth (Ogburn) 65
   Francis (Sr.) 65
   Francis (Jr.) 65
   Henry W. 65,66
   John 64,65
   Martha (Allen) 64,65
   Phoebe 65
   Sally (Winfield) 65
   Sarah W. 66
   Susan O. 66
   Thomas 65
   Thomas J. 66
Epps (See Epes, Eppes)
   Edward 55
   Edy 39
   Elizabeth 58
   Francis 58
   John 38,39,58
   John C. 39
   Moses 39
   Nancy 39
   Nathaniel 39
   Temperance 39
   William 39

Eric, James	47
Ervine, Alzina	77
Debora	77
Jared	77
Eskridge, Charles G.	100
Estes, Ambrose	50
Andrew	37
Elen	37
Etheridge, Eliza	83
Elizabeth M.	85
William B.	85
Evans, Charlotte	83
Jeremiah	83
Lt. Jesse	98
John W.	83
Evendon, Jonathan	44
Faison, James	35
Falconer, Elizabeth	35
Rev. James	34,35
Fannon, Col.	96
Fargeson, Ann	62
Samuel	62
Ferguson, Betsy (Jopling)	47
Daniel	47
Margarite	32
William	32
Farley, Joseph	58
Farmer, Fanny	97
Farrar, Richard	47
Thomas	47
Faubin, Diana (Rector)	33
Jacob	33
Fauntleroy, Eliza (Bowman)	53
Joseph M.	53
Fifer, Col.	96
Fishback, Owen T.	66
Fisher, Capt. Charles	44
Fitchett, Charles	82
Georgia	82
James P.	82
John E.	82
John T.	82
Joshua P.	82
Margaret M.	82
Margaret S.	82
Martha F.	82
Mary F.	82
Mary J.	82
Fitzgerald, Mrs. Anne	90
Charles	85
Clinton	39
Henry	87
Mary C.	87
Walter	87
Fitzpatrick, John	54
Fleming, Clara	81
Isabella V.	81
Margaret L.	81
Mary J.	81
Robert H.	81
Samuel	69
William W.	81
Flesher, Barbara	79
Christena	79
Hannah	79
Henry	79
Henry (Jr.)	79
John H.	79
Forbes, Elizabeth	85
James	85
Foster, Andrew	59
Fraley, Christian	51
Francis, Ann	83
Benjamin	83
John	83
John (Jr.)	83
Mariah	83
Sady E.	83
Thomas	83
Freeman, James	51
Fudge, John	45
Fulcher, William	46
Gale, Joseph	91
Mary	91
Sarah	91
Gamble, A. Hanson	80
Charles L.	80
Isabella S.	80
Mary L.	80
William A.	80
Gambol, John	83
Gann, Mrs. Frances	101,102,103
Garlick, Samuel	72
Garrard, Gov. James	54
Garrett, Eliza	84
W.	33
Garver, Martin	52
Samuel	52
Gatewood (Daut)	53
Philip	53
Gay, John	90
Gee, Benjamin	40
Bridget	40
Rebecca N.	40
George, Thos. J.	40
Gerrard, David	30
Ginn, Tralucia	50,51
William	50,51

Gibson, Elizabeth 86
Glascock, Aaron 63
  Acquila 63
  David O. 63
  Eda (Bishop) 63
  George 33,62
  Hannah 62
  Harrison 63
  Henry 62,63
  Hezekiah 63
  Jesse 62,63
  John 63
  Joseph 63
  Mary 62
  Moses 62,63
  Sally 63
  Sarah 63
  Thomas 62
  Thomas J. 63
  Winifred 63
Glasscock, George 54
  Gregory 54
  Hezekiah 54
  Jemima 54
  Jesse 54
  John Sr. 54
  John 54
  Levin 54
  Spencer 54
  Stephen 54
  William Sr. 54
Golding, Reuben D. 101
Gooch, John 41
  Susanna Duke 41
Good, Samuel 35
Goodrich, Edward 29
Gordon, Capt. Alexander 96
  Sally 46
Gore, William 54
Grant, Dr. A. 40
  Mary E. 40
Graves, Isaac 32
  Willis 27,28
Gray, Joseph A. 80
  Joseph E. 80
  Robert C. 80
  Sarah 80
  Sarah V. 80
Green, Ellen 79
  Margaret J. 79
  Mary 79
  Mary A. 79
  Gen. (Nathl.) 96
  Rawl B. 32
  (continued)

Green, William 79
  William (Jr.) 79
Greenswood (Greensword)
  Tralucia (Stegar) 50
Gresham, Ambrose 39
Griffin, John 48
  Sherod 47
Grigg, Thomas 34
Groom, John 32
Gross, Eamon 96
  William 97
Grove, Benjamin 78
  David 78
  Hannah 78
Gunn, Isaac 78
Gunther, John Conrad 73
Gwin, David 78
  Elizabeth R. 78
  James 79
  Laura M. 78
  Mahala 79
  Martha 78
  Mary V. 78

Hackett, Henry W. 57
  Margaret 57
Hadley, Capt. 94
Haggard, (Rev.) James 92
Hall, Hugh 42
  John 56
  John Jr. 56
  Capt. John 42
  Robert 44,56
Halterman, Andrew J. 80
  Elizabeth 80
  Louisa 80
  Sarah 80
  William 80
Hamilton, William S. 83
Hamlin, ____ 33,64
  Agnes (Cocke) 31
  Charles 31
  Elizabeth (Cross) 31
  John 35
  Thomas 31,35
Hand, Capt. (Henry) 57
Handson, Anderson 59
Hankins, Edward 60
  Feebe (Harrison) 60
Hardaway, Henry S. 66
  Joseph 56
  Stith 33
Harding, Polly 36

Hardison, Hester 85
   Matilda E. 85
   William 85
   William S. 85
Hardy, Mornin 49
   Solomon 49
Harper, William 41
Harrington, Isaac 84
Harris, Wm. Lee 48
Harrison, Ann (Chase) 61
   David 60,61
   Feebe 60
   Frances 29
   Jafamah 60
   John 40,60,61
   Zephama 60
Harwell, Ambrose 29
   Lemuel 30
Hasslen, F. E. 97
Hatchett, Abraham 58,59
   Mary 59
   William 59
Hays, Moses 54
Henderson, Major 95
Henes, John 70
Henry, Samuel 101
Herbert, Buller 42.43
Hevner, Philip 60
   Sally 60
Hickey, Rev. James 96
Hicklin, Sally 82
Hicks, Edward B. 39
High, James 78
   Jane 78
   John 78
   Mary E. 78
   Sarah E. 78
   William 78
Hill, Benjamin 66
   Captain 94
   Charles 66
Hillton, John 23
Hines, Caroline B. 35
   James 35,55
   Kelly 35
   Lucy K. 35
Hodsden, Henry 69
Holloway, Ann (Sterling) 65
Holsey, Joseph 83
   Mary 83
Hook, John 69
Hooper, Thomas 42
Hoover, Barbara 78
   Margaret 78
   Rufus 78
   Samuel 78

Hopkins, Charles C. 84
   John 23
Harmon, Edward 44
Houdeshell, Bridget 79
   John H. 79
   Michael D. 79
Hough, Barnett 63
Hubbard, John 42
Hudson, Elizabeth 43
   Francis 43
   James 56
Hufton, Joanah 84,86
   Joseph D. 84,86
   Joseph H. 84
   Mary 84
Hurst, Richard 35
Hurt, Elisha 48
   Mildred 48
Hutcheson, Charles 55
   John 55
   Richard 54

Irby, John W. 39
   Martha 39
Irvine, James 36
   Mary 36
Isaacs, Colonel 96
Isbell, Henry 36
   James 36
Isom, Ellen 91
   George 91
   Jones 91
   Mary 91
   Robert 91
   Sarah G. 91

Jackson, _____ 42
   Benjamin F. 82
   Cavel 55
   George 72
   Hannah E. 82
   Indiana 82
   John 23,82
   Mary (Glascock) 62
   Ruth 82
   Thomas 30
   Vincent 62
   Virginia J. 82
James, Rollings 96
Jeffreys, Simon 24
Jenkins, Enoch 44
Jett, Francis 63
Job, David 49
Johnson, Cave 90
   Edward 42
   Marmaduke 23

Johnston, Benjamin   69
Jolly, Captain   95
Jones, Anne   24,41
    Frances L.   41
    Henry Jr.   45
    Isaac   24
    John   24
    John (Jr.)   24
    Joseph   81
    Joseph (Jr.)   81
    Lew   39
    Littleberry A.   41
    Margaret   81
    Mary   84
    Richard   39
    Robert (Sr.)   44,45
    Robert Jr.   44
    Sarah   81
    Sarah (Jr.)   81
    Susanna H.   41
    Theodorick   41
    Thomas   45
    William A.M.   41
Jopling, Ann   47,48
    Benjamin   47
    Catharine   47
    Daniel   47
    Edward   48
    Hannah   48
    Holeman   48
    James   47,48
    Jane   47
    Jesse   48
    John   47
    Katherine   47
    Lucy   48
    Martha   47,48
    Mary   47
    Molly   46
    Nancy   47
    Patsey   47
    Ralph   47
    Ralph Jr.   47
    Rebeckah   48
    Sarah   47
    Thomas   46,47,48
    William   47
Jordan, David   53
    German   35
    Granville   37
Junkins, William   90

Keith, Cornelius   23
Kennedy, James   45
    John W.   45
    Joseph (Ens.)   98,99
        (Continued)

Kennedy, Joseph Jr.   46
Kennon, Richard   43
Kenyon, William   72
Key, John   97
Kidd, John   57
    Thomas   57
King Charles II   34
Kinser, Philip   60
Kirtley, John   29
    Simeon   28
    Thomas   27,29
Knight, Charles A.   84
    Matilda   84,86
    Mary E.   84
    Romulus   84,86
Knox, Thomas   71

Lafort, Isaac   34
Lambe, Captain   94
Lamkin, Jeane (Cross)   31
    Peter Jr   31
Lane, Major Isaac   97
Lansdoun, Johnson   38
    Mary   38
    Sarah   38
Lasellis, Gen. Perigrine   35
Lathropp, Thomas   43
    Thomas Jr.   43
Lawrence, Ann   87
    James   87
    James (Jr.)   87
    John   40,87
    Margaret   87
    Mary   87
    William   87
Lawton, Elizabeth Ann   35
    Thomas   35
Leake, John M.   41
Leaker, James   72
Lee, James F.   58
Leigh, David E.   85
Leith, James   50
Levi, Moses   87
Lewis, Abraham   29
    Catharine   27,29
    Colonel   93
    Henry   27,28,29
    Henry Jr   29
    James   29
    John   29
    Martha   27,28,29
    Simeon   29
    Thomas   29
    William   27,29
Lilly, Captain   71
Lindsey, David   34
    William   87

Link, Barton	39
Linn, William	31
Liverman, Franklin	83,86
Letta	83,86
Mary P.	83
Lock, Colonel	96
Logan, Col. Benjamin	98
Long, Major	92
Lorton, Israel	40
Rebecca	40
Lothian, Baillie John	73
Elizabeth	73
Love, Hugh	58
Lovell, John	90
Lowe, John	45
Sarah	45
William	42,45
Lowry, Alexander	90
Loyd, Edward	51
Lyell, Joseph	69
MacIver, Charles	73
MacKemie, Francis	55
McCarty, Isaac	49
McClannaham, Col.	99
McClure, Nathaniel	90
McDanal, John	81
McDowell, Lucy (Sterling)	65
McGary, Hugh	30
McGowan, Jarvis	85
McGrath, William	45
McHenry, Thomas	61
McKain, John	66
McKay, Abraham	49,50
James Sr.	49,50
James Jr.	49,50
Jeremiah	49
Leah	50
Mary	49,50
Moses	49
Nancy	50
Polly	50
Robert	49,50
Sally	49
Zachariah	49
McKinney, John H.	39
McMullan, Lewis	98
McMurray, James	54
McMurry, Wm. B.	59
McRea, Col. Turpin	94
Macklin, Col. Fred	92
Madison, James	36
Magel, Lieut.	30
Malone, Banister	36
Becky	36
Daniel	36
Daniel (Jr.)	36
Drury	36
Elizabeth	36
Jameson	36
John	36
Mary	36,65,66
Nathaniel	36
Peter	36
Polly	36
Susanna	36
Thomas	36,65,66
Thomas Jr	66
Man, John	78
Mary C.	78
Robert E.	78
Mann, Joel	57
Sarah M.	86
Marin, Thomas	79
Marshall, John W.	32
Martin, Abraham	46
Andrew	102
Anne	46
Dotia	101
Esther	24
James	46
John	24,46
Maj. John	46
I. W.	101
Margaretta	24
Mary	24
Pleasant	48
Rebecah (Jopling)	48
Ruth	46
Susan	46
Thomas	102
W. M.	101
Mason, George	84
Mateland, Emaline	85
John	85
Mattocks, Thomas	30
Meador, Bennet	48
Jimmy	48
John	48
John H.	48
Joseph	48
Jubal W.	48
Nancy	48,49
Melson, Elizabeth	84
Mary C.	84
William	84
Miers, Joseph	90

Miles, Ann M.	85
Benjamin F.	85
Edward	85
Franklin	85
Mary M.	85
Reuben	85
Miller, David	98
Hugh	63
William	92
,Mills, John	46
Mily, Amanda	82
Anton	82
Anton B.	82
John	80
Joshua	80
Mary J.	82
Salomeny	80
William E.	82
Minge, James Sr.	42
James Jr.	42
Minter, Anthony	38
Jonas	49
Mitchell, Thomas	70
Moir, Edward	71
Moore, Capt. Isaac	95
James	33
Osborne J.	39
Rebecca N.	39,40
Mrs. Robert P.	91
Thomas	77
Lt. William	98
Morgan, Capt.	99,100
General	96
Jacob	64
Jacob Philips	64
Morreen, William	87
Moseley, Richard	44
Moss, John	90
Motes, Christina	79
Mulenburg, Gen. Peter	92
Mullenax, Charity	78
Margaret	78
William	78
Munford, Ann Elizabeth	35
John	35
Edward	56
Robert	42,56,64
Maj. Robert	43
Murfrie, Col.	102
Murphie, Elizabeth	82
John	82
John Jr.	82
Polly	82
Murray, John	96

Mustain, Avery	55
Frances	55
Joel	55
John	55
Margaret	55
Margaret (Devin)	55
Martha	55
Mary	55
Myers, Aron	87
Nance, John	63
Neal, Joseph	63
Neelly, John	91
Neff, Dr. Jno. Henry	53
Nelson, Charles T.	39
Louisa	39
Nevil, Rachel	41
Roger	41
Newby, Thomas Jr.	41
Newell, Capt. James	98
Newton, Capt. George	34
Martha	38
William	38
Nicholson, Boling	94
Joshua	36,37
Robert	95
Nichleston, Isaac	94
James	94
Nord, Thomas	62
Norton & Son	73
Norvell, Holdcroft	57
Nowling, Elizabeth	55
Ogburn, Augustine	65
Elizabeth	65
Elizabeth (Massenburg)	65
Ormeston, John	69
Ormsby, Matthew	50
Ornsbey, John	63
Orsborne, John H.	59
Overton, Eliza	85,86
Frederick	85,86
Owen(s) Rev. Martin	98
Mathias	85,86
Olla	86
Patsy	86
William	38
William (Sr.)	98,99
Pace, George	42,45
Palmer, Capt. Joshua	95
Purmesion	95
Reuben	57
Richard	51
William R.	84

Parham, Daniel	58,59		Pray, Nelson	79
Susan	65		Phebe A.	79
Parker, Anderson	55		Preston, Col.	98
Charles	55		Price, Henry	28
Edward	55		Prichard, Swan	30
John	55		Prosser, Jonathan	69
Margaret Robins	55		Purvis, Col.	95
Richard	49		Puryear, Morgan	38
Pawlin, Capt.	100,102			
Peake, William H.	63		Quarles, Frances	32
Peck, Abraham	80		William	32
Elizabeth	80			
Jacob	80		Ramsey, Ann (Munford)	35
John	80		Booker	35
Susan	80		Elizabeth A.B.	35
Peete, Edwin H.	55		Caroline B.	35
Penn, Col. Abram	45,46		James	37
Abram (Jr.)	45,46		Lucy	35
Edmund	45		Randolph, Col. William	43
George	46		Rayford, Major	94
Sally (Critz)	45,46		Raynolds, Susanna	36
Sally (Gordon)	46		Read, Major	96
Thomas	45,46		Reams, Lemuel	58
Wilson	45		Reaves, George	39
Penner (Pinner)			Rector, Alfred	54
James	83,86		Diana	33
James H.	86		Henry	33,63
John	83		John	62,63
John B.	86		Joseph	63
Sarah	83,86		Nancy	33
Perault, Charles	34		Thomas Jr.	63
Daniel	34		Reed, John	33
Margaret	34		Reid, Hon. S.	100
Petit, John	34		Reynolds, Benjamin	83
Petty, Capt.	92		Emily	83
Peyton, Francis	99,100		James W.	83
Pike, Samuel	87		Matilda	83
Piles, William	41		Mary E.	83
Pledger, Henry A.	84		Rhoda C.	83
Pollard, Richard C.	48		William Sr.	83
Pope, John	56		William Jr.	83
John Jr.	56		William P.	83
Mathew	73		Rice, Capt.	102
Porter, Joseph	98		Enoch	96
Posford, John	44		Henretta	85
Powell, Davis	38		John W.	85
Edmund	48		Lemuel S.	85
Lucy (Jopling)	48		Sack E.	85
Mark	38		William C.	85
Powers, Charlotte	83,86		Richardson, Amos	96,97
Sarah	86		Daniel	37
Pray, Elizabeth	79		Dotia	101
John	79		Mrs. Fanny	97
Mary E.	79		Frances	101
(continued)			(continued)	

Richardson, Jesse 98,99
Joseph 99,100,101
Lt. Joseph 102
Nancy 100
Sally (Compton) 99,100,101
Sarah 102
Susannah 53
Thomas 97
William 100
William H. 53
Riddleburg, Francis 72
Riddlehurst, Francis 72
Roberts, Chastain 59
Polly 59
Robertson, Edward 29
Henry 50,51
Tralucia (Greenwood) 50
Walter 71
Rogers, William 58
Rorick, Edward 77
Ross, David 71
Ephraim 73
Routon, Susan 84
Zachariah 84
Rowe, Lt. Maurice 96
Ruck, Capt. Thomas 43
Ruckman, Asa 77
David V. 77
Margaret 77
Samuel 77
Runsberg, John 45
Rebecca 45
Russell, Capt. George 97
Wiley 41

Salle, Abraham 34
Sanders, Capt. Jesse 92
Sanford, Frances (Vivion) 32
Reuben 32
Sawyer, William C. 85
Scott, General 92
John 23
Seburn, Nathaniel 82
Sevier, Col. John 97
Seybert, Catharine 80
Jacob 80
Jacob (Jr.) 80
Mary 80
Mary E. 80
Sarah 80
Sharp, Elizabeth 79
Harriet 79
Henry 79
Jackson 79
(continued

Sharp, James 79
John 79
John Hilly 79
Martha 79
Mary 79
Polly 79
William 79
Shaws, Alexander 54
Andrew 54
James 54
Shelby, Col. 97
Isaac 90
Major 98
Shelor, Jacob 54
Shelton, Claiborne 46
Shepard, Col. Abram 95
Shepherd, Andrew 36
Shevalis, Emile 59
Shoemate, Albert 81
Augustus 81
Elizabeth 81
Elizabeth (Jr.) 81
Frances C. 81
Jacob 81
Louisa J. 81
Margaret 81
William 81
Shoky, Capt. 96
Short, William 45
Shurbey, Thomas 27
Zachariah 27
Shute, Samuel 43
Simmons, Sammuel 55
Sisson, Stephen 29
Sizemore, Daniel 38
Elizabeth 38
John 38
Skinner, William 71
Slaughter, James 61,62
Susanna 61,62
Smelt, John 82
Smith, Alfred 103
Augustine Jaquelin 90
Coleman 33
Dorothy Ann 66
Elizabeth 44
George W. 56
Guy 54
Hester 44
James 40
Joseph 44
Mary (Dunn) 56
Philip 35
Capt. Robert 93
(continued)

Smith, Robert W.	66	Strother, Capt. John	62
Susannah	90	Mary E.	62
William	44,54	Mary (Wade)	61,62
Snell, Judith (Dicken)	28	Samuel	62
London	28	Susanna	62
Snider, John	47	Sullivant, Joseph	65
Snoddy, Capt. John	98	Michael	65
Sowel, Col. Benj.	94	William	65
Spengler, Philip	49,50	Summers, Andrew	35
Spilac(?), Maj. James	35	John Sr.	35
Sprowl, Samuel	79	Sumner, General	94
William	79	Sutton, Mary L.	83
Stainback, George	58	Swain, Eliza A.	84
Stark, Robert	56	Franklin	85
Steed, Elizabeth	61	Joanna	86
Hannah	61	Swepston, Capt. Richard	92
John	61	Sydnor, Elizabeth (Cocke)	
Richard	61	(Cross)	31
Robert	61		
Stegar & Co.	51	Tabb, Capt. Edward	35
Hans Henrick	50,51	John	41
Hans William	50	Tabler, Andromache	81
Tralucia	50,51	Elizabeth	81
William	51	Hugh	81
Sterling, Ann	65	Jasper	81
Edmund	65	John T.	81
Jane	65	Mosheim	81
Lucy	65	Sarah E.	81
Lyne	65	Taff, Peter	90
Samuel	65	Thomas	90
Samuel M.	65	William	90
Thomas	65	Tandy, Henry	32
William	65	Tarkinton, John W.	85
Steuben, General	92	Tayford, Major	94
Stevens, Lewis Sr.	98	Taylor, Amelia C.	35
Stokes, Allen G.	87	Col. Edmond F.	39
Charles P.	87	Edmund P.	39
Margaret M.	87	Elizabeth	44
Stone, Richard	37	George	36
Stott, Eveline	87	Jesse	90
Stover, Joseph	49,50	John	63
Stringfellow, F.	32	Lewis S.	39
Strother, Ann	62	Martha	39
Charles O.	62	Richard	44
Francis	62	Sarah	39
Francis (Jr.)	62	Thomas	39
French	62	Waller	39
French (Jr.)	62	William	35,59
George	62	William H.	39
Mrs. Helen	62	W.M.H.	39
Henry St.G.	62	Tharp, Henry	77
Jeremiah	32	Thomas, Betsy	47
John	61,62	John	24
John (Jr.)	62	Col. John	95
(continued)		(continued)	

Thomas, Martha 47
   Mary 24,47
   Michael, Jr. 47
   Michael Jr. 47
   Patsey (Jopling) 47
   Ralph 47
Thompson, Elizabeth 62
   Lucy 93
   Mr. 69
   Wiley 98
   William F. 62
Thomson, Rhodes 32
   Sally 32
Thurmond, Gutheridge 47
   Katherine (Jopling) 47
Thweatte, Henry 43
   James 44
   Miles 44
Tillman, George 42
Tisdale, Jane 40
Townsend, Anna 38
   Austin 37,38
   Clement 37,38
   Daniel 40
   Frances 38
   John 38
   Joseph 37
   Lovina 37
   Maria A. 37,38
   Nancy S. 40
   Peter 37
   Richard 37,38
   Susan J. 37,38
   Thomas 37
   Wilcher J. 38
   William 37
Trail, James 47
Tranum, Clement 36
   Elizabeth 36
Tricett, Lettice 86
True, L. B. 101
Trump, James 70
Tuck, Edward 38
Turner, Benjamin 49
   John 48,54
   Lewis 48
   Mathew 55
   Mildred (Hurt) 48
   Thomas 82

Urquhart, John 95

Vass, Vincent, Jr. 32
Vaughan, Eaton P. 58
   Mary A. 58
   (continued)

Vaughan, Polly (McKay) 50
   Thomas 50
Vernon, Walter Jr. 42
Vickery, Benjamin 86
   Sarah 83,86
   William B. 83,86
Vivion, Charles 32
   Flavel 32
   Harvey 32
   Jackey 32
   Jane 32
   John 32
   Milton 32
   Thacker 32
   Thacker Smith 32
   Thomas 32
Voltaneier, John W. G. 45

Wade, James 61,62
   John Sr. 77
   Mary 61
Wafford, Col. 95
Walke, Anthony Sr. 33
   Anthony Jr. 33
Wall(s), James 59
   Miranda 82
   Sarah A. 82
Wallace, A. S. 95
   David 44
Walton, Elizabeth 51
Ward, John 57
   Plany 35
Warthen, Richard 42
Washington, General 96
   Colonel 96
Watson, Arthur 30
   Lydia 30
   Rhoda 77
   William 56
Waybright, Daniel 81
   Harrison 81
   Henry 81
   Nathan 81
   Rachel 81
Webb, Austin 32
   Charles 32
   Frances 32
   Garland 32
   Jane 32
   John Vivion 32
   Thacker 32
   William Sr 32
   William Jr 32
   Wyatt 32
Weeden, Harriett 32

West, Bransford   47
    Nancy (Jopling)   47
Westbrook, Ann   36
    James   36
    John   36,37
    John (Jr.)   36,37
    Samuel   36,37
    Samuel Jr.   36,37
    Sarah   36
    Thomas   36
    William   36,37
Wethers, Margaret   69
Wheelhouse, Dennis   66
White, Benjamin J.   55
Whitson, Joseph   49
Whitt, Abijah Jr.   60
Wigle, Barbary   61
    John   61
Wilkes, John   37
    Minor Sr.   37
Wilkinson, Frances   35
Williams, Edward   96
    K. B.   50
Willis, John   63
Willoughby, Isabella   85
    Truman   85
Wills, Robert   66
Wilson, George   72
    Isabella   82
    Lindsey   97
    Samuel   82
    Sarah H.   82
Wimer, Ann   80
    Ellener   80
    Philip   80
Wingali, Francis   70
Winfield, Sally   65
Winn, Edmund   37
    John   41
    Thomas W.   39
Wise, George D.   58
    George S.   58
    Peter   70
Withers, John   63
Woodbridge, John   90
Woodward, Christopher   43
    Elizabeth (Hudson)   43
    Nathaniel   42,43
    Samuel   42,43
Worrell, Ann L.   40
Worsham, W.   41
Wright, Joseph   48
    Thomas   81
Wyatt, Capt. Edward   42

Wygle, James   59,60
    John Jr.   59,60
    Sebastian Sr.   59,60
    Sebastian Jr.   59,60
    Sally (Hevner)   60
    William   59,60
Wynne, Joseph H.   83

Yager, Nancy (Dicken)   28
Yarbrough, Samuel   56
Yeates, Mary   85
    William   85
Young, Michael Cadet   23
    Sinnett   49

Zachary, Bartholomew   56
    David   56

VIRGINIA
ANCESTORS
AND ADVENTURERS

Volume 2

VIRGINIA
ANCESTORS AND ADVENTURERS, VOL. 2

TABLE OF CONTENTS

Dedication i

Foreword ii

Preface iii

SECTION ONE

County Court Records,

    Abstracts of I

    Marriage Records 64

SECTION TWO

The Virginia Gazette - Extracts 69

Census Records (selected) 79

SECTION THREE

Proof of Importations 87

Contributions by others 95

SECTION FOUR

INDEX

General 111

Dedicated to the memory
of an eminent Virginia Genealogist,
Beverley Fleet, Esq.
who had a most rare and pleasing
sense of humor and whom I wish
I could have known in his lifetime.

FOREWORD

        "We live in the past by a knowledge
of its history, and in the future by hope and
anticipation. By ascending to an association
with our ancestors; by contemplating their
example and studying their character; by par-
taking their sentiments and imbibing their
spirit; by accompanying them in their toils;
by sympathizing in their sufferings and re-
joicing in their successes and triumphs, we
mingle our existance with their's and seem to
belong to their age".

                              --Daniel Webster

        Remember the days of old,
        Consider the years of many generations.
        Ask thy father and he will show thee,
        Thy elders, and they will tell thee.

                        --Deuteronomy 32:7

PREFACE

Once again this compiler has managed to find enough "migration links", from records in the public domain, which prove legally and genealogically the fact of an individual (and/or family) settling in Virginia from somewhere else or leaving Virginia to settle some place else, to submit in book form.

As in our previous endeavors, we have obtained these type records (with full citation to original source) from Wills; Deeds; Court Orders; Census Records; Tax Records; Birth, Death, and Marriage Records; Church Records, Military Records; Powers of Attorney; Estate Settlements; and by contributions from others.

A compilation of these type records was first contemplated by this writer because he could find no such specific and organized attempt anywhere else. It is very gratifying to report, by this means, that others having been faced with the difficulty and frustration of proving that John Doe and Sarah, his wife, of Culpeper County, Virginia are the same, identical John and Sarah Doe who settled in Newberry District, South Carolina before the Revolutionary War, have been very encouraging for me to continue this series, with these type records. However, and moreover, everyone should be informed that there remain many thousands of like records to be discovered, compiled and presented in published form.

This Preface also gives me another chance to pay further tribute to that immortal Virginia gentlemen, the late Beverley Fleet, Genealogist Parfait, whose witty and delightful comments concerning the ancient records of Virginia he found in dusty and musty archives are not only superbly appropriate and humorous, but are priceless masterpieces. I was also delighted to find that he did not care too much about writing prefaces and have gleaned a few of the many remarks he incorporated within his own prefaces, to wit:

"My reader's patience with prefaces, no doubt, has given out, as well as my own."

"It would be nice to write a dignified and profound preface," etc.

"There is no preface. Perhaps an epitaph would be fitting."

"If you don't believe it, try it!"

"Poppycock! Any dunce should have brains enough to know that without any remarks on my part," etc.

"As age creeps upon me, that job will have to be left to others. All I can do is to drag our ancestors from their resting places."

"The best friends of this work are genealogists. They like names and dates. Here is a great pot full of that unappetizing fare."

"My best friends would cheerfully reduce me to the status of a hack copyist."

"Now, having complained and explained."

And so, respected reader, if my laborious preface fails to meet with your full approval, as it does with me, I hope you will concede that I did seek help from the best source available.

Charles Hughes Hamlin, C.G.
Route 2, Box C-44
Powhatan, Virginia 23139

July   1969

VIRGINIA
ANCESTORS AND ADVENTURERS, VOL. 2

SECTION 1

ABSTRACTS OF ORIGINAL COURT RECORDS
FROM VARIOUS COUNTIES OF VIRGINIA

Halifax Co., Va. Deed Book 12, page 126 -

15 June 1780 - Indenture in which Artha (sic) Brooks,
of CAZEWELL (sic) COUNTY, NORTH CAROLINA, of one part, sells to
Ruth Parrott, wife of John Parrott, deceased - and Elijah Parrott -
Susannah Parrott - Penelope Parrott - Elizabeth Parrott - James
Parrott - Judith Parrott - John Parrott - Nancy Parrott - Sally
Parrott and Mourning Parrott - heirs of the said John Parrott,
deceased, and Thomas Stanfield, executor of said Parrott, all of
Halifax Co., Va. - of the other part - for the sum of 40 pds. - a
tract of land in the County of Halifax, on waters of Lawson's
Creek containing 210 acres etc. Signed by Artha (sic) Brooks and
Sally (X) Brooks - (no witnesses listed) - acknowledged 16 August
1781 and Sally, wife of said Brooks relinquished her right of
dower.

Halifax Co., Va. Deed Book 14, page 545 -

20 July 1789 - William Warren, of CASWELL COUNTY, NORTH
CAROLINA sells to John Parrott, of County of Halifax, State of
Virginia - for 76 pds. - a tract of land in the County of Halifax,
Virginia on Holt's Mill Creek, containing 100 acres, etc. -
Witnesses: Thomas Stanfield - Timothy Holt - Esom Graves - James
Garrott - Proved by witnesses 25 January 1790 and ordered to be
recorded.

Halifax Co., Va. Deed Book 19, page 347 -

11 August 1802 - Indenture in which Ledford Parrott (by his
power of attorney to Charles Bostick) - of the COUNTY OF RUTHERFORD
STATE OF NORTH CAROLINA - sells to John Link Sr., of County of
Halifax, Virginia - for 6 pounds, 13 shillings, 4 pence - 21 acres
of land in County of Halifax and is part of a parcel of land formerly held by John Parrott, now deceased, and by him willed to
said Ledford Parrott and other children, legatees of said John
Parrott, deceased etc. Witnesses: William Chambers - Ransom
Turner - Thomas Link - Proved and recorded 27 September 1802.

Ibid, page 348 -

20 July 1802 - Indenture in which Elijah Parrott, of
COUNTY OF CHATHAM, STATE OF GEORGIA sells to John Link Sr., of
County of Halifax, Virginia for 6 pounds, 13 shillings, 4 pence -
21 acres of land in Halifax Co., which is part of the tract
formerly held by John Parrott, deceased, and by him willed to the
aforesaid Elijah Parrott and other children legatees of the said
John Parrott, deceased, etc. - Witnesses: Thomas Watkins -
Jesse Link - John Smith Jr. - Proved by witnesses 27 September
1802 and ordered recorded.

3

Spotsylvania Co., Deed Book M, page 209 -

4 January 1787 - I, Henry Willis, at present in
Spotsylvania County, but intending soon for the State of Georgia,
do hereby sell to John Whitaker Willis, of the County of
Spotsylvania, the following slaves (names seven); 40 head of
cattle; to sell same to pay an obligation to Gerard Banks, of
the County of Stafford. If this prove insufficient, etc., the
said Henry Willis doth empower the said John Whitaker Willis
to receive of Lewis Willis, Gentleman, out to the Lambs Creek
tract of land, as much as may be necessary etc.
Witnesses: P. Towles - Larkin Stanard - A. Dick.

Fauquier Co., Va. Deed Book 33, page 352 -

6 April 1833 - George Mann Jr. and Elizabeth, his wife,
of MIAMI COUNTY, STATE OF OHIO, sell to George Mann Sr. of
Miami County, State of Ohio, for $300.00, a certain parcel of
land in Fauquier Co., Va. being that part of the estate of
French Floweree, deceased, devised to the wife of the said George
Mann Jr. and designated in the division thereof as Lot #5, con-
taining 21 acres, 2 roods and 22 poles etc.
Witnesses: Robert Young - J. R. Young.
Certified by Justices of Miami Co., Ohio 6 April 1833 and
recorded in Fauquier Co., Va. April 25, 1833.

Ibid, page 433 -

6 April 1833 - George Mann Sr. and Hannah, his wife, of
MIAMI COUNTY, STATE OF OHIO, sell to Benjamin Brook, of the
County of Fauquier, State of Virginia - for $300.00 - a tract
of land in Fauquier Co., Va., being that part of the estate of
French Floweree, deceased, devised to the wife of George Mann Jr.
and designated in the division thereof as Lot #5 etc.
Witnesses: Robert Young - J. R. Young.
Certified by Justices of Miami Co., Ohio same day and re-
corded in Fauquier Co., Va. 7 September 1833.

Fauquier Co., Va. Deed Book 34, page 190-

25 March 1833 - Lewis Grigsby and Sharlott, his wife, of
the COUNTY OF CLARK, STATE OF KENTUCKY, sell to George Mann,
formerly of Fauquier Co., Va., for $120.00 - a certain lot of
land in the town of Rectortown, in Fauquier Co., Va., which lot
of land fell to me in the division of the estate of Daniel
Floweree, deceased, containing one acre, more or less, etc.
(The wife of Lewis Grigsby signs her name "Charlotte").
Certified by Justices of Clark Co., Kentucky the same day
and recorded in Fauquier Co., Va. 9 April 1834.

Ibid, page 274 -

16 June 1833 - Know ye that I, George Mann, of the COUNTY
OF MIAMI, STATE OF OHIO, owned, when I resided in the State of
Virginia, a black man named Nathaniel Nicholas, of the age of
40 years, that I brought into the State of Ohio in the month of
November 1831, and do by these presents manumit and set at liberty

the said slave as a free man, etc. (Signed at Troy, Ohio).
Certified by Justices of Miami Co., Ohio same day and recorded in Fauquier Co., Va. 29 July 1834.

Henry Co., Va. Deed Book 11, page 178 -

Christian Co., Ky. July 6, 1832 - George Dyer, of CHRISTIAN COUNTY, KENTUCKY constitutes and appoints James M. Smith, of Henry Co., Va. his true and lawful attorney to sell two certain tracts of land in the County of Henry, Virginia, one tract containing 300 acres on the waters of Smith River and the other tract containing 48 acres in same county on waters of Smith River etc.
Certified by Justices of Christian Co., Ky. 6 February 1832 and recorded in Henry Co., Va. 13 July 1832.

NOTE BY CHH: Ibid, page 281 - 17 May 1833 James M. Smith, attorney for George Dyer of Christian Co., Ky. sells 2 tracts of land in the County of Henry, containing 348 acres in the whole to Fontaine Dyer and Joseph F. Dyer of the County of Henry (Va) for $400.00. Acknowledged and recorded same day.

Richmond Co., Va. Account Book 1 (1724 - 1783), page 16

5 October 1727 - Deposition of Christopher Pridham, of North Farnham Parish, in Richmond Co., aged 53 years or thereabouts (thus born circa 1674) - that he well knew Walter Pavey of said county, deceased, and that he had one son named Webley Pavey who married one Sarah Tock about 25 years ago (ca 1702) which this deponent has not seen lately but by report of the neighbors verily believes that the said Sarah is now alive in this county and further saith that the said Walter Pavey's wife, mother to the said Webley Pavey, departed this life about 45 years ago (about 1682) - and that afterwards the said Walter Pavey intermarried with one Ann Newgent (Nugent) - and had by her one daughter named Sibella, which he believes to be about 29 years of age (thus born ca 1698) and to the best of his knowledge the said Sibella is the only surviving child of the said Walter Pavey and that it was commonly reported that the said Webley Pavey, together with one Sarah Yeats (a woman which he was supposed to keep company with) went away to North Carolina about 11 years ago (ca 1716) and further saith not.
Recorded same day.

Ibid, page 128 -

1 September 1740 - Power of attorney from Ann Pugh, widow - William Landman - Henry Pugh - Willoughby Pugh - Henry Headly and Lewis Pugh, of the COUNTY OF RICHMOND, COLONY OF VIRGINIA - appointing our well beloved David Pugh, of the County of Lancaster in said Colony to demand and receive for us from the executors of Lewis Pugh, formerly of Virginia aforesaid, but late of some part of South Wales in the Kingdom of Great Britain, deceased - all such sums of money, goods, chattels, etc. or other estate due and owing the aforesaid Ann Pugh, as her dower or thirds of the said deceased's estate and to the aforesaid William Landman -

Henry Pugh - Willoughby Pugh - Henry Headly and Lewis Pugh,
for their children's part of the same etc. Acknowledged and
recorded same day.

Ibid, page 129 -

Deposition of Ann Pugh, widow of Lewis Pugh, LATE OF THE
COUNTY OF RICHMOND, COLONY OF VIRGINIA, aged 60 years or thereabouts (thus born ca 1680) that on or about the year 1704 she
was lawfully married to the aforesaid Lewis Pugh and has had
by him seven children (to wit) - John - David - Elizabeth -
Henry - Willoughby - Ann - and Lewis (Pugh) and that about the
year 1731 her aforesaid husband receiving intelligance from his
brother-in-law, Benjamin Jones, of North Wales, in the Kingdom
of Great Britain, and Elizabeth, his wife (his sister) of an
estate, both real and personal, lying in South Wales, in Great
Britain, had descended to him from David Pugh, father of the
said deceased Lewis Pugh, went to England and took with him his
son, John Pugh and that they sailed out of Rappahannock River in
Virginia in the month of April 1731 on board Captain Loxam for
Liverpoole and that this deponent hath been lately advised that
her husband is dead in South Wales and together with her aforesaid five children, Elizabeth, now the wife of William Landman -
Ann, now the wife of Henry Headly - Henry - Willoughby and Lewis
have impowered her aforesaid son, David Pugh, to go over to
Great Britain and receive what is due to them for their parts of
the estate of her deceased husband's estate - and further saith
not.
Sworn to 1 September 1740 and ordered to be recorded.

Southampton Co., Va. Minute Book (1793 - 1799), page 300 -

21 September 1797 - John D. Haupman having for several
years discharged the duties of deputy clerk to this court with
great skill and diligence and being about to leave the state -
the court in consideration of his services feel themselves
bound to offer him an expression of their sentiment on that subject. It is therefore ordered that the clerk accordingly certify
to the said J. D. Haupman the sentiment of this court and offer
to him its best wishes for his future welfare.

(Contributed by Prentiss Price. Thank you Prentiss!)

Frederick Co., Va. Order Book 14, page 561 -

(Note: Indexed as "Aliens took oath of Allegience") -

5 September 1769 - Martin Scotzer - Alexander Hite and
Jacob Hite took the usual oaths to his Majesty's Person and
Government; took the oath of abjuration; repeated and subscribed
the test. It is ordered to be certified.

Frederick Co., Va. Superior Court Deed Book 2, pages 198-199-200 -

30 August 1794 - Tavener Beale and Elizabeth, his wife, of
SHENANDOAH COUNTY, said Elizabeth being one of the daughters of
Jacob Hite, late of the County of Berkeley, deceased - of one
part, and George Hite, son of the said Jacob Hite - Theodrick

Lee, of the County of Loudoun and Catherine, his wife - Alexander
Pitt Buchanan, of the Town of Baltimore, State of Maryland and
Sarah, his wife - and Mary Hite of the County of Frederick (in
Va.) - which said Mary - Catharine and Sarah are daughters and
co-heiresses of John Hite, deceased, eldest son and heir of the
said Jacob Hite, deceased - of the other part- Whereas the said
Jacob Hite unfortunately fell a sacrafice to savage cruelty without having made that provision for the said George Hite which it
is believed he would have done and whereas a Will made by the
said Jacob Hite, dated 17 March 1770 hath been recorded in the
County Court of Berkeley, the validity being contested by the
heirs of the said John Hite and a suit instituted by the said
George Hite etc. provision made by parties of 2nd part that
said Tavener Beale and Elizabeth, his wife - William Bushby and
Mary, his wife - James Hite and Frances Hite shall execute and
deliver such release and discharge as by the parties of the 2nd
part - etc. - to the said George Hite etc. various exceptions
including 1000 acres in the State of South Carolina etc.
  Recorded 2 September 1794.

COMMENT BY CHH: - A similar deed dated 26 August 1794 (Ibid
reference page 210) is indentured by William Bushby and Mary,
his wife, of Fairfax Co., Va. - which Mary is one of the daughters of Jacob Hite, deceased - etc.

  The Jacob Hite, deceased, has been proven as one of the
sons of Hans Yost Hite of whom many records are available.

  In Frederick Co. Superior Court Deed Book 3, page 57, is
another similar deed dated 27 August 1796 from James Hite, only
son and heir at law and devisee of Thomas Hite, deceased, one
of the sons of Jacob Hite, late of County of Berkeley, deceased
and Frances Hite, only daughter of the said Thomas Hite, deceased,
of one part and George Hite and the others named above as parties
of the 2nd part.

  Ibid reference, page 307 - 29 July 1794 -
Alexander Pitt Buchanan and Sarah, his wife, of Baltimore,
Theodrick Lee and Catharine, his wife, of Loudoun Co., Va. and
Mary Hite of County of Frederick sell to George Hite of the
County of Berkeley - for 300 pds. - 1000 acres of land in the
District of Ninety-Six in the State of South Carolina - etc.
  Recorded 6 October 1797.

(Deed Book 20, page 68 - 5 September 1783 - George Hite is shown
as administrator of Estate of Jacob Hite, deceased, late of
Berkeley Co., in a sale of land.)

Frederick Co., Va. Superior Court Deed Book 3, page 177 -

  3 March 1795 - George Hite and Deborah, his wife, of the
County of Berkeley sell to Joseph Myars of County of Frederick -
for 25 pds. - 2 tracts of land in the County of Frederick (bounds
and description) containing 150 acres, etc.
  Recorded 29 September 1797.

Spotsylvania Co., Va. Deed Book "V", page 224 -

6 July 1818 - Certified affidavit by Robert Swann, of the
COUNTY OF SPOTSYLVANIA, before a Justice of the said county that
a negro boy slave named Jonah, now his property, became his by
an intermarriage with Mary Ricketts, whom he married in the State
of Maryland and from which State he brought the said negro boy
slave into this State (Virginia) within 60 days last past, he
coming to the said Swann, under a distribution of the estate of
his wife's father made in April last (1818). The said boy being
about seven years old, etc. Acknowledged and recorded the same
day.

Wythe Co., Va. Deed Book 14, page 516 -

18 December 1838 - Indenture in which Barbara Hoppes*,
relict of Henry Hoppes* Senior, deceased - Henry Hoppes (Jr.)
and Polly, his wife, of the County of Wythe - Gasper Ritter and
Catherine, his wife - John Hedrick and Elizabeth, his wife -
David Wynn and Mary, his wife, of the County of Tazewell - John
Johnston and Margaret, his wife, of the County of Giles - John
Bonham and Juliana, his wife, of the County of Haywood, State of
North Carolina, heirs and distributees of Henry Hoppes, deceased,
parties of one part, sell to David Cline, of Wythe Co., Va. for
$3,000.00 - each of our respective rights, each being one-seventh
part of a tract of undivided land, in the County of Wythe, on the
head waters of Reed Creek, containing 300 acres, etc.
Recorded 11 May 1840 (Barbara Hoppes signed her name in
German script.)

NOTE: It is this writer's opinion that the name is misspelled
for Hopper.

Bedford Co., Va. Deed Book 22, page 456 -

24 October 1831 - Indenture between Leonard H. Williamson,
of one part and James Williamson Jr. of the other part -, both
of Bedford County, Virginia - whereas James Williamson Sr. of
Logan County, Kentucky authorized the above James Williamson Jr.
to take back from Henry Hatcher, a tract of land the said James
Sr. had previously sold, so much of said land as said Hatcher
had not paid for and the said Henry Hatcher did by deed dated
February 1827 convey to the said James Williamson Jr. 221¼ acres
of said land and the said James Williamson Jr. now holds said
land for the use, benefit and disposal of the said James Williamson
Sr. and by his written order requiring the said James Jr. to let
the said Leonard Williamson have the land and title to same - etc.
Recorded same date.

Giles Co., Va. Deed Book C, page 605 -

13 July 1829 - Indenture in which John Nida and Sally, his
wife, of the COUNTY OF GALLIA, STATE OF OHIO, sell to James
Dowdy, of County of Giles, State of Virginia - for value received -
a tract of land in the County of Giles, containing 60 acres, being
a survey granted John Nida by Letter Patent dated 10 July 1823,
adjoining land of Henry Coldwell - etc. Witnesses: Thomas J.

Ridenour - Joanna Ridenour.
Certified by Justice of Gallia County, Harrison Township, Ohio 16 July 1829.
Recorded Giles Co., Va. December Court 1829.

Campbell Co., Va. Order Book 3 (1786 - 1791), page 115 -

Buford vs. Early: (August Court 1787) - on the motion of plaintiff, leave is granted him to take the deposition of Richard Melcar (?) - Joseph Crockett - John Leftwich - Alexander Cummins - Joseph Pennell - Major Crutchfield, living in the State of Georgia. giving the defendant legal notice - etc.

Mecklenburg Co., Va. Deed Book 3, page 277 -

9 December 1771 - Indenture in which James Hopkins, schoolmaster of GRANVILLE COUNTY, PROVINCE OF NORTH CAROLINA, sell to Miner Cockerham, planter, of Mecklenburg, in Virginia for 30 pd - a tract of land in the County of Mecklenburg, Va., on the south side of Roanoke River - containing 400 acres, more or less, which is part of a larger tract of 4,950 acres in the name of Thomas Hopkins, deceased - etc. (witnesses not listed).
Acknowledged and recorded same day.

Lunenburg Co., Va. Deed Book 2, page 92 -

5 June 1749 - Indenture in which John Russill of GRANVILLE COUNTY, PROVINCE OF NORTH CAROLINA, sells to Peter Wilson, of the County of Lunenburg, Colony of Virginia - for the sum of 50 pds. - a tract of land in the County of Lunenburg containing 404 acres, more or less, on the south side of Dan River - on the county line - etc.
Witnesses: William Hogan - Redmond Gallon - Joseph Moor - Robert Wilkins - Abraham Arden.
Acknowledged in court and recorded 3 July 1750.

(NOTE BY CHH: The same day (ibid page 96) John Russell of Granville Co., N. C. sells Peter Willson another tract of land in Lunenburg Co. containing 344 acres, on the north side of Dan River.)

Amelia Co., Va. Deed Book 7, page 41 -

27 June 1759 - Indenture in which Isaac Farguson Sr., and Elizabeth, his wife, of the COUNTY OF HALIFAX, PROVINCE OF NORTH CAROLINA sell to James Lamkin, of the County of Amelia, Colony of Virginia - for 200 pds. - a certain tract of land containing 300 acres, more or less, on the south side of Whetstone Creek, in the said County of Amelia etc.
Witnesses: John Pace - Catharine Pace - John Pain - Samuel Smith.
Proved by witnesses 28th June 1759 and recorded 26 July 1759

Albemarle Co., Va. Will Book 2, page 356 -

Last Will and Testament of John Irwin, dated 17 June 1777, proven August Court 1777.

My cousin, John Hamilton, of Augusta, to collect the money due me from John Piper, of Cumberland County, Pennsylvania and remit the same to my brother, James Irwin, in Ireland, the same being 47 pds.

I give my friend, John Piper a (?chip) or (?ship) left in the care of James Kern.

Mentions money due him by Dr. Thomas Walker.

To my cousin, John Glasley Jr. of Augusta Co.

To Mrs. Margaret Coleman for her kind attendance on me in my illness.

Witnesses: George Gilman - Reuben Lindsay - Whittle Flannagan.

Cumberland Co., Va. Deed Book 10, page 264 -

22 September 1806 - Power of Attorney from Benjamin Harris and Joseph Harris, both of the County of Cumberland, appointing Francis Smith of Lunenburg Co. their true and lawful attorney to receive and recover any and all land being in the State of Kentucky which was willed to us and our brother, Allen Howard Harris, who is now an infant, said land which was willed to us by our father, Joseph Harris, deceased, of the County of Powhatan etc.
Acknowledged in Court same day and recorded.

(NOTE BY CHH:) (Ibid, page 265) - same day Benjamin Harris gives Francis Smith his power of attorney to recover for him all lands in State of Virginia left to him by the Will of his father, Joseph Harris, of Powhatan Co., deceased.
Recorded same day.

Cumberland Co., Va. Deed Book 11, page 162 -

27 February 1809 - Benjamin Harris - Joseph Harris - and Allen Howard Harris, of CUMBERLAND COUNTY, VIRGINIA, sell to Francis Smith, of Lunenburg Co., Virginia - for 200 pds. a tract of land containing 215 acres by actual survey, in the County of Montgomery, State of Kentucky, adjoining land of Aron Higgins - Jenkins Phillips - Lewis - William Ligget's claim, etc.
Acknowledged in Court and recorded February Court 1809.

Goochland Co., Va. Deed Book 9, page 207 -

25 September 1768 - Indenture in which Richardson Rowntree, of the PROVINCE OF SOUTH CAROLINA sells to Randol Rowntree, of the Colony of Virginia and County of Goochland - for 15 pds, 19 shillings, 1 penny, a tract of land in Goochland Co. containing

200 acres and is part of the tract on which William Rowntree, deceased, lived and devised by his Last Will to the said Richardson Rowntree, joining on the land of Josias Payne Jr. - Thomas Rowntree, etc.

Witnesses: John Payne - Josias Payne Jr. - Thomas Rowntree - Benjamin Woodson.

(In the recording, the clerk calls this a "Deed of Mortgage"). Proven 19 June 1769, and recorded. (Deed Book 10, page 123 dated 27 November 1770 - Richardson Rowntree makes a completed Bill of Sale of the above land to his brother, Randol Rowntree for 50 pds.)

NOTE BY CHH: William Rowntree, Sr. died testate in Goochland Co., Virginia. Will proven 16 September 1766 (Deed Book 9, page 38). He had removed to Goochland Co. in 1749 from New Kent Co; made deeds of gifts to two of his sons of his land in Goochland and himself, removed to Hanover Co., he later purchased other land in Goochland and returned to this county where he died in 1766. (Goochland Co. Deed Book 7, pages 203-204-206; - Deed Book 5, page 555).

In the 1790 Census of South Carolina, 96th District, Union Co., are found the following individuals of the surname "Roundtree Rountree, etc. (Pages 90-91)

Richardson	3 males;	7 females;	6 slaves
Turner	2 males;	2 females;	9 slaves
Woodson	1 male ;	1 female ;	3 slaves
James	1 male ;	2 females;	0 slaves

Prince William Co., Va. Deed Book "Q" (1763-1768), page 455 -

1 October 1766 - Power of Attorney from William Dawkins, of the PROVINCE OF SOUTH CAROLINA, appointing Thomas Dawkins and George Dawkins, of the County of Prince William, Colony of Virginia, his attornies in fact, to collect any and all debts, sums of money, and tobacco which are now due or owing to me, etc. And whereas I have lands and other effects in the said Colony (of Virginia), I do hereby impower my said attornies to sell and dispose of the said lands and effects and to make and convey a deed or deeds, etc.

Witnesses: Henry Peyton - Timothy Peyton - Rawleigh Chinn.

Proved by witnesses in Prince William Court 6 April 1767 and recorded. (In the margin by the clerk "examined and delivered to Thomas Dawkins.")

(Contributed by Mr. Thomas P. Hughes, of Memphis, Tennessee, a descendant of William Dawkins.) Thank you Tommy.

NOTE BY CHH: Reference is made to "Land Causes of Prince William County, Virginia (1793-1811) pages 331-380" which includes among other documents the Last Will and Testament of John Dawkins Sr. of Dettigen Parish, Prince William County, dated 16 October 1746, proved 26 January 1746/7 which names his wife, Frances Dawkins and the following children, viz: (sons) John - Joseph - William - Thomas - and George Dawkins and daughter, Hannah Dawkins.

11

Chesterfield Co., Va. Deed Book 13, page 533 -

24 October 1796 - Power of Attorney from Abraham Collins - Martin Roberts - Joshua Burnett - Hugh Queen - John Roberts - and Thomas Roberts, of the COUNTY OF LINCOLN, STATE OF NORTH CAROLINA, children and heirs of Morris or (Maurice) Roberts and Eunity, his wife, late Eunity Martin, appointing Joshua Roberts, of the county and state aforesaid, their true and lawful attorney, to collect any and all money, legacies, etc., with full power to make deeds of conveyance for land belonging to the estate of John Martin, deceased, late of Virginia etc. (NOTE: signed by all the above named and also signed by the following wives - Susannah Collins - Mary Burnett - and Jean Queen.)
Certified by Justice of Lincoln Co., North Carolina (John Carruth, Esq.) 14 November 1796 and recorded in Chesterfield Co., Virginia October (sic) Court 1796.

Chesterfield Co., Va. Deed Book 14, page 228 -

28 November 1796 - Indenture in which Thomas Martin and Anna*, his wife - John Roberts and Rebecca, his wife, of the COUNTY OF CHESTERFIELD, VIRGINIA and Joshua Roberts and Esther, his wife - Abraham Collins and Susanna, his wife - Joshua Burnett and Mary, his wife - Hugh Queen and Jean, his wife - Martin Roberts - John Roberts and Thomas Roberts, of the State of North Carolina, which said Thomas Martin is brother, and Rebecca, wife of John Roberts, is sister of John Martin, late of the County of Chesterfield, deceased, and the said Joshua Roberts - Susanna Collins - Martin Roberts - Mary Burnett - Jean Queen - John Roberts and Thomas Roberts are children and heirs of Unity Roberts, deceased, who was sister of the said John Martin, deceased, parties of the one part, sell to Daniel Trabue, of the County of Chesterfield - a tract of land in said county, formerly belonging to John Martin, deceased, containing 202½ acres on northeast side of Falling Creek (gives bounds and description) (names Unity, sister of John Martin, deceased as widow of Maurice Roberts, deceased) for 500 pds. current money of Virginia etc.
Witnesses: Robert Wooldridge - Thomas Wooldridge - Cornelius Ellitt.
Recorded April Court 1797.

*Anna, wife of Thomas Martin is rendered as "Amey" Martin, in a commission to obtain her relinquishment of Dower. (Chesterfield County Marriages, by Knor, page 84. 8 September 1778 Thomas Martin married Amey Bowman, John Bowman, sec.)

Amelia Co., Va. Deed Book 2, page 1 -

2 July 1742 - Deed of Gift by William Eaton, of the PROVINCE OF NORTH CAROLINA to Anthony Haynes, of the County of Prince George, in the Colony of Virginia - for natural love and affection he hath for his daughter, Jane Haynes, the wife of the said Anthony Haynes - conveys a tract of land in the County of Amelia, Colony of Virginia containing 204 acres which was granted to the said William Eaton by patent dated 28 September 1732 etc.
Witnesses: John Jones - Wood Jones - Clement Read.
Finally proved in full by witnesses 21 June 1745.

Charles City Co., Va. Records (1766-1774), page 547 -

    1 January 1774 - Indenture in which Francis Irby, of Charles City County sells to Roger Jones, of Bute County, North Carolina - for 30 pds. all interest, claim, right and title that the said Irby has in and to six negroes now in the possession of Sarah Hight, of the aforesaid County of Bute, North Carolina, which negroes were devised the aforesaid Sarah Hight during her life by her late husband, Robert Wynn, deceased, of Dinwiddie Co. etc.
    (Date of recordation obliterated).

Ibid, page 125 -

    1 May 1769 - Indenture in which Edward Munford and Betty, his wife, of the COUNTY OF HALIFAX, PROVINCE OF NORTH CAROLINA, sell to Paul Jones, of the County of Charles City, Colony of Virginia for 100 pds. all right, title, interest and claim in a tract of land in Charles City Co. devised by the Last Will and Testament of Edward Broadnax unto Betty Broadnax, now Betty Montfort (sic) during her natural life etc.
    Witnesses: William Holme - Jacob Carter - Benjamin Bradley.
    Proved 3 May 1769 and ordered recorded.

Ibid, page 218 -

    22 May 1770 - John Jolly, of the PROVINCE OF NORTH CAROLINA sells to Robert Pleasants, of the County of Henrico, Colony of Virginia for 20 pds. a tract of land containing 100 acres in the County of Charles City which land was given to the aforesaid John Jolly by Edward Jolly, his father, by his Last Will as records in Charles City Co. will show, adjoining lands given by the said Edward Jolly to Thomas Jolly etc.
    Witnesses: Thomas Jolly - Thomas Childers - William Binford Robert Pleasants, Jr.
    Proved 1 August 1770.

Brunswick Co., Va. Deed Book 14, page 378 -

    21 July 1788 - William Collingsworth of the COUNTY OF NORTHAMPTON, STATE OF NORTH CAROLINA and Abby, his wife, sell to William Justice of County of Brunswick, Virginia for 60 pds. current money of Virginia - all that tract of land in (Brunswick Co.) adjoining land of William Justice - Caleb Manning - John Wesson - John Moore - (and others) containing 75 acres etc.
    Witnesses: Owen Hyrick - James Johnson - Owen M. Fletcher.
    Acknowledged 28 July 1788 and ordered to be recorded.

Brunswick Co., Va. Deed Book 15, page 11 -

    20 May 1790 - Heartwell Rains, of COUNTY OF BRUNSWICK IN VIRGINIA - sells to Nathaniel Thrift, of County of Northampton, in North Carolina - said Rains being indebted to said Thrift in sum of 95 pds., 4 shillings, and 2 pence, to secure which he mortgages, sells, etc., six negroes (named) - (names Francis Dancy trustee, etc.)
    Witnesses: William Thrift - William Jones - Richard Putney.
    Proved and recorded 22 November 1790.

Brunswick Co., Va. Deed Book 19, page 444 –

7 April 1806 – Lyson Lewellin and Sally, his wife, of
COUNTY OF NORTHAMPTON, STATE OF NORTH CAROLINA, sell to Mark
Justis, of County of Brunswick, Virginia – for $100.00 a tract
of land in the County of Brunswick containing 62½ acres etc.
Recorded 28 April 1806.

Surry Co., Va. Deeds #2 (1799-1804), page 514 –

24 July 1804 – Captain James Bailey, of Surry Co., purchases
from John Justiss, of same county, attorney in fact for James
King and Peggy, his wife, of Granville Co., North Carolina for
22 pds., 10 shillings – a tract of land in Surry Co., Virginia
containing 100 acres adjoining lands of Benjamin Putney – Captain
James Bailey – Captain Thomas Peter, Samuel Lucas, deceased, etc.
Acknowledged by John Justiss same day and recorded.

Essex Co., Va. Deed Book 24, page 339 –

28 March 1749 – Power of Attorney from William Moseley, of
the COUNTY OF BEAUFORT, IN THE PROVINCE OF NORTH CAROLINA, only
heir at law to William Moseley, deceased, who was the son of
Benjamin Moseley, the son of Robert Moseley, deceased, of the
County of Essex, Colony of Virginia, constituting and appointing
his friend, Robert Brooke, of the said County of Essex, Colony
of Virginia, his true and lawful attorney to recover of Henry
Crittendon, of the said county and colony (Va.) who was the late
guardian to the said William Moseley, the son of Banjamin Moseley,
who was the son of Robert Moseley aforesaid, all the estate
personal of the said William Moseley under the guardianship of
Henry Crittenden, deceased, etc.
Witnesses: John Rowzee – John Thomas.
Recorded 16 May 1749.

NOTE BY CHH: The above is a beautiful example of a genealogical
record proving four generations and migration in a single record
and was used by me in my column "Happy Hunting" in the Genealogical
Acorn of Tampa, Florida. See also ibid reference, page 315 for
the sale of several tracts of land to Robert Brooke by William
Moseley, of the County of Beaufort, North Carolina etc.

Powhatan Co., Va. Deed Book 12, page 151 –

9 April 1832 – Power of Attorney from Nancy Maxey, of the
COUNTY OF HART, STATE OF KENTUCKY, appointing Thomas Jefferson
Maxey, of the same county and state, her lawful attorney, etc.,
"for me and in my name, as one of the legatees and devisees of
Samuel Woodfin, late of the County of Powhatan, State of Virginia,
deceased" etc., all property, real, money, or slaves, etc. to
which she may be entitled, etc.

Pittsylvania Co., Va. Deed Book 16 (1808-1810), page 42 –

2 June 1808 – I, Sherwood Peerson, heir at law of my son,
Joe Peerson, deceased, in the STATE OF KENTUCKY, MERCER COUNTY,
give my Power of Attorney to my son, Richmond S. (or L.) Peerson,

of Mercer Co., Kentucky to sell the land of the said Joe, on the
waters of Green Creek, in Green Co., Kentucky, on Russell's
Creek, etc., conveyed to him by Morgan Bryant by Deed of Record
in Henry Co., Kentucky, etc.
    Witnesses: Hartwell Allin - Jabez Smith - James Hamlet -
Mastin Peerson - Thomas Peerson.
    Proved 20 June 1808 and recorded.

Pittsylvania Co., Va. Deed Book 25 (1822-1823), page 571 -

    18 August 1823 - Thomas Peerson, of LAURENCE COUNTY, ALABAMA
to Mastin Peerson, of Pittsylvania Co., Virginia - WHEREAS,
Sherwood Peerson, deceased, by his Last Will and Testament devised
to Elizabeth Peerson, his wife, a tract of land on both sides of
Turkey Cock Creek, for her natural life, supposed to be 450 acres,
and then equally to four of his sons (namely) Mastin - Thomas -
Charles - and William Peerson, etc., the aforesaid Thomas Peerson
sells his right, title, and interest in the land (after the death
of the said Elizabeth) to Mastin Peerson, for $300.00 etc.
    Witnesses: John M. Hart - Benjamin Walker - Pleasant
Thacker.
    Proved 20 October 1823 in Pittsylvania Co. and recorded.

Lunenburg Co., Va. Deed Book 21 (1806-1808), page 96 -

    20 May 1807 - Power of Attorney from Richmond Pearson,
of ROWAN COUNTY, NORTH CAROLINA to Jesse A. Pearson, of the same
county and state to receive from David Street, of Lunenburg Co.,
Virginia, Administrator of (Colonel) David Stokes, deceased,
(of Mecklenburg Co., Virginia) property due me as Administrator
of (Colonel) John Stokes (of North Carolina), deceased, and as
guardian of his only son, Richmond Stokes, etc.

Prince Edward Co., Va. Deed Book 4 (1771-1772), page 163 -

    1 May 1772 - George Walton (the younger) of SAVANNAH, in
the PROVINCE OF GEORGIA, etc., WHEREAS, Robert Walton, of the
County of Cumberland, Colony of Virginia, Gent., deceased, by his
Last Will and Testament dated 5th September 1749 did bequeath
unto Sarah Walton, who has since intermarried with one Thomas
Watkins, and to the aforesaid George Walton, (the younger),
several negro slaves, to be equally divided when the said Sarah
and George should marry or come of age and also 200 pds., and
did appoint George Walton (the elder) now of Prince Edward Co.
and Tucker Woodson (the elder), of Goochland Co., Gents., his
executors, and the said George Walton (the younger) is desirous
of having his said part alloted to him (with these presents)
gives Power of Attorney to Joseph Pearson, late of the County of
Charlotte, Virginia, but now of Savannah, Gent., (George Walton,
the elder, acting executor, lately guardian to me, George Walton,
the younger.)
    Witnesses: Thomas Lloyd - James Robertson.
    Proved 1 May 1772 at Savannah, Georgia and recorded July
Court 1772, Prince Edward Co. Virginia.

NOTE BY CHH: This was George Walton, "Signer" of the Declaration
of Independence and later Governor of Georgia.

<u>Prince William Co., Va. Deed Book Z, page 45</u> -

1 December 1796 - Indenture in which Lynn West, of the COUNTY OF SCOTT, STATE OF KENTUCKY sells to Enoch Renoe, of the County of Prince William, State of Virginia for 120 pds. current money, a tract of land in Prince William County which descended to the said Lynn West from his father, James West, containing 102¾ acres, adjoining land of Francis Reno, Isaac Farrow, William Pearson, etc., excepting 2¾ acres sold by Lewis Renoe when said land was in his possession, to William Ashmore for a mill seat, etc. Recorded 5 December 1796.

<u>Ibid, page 116</u> -

12 October 1796 - Indenture in which Robert H. Courts and Catharine, his wife, of the COUNTY OF NELSON, STATE OF KENTUCKY sell to Enoch Renoe of the County of Prince William, in Virginia, for 18 pds. - a tract of land in Prince William Co. containing 37⅓ acres being the one-third part of a tract of land formerly the property of Thomas Renoe, first husband of the above Catharine Courts, which land was set apart as her dower etc. Recorded 1 May 1797.

COMMENT: Francis Renoe, Sr., of Prince William Co., dated his Will 18 October 1794 (Proven 2 October 1797) (Will Book H, page 224) and named therein his sons, Enoch - Francis - George - and Baylis Renoe - leaving them each land and slaves. He also left a slave or slaves to each of his daughters, namely - Lidia More - Nancy Whitledge, wife of Robert - Fanny Tackett - Milley Jamison - Dolley Renoe - Jane Renoe and Susanna Crosby.

<u>Charlotte Co., Va. Deed Book 13, page 127</u> -

10 April 1815 - Indenture in which John Watkins, for himself, and as attorney in fact for Nancy Ferguson, wife of Bryant Ferguson and Fanny Hamletts heirs - John Redd, attorney in fact for Sarah Moore and James D. Cole and Robert Smith, all legatees of George Moore, deceased, of the one part, and William Davis of the County of Charlotte, of the other part - for $1,350.00 - a tract of land in County of Lunenburg containing 900 acres, etc. Recorded 3 July 1815.

<u>Ibid, page 201</u> -

24 February 1816 - We, Bryant Ferguson and Nancy Ferguson, his wife, late Nancy Moore, daughter and one of the heirs of George Moore, deceased, late of Charlotte Co., State of Virginia - of the COUNTY OF FAYETTE, STATE OF KENTUCKY, constitute and appoint William T. Davis, of County of Charlotte, Virginia our true and lawful attorney, to convey to Joel Watkins, of the County of Prince Edward, Virginia all our interest as heirs of the said George Moore, deceased, to a tract of land containing 500 acres in the County of Prince Edward and to convey to William Dabbs, of the County of Charlotte, all our interest to a tract of land containing 800 acres and upwards, in the County of Lunenburg, etc. Certified before John D. Young, notary public of Lexington,

County of Fayette, State of Kentucky etc., on 24 February 1816.
Recorded Charlotte Co., Virginia 3 June 1816.

Lunenburg Co., Va. Deed Book 24, page 428 -

3 June 1816 - William Davis of COUNTY OF CHARLOTTE, VIRGINIA,
by Power of Attorney from Bryant Farguson and Nancy, his wife,
of the County of Fayette, State of Kentucky sells to William
Dabbs of the County of Charlotte, Virginia their part of a tract
of land in the County of Lunenburg, Virginia of which George Moore
died seized of, known by the name of Moore's Old Mill tract, containing by a late survey 903 acres etc.
Acknowledged in Court same day and recorded 13 August 1818.

Charles City Co., Va. Deed Book 4, page 124 -

24 August 1792 - Indenture in which Burwell Brown, of
GREEN COUNTY, in the STATE OF GEORGIA, sells to John Irby, of
Charles City Co., Virginia for 100 pds. - a tract of land in said
County of Charles City containing 200 acres etc.
Witnesses: Stith Hardyman - Esek Brown - Francis H. Dancy.
Proved 21 February 1793 and ordered recorded.

(Old) Rappahannock Co. (Va.) Orders (1683-1686), page 19 -

2 April 1684 - Whereas John Camell hath a long time been
wrongfully called by the name of John Bayley, who came to this
country as a lad, was forced by his brother (as he pretends) to
change his name - therefore, he, the said Camell, did in open
Court utterly deny and renounce the name of Bayley and doe declare
his name to be John Camell.

New York Genealogical and Biographical Record, Vol. 99, page 13 -

3 November 1766 - John De La Somet, banished from France
in 1684 for his religion, died in early October in Fauquier Co.,
Virginia, aged upward of 130 years (thus born ca 1636).

Prince George Co., Va. Records (1733), page 585 (Accession)

8th - 9th October 1733 - Indenture in which Moses Beck, of
the PROVINCE OF NORTH CAROLINA, sells to his brother, Andrew
Beck, of the County of Prince George, Parish of Bristol, Colony
of Virginia (lease 5 shillings - release 12 pounds) 166 acres of
land in Prince George Co. etc.
Acknowledged 9 October 1733.

Albemarle Co., Va. Deed Book 3, page 190 -

8 July 1762 - John Mitchell, of Great Britain, and Andrew
Shepherd, of the County of Orange in Virginia, Merchant, his
certain attorney, of one part, sell to William Dalton, of the
County of Albemarle - for 30 pds. - a tract of land in the County
of Albemarle containing 277 acres, adjoining land of John Ennis -
etc.
Recorded same day.
(No witnesses listed.)

NOTE BY CHH: This deed is followed (page 191) same date, by
another deed from the same parties of the first part, as above,
selling 204 acres in Albemarle Co. to Gabriel Maupin of Albemarle
Co. They also sell Gabriel Maupin, the same day, (Ibid, page 192)
another tract of land containing 318 acres. On page 194 (same day)
Andrew Shepherd, attorney for John Mitchell, of Great Britain, sells
230 acres in Albemarle Co. to William Keaton Jr. (A busy and
profitable day.)

Albemarle Co., Va. Deed Book 9, page 271 -

4 May 1785 - Indenture in which Robert Harris, of the
COUNTY OF SURRY, PROVINCE OF NORTH CAROLINA, sells to William
Dalton, of the County of Albemarle, Colony of Virginia - for 350 pds.
a tract of land in the County of Albemarle (Va.) - containing 400
acres on the branches of Doyles River, at the foot of the Blue
Ridge Mountains etc.
    Witnesses: Lewis Raddell - Thomas Burrus - Stephen Smith -
Charles Smith.
    Proved by witnesses 12 October 1786 and ordered recorded.

NOTE BY CHH: A Robert Harris made a Deed of Gift of two negro
slaves to his son-in-law, William Dalton, on the 25th day of
November 1761 and on the same day, Samuel Dalton Sr., and wife,
Anne, made a Deed of Gift of 404 acres of land to their son,
William Dalton (Albemarle Deed Book 3, page 124).

Giles Co., Va. Deed Book C, page 567 -

10 February 1829 - Indenture in which William Caldwell and
Polly, his wife, LATE OF THE COUNTY OF GILES, STATE OF VIRGINIA,
sell to John K. Clark, of Chicago, State of Illinois, etc:
Whereas Thomas Clyborne, now deceased, in his lifetime sold to
his son, Jonas Clybourn, a tract of land in Giles County, on the
west side of Walkers Creek estimated at 28 acres, but failed to
convey the said land to the said Jonas Clyburn and having departed this life, intestate, the legal title to the said land
descended and vested in his children, to wit: the above named
William Coldwell (sic) and Polly, his wife, late Polly Clybourn -
Jonas Clybourn - John Clybourn - Archibald Clybourn - Lemuel
Clybourn - James Clybourn and William Clybourn - and the said
Jonas Clybourn, having sold his piece of land to the above named
John Clark, etc.
    Certified before Justices of Harlen County (State of Kentucky),
by William Caldwell 10 February 1829, who make affidavit.
    Recorded Giles Co., Virginia June Court 1829.

Giles Co., Va. Deed Book E, page 113 -

18 November 1833 - Indenture in which Joseph Peck and
Elizabeth, his wife, of the COUNTY OF LAURENCE, STATE OF KENTUCKY
sell to John Caldwell, of the County of Giles, State of Virginia -
for $75.00 - a tract of land in the County of Giles, on Sinking
Creek, containing 56 acres, adjoining the lands of William Fairer
(Ferrier) - Adam Peck, etc.
    Certified and acknowledged before Justices of Lawrence Co.,
Kentucky who make affidavit on the above date.

18

Recorded Giles Co., January Court 1837.

Montgomery Co., Va. Will Book 4, page 98 -

7 October 1824 - Power of Attorney from Ann Price, formerly
Ann Grissom, child and heir at law of Robert Grissom, LATE OF THE
COUNTY OF MONTGOMERY, STATE OF VIRGINIA, deceased, and Henry
Price, of the County of Preble, State of Ohio, do appoint William
Thomas of the County of Montgomery in Virginia our lawful attorney,
to sell and convey a tract of land in Montgomery Co. (Lot #3)
containing 30 acres, it being a part of the land of which Robert
Grissom died seized and possessed and divided among his heirs
by order of Court of Montgomery Co.
    Signatures certified by Justices of Preble Co., Ohio.
Recorded Montgomery Co., Virginia Courthouse February 1825.

Loudoun Co. Va. Deed Book F, page 48 -

4 June 1766 - Power of Attorney from Margaret and Mary
Conners, daughters lawful and only children, now in life, of the
deceased, Robert Conner, Mariner, of Greenock; sisters German
and nearest heirs to the also deceased, Edward Conner, late
storekeeper at Alexandria, in the County of Loudoun, on the Potomac
in Virginia, appointing Mr. Alexander Henderson, Merchant, in
Colechester, Fairfax Co., Virginia their true and lawful attorney
to secure for them and in their names the estate, etc., of the
aforesaid Edward Conner etc.
    Witnesses: Hugh McLean - Arch: McAdam.
    Proven by the witnesses on 4 June 1766 in the City of
Glasgow (Scotland) before John Bowman, Esq., Lord Provost of
the City of Glasgow. Followed by an affidavit dated the same
day, in Glasgow, by Thomas Donald, Merchant in General and William
Rodger, at Town Melne, of Glasgow who deposed, on oath, that they
were well acquainted with the within mentioned Edward Conner,
before he went abroad and also with the within mentioned Margaret
and Mary Conner and know them to be brother and sisters German
and to be lawful children of the within deceased Robert Conner,
Mariner.
    Recorded Loudoun Co., Virginia 10 August 1767.

Campbell Co., Va. Deed Book 7, page 351 -

25 February 1806 - Indenture in which Stephen Stepp, of
the COUNTY OF OGLETHORPE in the STATE OF GEORGIA, sells to Dennis
Kelly of the County of Campbell in Virginia - for 100 pds. current
money - a tract of land in Campbell Co., Virginia containing 100
acres, on both sides of Schoolhouse Branch being part of a greater
tract granted by patent to Joseph Akins of 260 acres, etc.
    Witnesses: J. D. Harvie - William Lamott - Solomon Sharp.
    Certified by officials of Oglethorpe Co., Georgia and
recorded in Campbell Co., Virginia 9 June 1806.

Loudoun Co., Va. Deed Book 2L, page 83 -

18 October 1800 - Power of Attorney from Walker Ansill
of KENAWAY COUNTY, STATE OF VIRGINIA (misspelling for Kanawha
Co., now West Virginia) to his friend and brother, Leonard Ansill,
of County of Loudoun, Virginia to sell and convey his interest
or part of the land which fell to him from the plantation of his
father, Leonard Ansill, deceased, etc.

NOTE BY CHH: His signature is written in an unreadable (by me)
German script.

Recorded January Court 1810.

Loudoun Co., Va. Deed Book E, page 248 -

10 November 1766 - Daniel Conner and Mary, his wife, of
LOUDOUN COUNTY, COLONY OF VIRGINIA sell to John Moore, of County
of Hunterdon, Province of New Jersey - (lease 5 shillings - release 61 pounds), a tract of land in County of Loudoun which fell
by descent to Elizabeth Stripling - Frances Ashby and Dollothy
Winn, by the death of Francis Right (Wright) their father, etc.,
containing 261½ acres etc.
    Witnesses: Andrew Campbell - John Lewis,- Phil. Noland.
Recorded 11 November 1766.

Stafford Co.,Va. Deeds (1722-1728), page 92-94 -

3 April 1724 - Prior Smallwood of CHARLES COUNTY in PROVINCE
OF MARYLAND, Gent., sells to George Mason, of County of Stafford,
Colony of Virginia, Gent., (lease 5 shillings, release 3,000 lbs.
tobacco) that tract of land called or known by the name of
Cockpit Point, on the Potomac River, containing 200 acres, in
Stafford Co., etc.
    Witnesses: William Taliaferro - Richard Hubbard - (By
Power of Attorney to Benjamin Berry, Gent.). Elizabeth, wife
of Pryor Smallwood, relinquishes her right of dower.
Recorded 8 April 1724.

NOTE BY CHH: An account of the Smallwood family of Maryland,
by Professor Arthur L. Keith, in Maryland Historical Magazine
(Vol. 22, page 139 et seq) proves Pryor Smallwood born ca 1680
died 1734 as son of Colonel James Smallwood, immigrant to
Maryland in 1664 who died testate 1714/15. Prior Smallwood
and his wife, Elizabeth, had the following children: Bayne -
William - Ann - Elizabeth - Hester (Smallwood).

Stafford Co., Va. Liber S - 1780-89, page 359 -

Last Will and Testament of William Mathews dated 3 December
1785, probated 14 August 1786.

My loving mother, Ann Thomson - 50 pds.

I believe my wife to be with child, and if so, my whole
estate, real and personal, to said child. If not, to my loving
wife.

Whereas I am entitled to a considerable sum of money in Great Britain, by right of my wife, etc. said money (when got) to be laid out in lands etc.

Executors: My loving wife - and my friends, Mr. Thomas Short of King George Co. and Benjamin Harrison of Fauquier Co.

(Will was presented in Court by Margaret, widow of said William Mathews - Bond was 3,000 pds.)

Loudoun Co., Va. Will Book A, page 122 -

Last Will and Testament of Thomas Long dated 27 October 1764, probated 11 March 1765.

I, Thomas Long, LATE OF HARFORD COUNTY IN NEW ENGLAND, but now of Loudoun Co. in Virginia.
To my much esteemed friend, James Long, of Loudoun Co., all my lot of land and buildings situate in the Town of Harford, in the County of Harford and also 11 acres of land near the said Town - the Title and Deeds of both and all my other papers I left in the care and custody of Mr. George Smith of said town.

I constitute and appoint the said James Long my whole and sole executor, etc. (Signed by his mark "X").
Witnesses: Lee (?) Massey and Frederick Weisel (signature in German).

NOTE: A check of Maine, Vermont, Rhode Island, Massachusetts, and New Hampshire does not reveal a Harford Co. There is a Hartford Co. in Connecticut.

Fairfax Co., Va. Deed Book 1-A (1729-1735), page 99 -

20 August 1730 - Power of Attorney from Angus Mackay, of INVERNESS, IN THE KINGDOM OF GREAT BRITAIN, now of the County of King George, in the Colony of Virginia, Merchant, appointing William Strother, Gent., of the County of King George aforesaid, his true and lawful attorney etc.
Witnesses: Thomas Moore - Nicholas Smith - Edward Barradall.
Recorded 5 November 1730.

Ibid, page 133 -

14 July 1729 - Power of Attorney from Jane Sargant, wife of William Sargant, of the CITY OF BRISTOL (KINGDOM OF GREAT BRITAIN, Merchant) to Thomas Waring, Gent., of the County of Essex, Colony of Virginia - to relinquish her right of dower in all lands in the County of King George, Virginia which her said husband shall make sale of, etc.
Witnesses: William Loyd - Joseph Smith.
Proved and recorded, Essex Co., Virginia 16 December 1729.
Recorded King George Co., Virginia 7 May 1731.

Ibid, page 217 -

    28 March 1732 - Power of Attorney from Thomas Seed, of the
CITY OF BRISTOL, COOPER, and Elizabeth, my wife, one of the daughters
and co-heirs of Francis Barnard, late of the same city, Merchant,
deceased, and Francis Brown, of the said City of Bristol, Cooper,
son of Nathaniel Brown, late of the said city, baker, also deceased,
on the body of Mary, his wife, begotten, (who was) one other of
the daughters and co-heirs of the said Francis Barnard, appointing
Jeremiah Murdòck, of the Colony of Virginia, Merchant, their
lawful attorney to receive and recover all rents now or hereafter
due and payable in respect of that tract or seat of land containing
200 acres, with the dwelling house and two tobacco houses, being
in the Parish of Washington, County of Westmoreland, Colony of
Virginia, near to Rozier's Creek of the South Potomack which land
was formerly purchased by the said Francis Barnard, deceased,
(in his lifetime) from John Jones, of the said City of Bristol,
Mariner, to whom the same, before that time, had been granted, etc.
    Witnesses: Daniel Williams - Thomas Smith.
    Recorded King George Co., Virginia 4 August 1732.

Halifax Co., Va. Deed Book 27, page 368 -

    4 July 1818 - Larkin Simore, of GRAINGER COUNTY, STATE OF
TENNESSEE gives a Power of Attorney to Coleman Cox and William
Webb, of County of Halifax, State of Virginia, to receive a ba-
lance of his part of the estate of John Bruce, Sr., left to me
in his Last Will, Jesse Munsay, (or Munday?), Administrator, etc.
    Witnesses: Benjamin Anderson - Edward Roberts - William
C. Yates.
    Recorded Halifax Co., Virginia 25 January 1819.

Washington Co., Va. Deed Book 7, page 286 -

    15 November 1820 - James Reamy, of the COUNTY OF FLOYD,
STATE OF KENTUCKY, sells to George Hayton and Margaret Hayton,
widow of John Hayton, deceased, for $300.00 - a tract of land
in the County of Washington (State of Virginia) containing 90
acres, on the north side of the middle fork of the Holstein River
adjoining land of John Byars - Nathaniel Harris land purchased
of the heirs of John Hayton, deceased, Jacob Wolf's line - Jacob
Roman's land - etc.
    Witness: James Meek (J.P.)
    Acknowledged in Court 16 November 1820 and recorded 19
December 1820.

Augusta Co., Va. Deed Book 24, page 312 -

    6 July 1784 - Power of Attorney from William Hadden, of
the COUNTY OF FAYETTE, COMMONWEALTH OF VIRGINIA (now Kentucky),
to his trusty friend, David Hadden to make a sufficient general
warrant and title to John Waneck (?) for a tract of land containing 186 acres in Monongehala Co. in Virginia (now West
Virginia) etc.
    Witnesses: William Monnell - James Gay - Alex Dunlap.
    Proved by witnesses 17 August 1784 and ordered recorded.

Culpeper Co., Va. Deed Book B, page 8 -

    16 August 1753 - Indenture in which James Hume, orphan of William Hume, LATE OF THE KINGDOM OF GREAT BRITAIN, deceased, of one part, and Roger Dixon, Gent., attorney at law and clerk of the County Court of Culpeper, of the other part - Witnesseth that the said James Hume by advice and consent of his mother, Mrs. Sarah Hume, and the approbation of the County Court of Culpeper, and of his own free will; doth voluntarily bind himself an apprentice, by these presents, to the said Roger Dixon, to learn the profession or calling of an attorney at law and scrivener for the term of seven years, next ensuing etc.
    Acknowledged by James Hume 17ᵗʰ August 1753 and ordered to be recorded.

COMMENT: He must have been 14 years of age at this time, as he bound himself for seven years. Thus born ca 1739. His father, William, and probably his mother, Sarah, were therefore the immigrant progenitors of this branch. The above James would therefore have reached his majority in the year 1760.

Frederick Co., Va. Deed Book 23, page 431 -

    3 October 1792 - Solomon Niswanger and Elizabeth, his wife, of Frederick Co., sell to John Marlow, late of Montgomery Co. Maryland - for 75 pds. current money - all that estate, real and personal, devised and bequeathed to him as a legatee in the Will of his father, John Nisewanga, deceased, which Will was dated 23 September 1788, now of record in the County Court of Frederick, and the landed estate therein is in the said County of Frederick on the long marsh or drains of Cedar Creek etc.
    Acknowledged and recorded same day.

NOTE BY CHH: Frederick Co., Virginia Marriages by Chappalier, page 56 -
    May 10, 1787 - Solomon Nighswanger (sic) and Elizabeth Kern.

Frederick Co., Va. Deed Book 4, pages 83 - 84 -

    29 and 30ᵗʰ December 1755 - Christian Funkhouser, of the COUNTY OF FREDERICK, COLONY OF VIRGINIA sells to Henry Mire, late of the Province of Pennsylvania - (lease 5 shillings - release 33 pounds, 15 shillings) 200 acres of land in the County of Frederick, being part of 444 acres of land granted to the said Christian Funkhouser, by Lord Fairfax 2 March 1752, on Holeman's Creek, a branch of the North River of Shenandoah, etc.
    Witnesses: Abraham Denton - Caleb Odell.
    Recorded 4 February 1756 - and Christinah, wife of Christian Funkhouser, acknowledged her release of said land. (Christian signs by his mark (CH) and Christene (sic) by her mark (CI)).

Frederick Co., Va. Deed Book 6, page 85 -

    4 November 1760 - Thomas Palmore, of PROVINCE OF NEW YORK, sells to John Rhodes of County of Frederick, Colony of Virginia -

for 250 pds. - a tract of land in the County of Frederick on
the North Branch of the Shenandoah River, containing 500 acres
granted to the said Thomas Palmore by Lord Fairfax 22 May 1751
etc.

Acknowledged and recorded same day - (no witnesses listed).

Loudoun Co., Va. Deed Book P, pages 485-487 -

15ᵗʰ and 16ᵗʰ February 1787 - Indenture in which Mahlon
Smith, of WINCHESTER, COUNTY OF FREDERICK, sadler, and Mary,
his wife, sell to John Wilson, lately of London, in old England,
Gent., (lease 5 shillings - release 130 pounds) - a tract of
land in the County of Loudoun, adjoining land of John Piggot,
near the meeting house - Edward Thompson - containing 47¾ acres,
13 perches, more or less, etc.

Witnesses: Joseph Pool - Nathan Updegraff - Thomas Ouram.
Recorded 11 June 1787.

Loudoun Co., Va. Will Book C, page 32 -

Last Will and Testament of John Wilson, Gent., formerly
of the CITY OF LONDON, IN OLD ENGLAND, but now of the Parish of
Shelburn, in the County of Loudoun, State of Virginia, Planter,
(dated 10 July 1787 - proved 14 April 1788).

Loving wife, Mary Wilson -

Sons:
    John Jefferson Wilson
    Henry Lawrence Wilson

Daughters:
    Maria Wilson
    Kezia Wilson

Wife, Mary, sole executrix.
Witnesses: James Dillon - Isaac Hook - Mary Hook.

Executors Bond 500 pds., Mary Wilson qualified, with William
Janny and James Dillon her securities.

NOTE BY CHH: The Will of Peter Carr (Loudoun Co. Will Book K,
page 96) dated 13 April 1810 proves that he married Mary Wilson,
widow of John Wilson, and her Will, (Mary Carr) (Loudoun Co.
Will Book M, page 42) - dated 15 August 1815 names some of her
Wilson children. Incidently, another record proves the full and
proper name of "Kezia" Wilson as Hezekiah Wilson.

Stafford Co., Va. Liber S (1780-1789), page 360 -

Last Will and Testament of William Ballard, of STAFFORD
COUNTY, VIRGINIA, dated 19 March 1786 - (no date of probate).

"Being about to remove to the Western Waters of Kentucky
and this life being in general very uncertain" -

My brother-in-law, George Hampton, who married my sister,
Mary, to be my whole trustee and manager of my estate, both real
and personal, to the interest of the children of my sister, Mary,
may inherit my whole estate - I dying without issue.

To my niece, Frankie, a negro girl.
To my niece, Susanna, a negro girl.

Refers to his land in Stafford to Deed dated 25 December
1778 (?) and his land claimed on Western Waters as preempton of
250 acres and balance of military right, 2,000 acres.
  Witnesses: George F. Luck - Lewis Cobbs - Timothy Parish -
Bernard Renolds - Henry Chiles - Richard Burch.

COMMENT: Register of Officers, by Hertman, page 84, lists a
William Ballard, Virginia Service, as Lieutenant of Virginia
Regiment in 1780-1781.

Fauquier Co., Va. Land Causes (1833-1850), page 367 -

  STATE OF INDIANA, COUNTY OF SWITZERLAND - 5 May 1837 -
  Be it remembered that on this fifth day of May in the year
of our Lord 1837, personally appeared before us, two Justices
of the Peace within and for said county, Stephen Rogers, of said
county who being by us duly sworn, on his oath deposeth and saith,
that he is a son of John Rogers and a brother of Henry Rogers,
both late of the County of Fauquier, in the Commonwealth of Virginia
and that he is the identical Stephen Rogers, named in a lease
giving to John Rogers, his father, and Henry Rogers, his brother,
and himself, by Lord Fairfax, for a tract of land in the County
of Fauquier and that he, the said Stephen Rogers is still living
and residing in the County of Switzerland and State of Indiana
and further saith not - (Newton H. Tapp and Perret Dufour, J.P.)

NOTE BY CHH: This lease of land by Lord Fairfax, to John Rogers
and Henry and Stephen Rogers, his sons, was dated 28 July 1763,
reference, Fauquier Co. Deed Book 2, page 50.

Brunswick Co., Va. Deed Book 17, page 151 -

  27 March 1787 - Joseph Carter, of COUNTY OF HALIFAX, NORTH
CAROLINA, sells to Thomas Barker, of the County of Greensville,
Virginia - 63 pds. - a tract of land in the County of Brunswick,
Virginia - containing 196 acres adjoining lands of James Maclin -
Adams - Harris - Gower - on the Meherrin - etc.
  Witnesses: Robert Spencer - Thomas Spencer - Edward
Delbridge.
  Recorded 25 September 1797 (sic).

Brunswick Co., Va. Deed Book 7, page 62 -

  20 February 1762 - Abraham Jones, of the COUNTY OF HALIFAX,
PROVINCE OF NORTH CAROLINA - sells to Lewis Barker, of the County
of Brunswick, Colony of Virginia - for 8 pds. - a tract of land
in Brunswick Co., adjoining land of John Barker, containing 186
acres, more or less, etc.
  Witnesses: Benjamin Moseley - Thomas Moseley - Isaac
Moseley.
  Recorded 22 February 1762.

Montgomery Co., Va. Deed Book G, page 309 -

20 January 1820 - Joseph Thompson, Attorney in fact for Meredith Akers, of the COUNTY OF ROCKCASTLE in the STATE OF KENTUCKY sells to Richard M. Crump, of the County of Montgomery, State of Virginia - for $100.00 - all his right, title and in-terest of and in to a certain tract of land in the County of Montgomery, on the head waters of one branch of Wilson's Creek, of the north fork of Roanoke (River) which tract of land was conveyed to Claiborne Akers, father of the said Meredith Akers, by Samuel Langdon and wife, etc.
Acknowledged and recorded same day.

NOTE BY CHH: Montgomery Co. Marriage Register, page 29.
17 April 1789 - Clayburn Acres and Elizabeth Thompson, daughter of George Thompson - John Thompson, Security (page 349, Richard Whitt, Minister).

Pittsylvania Co., Va. Deed Book 12, page 133 -

25 January 1800 - Humphrey Marshall, of the COUNTY OF WOODFORD, KENTUCKY sells to Josiah Maples of County of Pittsylvania, Virginia - for 20 pds. - 100 acres of land in County of Pittsylvania-on the waters of Cherrystone Creek etc. signed by Thomas Marshall, attorney in fact for Humphrey Marshall.
Witnesses: George Long - Henry Polley - George Craft.
Recorded 16 June 1800.

NOTE: This record is followed (page 134) by another record of sale of 300 acres of land in Pittsylvania Co. by Thomas Marshall, attorney for Humphrey Marshall, of Woodford Co., Kentucky to George Long and Peter Maples of Pittsylvania Co., Virginia - (Recorded 16 June 1800).

Pittsylvania Co., Va. Deed Book 22, page 362 -

7 October 1813 (or 1815?) - Power of Attorney from Edward Long, son of William Long, of the COUNTY OF MADISON, STATE OF KENTUCKY to his friend and brother, Richard Long, of the same county and state - to receive in his name any money or property coming to him by the Last Will and Testament of his grandfather, Edward Long, deceased, of Pittsylvania Co., Virginia, etc.
(Followed by several certifications of Justices of Madison Co., Kentucky).
Recorded 19 July 1819.

NOTE: The above Edward Long is named as "grandson" in (D & W 11, page 296) the Will of Edward Long of Pittsylvania Co. dated 30 October 1804.

Frederick Co., Va. Land Book 1 (and Causes) 1758-1832, page 179 -

Last Will and Testament of the Right Honorable Thomas, Lord Fairfax, Baron of Cameron in that part of Great Britain called Scotland and proprietor of the Northern Neck of Virginia, dated 8 November 1777, probated 5 March 1782.

My undivided sixth part of my lands and plantations in

Colony of Virginia, known as the Northern Neck of Virginia, being formerly the Estate of the Honorable Alexander Culpeper, Esq., deceased, to the Reverend Mr. Denny Martin, my nephew, now of the County of Kent, in Great Britain if he be alive - if dead, then to Thomas Bryan Martin, Esq., his next brother, now living with me and in case of his death before me, to my other nephew, Philip Martin, Esq., brother to the aforesaid Denny and Thomas, etc.

My nieces, Frances Martin - Sybella Martin - and Ann Susanna Martin, to each an annuity of 100 pds. sterling during their natural lives.

Provided he, the said Denny Martin or he to whom the said sixth part shall pass, shall procure an Act of Parliament to pass to take upon him the name of Fairfax and Coat of Arms. Whereas by a previous Will, now cancelled, I did give a considerable pecumary legacy to my brother, The Honorable Robert Fairfax, Esq., which sum of money I have since advanced to him and paid to him, therefore, I now only give him the further sum of 500 pds. sterling and to my sister, Frances Martin, 500 pds. sterling.

All the rest and residue of my estate, real and personal, I give, devise, and bequeath to my elder nephew, the aforesaid Reverend Denny Martin.

My executors: My nephew, Thomas Bryan Martin - Peter Hog and Gabriel Jones of County of Augusta, Colony of Virginia - and to said Peter Hog and Gabriel Jones, to each 500 pds. current money of Virginia.

Codicil dated 27 November 1779 - changes the item concerning his slaves left to his nephews, Denny Martin - Thomas Bryan Martin and Philip Martin, Esq., to be now divided in four equal parts and to include Bryan Fairfax, Esq., and as to the 100 pds. sterling per annum bequeathed to his three nieces, upon their death the annuity of each is to descend to the first three children of the said Bryan Fairfax etc. during his or her natural life - and further and lastly do direct that 500 pds. sterling money of Great Britain be paid to his executors instead of the same sum given them in current money.
    Witnesses: John Hite - Angus McDonald - Richard Rigg - John Lagarde - Thomas Smithers.
    Witnesses to codicil: Robert Macky - Peter Catlett - John S. Woodcock - John Hite.

NOTE: Thomas Bryan Martin and Gabriel Jones, surviving executors therein named qualified.

FURTHER NOTE: Later records are found issued by Denny Fairfax, who must have been able to legally change his name from Martin.

Norfolk Co., Va. Will Book 2 (1772-1788), page 101 -

    Last Will and Testament of Robert Kerr, Sergeant in the 2nd Company of Charles Harrison Esq's. Regiment of Artillery etc., dated 13 November 1777, probated February Court 1778.

To my eldest brother, James Kerr, one-half my personal and real estate.

To my other brother, Samuel Kerr, the other half of my estate, real and personal, he paying to each of my next heirs one English guinea each.

My lands being and laying as follows - in West Augusta. Vizt: 600 acres on Hog Run - 600 acres bought of Francis Purley joining Michael Chrisup's land on Bull Runn - and 600 acres on south side of Middle Island and 600 acres on French Creek.

Likewise a Bill of Sale of a house and lot in Kentucky in Herods Town (sic) half acre in lot and ten acres in out lots - etc. Various notes of hand due by (named) - papers above mentioned left in possession of Abraham Lean at the mouth of Wheeling in West Augusta, in Virginia.

I do appoint my father, James Kerr, in Bedford Co., Pennsylvania and Thomas Brown Sr. in West Augusta, Virginia my lawful executors, etc. Teste - William Poythress - William Daniell.

Norfolk Co., Va. Deed Book 15, page 35(A) -

20 November 1750 - Power of Attorney from Samuel Knight, of the PARISH OF ST. PETER, ISLAND OF BARBADOS, appointing his good friend, Max(Millan) Calvert of the Borough of Norfolk, Colony of Virginia, his true and lawful attorney, etc.
Recorded by Captain Maxmillan Calvert 22 March 1750/51.

Norfolk Co., Va. Will Book 2A (1772 - 1788 original), page 218
(Transcript page 267)

Will of Thomas Dickinson, of the Town of Portsmouth, County of Norfolk dated 24 March 1785, probated 19 May 1785.

15 pds. be laid out to purchase a piece of land near Court Street and a house to be built thereon 24 x 16 and Deed made to my daughter, Sarah Dickinson and her heirs.

To beloved wife, Ann Dickinson, all my lands in Town of (Sunbury? Lunbury?) in County of St. Johns, State of Georgia and all lands that shall hereafter fall to me, also to her my negro wench Dinah and a negro boy, Jack.

Mentions money due him from Mr. McCully Righton and Mr. Thomas Evelich (?) both of City of Charlestown, State of South Carolina.

Mourning rings to both of my sisters -

Nephew Thomas Nelme -

Executors - loving wife and brother-in-law, Robert Thompson.

Witnesses: Thomas Craft - Andrew Kidd - Mort (?) Brian.

NOTE BY CHH: Norfolk Marriages by Wingo, page 20 - 17 July 1783 - Thomas Dickinson and Ann Thompson - Thomas Crafts, Security.

Ibid, page 243 -

Will of William Dudley of Town of Portsmouth, County of Norfolk dated 25 March 1787, probated 21 June 1787.

To dearly beloved wife, Mary Dudley, all my property.

To my only child and daughter, Anne Sheldon Dudley, a certain tract of land in the County of Tipperary and Kingdom of Ireland, which was devised to me by my father, John Dudley bearing date, October 10, 1780.

Executors: My well beloved wife, Mary Dudley and her brother, Moses Bryant, of Philadelphia.
Witnesses: Martin Heily - Christopher Coffin - William Leary.

COMMENT: His widow is very probably the Mrs. Mary Dudley who remarried to James Dickinson, 18 April 1789 (Wingo, page 20) Norfolk Co.

Frederick Co., Va. Superior Court Deed Book 2, page 379 -

Commonwealth of Virginia William Maxwell, Judge of Court of Common Pleas and John Maxwell, a Justice of the Peace of Sussex Co. in State of New Jersey, Greeting -

Whereas Thomas Hamlin and Sarah, his wife, by their certain indenture dated 29 December 1794 have bargained and sold unto Robert Sherrard the fee simple estate of and in a tract of land in the County of Berkeley in the Commonwealth of Virginia (this is now in West Virginia) containing 225 acres etc., etc., and whereas the said Sarah cannot conveniently travel to our District Court holden at Winchester to make her acknowledgment thereof - etc

State of New Jersey, Sussex Co. - 19 May 1795 - certified by William Maxwell, Judge etc. and John Maxwell that Sarah, wife of Thomas Hamlin, acknowledged her full consent to the within mentioned bargain and sale.
Recorded 1 September 1795.

Fairfax Co., Va. Deed Book 1-A (1729 - 1735), page 120 -

5 February 1730/1 - The deposition of Ann Mackfereson (sic) of Stafford Co., aged about sixty-three years (thus born ca 1667/8), the deponent being duly sworn sayeth that Frances Golbee came to her and asked her, the aforesaid Ann, whether or no she was the daughter of Francis Warrington's wife, which the aforesaid Ann said she was. Then replyed Frances Golbee, you are my own cousin for your mother and my mother is (sic) two sisters. The deponent further says that her mother which was then Warrington's wife, but sometime before had been the wife of John Martin,

deceased, informed her several times that Frances Golbee was her own sister's child and the deponent further declareth that the aforesaid Frances Golbee, which was afterwards the wife of Thomas White, deceased always acknowledged Warrington's wife to be her aunt and further the deponent sayeth not. (Ann Mackfereson signs by her mark "X".)
Recorded same day.

Ibid, page 120-121 -

5 February 1730/1 - The deposition of Mary Reynolds, of King George Co., aged about ninty-one years (thus born ca 1639/40) the deponent being duly sworn sayeth that Frances Golbee, afterwards wife of Thomas White, deceased, informed her about thirty years ago (i.e. about 1700) that she had heard that Francis Warrington's wife, who sometime before was the widow of John Martin, deceased, was her kinswoman and desired the said Mary Reynolds to go with her, the said Frances Golbee, to know the certainty, whether or no Warrington's wife was related to her, which the said Mary did and when they came to Warrington's house, Warrington's wife, after some discourse with the aforesaid Frances Golbee concerning the place of their nativity; Frances Golbee asked Warrington's wife if she know such a woman; which the aforesaid Warrington's wife replyed, I did know her very well some years ago for she is my own sister. Then replyed Frances Golbee, you are my aunt; then says Warrington's wife, you are my own sister's child. I, the aforesaid Mary Reynolds, further declare that Warrington's wife, as far as ever she heard afterwards, was went for Frances Golbee's aunt and further the deponent sayeth not. (Mary Reynolds signs by her mark "X".)
Recorded same day.

NOTE BY CHH: I believe, but have not so proven, that "GOLBEE" is a misspelling by the clerk for "GOLDSBY".

Pittsylvania Co., Va. Deed Book 10, page 221 -

5 August 1795 - Thomas Oliver of FAYETTE COUNTY, KENTUCKY gives his Power of Attorney to his mother, Mary Oliver, of Pittsylvania Co., Virginia to claim any negroes which shall be or may be given or left to him by his grandmother, Elizabeth Oliver, after her decease etc.
Proved by witnesses and recorded 21 September 1795.

Norfolk Co., Va. Deed Book 22, page 27-28 - (Lease and Release)

1 December 1763 - Henry Culpeper and Christian, his wife, of COUNTY OF CURRITUCK in the PROVINCE OF NORTH CAROLINA sell to John Rutter of County of Norfolk, Colony of Virginia - 25 acres of land in County of Norfolk, on the south side of Deep Creek, of the Southern Branch of Elizabeth River, which land did formerly belong unto Henry Culpeper and by descent fell unto his son, Henry, being heir at law to the said land, etc.
Witnesses: Thomas Williams - John Williams - Phebe Williams - Sarah Williams.
Recorded 18 October 1764.

Augusta Co., Va. Order Book 6, page 85 –

21 December 1757 – Deposition of Margaret Anderson, who swears on oath, that she was well acquainted with William Francis, of CHESTER COUNTY, TOWNSHIP OF EAST NOTTINGHAM (PENNSYLVANIA) now deceased, and that John Francis, of this county of Augusta (Va) was the eldest male issue of the said William (Francis) by Ann, his first wife, which on the motion of John Francis is certified.

COMMENT: John Francis married Mary Erwin, daughter of Mathew Erwin and Elizabeth, his wife, who died testate in Augusta Co., Virginia (Will Book 3, page 178) in 1762 and who named among seven daughters, "Mary Erwin", alias "Francis" and instructed that John Francis be the overseer of his Will. It is of further interest to note that John Francis was listed as a soldier in Captain John Smith's Company of Augusta County Militia in 1742 (8V279) and appears again on a "Size Roll" of the 7th Company of the Virginia Regiment (Captain J. Lewis) and on which "Roll" it is shown that he, John Francis, enlisted November 5, 1754 – age 35 – planter – 5 ft. 1 inch – and was born in Maryland. It is therefore obvious that his parents, William and Ann Francis, had removed from Maryland sometime after 1719 to Chester Co., Pennsylvania (1V390).

Pittsylvania Co., Va. Deed Book 7, page 128 –

1 January 1783 – Power of Attorney from James Dalton of PITTSYLVANIA COUNTY, VIRGINIA, eldest son and heir and executor of Timothy Dalton, deceased, appointing Nathaniel Williams Esq., of Guilford Co., North Carolina, his true and lawful attorney to take possession of his right and title to land in Pittsylvania Co. and Bedford (?) on both sides of Stanton River where my father Timothy Dalton died and claimed by John Chiles and others by their getting possession and standing a suit for same, etc.
        Witnesses: Randolph Dalton – William Arthur – Joseph Cook.
        Recorded 16 September 1783.

Powhatan Co., Va. Deed Book 1, page 262 –

1 October 1783 – Agreement between Edward Maxey and George Smith – whereas the said Edward Maxey is proprietor of and possessed of land warrants to the amount of 14,218 acres in different warrants one for 10,018 acres and one for 1,800 acres #6819 the remainder of 2,400 acres and which he has committed to the care of George Smith of said county on 22 October (?) – and he, the said Smith being then about to set out for the western country (i.e. Ky.) in order to take up lands and he to receive one half part thereof, etc.
        Recorded 19 August 1784.

Mecklenburg Co., Va. Deed Book 3, page 344 –

30 December 1771 – Richard Wilkins of COUNTY OF GRANVILLE, PROVINCE OF NORTH CAROLINA sells to Alexander Carter of County of Mecklenburg, Colony of Virginia for 75 pds., 80 acres of land in

County of Mecklenburg on the north side of Great Buffalo Creek, etc.
Recorded 13 April 1772.

Mecklenburg Co., Va. Deed Book 4, page 404 -

14 January 1775 - Giles Carter of COUNTY OF GUILFORD, PROVINCE OF NORTH CAROLINA to Robert Carter Jr. of County of Mecklenburg, Colony of Virginia for 35 pds. a tract of land in County of Mecklenburg containing 200 acres on south side of Kieths Branch being the same land the said Giles Carter purchased of Charles Carter and whereon Robert Carter the elder now lives, bounded by lands of Daniel Johnson orphans - Samuel Hopkins - Robert Burton Newton - John Hendrick - Thomas Stephens and James Kidd, etc.
Recorded 13 March 1775.

Henrico Co., Va. Deeds and Wills (1714 - 1718), page 108 -

Last Will and Testament of James LeGrand, dated 20 August 1716; proven 3 September 1716.

"Late of LaHaye, in Holand" (sic) -

To my dear brother, John LeGrand, the one-half of a tract of land containing in the whole 365 acres, being upon the Great Swamp and main run of Swift Creek, joyning (sic) the lands of Richard Womack and Anthony Trabue, etc.

To my dear and well beloved wife, Elizabeth LeGrand, the other halfe (sic) of the land above mentioned and the piece of land where I now live, my said wife to be executrix, etc. (Signature - Jacque LeGrand - Seal).
Witnesses: Bartholomew Dupuy - Forquieran - Moses Levereau - Abraham Salle.

Powhatan Co., Va. Deed Book 7, page 212 -

21 March 1819 - Power of Attorney from William Bentley, of the COUNTY OF POWHATAN, STATE OF VIRGINIA, appointing his worthy friend Joseph T. Allyn, his lawful attorney, the said William Bentley being entitled to certain lots of land in the western country, State of Kentucky for military service as a Captain in the Revolutionary War, etc., the said Allyn to act in his behalf as his representative etc. and do further authorize him to search for the lands of Henry Moss, deceased, who was also a Captain in the Revolutionary War, who by his Last Will, of record in Powhatan Co., bequeathed to me all his property not particularly disposed of etc.
Acknowledged 19 August 1819 and recorded.

Ibid, page 495 -

20 November 1820 - Power of Attorney from Joseph Bondurant and Elizabeth Bondurant, of SHELBY COUNTY, STATE OF KENTUCKY appointing Jeffrey William Bondurant of the same county and

state and Joseph B. Davis and Benjamin T. Davis, of Powhatan
Co., State of Virginia - our true and lawful attornies to act
and collect, recover and receive our full proportion or part
of the negroes, land, and estate of George Davis, deceased, and
the negroes bequeathed to the children of Mary Davis, deceased,
by William Maxey, deceased, etc.
      Witnesses: Seth Cook - Charles Mitchell.
      Certified by Justices of Shelby Co., Kentucky the same day
(stating that Elizabeth Bondurant was the wife of Joseph
Bondurant).
      Recorded Powhatan Co., Virginia 17 May 1821.

Powhatan Co., Va. Deed Book 18, page 465 -

      13 September 1849 - Indenture in which Joshua Flood and
Mary, his wife - Elizabeth Lewis - John Blaydes and Kesiah,
his wife - Richard Radford Sr. and Rebecca, his wife - William
H. Watson and Benjamin Watson, heirs and legal representatives
of Joseph Bondurant, deceased, and Elliott Bondurant and George
W. Bondurant, heirs and legal representatives of Benjamin
Bondurant, deceased, all of the COUNTY OF SHELBY, STATE OF
KENTUCKY, parties of the first part, sell to Jeffrey W. Bondurant
of the County of Oldham, State of Kentucky, party of the second
part - for $1.00 - all that tract of land in the County of
Powhatan, State of Virginia - being the same tract of land conveyed by George Davis Sr. to George Davis Jr., and which land
was inherited by Joseph Bondurant* and Benjamin Bondurant by
the Will of George Davis Jr. of the County of Shelby, State of
Kentucky supposed to contain about 25 acres etc.
      Certified by Justices of Shelby Co., Kentucky and recorded
in Powhatan Co., Virginia 5 November 1851.

*Powhatan Co., Va. Marriages by Knorr, page 8

      15 January 1778 - Joseph Bondurant and Elizabeth Davis,
daughter of George Davis, who is security.
      Witness: George Miller.

COMMENT: The above cited Joseph and Benjamin Bondurant must
have been sons of Joseph Bondurant and Elizabeth Davis of the
above marriage.

Ibid, page 463 -

      26 January 1850 - Indenture in which Jeffrey W. Bondurant,
of the COUNTY OF OLDHAM, STATE OF KENTUCKY, sells to William T.
Davis, of the County of Powhatan, State of Virginia - for $75.00 -
a tract of land in the County of Powhatan (Va.) it being the same
land conveyed by George Davis Sr. to George Davis Jr. and also
being the same tract of land inherited by Joseph and Benjamin
Bondurant by the Last Will and Testament of George Davis Jr. -
which Will is recorded in the Clerk's Office for the County of
Shelby and Commonwealth of Kentucky, it also being the same tract
of land conveyed by the heirs of the said Joseph and Benjamin
Bondurant to the said Jeffrey W. Bondurant by Deed bearing date
13 September 1849, supposed to contain about 25 acres, more or
less, etc.

NOTE BY CHH: The above Deed is also signed by Lucinda Bondurant identified as wife of Jeffrey W. Bondurant.

      Certified by Justices of Oldham Co., Kentucky and recorded in Powhatan Co., Virginia 1 November 1851.

Cumberland Co., Va. Will Book 3, page 249 -

      Will of George Bondurant dated 18 October 1803, proven 27 February 1804.

      As I have never received any part of the estate of Charles Palmore, deceased, I do not conceive it my duty to leave anything now in my possession to my wife, Sally Bondurant.

      I give to my son, Charles P. Bondurant - etc.

      My brother, William Bondurant, my executor.

NOTE BY CHH: It is evident by the above Will that George Bondurant married Sally (Sarah) Palmore, daughter of Charles Palmore. The marriage of his son, Charles P (almore) Bondurant is found in Cumberland Co. Marriage Bonds (DAR Magazine, Vol. 65, page 43) to Caroline E. Smith, with consent of guardian, John R. Palmore, 8 April 1833 (bond).

Powhatan Co., Va. Will Book 5, page 64 -

      Will of George Davis, Sr. dated 15 October 1813, proven 20 March 1816.

      Property to wife but does not name her.

Sons	Daughters	Grandchildren
Samuel - ½ land	Elizabeth	Sally Carter
Benjamin - ½ land	Mary	Lucy Carter
William	Kissey	Joseph B. Davis
Jeffrey		
George *(Jr.)		

      Executors: My sons, William and Samuel Davis and my grandson, Joseph B. Davis.
      Witnesses: Daniel Bass - Benjamin T. Davis - James Smith.

*We have seen by the preceeding records that George Jr. died testate in Shelby Co., Kentucky.

Halifax Co., Va. Deed Book 10, page 191 -

      10 October 1776 - Charles Mulholland of PROVINCE OF NORTH CAROLINA, COUNTY OF ORANGE sells to Addam Gann of County of Halifax, Colony of Virginia - for 50 pds. - a tract of land in the County of Halifax, in Virginia containing 300 acres on the waters of Ann Smith's Mill Creek etc.
      Witnesses: Thomas Carter - Micager (sic) Snead - William Dye.

34

Proved by witnesses 15 May 1777 and ordered recorded.

Halifax Co., Va. Deed Book 12, page 402 -

14 December 1783 - John Gan and Hannah, his wife, of the
COUNTY OF HALIFAX, sell to James Reylye, of the County of Caswell
(State of North Carolina) - for 11 pounds, 10 shillings - a tract
of land in the County of Halifax, Virginia containing 100 acres
adjoining land of Adam Gans, Nathaniel Sims, William More, being
the land the said John and Hannah Gans now has in (their) possession
etc. (Both sign by X).
    Witnesses: John Connally - Jesse Moore - Christopher
Hinton.
    Proved by witnesses 18 March 1784 and recorded.

Ibid, page 405 -

10 December 1782 - John Gan and Hannah, his wife, of COUNTY
OF HALIFAX, VIRGINIA sell to William Moore, of Orange Co. -
(note: may be Virginia or North Carolina) for 50 pds. - 100 acres
of land in Halifax Co., Virginia, on William Lee's line - George
Connally - John Lewis - Nathaniel Sims and John Carter, being
the land John and Hannah Gans now has in (their) possession, etc.
(Signed by both by mark X).
    Witnesses: John Connally - Jesse Moore - Christopher
Hinton.
    Certified by 2 witnesses 17 July 1783 and proven by 3rd
witness 18 March 1784 and recorded.

Halifax Co., Va. Deed Book 14, page 48 -

6 February 1787 - John Gann, of WASHINGTON COUNTY, NORTH
CAROLINA, sells to James Reyley, of Halifax Co., Virginia - for
25 pds. - a tract of land in Halifax Co., Virginia on the waters
of Dan River, containing 50 acres, bounded on lines of Gordon,
the said Reyley and Edmond Bryant, etc.
    Witnesses: Jesse Moore - Vallentine More - Charles Little -
David Little.
    Proved by three witnesses 15 February 1787 and recorded.

Ibid, page 64 -

6 February 1787 - John Gann, of WASHINGTON COUNTY, NORTH
CAROLINA sells to Jesse Moore, of Halifax Co., Virginia - for
25 pds. - a tract of land in said County of Halifax, on waters
on Dan River, containing 50 acres bounded on lines of James
Reyley - Edward Bryant and said Jesse Moore, etc.
    Witnesses: James Reyley - Charles Little - David Little -
Valentine More.
    Proven and recorded 15 February 1787.

Pittsylvania Co., Va. Deed Book 16, page 104 -

15 August 1808 - Indenture in which Pierce B. Pannill and
Elizabeth, his wife, of the COUNTY OF CASEY, STATE OF KENTUCKY,
of one part, sell to Joseph Morton, of the County of Pittsylvania,

State of Virginia - for $1,133.00 - a tract of land in
Pittsylvania Co. on the north fork of Sandy River containing
200 acres, which land the said Pierce B. Pannill purchased of
Daniel Johnson and also another tract of land containing 150
acres, on Hutchinson's Branches which the said Pannill also
purchased from Daniel Johnson, etc.
  Witnesses: William F. Golden - Richard B. Beck.
  Acknowledged in Pittsylvania Co. Court by the said Pierce
B. and Elizabeth Pannill to be their Act and Deed and ordered
recorded.

NOTE BY CHH: Pierce Butler Pennell (Pannill) was a Revolutionary
War soldier who served in the Bedford Co., Virginia Militia in
1781-1782. He was probably born about 1753 by other records.

Ibid, page 107 -

  1 August 1808 - Power of Attorney from Ezekiel Murphy, of
the COUNTY OF RUTHERFORD, STATE OF TENNESSEE in which he appoints
his trusty friend, James Blackley, of Pittsylvania Co., Virginia
his attorney to sell for him a tract of land in Pittsylvania Co.,
Virginia on both sides of Long Branch and Pole Bridge Branch
containing by patent 272 acres and also another tract joining
the above lands etc.
  Witnesses: Benjamin Thomas - Edward W. Smith - John (?) -
Smith Fulton - James Fulton.
  Proven by witnesses 15 August 1808 (by affirmation of James
Fulton) and ordered recorded.

Prince Edward Co., Va. Deed Book 11, page 76 -

  3 April 1797 - Power of Attorney from George Moore, of
COUNTY OF PRINCE EDWARD, VIRGINIA appointing Bryant Ferguson,
of the County of Fayette, State of Kentucky his true and lawful
attorney to sell for him a tract of land containing 1,000 acres
granted him by patent dated 29 April 1788, in County of Fayette,
Kentucky on waters of the North Fork of Licking adjoining land
of Joseph Moore, etc.
  Recorded 19 June 1797.

Henrico Co., Va. Deed Book 6, page 85 -

  30 December 1800 - John Payne of the County of Henrico
and William G. Payne, of the County of Monongahalia (now West
Virginia) of one part, sell to Robert Priddy of the County of
Henrico - for 700 pds. - a tract of land in Henrico Co. con-
taining 418½ acres, it being the tract of land owned by us and
bought by Frances Payne of Julius Curle etc.
  Witnesses: James Mann - John C. Payne - Zachariah Toler -
Jesse Payne - John Wade.
  Recorded 3 February 1801.

Pittsylvania Co., Va. Deed Book 11, page 391 -

  12 December 1798 - William Maples of the COUNTY OF JEFFERSON,
STATE OF TENNESSEE sells to Robert Adams - for 20 pds. - a tract

of land in the County of Pittsylvania, Virginia, on the branches
of Strawberry Creek, containing 126 acres by survey etc.
    Witnesses: Joseph Carter - Josiah Maples - John Long.
    Proved and recorded 17 December 1798.

NOTE BY CHH: This 126 acres was a land grant to John Long and
William Maples (the younger) dated 3 December 1796 (Book 36,
page 200).

Pittsylvania Co., Va. Deed Book 20, page 20 -

    6 October 1815 - Indenture in which Thomas Chattin - John
Chattin - Joseph Chattin - Ephraim Giles and Nancy, his wife
(late Nancy Chattin) - Silvanus A. Vaden and Polly, his wife
(late Polly Chattin) - Bazel Nelson and Elizabeth, his wife
(late Elizabeth Chattin) - all of the County of Pittsylvania,
and William Williams and Sally, his wife, (late Sally Chattin)
of the County of Tazwell, in Virginia - and Harris Adams, of
the County of Clark, and State of Kentucky, heirs of John
Chattin, deceased, of one part - sell to Wesley Shilton, of
County of Pittsylvania, Virginia of the other part - for
$1,016.00 - a certain tract of land in the County of Pittsylvania
on the north side of Banister River, containing 253 acres, more
or less, etc.
    Witnesses: Thomas H. Clark - Will Tunstall - William Holt.
    (Several certifications by several justices of the several
counties, etc.)

Ibid, page 291 -

    16 July 1816 - Indenture in which Basel Nelson and Elizabeth,
his wife, of the COUNTY OF MONTGOMERY, STATE OF TENNESSEE sell
to Thomas Chattin of the County of Pittsylvania, State of Virginia
for $400.00 - a certain tract of land in County of Pittsylvania,
Virginia containing 174 acres which land was heretofore conveyed
by John Chattin to Basel Nelson, etc.
    Certified by Justices of Montgomery Co., Tennessee and
recorded Pittsylvania Co., Virginia 17 February 1817.

NOTE: Abstracts of original records in my files prove the above
Basil Nelson (Junior) as the son of Basil Nelson Sr., who was
the son of Ambrose Nelson (died testate 1799 in Pittsylvania Co.,
Virginia.

Pittsylvania Co., Va. Deed Book 12, page 295 -

    18 April 1801 - Indenture in which James Nelson, of
PITTSYLVANIA COUNTY, VIRGINIA sells to Matthew Moor (sic) of
Stokes Co., North Carolina - for 40 pds. - a tract of land in
Pittsylvania Co. containing 100 acres being part of a survey
of 166 acres granted by patent to the said James Nelson, dated
7 August 1788, on Lawless Creek etc.
    Acknowledged in Court 20 April 1801 and recorded.

Pittsylvania Co., Va. Deeds and Wills 10, page 442 -

    13 October 1795 - Indenture in which Benjamin Twedel and

Silas Twedel of COUNTY OF PITTSYLVANIA, VIRGINIA, of one part,
sell to James Nelson, of County of Stokes, State of North Carolina -
whereas William Twedell, in his lifetime published his Last
Will and Testament dated 8 February 1794 whereby he did give
and devise to his wife, Abigail, the land on which he lived
containing 200 acres during her natural life and then to his
son, Benjamin (party to these presents) and reversion to his
son Silas, and the said James Nelson, having contracted and
agreed with the said Silas Twedell for the purchase of said
land, do sell him for 70 pds., 210 acres etc.
    Witnesses: W. Wright - Ezekiel Russell - Thomas McNeely -
Robert Wright.
    Proven by witnesses 15 February 1796 and further proven
18 July 1796.
    Certified and recorded 19 September 1796.

NOTE BY CHH: William Twedle made his Will in Pittsylvania
Co., Virginia 8 February 1794; proved 16 June 1794 (Deeds and
Wills 10, page 6) and named therein his wife Abigail - his sons:
Benjamin - Silas - William - and John. He also bequeathed pro-
perty to his son-in-law, James Nelson, and appointed him one of
his executors.

Pittsylvania Co., Va. Deed Book 33, page 49 -

    22 July 1831 - Indenture in which William B. A. Nelson
and Susanna, his wife, of the COUNTY OF LINCOLN, STATE OF
MISSOURI, sell to Thompson Robertson, of the County of
Pittsylvania, State of Virginia - for $150.00 - a tract of land
containing 120 acres in the County of Pittsylvania, on both
sides of Mill Creek, being the same tract of land laid off by
commissioners appointed by the Court to Susanna Shelton, the
daughter of Benjamin Shelton, deceased, who has since intermarried
with the aforesaid William B. A. Nelson, etc.
    Certified by Justices of County of Lincoln, State of Missouri
22 July 1831 and recorded Pittsylvania Co., Virginia 19 September
1831.

Pittsylvania Co., Va. Deed Book 35, page 172 -

    28 February 1833 - Indenture in which Samuel Nelson and
Abraham Landers, Executors of James Nelson, deceased, of CASWELL
COUNTY, NORTH CAROLINA, of one part, sell to John Terry Crain,
of County of Pittsylvania, State of Virginia - agreeable to the
Last Will and Testament of James Nelson, deceased, for $213.90 -
a tract of land in Pittsylvania Co., adjoining land of Jeduthan
Carter - Freeman - John Kirby - Thomas Cusins - James Sawyer Sr. -
and others - on the head branch of Fall Creek containing 186
acres etc.
    Proven by witnessess 15 July 1833 and recorded.

Charlotte Co., Va. Deed Book 17, page 102 -

    29 November 1824 - Power of Attorney from Alexander Rudder,
of the COUNTY OF CHARLOTTE, STATE OF VIRGINIA, to Edward Rudder
Sr. of the same county, to recover of Samuel Sparrill, Administrator
of Samuel Rudder, deceased, of Tyrrell Co., North Carolina,

38

"my full proportion of the sale of the land whereof Samuel
Rudder died possessed of lying in the County of Tyrell, North
Carolina." etc. (Signed by Alexander Rudder Sr.)
Witnesses: Jennings M. Jeffress - Henry Robertson - Francis
Barnes Jr.
Recorded 6 December 1824.

Marriages of Charlotte Co., Va. by Knorr - page 74

23 December 1793 (bond) - Samuel Rudder and Rebecca Brown.
Surety, Burwell Brown. Married 24 December (1793) by Rev. Thomas
Dobson.

Fauquier Co., Va. Deed Book 12, page 304 -

23 May 1795 - James Dunlop, of the STATE OF MARYLAND, to
Rhodam Rogers, of the County of Fauquier, Virginia - rents and
leases a lot of land in County of Fauquier (#14) on Little
River - containing 158 acres - for the space and term of the
natural lives of said Rhodam Rogers, his wife, Mildred, and son,
Rhodam Rogers Jr.
Witnesses: John P. Harrison - William Metcalfe - Thomas
Weeks - James Weeks.
Proven and recorded 28 September 1795.

Ibid, page 382 -

10 July 1795 - William Metcalfe and Elizabeth, his wife,
of the COUNTY OF FAUQUIER sell to Joseph Rice, of the Town of
Baltimore, State of Maryland - for 732 pds. - that tract of land
in County of Fauquier, on Hunger Run, Waters of Little River -
containing 434 acres, etc.
Witnesses: James Hennen - Joshua Ownes - Thomas Jett.
Recorded 28 December 1795.

Albemarle Co., Va. Deed Book 9, page 140 -

(-) September 1785 - Andrew Trible, of the COUNTY OF LINCOLN
(KENTUCKY) sells to David Humphrey, of County of Albemarle, in
Virginia - for 175 pds. - a tract of land in the County of
Albemarle containing 174¾ acres etc.
Acknowledged by Andrew Trible September Court 1785 and
ordered to be recorded.

NOTE BY CHH: Rev. Andrew Tribble, born March 22, 1741 died
December 30, 1822 (Gravestone marker in old Tribble Graveyard,
4 miles north of Richmond, Madison Co., Kentucky). He married
in 1768, Orange Co., Virginia, Sarah Ann Burrus, born September 3
1753 Orange Co., Virginia, died December 15, 1830, daughter of
Thomas and Frances Burrus. (See "They Went Thataway", Vol. 3,
pages 47, 48 by C. H. Hamlin.

Norfolk Co., Va. Deed Book 13, pages 60-61 -

19 February 1742 - John Dickinson and Sarah, his wife, of
NORTH HAMPTON COUNTY OF NORTH CAROLINA - sell to William Manning
of Norfolk Co., Colony of Virginia - for 16 pds. - 40 acres of

land in Norfolk Co. - on Julians Creek - adjoining the land the said William Manning now lives on, etc.
Witnesses: Malachy Manning - Edward Grant - Mathew Manning - William Waller (?).
Recorded 18 March 1742/3.

Norfolk Co., Va. Deed Book 34, page 30 -

15 October 1792 - Cornelius Calvert Jr., of the COUNTY OF PRINCESS ANNE, VIRGINIA sells to Elisha Dickinson and Mathias Aydelotte, of the State of Delaware - for 47 pounds, 2 shillings - 157 acres of land in County of Norfolk near the head of New Mill Creek, etc.
Acknowledged 15 October 1792 and ordered to be recorded.

Ibid, page 34 -

23 May 1792 - John Murden Jr. and Elizabeth, his wife, of COUNTY OF HALIFAX, STATE OF NORTH CAROLINA, sell to Andrew Martin, of the County of Norfolk, State of Virginia - for 150 pds. - a tract of land in County of Norfolk, Parish of St. Brides, containing 220 acres - being part of a tract called the Reeds; 50 acres of the tract conveyed being devised by John Hopkins to his daughter, Elizabeth Murden, from whom it descended to her son and heir, the aforesaid John Murden - 100 acres were devised by Jeremiah Murden to the said John and the remaining 70 acres were devised by said Jeremiah to Edward Murden, who conveyed it to the said John Murden. Mentions a decree of court dividing the land of Jeremiah Murden.
Proved 17 December 1792.

Lunenburg Co., Va. Deed Book 11, page 124 -

7 March 1768 - Drury Allen of COUNTY OF GRANVILLE, PROVINCE OF NORTH CAROLINA sells to Isaac Brizendine, of the County of Lunenburg and Government of Virginia - for 70 pds. - a tract of land in Lunenburg Co. on the head branches of Couches and Tucking Creeks - containing 300 acres - being part of a quanity of 404 acres, etc.
Witnesses: Lyddal Bacon - Anthony Street - Allen Stokes.
Acknowledged 11 March 1768 by Drury Allen and Elizabeth, his wife, relinquished her right of dower and ordered to be recorded.

Frederick Co., Va. Deed Book 44, page 161 -

22 January 1821 - Power of Attorney from Joseph Berry Sr. and Joseph Berry Jr, of the COUNTY OF MASON, STATE OF KENTUCKY appointing our friend, William Kennon, of Fleming Co., Kentucky, our lawful attorney and agent to receive in our names any estate to which we may be entitled to or have claim to in the State of Virginia or elsewhere as heirs at law or devisees of Thomas Berry, deceased, and William Berry, deceased, or either or both of them.
Acknowledgement of above certified by Justices of Mason Co., Kentucky same day and recorded in Frederick Co., Virginia 13 April 1821.

NOTE BY CHH: Identification of the above individuals is to
be found in the Will of Thomas Berry, of Frederick Co., Virginia
(Will Book 10, page 393) dated 20 February 1806 - probated
4 March 1819 in which, among other legatees, he names the above
Joseph Sr., as 'son'; Joseph Jr. as 'grandson'; William Kennon
as 'son-in-law' (married his daughter, Sally); and William Berry
as 'son'. In addition to the above, he also named another son,
Samuel Berry, and daughter, Peggy Rankins, wife of Col. Robert
Rankins; Jane, wife of John Kercheval and grandchildren, Fanny
Kennon - Matilda Kercheval, Thomas B. Kercheval, Lewis C. Kercheval
and Samuel Berry, son of my son, Joseph Berry (Sr.).

Frederick Co., Va. Deed Book 31, page 180 -

4 April 1808 - William Wilson, of COUNTY OF BERKELY (NOW
WEST VIRGINIA) Jacob Jenkins and John Jenkins, of the COUNTY
OF HAMPSHIRE (NOW WEST VIRGINIA), Executors of the Last Will
of Joseph Berry, late of said County of Hampshire (now West
Virginia), deceased, sell to David Rees (?) - for $1.00 - a
tract of land on Sleepy Creek, in County of Frederick, Virginia,
formerly sold to John Berry, deceased, the father of the said
Joseph Berry, deceased, 4th April 1786 - and bequeathed by Will
of said John Berry, deceased, to his said son, Joseph Berry,
deceased, who by his Last Will ordered the same to be sold,
which part of 170 acres is to David Rees, etc.
    Recorded 5 September 1808.

NOTE BY CHH: The Will of the above cited John Berry is to be
found in Frederick Co., Virginia Will Book 6, page 499, dated
6 October 1792, probated 31 March 1800 (more later).

Frederick Co., Va. Deed Book 27, page 685 -

25 March 1802 - Articles of Agreement between Patience
Berry, of FREDERICK COUNTY, VIRGINIA and Joseph Berry, of
HAMPSHIRE COUNTY (NOW WEST VIRGINIA). (This is a land trade,
of the dower left Patience by Will of her husband and she is to
receive maintainence for life, stock, furniture, etc.)
    Recorded 7 December 1802.

NOTE BY CHH: John Berry dated his Will in Frederick Co.,
Virginia 6 October 1792, recorded 31 March 1800. His legatees
were his wife, Patience - sons, Joseph, Samuel, David, John,
Aaron and daughters, Lydia Berry, Margaret Tucker, and Patience
Dick. Frederick Co. Marriages by Davis - July 21, 1791 Margaret
Barry (sic) married Joseph Tucker - May 12, 1789, Patience Berry
married Charles Dick.

Frederick Co., Va. Deed Book 16, page 642 -

Indenture sexpartite dated 30 November 1774 by George Mercer,
of Colony of Virginia, Esq., but now of the City of London, of
one part - Richard Gravatt of City of London, of second part -
Mary Wroughton, of the City of Bath, spinster, of third part -
John Taylor and George Washington, of Colony of Virginia, of
fourth part - attorneys in fact for the said George Mercer-

Richard Gravatt and Mary Wroughton - James Hunter and Charles
Dick, of Colony of Virginia, Esq., of the fifth part and Benjamin
Berry, of Frederick Co., son of Henry Berry, late of King George
Co., of the sixth part - etc. (concerns the various mortgages
on 6500 acres of land, of which Benjamin Berry purchased 2 tracts
of 560 acres for 272 pds. and proceedure to give him a full and
clear title etc.
    Recorded 6 December 1774.

Frederick Co., Va. Deed Book 18, page 244 -

    13 November 1775 - Benjamin Berry of COUNTY OF FREDERICK
PROVINCE (sic) OF VIRGINIA sells to Elisha Williams of the
COUNTY OF FREDERICK, PROVINCE OF MARYLAND, for 20 pds., the
remainder of a lot of land (#15) being part of a tract formerly
the property of George Mercer, on Shenandoah River - containing
160 acres, etc.
    (A Benjamin Berry and a Thomas Berry are witnesses.)
    Recorded 5 March 1776.

NOTE: Ibid, page 246 - the same day (13 November 1775) Benjamin
Berry sells to James Alnutt, of Frederick Co., Maryland - for
316 pds. - all that lot of land (#13) late the property of Col.
George Mercer, containing 400 acres in County of Frederick,
Virginia, etc.
    Recorded 5 March 1776.

Montgomery Co., Va. Deed Book "B", page 507 -

    12 August 1801 - Barbary Wigle, widow and relict of John
Wigle, deceased, of the COUNTY OF JEFFERSON, STATE OF KENTUCKY,
sells to John Crow of the County of Montgomery, State of Virginia -
for $20.00 her right of dower, as widow to the said John Wigle,
deceased, in a tract of land in Montgomery Co. adjoining land of
the said John Crow and others, etc.
    Certified by Worden Pope, Clerk of County Court of Jefferson,
State of Kentucky 14 August 1801 and recorded Montgomery Co.,
Virginia March Court 1802.

NOTE: Deed Book "D", page 370 - 7 October 1806 - Adam Wygal -
Sebastian Wygal - James Miller and Peggy, his wife, (formerly
Wygal) Meredith Rains and Mary, his wife (formerly Wygal) and
Thompson Farmer, (in right of his wife, Catharine, now deceased)
children and heirs of John Wygal (Waghill) sell a tract of land
to John Crow containing 91 acres by survey dated 9 March 1774, etc.
    Recorded October Court 1806.
    John Wygal later sells his portion of this land to John
Crow (Deed Book "D", page 415) and in Deed Book "E", page 67
dated 2 October 1810, Anne Christina Wiley, daughter and co-heiress
of John Wygal, deceased, of the County of Garrett, State of
Kentucky, sells her portion or share of the 91 acres to John
Crow (Anna Christina signs her name by her mark (X) as "Wylie".)
    Recorded December Court 1810.

Fluvanna Co., Va. Deed Book 7, page 251 -

    27 May 1818 - Indenture in which Jesse Hatton, of the TOWN

OF MOBILE, TERRITORY OF ALABAMA, sells to John R. Perkins -
William Pasteur - John Winn - John Johnson Jr. - of the County
of Fluvanna, State of Virginia - for $400.00 - all that tract
of land in the said County of Fluvanna, on Mechunk Creek, a
water of the James River, containing 300 acres, purchased by
the said Jesse Hatton 2nd December 1817 from James McCally and
Reuben Jaes, etc.
    Witnesses: Thomas W. Glass - Reuben Martin - Abraham
Applebury.
    Proved by witnesses 25 January 1819 and ordered to be re-
corded.

Mecklenburg Co., Va. Deed Book 10, page 140 -

    3 January 1800 - Indenture in which Secretary Carter of
COUNTY OF OGLETHORPE, STATE OF GEORGIA and Henry Fleeman (sic)
and Mary Fleeman (sic) of the County of Granville, State of North
Carolina, parties of one part sell to Christopher Haskins of
County of Mecklenburg in Virginia - for 189 pds. - a tract of
land in Mecklenburg Co. on the south side of Kieths Branch con-
taining 200 acres adjoining lands of John Johnson - Jonathan
Tanner - John Kendrick - Robert B. Newton and the orphans of
John Johnson Sr., deceased, etc.
    Recorded 11 January 1800.

COMMENT: The names of Henry and Mary are in other records as
"Freeman". Mary Freeman was named in Will of Thomas Carter
(D 1796) as his daughter and Secretary Carter as his grandson
(son of his deceased son, Robert Carter).

Wythe Co., Va. Deed Book 18, page 535 -

    10 November 1849 - Indenture in which Moses B. Lloyd and
Matilda, his wife - Nancy R. Hoge - Moses H. Hoge - and John
M. Hoge - executors of the Will of John Hoge, deceased, of
Pulaski Co., Virginia - and John Peterman and Jane R., his
wife, of Montgomery Co., Virginia - William P. Hickman and
Margaret, his wife, of the County of Wythe, Virginia - and
Dugald McIntyre and Rebecca, his wife, of the County of Montgomer
State of Indiana, parties of the first part, sell to David Graham
of Wythe Co., Virginia - for $3,000.00 - a tract of land in the
County of Wythe, containing (by survey for John Hoge, deceased,
11 August 1837) 420 acres, etc.

NOTE: Also included in the above Deed is mention of Eliza A.
Long as entitled to a one-sixth portion by Will of John Hoge,
deceased.
    All signatures certified by Justices of various counties
of residence as given above.
    Recorded Wythe Co., Virginia 11 March 1851.

Montgomery Co., Va. Marriages (Photostat of Original), page 234

    19 December 1832 (Bond) - Dugald McIntyre and Rebecca S.
Hoge - daughter of John Hoge - William H. Howe and Moses B.
Lloyd, Security and witness - (page 390) married 20 December
1832 by John H. Wallace, Minister, who calls him Rev. Dugald
McIntyre.

Isle of Wight Co., Va. Deed Book 8 (1747-1752), page 42 -

    8 December 1747 - Thomas Summerell of NORTH CAROLINA sells
to William Cooper at Nansemond County in Virginia, for 12 pounds,
18 shillings - 295 acres in Isle of Wight Co. on the north side
of Nottoway River, being a patent dated 16 June 1744 to Edward
Cobb adjoining John Barnes, John Turner, Cypress Swamp.
    (James Gardner, Thomas Sharp, Witnesses.)
    Acknowledged 10 December 1747 in Isle of Wight.

NOTE BY CHH: Isle of Wight Co., Va. Wills and Accounts #4, page 428
Will of Edward Cobb dated 22 August 1742, proved 27 September 1742
names a son, Edward Cobb, and his well beloved son-in-law,
Thomas Sumerell, among other legatees.

Mecklenburg Co., Va. Deed Book 11, page 349 -   (Deed of Trust)

    5 December 1802 - Indenture in which Robert Wright of the
COUNTY OF MECKLENBURG, STATE OF VIRGINIA, sells to Richard Russell,
of the County of Warren, State of North Carolina, and Curly
Langford of the same state and county, the said Robert Wright
being indebted to said Richard Russell in the sum of 89 pounds,
14 shillings, 3 pence, etc. secures debt with a lien on 172
acres of land in Mecklenburg Co., etc.
    Acknowledged 14 March 1803 and recorded.

Powhatan Co., Va. Deed Book 4, page 100 -

    27 October 1809 - Power of Attorney from Francis E. Harris
of COUNTY OF POWHATAN, STATE OF VIRGINIA, "Being about to remove
from this State" appoints John Ford, of County of Cumberland, in
Virginia, his true and lawful attorney, to handle all his business of every sort, etc.
    Witnesses: Peyton Powell - Samuel Hobson - Robert Mosley -
Henry Daniel - L. Mosley.
    Recorded 15 November 1809.

Powhatan Co., Va. Deed Book 11, page 172 -

    19 May 1830 - Power of Attorney from Francis Harris of
COUNTY OF POWHATAN, STATE OF VIRGINIA, appointing John F. Harris,
of the County of McCracken, State of Kentucky, his true and
lawful attorney, to prevent squatters from settling on the land
of me, the said Francis Harris lying in County of McCracken,
Kentucky and to prevent depredations, etc.
    Acknowledged in Court same day by Francis Harris and recorded
and ordered to be certified to the State of Kentucky.

NOTE BY CHH: These are two different Francis Harris'es.

Ibid, page 173 -

    26 February 1830 - Francis Harris of POWHATAN COUNTY, STATE
OF VIRGINIA to Chiles Terrell, of Jefferson Co., State of Kentucky,
for consideration of the services rendered by the said Terrell
to the said Harris in the survey and division of lands located

for Colonel John Harris, deceased, of Powhatan Co., Virginia (father of the said Francis Harris) by Green Clay on the waters of the Ohio, in the County of McCracken, State of Kentucky, upon Treasury Warrants, etc., conveys to said Terrell 400 acres of land on the Ohio River, adjoining land of the said Francis Harris - Jordan Harris, etc.

Acknowledged in Court 15 May 1830, recorded and ordered to be certified to State of Kentucky to be recorded there.

Fauquier Co., Va. Will Book 6, page 133 -

Will of Robert Embry, dated 15 June 1815 and proven 24 July 1815.

To my daughter, Sarah Courtney, of Kentucky, slaves (named) - (see note 2).

Whereas my daughter, Elizabeth, died without heirs, her husband to receive nothing further - (see note 1).

Balance of my estate to my son, John Embrey - (see note 3).

(Mentions Walker, son of John - John Thompson Embrey, son of John - Albert G. Embrey, son of John, all underage and also John's daughters, not named or numbered.)

Executor: Son, John Embrey.
Witnesses: William Thompson - John Fallen - William Embrey.

NOTE 1 by CHH: Fauquier Co. Marriage Bonds by Chappaliar and Gott, page 37 reveals that Elizabeth Embry, daughter of Robert Embry, married Robert Embry 21 December 1795.

NOTE 2 by CHH: Ibid, page 27 - 22 December 1794, Sarah Embry, daughter of Robert Embry, married James Courtney.

NOTE 3 by CHH: Ibid, page 37 - 21 December 1795 John Embry married Elizabeth Homes, daughter of Edmund Homes and 23 May 1803, John Embry married Anne Walker, Solomon Walker, bondsman.

Frederick Co., Va. Superior Court Will Book 3 (1815-1830), page 21

Last Will and Testament of Lawrence Augustine Washington, dated 30 October 1823 and proven March Term 1824.

States that he was formerly a resident of the Counties of Jefferson and Frederick and lately of Mason, but now of Ohio, in the State of Virginia.

Wife - Mary Dorcas Washington.

Legacies to his underage children (male and female) but does not name or number them.

Frederick Co., Va. Superior Court Will Book 4 (1830-1859), page 6

Last Will and Testament of John Barrow of HIGHLAND COUNTY,

STATE OF OHIO, dated 18 September 1830 and proven April Term 1832.

Wife - Elizabeth.

Sons:
Ezra
Elias
Thomas
John (Jr.)
Randolph

Daughters:
(Mrs.) Elizabeth Pugh
(Mrs.) Jane Thompson

Executors: Sons, Ezra and Elias Barrow.

Certified by Clerk of Highland Co., Ohio.

Ezra Barrow certifies before an associate Judge of Highland Co., Ohio that he has settled with Jane Thompson - Thomas Barrow - Randolph Barrow - Robert Pugh and Elizabeth, his wife, (formerly Barrow) and the above named Thomas Barrow, in his capacity of Administrator of his deceased brother, John Barrow Jr., also mentions 11 notes of $100.00 and 1 note of $193.00 due the estate by Eleazer Barrow of Frederick Co., Va. (now dead) to the testator, John Barrow (deceased) and which were part of the assets of the said estate, etc. (Dated 11 September 1833).
Recorded 29 November 1833.

Northumberland Co., Va. Record Book 19 (1811-1815), page 1 -

2 January 1811 - John Yerby and Mary, his wife, of George Town (sic) District of Columbia, sell to Charles Haydon, of the County of Northumberland, State of Virginia - for $800.00 - 200 acres of land in the County of Northumberland, being the land the said John Yerby heired by and under his deceased father's Will, recorded in the County Court of Northumberland, bounded on the lands of Mr. Ezekiel Haydon, deceased, (and others), etc. (Mary signs as Mary M. Yerby.)
Witnesses: James Sutton - Hopkins Harding - Stephen Haynie - William Goodridge.
Proved and recorded 12 August 1811.

NOTE BY CHH: Northumberland County Record Book #15 (1794-1799) page 100, has the Will of Charles Yerby dated 15 February 1794; proven 13 October 1794, which includes as his legatees his wife, Judith, and children, Betsey - John - Thomas - Charles and a possible unborn child.

Essex Co., Va. Deed Book 24, page 339 -

28 March 1749 - Power of Attorney from William Moseley, of BEAUFORT COUNTY in NORTH CAROLINA, only son of William Moseley, deceased, who was the son of Benjamin Moseley, the son of Robert Moseley, deceased, of the County of Essex, in Virginia to friend, Robert Brooke, of Essex Co., to recover of Henry Crittenden, of Essex Co., late guardian of the above said William Moseley, the son of Benjamin Moseley, all the estate possessed by said Henry Crittenden, deceased, as guardian, etc.

Frederick Co., Va. Deed Book 25, page 357 -

27 February 1796 - Power of Attorney from Catharine Douglas Sr. - Archibald Douglas - Margaret Douglas - and Catharine Douglas Jr., of that part of the ISLAND OF GREAT BRITAIN called SCOTLAND - appointing Alexander Henderson, of the County of Prince William, Virginia to convey to the heirs of a certain Robert Scott, deceased, late of the County of Fauquier, Virginia - all their right, title and interest in a parcel of land in Frederick Co., Virginia, which was granted by the late Thomas, Lord Fairfax, to a certain James Douglas, formerly husband of Catharine Douglas Sr., party to these presents the 15 day of September 1766, who was father to the afore mentioned Archibald - Margaret and Catharine Jr., etc.
    Witnesses: Archibald Henderson - Andrew Mitchell.
    Certified by and before Andrew Mitchell of the City of Glasgow, Scotland 27 February 1796.

Ibid, page 360 -

15 September 1797 - Catharine Douglas, widow of James Douglas Archibald Douglas, son of the said James, and Margaret Douglas and Catharine Douglas Jr., daughters of the same James Douglas, who was formerly of the Town of Dumfries, State of Virginia, of one part, sell to Charles Robert Scott - Christopher Chinn - Thomas Chinn - Mary I.Chinn and Jannett Withers, heirs of Robert Scott, late of the County of Fauquier, deceased - a tract of land in Frederick Co., Virginia granted 15 September 1766 by Thomas, Lord Fairfax, to the said James Douglas containing 442 acres etc., by their Power of Attorney to Alexander Henderson, of Dumfries, in the County of Prince William, Virginia, etc. (Brings out the fact that the late Robert Scott of Fauquier Co., deceased, had a brother named William Scott who was the father of the said Charles Robert Scott and a sister named Jannett who intermarried with Thomas Chinn who died leaving the said Christopher Chinn - Thomas Chinn - Mary I. Chinn and the said Jannett Withers, etc.)
    Recorded 30 April 1798.

Orange Co., Va. Deed Book 21, page 143 -

27 September 1794 - John Snell, of the STATE OF KENTUCKY and COUNTY OF SCOTT and Philemon Snell, of the COUNTY OF ALBEMARLE STATE OF VIRGINIA - of one part - convey to Robert Snell, as Executors of their father, John Snell, late of Orange Co., Virginia, deceased, for 300 pds., the tract of land formerly possessed by the deceased John Snell, containing 389 acres, in the County of Orange etc.
    Witnesses: John Williams - Haskew Foster - Catharine Foster Richard Payne.
    Recorded 26 December 1795.

Orange Co., Va. Deed Book 26, page 38 -

1 December 1812 - Richard Roberson and Polley, his wife, of the STATE OF KENTUCKY and COUNTY OF WOODFORD - sell to Thomas Roberson of the County of Orange (Virginia) - whereas John

Roberson, deceased, formerly of Orange Co., Virginia and father
to the said Richard and Thomas Roberson, in the year 1811 died
possessed of considerable property and made his Will dated 8 March
1811 in which he lends his beloved wife, Aley Roberson, his
whole estate, real and personal, during her natural life or widowhood and at her death or marriage, to be divided among his
children named - (seven). The aforesaid Richard sells for 42 pds.
his portion, right, title, interest and claim, etc.
  Witnesses: John Payne - James Jones - William Payne.
  Certified by Clerk of Court of Woodford Co., Kentucky 3 May
1813.
  Recorded Orange Co., Virginia 23 August 1813.

Orange Co., Va. Deed Book 24, page 239 -

  11 May 1807 - Power of Attorney from John Robertson, of
the COUNTY OF WILKS, STATE OF GEORGIA to his friend, John Taylor,
of the County of Orange, State of Virginia to recover and receive
from his brother, William Robertson, Executor of the Will of my
deceased father, William Robertson, property bequeathed to him,
etc.
  Witnesses: John Darracott - George D. Willis - William
G. Gilbert.
  Recorded 28 September 1807.

Bute Co., North Carolina Will Book A, page 105 -

  Last Will and Testament of Thomas Christmas, of ST. MARTIN'S
PARISH, HANOVER CO., VIRGINIA dated 29 December 1768; recorded
Hanover Co., Virginia 7 September 1769; attested copy recorded
Bute Co., North Carolina February Court 1770.

  To son John Christmas (and his son, Thomas) -

  To daughters - Elizabeth Paulett - Catey Higgason -
      and Rachel Chisolm -

  Mentions land purchased of John Flannaken (sic). Son,
Thomas, deceased, his children, namely, John - Mary - Thomas -
Richard - and William (the youngest) - also names Temperance,
widow of Thomas.

  Six grandchildren: Charles Whitlock - James Whitlock - Mary
Jones - Anne Austine - Thomas Whitlock and Nathaniel Whitlock.

  To my five grandchildren, John Sanders - Elizabeth Simms -
Nancy Sanders - Mary Sanders - and Rietter Sanders.

  To John Christmas, son of Elizabeth Paulett -

  Residue in five parts to my four children - John Christmas -
Elizabeth Paulett - Catey Higgason - Rachel Chisholm - and children
of my deceased son, Thomas Christmas, etc.

  Executors: Son, John Christmas and John Higason (sic).
  Witnesses: David Anderson - Richard Higgason - John Higgason.

Halifax Co., Va. Deed Book 25, page 103 -

20 August 1814 - Indenture in which Thomas Stewart - Agnes
Stewart - Elinor Stewart - Leonard Oden and Ruth, his wife -
of the COUNTY OF WARREN, STATE OF KENTUKCY - Robert Fambrough
and Hannah, his wife, of the COUNTY OF RUTHERFORD, STATE OF
TENNESSEE - Rachel Stewart, of the MISSOURI TERRITORY - Robert
W. Stewart, and Rebeckah, his wife, of the COUNTY OF PITTSYLVANIA,
STATE OF VIRGINIA (parties of one part), sell (for $1,276.00)
to William Logan of County of Halifax, Virginia - a tract of land
in Halifax Co. on both sides of Elkhorn Creek, containing 232
acres and being the same land Charles Stewart, by his Last Will,
devised to his three sons, to wit: Robert - Thomas and Charles
(Jr.), which Will is of record in Halifax Co., etc.
        Recorded 24 October 1814.

NOTE BY CHH: The Will of Charles Stuart is to be found in
Halifax Co. Will Book 1, page 302, dated 11 January 1780; proven
16 March 1780. In addition to the three sons named above, he
also bequeathed property to his wife, Agnes, and four daughters,
Rachel - Ruth - Eliner and Hannah.

Halifax Co., Va. Deed Book 1, page 125 -

9 December 1754 - John Stewart of LUNENBURG COUNTY sells
Cornelius Short of Halifax - 40 pds. - 318 acres in Halifax on
both sides of Buffalo Creek, which was granted him by patent
dated 10 February 1748, etc.

Ibid, page 178 -

8 April 1756 - Indenture in which John Stewart of the
COUNTY OF "SOLSBERY" (sic) in SOUTH CAROLINA (sic), sells to
Charles Stewart, of the COUNTY OF LUNENBURG, COLONY OF VIRGINIA -
for 40 pds. - a tract of land in the County of Halifax containing
400 acres, on both sides of Elkhorn Creek, adjoining land of
David Logan, etc.
        Witnesses: James Stuart - John Stuart - Charles Stuart.
        Proved by witnesses 20 May 1756 and ordered to be recorded.

Halifax Co., Va. Deed Book 6, page 308 -

19 March 1767 - Deed of Gift from Thomas Stewart of COUNTY
OF CHARLOTTE, Planter, to Charles Stewart of same county, Planter
for natural love and affection for his said son - conveys a
tract of land on both sides of Elkhorn Creek in County of Halifax
containing 200 acres, being part of a greater tract of 400 acres,
which descended to the said Thomas Stewart as eldest brother
and heir at law of Charles Stewart, deceased, which 200 acres is
at lower end of said tract adjoining lines of John Logan - Robert
Caldwell and James Stewart, etc.
        Acknowledged in Court same day and recorded.

Stafford Co., Va. Deed Book (1722-1728), page 94 -

4 April 1724 - Prior Smallwood, of CHARLES COUNTY, PROVINCE
OF MARYLAND, Gentleman, sells to George Mason, of the County of

Stafford, Colony of Virginia, Gentleman, sells and conveys a tract of land called Cockpitt Point, on the Potomack River, containing 200 acres, for 3,000 lbs. tobacco - (his mark "P").

Witnesses: William Taliaferro - Richard Hubbard - (Power of Attorney to Benjamin Berryman, Gentleman, from Elizabeth, wife of Prior Smallwood, to relinquish her right of dower, etc.) Recorded 8 April 1724.

Hoyts Index of Revolutionary War Pension Applications -

John Darwin, (Abstract) Virginia and South Carolina, S21155.

John Darwin, born 19 March 1755 in LOUISA COUNTY, VIRGINIA, enlisted from that County 2 February 1776 as a private in Captain Thomas Johnston's and Powel's companies, Colonel Mercer, Weadon and Marshall's Virginia regiment.

He was in the Battle of Fort Washington where he was wounded in the arm and at Battles of Brandywine and Germantown. Discharged 3 February 1778.

In fall of 1778, he moved from Louisa Co., Virginia to York District, South Carolina. Served with South Carolina troops; promoted to Captain in one campaign.

Allowed pension on his application executed 22 October 1834 at which time he was living in York District, South Carolina. He died 13 July 1837.

He is the only one of his name found in Revolutionary War Records.

NOTE: 1790 Census of South Carolina, page 30 -
John Dervin - 1 male over 16 (himself)
          1 male under 16 (son)(William)
          4 females (including wife)
(Camden District, York County)

Botetourt Co., Va. Will Book F, page 115 -

Last Will and Testament of Samuel Noftsinger, proved August Court 1839 (signed 11 May 1839).

"Being infirm and of advanced age" -

To my daughter, Elizabeth, who intermarried with Thomas Bilbro, $750.00.

To my grandson, Samuel Noftsinger Howard, of Kentucky, son to my daughter, Elizabeth, $100.00 when he reaches age 21.

To my daughter, Polly Mace, wife of Peter Mace, 100 acres of the land whereon I now live, which she has sold to my son, Isaac, and a Deed to be made to him (she retaining a life interest).

To my son, Abraham, 105 acres, part of tract whereon I live - (his present residence).

50

To my son, Isaac, 100 acres including my dwelling house.

To my daughter, Sally or Sarah, 100 acres, part of land I live on.

To Polly Tabscott, who now lives with me, bed, furniture, flax wheel and cow.

To my two sons, 600 acres of land in the County of Bedford.

Executors: My two sons, Abraham and Isaac.
Witnesses: Ralph Schenck - George Delong - William P. Ferrile - Thomas Armstrong. (Signed by testator in German Script.)

Fairfax Co., Va. Liber B-1 (1746-1750), page 96 -

19 August 1746 - Indenture in which Joseph Dixon of KENNOT TOWNSHIP, in the COUNTY OF CHESTER, PROVINCE OF PENNSYLVANIA, Yeoman, and Mary, his wife, to John Dixon, of New Garden in the said county, Yeoman - whereas the said Joseph Dixon has become lawfully siezed of a certain tract of land by virtue of a Deed from Thomas, Lord Fairfax, Proprietor of the Northern Neck of Virginia dated 1 November 1742 registered in Book E, page 518, in the County of Fairfax, (Colony of Virginia) on a branch of the northwest fork of Goose Creek, containing 670 acres - sell to said John Dixon for 20 shillings the above described tract of land, etc.
Witnesses: Thomas John - Harmon Cox - John Carlton - William Ferrell - Jane Cox.
Proved by the affirmation of Thomas John - Harmon Cox and Jane Cox (Quakers?) and recorded 21 October 1746.

Ibid, page 100 -

19 August 1746 - (same date as above) - Indenture in which James Phillips Jr. of Millcreek Hundred in the COUNTY OF NEWCASTLE upon DELAWARE, Yeoman, and Ruth, his wife, sell to John Dixon, of New Garden, in the County of Chester, Province of Pennsylvania, Yeoman - whereas the said James Phillips is seized of a tract of land duly executed by Thomas, Lord Fairfax, etc. by a Deed dated 21 June 1744 (Book F, folio 174) in the County of Fairfax (Va.) containing 156 acres and also by another conveyance dated 6 April 1742 (Book E, folio 431) situated in the County of Prince William containing 515 acres - to have the two tracts of land, etc. - containing in the whole 671 acres, etc.
Witnesses: Thomas John - Harman Cox - John Carlton - William Ferrall - Jane Cox.
Proved and recorded 21 October 1746.

Fairfax Co., Va. Liber C-1 (1750-1754), page 808 -

Indenture dated 16 July 1754 in which Joseph Dixson, of the COUNTY OF FAIRFAX, Blacksmith, sells to Eneas Campbell, late of St. Mary's Co., Province of Maryland, Planter, for 169 pds., 2 shillings, 9 pence, a tract of land in the County of Fairfax on the branches of Limestone Run, containing 393 acres, which land was granted the said Joseph Dixon 2 July 1731 and registered in Liber C, folio 181, etc.

Witnesses: Thomas Sorrell - John Moss - Thomas Davis - John Mears - Mathew Cartwright.

Proved 17 July 1754 and Susannah, wife of Joseph Dixon, relinquished her right of dower.

Recorded 18 September 1754.

Fairfax Co., Va. Liber B, page 314 -

15 March 1747 - Joseph Dixon and Susannah, his wife, of Fairfax Co., Blacksmith, sells to Isaac Walter, of same county, Weaver, a tract of land in said county containing 313 acres, being part of a tract surveyed for the said Joseph Dixon containing 426 acres - for 20 pds. - which land was granted the said Joseph Dixon 13 June 1744 (Book F, folio 183).

Acknowledged and recorded 16 March 1747.

Fairfax Co., Va. Liber D-1 (1755-1761), page 438 -

21 June 1757 - William Ramsay, of the TOWN OF ALEXANDRIA, COLONY OF VIRGINIA, Merchant, of one part and John Dixon, of the COUNTY OF CUMBERLAND, in the KINGDOM OF ENGLAND, Merchant, of the other part - heretofore joint Merchants and partners, agree to dissolve partnership, etc.

Acknowledged in Court 22 June 1757 by John Dixon and William Ramsay and recorded.

NOTE BY CHH: (Ibid, page 450) 20 July 1757 - William Ramsay and Anne, his wife, of County of Fairfax, Merchant sells to John Dixon, Merchant, of County of Cumberland (England) a tract of land said William Ramsay purchased of Henry Awbery - Francis Awbery and Thomas Awbery, 9 March 1749 containing 1,261 acres and also several lots in the Town of Alexandria, County of Fairfax (consideration being 810 pounds, 7 shillings sterling money of Great Britain) which is actually a Deed of Trust and Mortgage.

Brunswick Co., Va. Will Book 3, page 33 -

Will of Walter Campbell dated (not dated), proven 24 September 1751.

Wife, Tabitha, the negroes I had by her father, which was many, cattle, 150 acres of land and which afterwards shall descend to my sister, Sarah Campbell, in Scotland or Sarah Hogg (or Hagg?) and her and their heirs and assigns forever.

Mentions his lands in Brunswick and Lunenburg to be subject to his debts, etc.

(No witnesses listed).

Widow, Tabitha Campbell qualified as Executrix and gave bond in sum of (? five) thousand pds. with John Wall, Gentleman, her security.

52

Lunenburg Co., Va. Deed Book 24, page 225 -

State of Georgia, County of Washington -
12 December 1816 -

Power of Attorney from Ann Dixon, being heir at law to
part of the estate of Lydal Bacon, deceased, of Virginia and
further that we, Ann Dixon and Henry Dixon, being Executor and
Executrix of the Last Will and Testament of Robert Dixon, deceased,
who was one of the Executors of the said Lydal Bacon and we
(therefore) being as such the only persons authorized to settle
the estate of the said Lydal Bacon, etc., do now ordain, appoint,
etc., our trusty friend, Tilman L. Dixon, our true and lawful
attorney, etc.
Certified by Justices of Washington Co., Georgia and recorded in Lunenburg Co. Court 9 January 1817.

Lunenburg Co., Va. Deed Book 9, page 40 -

8 January 1763 - Robert Dixon, of the COUNTY OF DINWIDDIE,
buys from Stephen Dewey, of the PROVINCE OF NORTH CAROLINA - for
175 pds. - a tract of land in Lunenburg Co. (formerly Brunswick)
containing 588 acres, on Nottoway River - which land was granted
the said Stephen Dewey by patent dated 1 March 1743, etc.
Witnesses: Thomas Jackson - Henry Dixon - Archelaus Carlos -
William Vaughn - (?Nat) Jackson.
Proved and recorded 10 March 1763.

Lunenburg Co., Va. Will Book 7, page 347 -

Last Will and Testament of Elizabeth Gordon, dated 9 August
1816; recorded Washington Co., Georgia 17 November 1817; recorded
Lunenburg Co., Virginia 29 January 1818.

Sons	Daughters	Grandchildren
Thomas Gordon of North Carolina - Lyddal Gordon of South Carolina - Langston B. Gordon, (deceased) of North Carolina - Richard Gordon, of Georgia -	Sarah Hopson - Jane Allen Tucker of Tennessee - Lucy Bruce, of North Carolina - Mary Adkins, of Georgia - Elizabeth Buckannon, of Georgia - Martha C. Tucker, of Tennessee -	Roderick ___ ? (see note)

Mentions the Will of her father, Lyddal Bacon, of Lunenburg
Co., Virginia and her mother, Mary Bacon - son, Richard Gordon,
Executor.
Witnesses: T. Dixon - Kedar Parker - Lea Adkins.

NOTE BY CHH: Refer to Lunenburg Co. Marriages by Matheny and
Yates, page 52 - 22 May 1756 (or 1754?) William Gordon and
Elizabeth Bacon, Spinster. Surety, Nathaniel Bacon. (Ibid)
25 December 1787 a Roderick Gordon, of Lunenburg,married

Susanna Stokes Ellis.

Virginia Marriages by Wulfeck, Vol. 1, page 49 states that Lydall Bacon (born 1719) married 1740 Mary Allen.

<u>Cumberland Co., Va. Deed Book 6 (1779-1790), page 468 -</u>

14 February 1788 - Nathaniel Glenn of the State of South Carolina and County of Union, to Gulielmus Coleman of the State of Virginia and County of Cumberland, for 300 pds., 350 acres in Cumberland on both sides of the double Horsepen Branch, adjoining Thomas Wright, Nathan Womack, James Glen, William Glenn, John Macon.
Elliott Coleman, William Glenn, Robert Glenn, Witnesses. Proved 28 July 1788. (Signed "Nathan" Glenn).

<u>Richmond Co., Va. Wills and Inventory (1709-1717), page 304 -</u>

Last Will and Testament of Robert Paine, dated 16 March 1716/17, proved 3 April 1717 by witnesses Simon Miller - William Sies and Lewis Jones.

To the poor people of Sepulchers Parish in London - money I have in the hands of Mr. William Dawkins, Merchant in London.

To my wife's brother in London, Mr. Henry Williamson, his sister, Elizabeth, and his sister, Jane.

To my goddaughter, Barbarie, daughter of William Carter - To Elinor Carter - To William Carter - To my goddaughter, Barbary, daughter of Samuel Kershavell - To Mr. Owen Jones, one gold ring - To Mrs. Elizabeth Gipson, one gold ring - To my godson, Robert Strother - To David Jones, son of Lewis Jones - To Robert Taylor - To my goddaughter, Mary Tutt - To Halbert Raphell, my boat and oars - All the balance of my estate, real and personal, negroes, plate, etc. to my two loving friends, Francis Slaughter Sr. and Samuel Wharton and they, my Executors.

<u>Loudoun Co., Va. Will Book D (1788-1793), page 24 -</u>

Last Will and Testament of Alexander McIntyre dated 21 October 1788 and proven 15 April 1789.

"of the Town of Leesburg" -

To beloved wife, Jane, whole of my estate, real and personal, for her natural life.

My children to be educated and at a suitable age to be bound to a trade of their choice.

My son, John, already of age - 500 acres located in name of Robert Ferguson by Colonel William Ellzey Jr. and conveyed to me, reference to which may be had in Register's Office of Kentucky.

To son, Robert McIntyre, 500 acres, part of the above described land.

To sons, Alexander and Daniel McIntire, 500 acres, being part of the land bequeathed to my two oldest sons.

My Kentucky land thus devised to my four sons aforesaid of the quantity of 500 acres each, shall be divided equally by some judicious person.

My three sons, John, Robert and Alexander to also have the overplus of my lands on the Western Waters, being 400 acres. To my daughter, Catharine McIntyre, house and lot. To my son, Charles McIntyre, my plantation in Loudoun Co.

To my son, Patrick McIntyre, the house I now live in, etc.

My two daughters, Catharine and Elizabeth -

To my son, William McIntyre, residue of my land.

Executrix: My wife, Jane.
Witnesses: Pat Cavan - James Murdock - Burnett Hough.

Ibid, page 161 -

Inventory and appraisement of estate of Alexander McIntyre, deceased, as per Court Order dated 7 January 1791, includes names and ages of nine slaves. Total 525 pounds, 6 shilling, 0 pence.
Recorded February 16, 1791.

Middlesex Co., Va. Will Book F (1772-1787), page 63 -

Last Will and Testament of Sarah Crisp, of BUCKINGHAM in COUNTY OF MIDDLESEX, VIRGINIA - born on Great Tower Hill and registered at Barking Church, Tower Street, June 29, 1716 as daughter to Peter Crisp and Sarah, his wife.

If any legacies should be left to me by any of my relatives or connections, etc., to be given to Mrs. Joanna Corbin for her many kindnesses and tenderness to me, and the remainder, at her death be vested in her eldest daughter, Betty Tayloe Turbeville, etc.

George Lee Turbeville, Esq., to be my Executor.

Dated 24 February 1783, proved 28 July 1783.
Teste: Edward Ware - Ann Corbin.

Executors Bond 500 pds. - Executor named in Will qualified.

NOTE BY CHH: Gawin Corbin, of Buckingham House, Middlesex
Co., born 29 December 1738 at "Corbin Hall" died July 1779;
son of Colonel Richard Corbin and his wife, Elizabeth (Tayloe),
married 17 November 1762 - his cousin, Joanna Tucker, daughter
of Colonel Robert Tucker and his wife, Joanna (Corbin). Colonel
Robert Tucker's Will, on file in Williamsburg 1769 names daughter
Joanna Corbin. (30V,p312) (Colonial Families, p176) George Lee
Turbeville married 4 January 1782 Betty Tayloe Corbin with consent
of her grandfather, Richard Corbin. (30V,p313)

Chesterfield Co., Va. Will Book 3, page 322 -

Last Will and Testament of John Crisp, dated 2 October
1778, proven - no date listed.

All my estate to my only son, John Crisp, and if he should
die without a lawful heir of his body, then to my two brothers
and my sister in the Town of Estone, Suffolk Co., in England -
i.e., Moses - Samuel and Mary Crisp to be equally divided.

Executors: My son, John Crisp - Robert Donald and John
Osborn.
Witnesses: James Hatcher - David Chockley - Malcolm McLeland.

Ibid, page 342 -

Inventory and appraisement of estate of John Crisp, deceased,
includes names of six slaves - (valuation 218 pounds, 4 shillings,
3 pence). By Order of Court dated September 1782. Returned
8 November 1782.

John Crisp, Executor.

NOTE BY CHH: (Chesterfield Co. Marriages, Knorr, page 37 -)
5 May 1780 - John Crisp and Anne Farmer. Surety, James Turner -
(page 11).

Land Bounty Warrant For Revolutionary War Service - (Originals in Archives of Virginia State Library.)

To His Excellency John Floyd, Governor of Virginia -

Your petitioner, John Ashby, of LIMESTONE COUNTY, STATE OF
ALABAMA, late a Captain of the Continental Line of Virginia,
on State Establishment, represents to your Excellency that he
entered the service as Captain in the 3rd Regiment, of said
line, in July 1776. That while he was in the service, he received a wound which so disabled him as to render him incapable
of active duty and that in consequence thereof, he was placed
on the list of invalid officers and continued in that situation
to the end of the war.

Your petitioner has received no part of his bounty land
and therefore prays your Excellency to grant him an order on the
Register for a Warrant for the same and he will pray, etc.

                              John Ashby
                              (by his attorney)

Petition of the heirs of John Ashby received 26 April 1834. (Notation by the Clerk that the Commissioner reported he is entitled for more than three years service as a Captain in the Continental Line.)

The names of the heirs are listed as follows:-

Children of Samuel Ashby	Children of John Ashby (Jr.)

	Children of Samuel Ashby	Children of John Ashby (Jr.)
Thomson Ashby	Jamison Ashby	William Ashby
William Ashby	William C. Ashby	Mary T. Ashby
Turner Ashby	Maria Chanceller	Lucy S. Ashby
Marshall Ashby	Mary Grantham	Susan Ashby
Martha Withers	Kitty Tutt	Eliza M. Neal
Elizabeth T.	Martha Ashby	
Ashby, Wife	Caroline Ashby	
of Nimrod Ashby		

John Tutt, the husband of
Elizabeth Tutt (formerly Ashby).
Alcinda Ashby, wife of Henry Ashby, deceased.
Gabriel Jones
Polly Lightfoot, formerly Jones.
Betty Hughs, formerly Jones.
Harriett Adams, formerly Jones.
Juliett Jones
John A. Jones
Francis Slaughter Jones
Robert Jones

Fauquier Co., Va. Will Book 6, page 140 -

Will of John Ashby dated 18 January 1812 and probated 28 August 1815.

To son Samuel, (½) or 400 acres on waters of Horner's Fork of the Licking containing by patent 800 acres, also 200 acres adjoining a tract of 500 acres entered in the name of John Marshall near the Kentucky River - both these tracts are in State of Kentucky - also a lot of land in the Manor of Leeds and two negroes.

To my son, John Ashby (½) or 400 acres on Licking in State of Kentucky, adjoining land of his brother Samuel - also a lot of land in Manor of Leeds - also two negroes.

To daughter, Martha Withers - negro, and after her mother's death, 60 pds. in money.

To daughter, Dolly Jones - negro Abraham, and also lend to her two other negroes for her natural life and the latter two negroes then to her children.

To daughter, Elizabeth Tutt - two negroes.

To my three daughters named above, ½ of a tract of land on waters of Licking in State of Kentucky containing by patent

1,693 acres.

    To my son, Nimrod Ashby - two negroes.

    I give and bequeath to my son, William Ashby, negroes Milly and George, also a lott of land in the Manor of Leeds adjoining the land of Nimrod Farrow - 2 cows and calves and 6 sheep to him and his heirs forever.

    To my son, Thomson Ashby, lot of land in Manor of Leeds known by name of My Mountain Plantation - and 2 negroes.

    To my son, Turner Ashby, a lot of land on Goose Creek adjoining Thomas Adams - also 2 negroes, Lewis and Fanny and her 4 children, etc.

    To my son, Marshall Ashby, 6 negroes.

    To my 2 sons, Turner and Marshall, the land I live on after their mother's death - the land I purchased from John Hickman and the land I purchased from John Adams.

    To my 3 sons, Nimrod, William and Thomson, ½ of a tract of land on north fork of Licking in State of Kentucky containing 1,693 acres - the other half devised to the 3 sisters - also all my land on main branch of Licking containing 1,450 acres to be equally divided.

    To my beloved wife, Mary Ashby, for her natural life, negroes Milly - Jook's daughters and her 2 children, Sanford and Edward, and after her death, to my son Marshall - also negroes (9 named and the land I live on).

    Wife - sons, Samuel and Nimrod, my Executors.

Fauquier Co., Va. Will Book 9, page 425 -

    Will of Mary Ashby dated 24 February 1826 and proven 23 May 1826.

Legacies to Sons	Daughters	Grandchildren
Marshall	Martha Withers,	Edwin Thomas Ashby, Son
Nimrod	wife of William	of Nimrod -
William	Withers -	Children of my
Thompson	Elizabeth Tutt	daughter, Dolly Jones,
		deceased, 1/6th
		part of estate -
		Eliza - Mary -
		Samuel - and Martha
		Withers -

    Executors: Sons, Nimrod, William and Thomson.
    Executors refused and Administrator of Estate given to John Tutt with William Ashby and John Ashby his securities.

58

NOTE BY CHH: Fauquier Marriage Bonds, by Chappaliar and Gott, page 5 - 22 February 1768, John Ashby Jr. and Mary Turner - Benjamin Piper, bondsman.

Campbell Co., Va. Will Book 3, page 122 -

CLARK COUNTY, GEORGIA, Last Will and Testament of William Robison, of aforesaid county and state, dated 17 January 1809 and proven in Clark Co., Georgia 6 March 1809.

Bequeaths to his beloved brother, John Robison, two slaves, Toney and Haney, and the land and plantation whereon he now lives, and also one lot of land in the Twenty-fifth District in Wilkison Co., known as lot #91 drawn in his name, etc.

Bequeaths two slaves, Cloe and John, to his beloved sister, Elizabeth Sandies (sic).

Bequeaths 25 cents to the heirs of his beloved sister, Ann Wade.

Executors: Brother, John Robison and William Strong and James Turner.
Witnesses: John Martindale - Arthur L. Simes (sic) and Shadrick Hutson.
Recorded in Campbell Co., Virginia 8 December 1811.

Campbell Co., Va. Deed Book 2, page 261 -

1 December 1787 - Indenture in which John Talbot, of the COUNTY OF WILKES, STATE OF GEORGIA, sells to John Haden, of the County of Campbell, State of Virginia, for 100 pds. current money, a tract of land containing 438 acres in the County of Campbell, in Virginia, on the south side of Otter River, adjoining Haden's land (and others) etc.
Witnesses not listed.
Recorded Campbell Co., Virginia 6 December 1787.

Ibid, page 440 -

21 January 1787 - Indenture in which John Welch, son and heir of John Welch, deceased, and Chloe, his wife - John Booker Hoy, and Mary, his wife, of the COUNTY OF ROWAN, in NORTH CAROLINA - of one part - sell to Anthony Haden, of the County of Campbell, in Virginia - for 140 pds. - a tract of land containing 432 acres, in the County of Campbell on the north side of Seneca Creek and another 32 acres deeded by gift by Samuel Gilbert, deceased, to his daughter Mary Welch, it being the plantation where John Welch lived and died etc.
Witnesses: Samuel Welch - Isham Welch - James Welch - Thomas Hoy - Edward Burton - Jesse Stanley.
Proved by "affirmation" of Samuel Welch and James Welch and Isham Welch.
Recorded 1 October 1789.

Fluvanna Co., Va. Deed Book 2, page 481 -

1 November 1791 - Thomas Rountree and Lottishea, his wife, of the COUNTY OF RUTHERFORD, STATE OF NORTH CAROLINA, sell to Anthony Haden of COUNTY OF CAMPBELL, STATE OF VIRGINIA - for 30 pds. - a tract of land in the County of Fluvanna, in Virginia, containing 25 acres, more or less, on the north side of the north fork of the James River, which land was conveyed by Colonel John Payne, of Goochland Co., to Thomas Rountree by Deed recorded in Albemarle Co., Virginia, etc. (Both Thomas Rountree and his wife sign by their own signatures and seal.)
Witnesses: John Rountree - Sarah Byras - Stripling Byras. Recorded 1 December 1791.

Fauquier Co., Va. Deed Book 40, page 15 -

11 September 1840 - Mary Allison - John Alif and Catherine, his wife, of the STATE OF KENTUCKY - (at present in Virginia) - James Germain and Nancy, his wife, of Fauquier Co., Virginia and John McCanalty and Fanny, his wife, of the same place - of one part - sell to Joseph Blackwell Smith, of Fauquier Co., Virginia - Whereas: by the Last Will and Testament of William Allison, deceased, certain lands in Fauquier Co. were devised to his wife, Mary, during her life and after her death 50 acres thereof to his son, Martin Allison, and the remainder to his 3 daughters, Catharine - Fanny - and Nancy, above named, etc.
Certified before Justices and recorded the same day.

Halifax Co., Va. Deed Book 22 (1808-1811), page 545 -

25 December 1809 - David Marshall and Rebeccah (X), his wife, of WILSON COUNTY, TENNESSEE, sell to Richard Waller of Halifax Co., Virginia for 400 pds., 353 acres in Halifax on the waters of Tinsley's Creek.
Acknowledged 28 December 1809 in Wilson Co., Tennessee. Recorded in Halifax 28 November 1810.

Lee Co., Virginia Deed Book 3, page 393 -

14 April 1818 - Indenture in which Abner Hatfield of the COUNTY OF CLAIBORNE, STATE OF TENNESSEE sells to Philip Nance of County of Lee, State of Virginia - for $100.00 - a tract of land lying and being in the County of Lee, (Virginia) containing 115 acres on the waters of the Lick Branch, etc.
Acknowledged before the Clerk of Lee Co. 24 November 1818.

Lee Co., Va. Deed Book 2, page 468 -

25 August 1812 - Indenture in which Peter Fisher of the COUNTY OF RUTHERFORD, STATE OF NORTH CAROLINA and Tench Cox of PHILADELPHIA, PENNSYLVANIA, parties of one part - sell to Moses Ball of the County of Lee, State of Virginia, of the other part, for 5 pds. Virginia currency, a tract of land in said County of Lee (Virginia) containing 100 acres adjoining land of David Chadwell, Sr. - Robert Preston - Fishers and Coxes land, etc.
Recorded 28 July 1812 (sic) and signed by Martin Beaty, Attorney in fact for Fisher and Cox.

60

Lee Co., Va. Deed Book 8, page 56 -

7 August 1838 - Deed of Gift from John Russell Sr. of
Lee Co., Virginia - for natural love and affection he has and
bears to Peggy Evans of BARTHOLOMEW COUNTY, STATE OF INDIANA -
Ruth Yeary and Faith Orr of County of Lee, Virginia - one hundred
acres of land, it being the same land I purchased of Peter Fisher,
etc.
   Witnesses: Robert W. Wynn - Abraham Crabtree - Job Crabtree.
   Recorded 14 August 1838.

Ibid, page 359 -

21 January 1841 - Jacob Fisher, of the COUNTY OF LIMESTONE
and STATE OF ALABAMA, by John D. Sharp and Elijah Hill, his
attorneys in fact, of one part, sell to Jesse Evans and Peggy,
his wife, (formerly Peggy Russell) - Henry Yeary and Ruth, his
wife, (formerly Ruth Russell) and Alexander Orr and Faithy,
his wife, (formerly Faith Russell), the said females being the
children of John Russell, deceased, and all of Lee Co., Virginia -
$100.00 - $50.00 hereof paid to him and the other $50.00 thereof
paid to his father, Peter Fisher, deceased, in his lifetime,
100 acres of land in County of Lee, State of Virginia, etc.
   Recorded same date.

Lee Co., Va. Deed Book 9, page 25 -

6 September 1841 - Indenture in which Adam Yeary and
Henrietta, his wife, of COUNTY OF CLAIBORNE, STATE OF TENNESSEE,
of one part, sell to Benedict M. Yeary of County of Lee, State
of Virginia - for $75.00 all his right, title, claim and interest
in a tract of land (which he now has or shall hereafter have)
which was devised to Matilda Yeary by her father, Henry Yeary,
so long as she remained a single woman - lying in Lee Co.,
Virginia and also all his interest in one other tract of land
containing 75 acres joining said tract on the south side of
Indian Creek, etc.
   Recorded 28 September 1841.

COMMENT: (Lee Co. Deed Book 2, page 279) - 18 September 1809 -
John Ball of County of Lee by Deed of Gift conveyed to Henry
Yeary of said county - 74 acres, more or less, on south side
of Indian Creek, etc. Further comment: There is certain evidence
that the maiden name of Henrietta (called Ritter) was Morgan.

Lee Co., Va. Deed Book 8 (1838-1840), page 56 -

7 August 1838 - Deed of Gift from John Russell Sr. of Lee
for natural love and affection to Peggy Evans of BARTHOLOMEW
COUNTY, INDIANA, Ruth Yeary and Faith Ourr of Lee Co., and $1.00,
100 acres, all my household and kitchen furniture, livestock,
farm utensils.
   Proved 14 August 1838.

Ibid, page 359 -

21 January 1841 - Jacob Fisher of LIMESTONE COUNTY, ALABAMA,

by John D. Sharp and Elijah Hill, his attornies in fact, sell
to Jesse Evans and Peggy, his wife, (formerly Peggy Russell) -
Henry Yeary and Ruth, his wife (formerly Ruth Russell) and
Alexander Orr and Faithy, his wife (formerly Faithy Russell) the
said females being children of John Russell, deceased, of Lee
County for $100.00 ($50 paid to him and the other $50 paid to
his father, Peter Fisher, deceased). (Same in Deed of John
Russell above.)
    Acknowledged by the attorneys 15 February 1841.

Ibid, page 424 -

    27 September 1841 - Henry (X) Yeary and wife, Susannah (X)
of Lee to Matilda Yeary for $75, all interest in 190 acres devised
to said Matilda by her father Henry Yeary Sr. so long as she remained single.
    Acknowledged 29 September 1841.

Louisa Co., Va. Deed Book H, page 473 - (1783-1785, Reel 5)

    10 March 1785 - Articles of Agreement between Waddy Tait,
of the COUNTY OF CASWELL, STATE OF NORTH CAROLINA, brother of
Zedekiah Tate, deceased, of Louisa Co., Virginia of the 1st part,
and Zachius Tait, of the County of Orange, State of North Carolina,
brother of the said Zedekiah Tait, deceased, of the 2nd part, and
Zephaniah Tait, of the COUNTY OF GUILFORD, STATE OF NORTH CAROLINA,
brother to the said Zedekiah Tait, deceased, of the 3rd part, -
and Joseph Street, representative of Sarah, his wife, sister to
the said Zedekiah Tait, deceased, of the 4th part - and Charles
Snelson, of the County of Halifax, State of Virginia, representative
of Mary, his wife, sister to the said Zedekiah, deceased, of the
5th part and Anthony Winston, of the County of Louisa, State of
Virginia, representative of his late wife Uphan, sister to the
said Zedekiah Tait, deceased, of the 6th part, and Henry Anderson,
of the county and state aforesaid, representative of Mary, his
wife, niece to the said Zedekiah Tait, deceased, brother (in-law)
to the said Zedekiah and John Tait, of the COUNTY OF ORANGE,
STATE OF NORTH CAROLINA, son of Zacharias Tait, deceased, brother
to the said Zedekiah Tait, deceased, representative of his father,
as administrator to his estate, also of his father's orphan
children, Vizt:Sarah Tait - Anderson Tait and Richard Tait, being
guardian to them, of the 8th part and Zephaniah Tait, aforesaid,
as representative for John Tait - Fanny Tait - Sally Tait -
Hannah Tait - Caswell Tait and Anthony Tait, orphan children of
John Tait, deceased, brother of the said Zedekiah Tait, deceased,
being guardian lawfully appointed for them, of the 9th part etc.,
etc. - refers to Will of Zedekiah Tait dated 21 May 1784, County
of Louisa in Virginia (which see) aforesaid heirs appoint
Zephaniah Tait, of the parties hereto their attorney and agent
to settle the estate, etc. The signatures appear as follows -
Waddy Tate - Zacekias Tate - Zephaniah Tate - Joseph Street -
Charles Snelson - Anthony Winston - Henry Anderson - John Taite,
administrator and guardian - Zephaniah Tait, guardian.
    Proved and recorded Louisa Co., Virginia 14 March 1785.

Louisa Co., Va. Will Book 3, page 20 -

Will of Zedekiah Tate dated 21 May 1784, probated 13 September 1784.

To mother, Mary Tate, land devised me by my father John Tate, deceased, for life - at her death sold and divided - my brother's, Waddy and Zaphanial Tate and my sisters, Sarah Street, Mary Snelson and Uphan Winston - and my niece Mary Anderson.

Reserving 1/9 of money to the children of Zacharias Tate, deceased, and another ninth to the children of John Tate, deceased.

My nephews John Tate Street and John Tate Winston -

I appoint my brother, Zephaniah Tate and my friends, Anthony Winston and William (?Terrell - Sorrell - Lovell) Executors

Ibid, page 492 -

Will of Abigail Tate dated 28 August 1784 and probated 8 August 1792.

Sons	Daughters
Robert Tate	Abigail McAlister
	Margaret Tate

Executors: Friends - Garrett Minor - William Quarles

Louisa Co., Va. Deed Book H, page 477 -

10 March 1785 - Articles of Agreement between Zackeus Tait, of the COUNTY OF ORANGE, STATE OF NORTH CAROLINA, son of John Tait, deceased, formerly of the County of Louisa, Virginia, of 1st part - (Zenas) Tait of City of Richmond, Virginia, son of John Tait, deceased, of 2nd part - Waddy Tait, of COUNTY OF CASWELL, STATE OF NORTH CAROLINA, son of said John Tait, deceased, of 3rd part and Zephaniah Tait, of the COUNTY OF GILFORD (sic) STATE OF NORTH CAROLINA, son of the said John Taite, deceased, of the 4th part - Charles Snelson of the County of Halifax, State of Virginia, representative of Mary, his wife, daughter of John Tait, deceased of 5th part - and Joseph Street, of County of Louisa, Virginia, representative of Sarah, his wife, daughter of John Tait, deceased, of 6th part - and Anthony Winston, of county and state aforesaid, representative of his late wife, Uphan, daughter of John Tait, deceased, of the 7th part - and John Tait, of the COUNTY OF ORANGE, STATE OF NORTH CAROLINA, son of Zacharias Tait, deceased, son of the said John Tait, deceased, representative of his father as administrator of his estate and also of his father's orphan children, Sarah Tait - Anderson Tait and Richard Tait, being their guardian, of the 8th part and Zephaniah Tait, aforesaid, as representative for John Tait - Fanny Tait - Sally Tait - Hannah Tait - Caswell Tait - and Anthony Tait, orphan children of John Tait, deceased, being their guardian lawfully appointed, of the 9th part, etc., etc.

Refers to Will of John Tait of Louisa Co., Virginia dated 25 November 1768 (which see) and his wife (and relict) Mary Tait, his ten children, etc., aforesaid heirs appoint Zephaniah Tait their legal attorney and agent, etc.

The signatures of the parties appear as Zacekis Tait - Zenas Tait - Waddy Tait - Zephaniah Tait - Charles Snelson - Joseph Street - Anthony Winston - John Tait, administrator and guardian and Zephaniah Tait, guardian.
Proved and recorded Louisa Co., Virginia 14 March 1785.

Ibid, page 481 -

10 March 1785 - Mary Tait, of County of Louisa, widow of John Tait, deceased, - for 90 pds. - Specie, relinquishes and quit-claims to the legatees of her said husband, her part of said estate and also her part of her son, Zedekiah Taite, deceased, estate, etc.
Recorded 14 March 1785.

Louisa Co., Va. Will Book 2, page 63 -

Will of John Tait of Parish of St. Martins dated 20 November 1768 and probated 11 September 1769.

Wife, Mary - 18 slaves.

Sons:	Daughters:
Zacharias - negro Charles	Mary Snelson
Zacheus - Davey - Rachel	Sarah Tait
Zeneus - Liger	Uphan Tait
John - Jupiter - Aggy	mentions
Waddy - Tom and Cecilia	(my 10
Zephaniah - Boy (Ben) and girl (Keziah)	children)
and 1 rifle gun	
Zedekiah - 412 acres land I live on and Robin.	

Executors: Wife, Mary - son, Zacharias - friend, David Anderson.

Executors Bond 2,000 pds. 11 September 1769 - by Mary Tait with Zacharias Tait, Waddy Thompson, John Hawkins - and James Tait, security. (Note: the inventory included names of 31 slaves).

Louisa Co., Va. Will Book 3, page 507 -

Aron Fontaine and Garrett Minor, examine and approve the account produced to them by Enos Tait, acting executor of James Tait, deceased, and find the said James Tait's personal estate to amount to 646 pounds, 9 shillings, 7 d - etc. The Court will decide what is the widow's part.

We find that Rachel Hesther, daughter of the same James Tait, deceased, died before him, leaving a son, Charles Hesther, now living. We find also that John and Nathan Tait, sons of the said James Tate, deceased, entered into the Continental Army previous to the said James' death and that they have not been

heard from since, in this part of the country and we also find
that the said James Tait, deceased, has seven other children,
Viz:- Uriah - James - Robert - Elizabeth - Cisley - Abigail -
and Peggy.
Returned and recorded 9 July 1793.

NOTE BY CHH: Louisa Co., Va. Marriage Register (1766-1861),
page 5 -
9 September 1772 - Enos Tate married Elizabeth Tate (under 21),
daughter of James Tate. Security and witness, Uriah Tate and
Robert Tate.

Albemarle Co., Va. Deed Book 2, page 88 -

8 March 1755 - Indenture in which Joseph Tate of the COUNTY
OF ROAN (sic) in NORTH CAROLINA sells to John Haden of the
County of Goochland, (Colony of Virginia) for 80 pds. -
400 acres of land, in the county aforesaid - by the side of
the Byrd - adjoining land of John Clark - near the fork of Elk
River - line of Richard Adams - and also one other tract containing
400 acres, in the county aforesaid on the branches of Elk Run
of the Byrd, etc.
Witnesses: Tandy Holman - Archelaus Michell - G. Marr.
Acknowledged and recorded same day and Alice, wife of
Joseph Tate, relinquished her right of dower.

COMMENT: Albemarle Co. was formed from Goochland Co. in 1744.

Loudoun Co. Marriage Records (Fairfax Monthly Meeting (1751-1892)

(Microfilm Reel 93 - Virginia State Library) -

Page 1 - 9 October 1760 - William Pidgion, son of Charles Pidgion
of Menallen Township, County of York and Province of Pennsylvania
and Rachel Everett, daughter of John (Everett) of county aforesaid.

Page 2 - William Ballinger, son of Henry Ballinger, of Frederick
Co., Province of Maryland and Cassandra Plummer, daughter of
Samuel Plummer, of Prince George's Co., Maryland August 3, 1751.

Page 3 - 13 October 1759 - James Brooke (Jr.) of Frederick Co.,
Maryland and Hannah Janney, of County of Loudoun, Colony of
Virginia.

Page 6 - 29 August 1758 - Mahlon Janney, of Loudoun Co., Virginia
and Sarah Plummer, of County of Frederick, Maryland, daughter of
Samuel and Sarah Plummer, of Prince George's Co., Maryland.

Page 7 - 29 April 1761 - Thomas Plummer, of Frederick Co.,
Maryland and Elener (sic) Poultney, of Loudoun Co., Virginia.

Page 9 - 13 September 1762 - Richard Richardson, son of Richard
Richardson, and Mary Pierpoint, daughter of Francis Pierpoint,
both of Frederick Co., Maryland.

Page 10 - James McGrew, of Township of Monalen, York Co.,

Province of Pennsylvania and Mary Ridgeway, of Pipe Creek,
Frederick Co., Province of Maryland 12 December 1760.

Page 11 - 9 April 1761 - Joseph Wright, son of John and Elizabeth
Wright, of Menallen Township, York Co., Pennsylvania and Mary
Farqar, daughter of William and Ann Farqhar, of Pipe Creek,
Frederick Co., Maryland.

Page 13 - 7 October 1762 - Thomas Gregg, of Kennett, Chester
Co., Pennsylvania and Rebeccah Janney, daughter of Jacob Janney,
of Loudoun Co., Virginia.

Page 15 - 18 February 1764 - Samuel Plummer, of Frederick Co.,
Maryland, son of Samuel Plummer and Sarah, his wife, of Prince
George's Co., Maryland and Mary Tucker, of the same place,
daughter of Robert and Lydia Tucker, of Bucks Co., Pennsylvania
(married at Bush Creek Meeting House, Frederick Co., Maryland).

Page 16 - 10 October 1765 - Micajah Standley, of Roannand (sic)
(misspelled for Roane), Province of North Carolina, and Barbara
Walker, of Loudoun Co., Virginia (married at Bush Creek,
Maryland).

Page 18 - 7 April 1773 - Obed Pierpoint, of Frederick Co.,
Maryland and Esther Myres, of Loudoun Co., Virginia.

Page 19 - 31 December 1772 - Samuel Waters, of Frederick Co.,
Maryland, son of Samuel and Artrage Waters, of Prince George's
Co., Maryland, and Susannah Plummer, daughter of Joseph and
Sarah Plummer, of Frederick Co., Maryland (at Bush Creek,
Maryland).

Page 33 - 12 December 1770 - Gideon Gipson, of Linganore,
Frederick Co., Maryland and Hannah Norkles, of Pipe Creek, of
aforesaid county and province.

Page 39 - 1 July 1772 - Joel Wright, son of John and Elizabeth
Wright, of Monalellen Township, York Co., Pennsylvania, and
Elizabeth Farquhar, daughter of William and Ann Farquhar, of
Pipe Creek, Frederick Co., Maryland.

Page 46 - 4 January 1775 - Joseph West Plummer, son of Joseph
and Sarah Plummer, and Mary Taylor, daughter of Thomas and
Caleb (sic) Taylor, both of Frederick Co., Maryland, at the
house of Thomas Taylor, of Menoquesy.

Page 67 - 26 October 1779 - John Pancoast, of Montgomery Co.,
Maryland, and Ruth Nickols, of Loudoun Co., Virginia (at Goose
Creek).

Page 74 - 29 November 1780 - Oliven Rogers, of Hampshire Co.,
Virginia (now West Virginia) and Mary Roach, daughter of Richard
and Hannah Roach, of the County of Loudoun, Virginia (at Fairfax).

Page 77 - 10 January 1782 - Constantine Hughes, son of Matthew
and Elizabeth Hughes, of Bucks Co., Pennsylvania, and Elizabeth
Nickols, widow of Thomas Nickols, deceased; daughter of William

and Elizabeth Janney, of Loudoun Co., Virginia (at Goose Creek).

Page 82 - 27 August 1783 - George Chandler, of Frederick Co., Maryland, and Deborah Brooke, of County of Loudoun, Virginia (at Fairfax).

Page 99 - 2 January 1788 - John Roberts, son of Richard and Mary Roberts, of Frederick Co., Maryland, and Rebeckah Scott, daughter of Jacob and Elizabeth Scott, of Loudoun Co., Virginia (the former deceased) (at Fairfax).

Page 101 - 30 December 1788 - Abraham Griffith, son of Isaac Griffith, of Baltimore Co., Maryland, and Rachel Taylor, daughter of Thomas Taylor, of Loudoun Co., Va. (at Fairfax).

Page 109 - 29 August 1792 - Samuel Hopkins, son of John and Elizabeth Hopkins, of Ann Arundel Co., Maryland and Hannah Janney, daughter of Joseph and Hannah Janney, of the County of Loudoun, Virginia (at Fairfax).

Page 110 - 15 November 1792 - Bernard Taylor, son of Timothy Taylor, late of Newtown, County of Bucks, Pennsylvania, deceased, and Sarah Smith, daughter of Henry Smith, late of Loudoun Co., Virginia, deceased.

Page 111 - 8 November 1792 - Mordecai Miller, of the Town of Alexandria, Virginia, son of Warwick and Elizabeth Miller, deceased, of Chester Co., Pennsylvania and Rebecca Hartshorne, daughter of William and Susannah Hartshorne of Fairfax Co., Virginia (at Alexandria).

Page 112 - 12 December 1792 - Edward Potts, of Loudoun Co., Virginia and Mary Backhouse, daughter of John Backhouse and Mary, his wife, of County of Newcastle, State of Delaware (at Fairfax).

Page 116 - 29 January 1795 - John Brown, son of Isaac Brown and Margaret, his wife (deceased) of County of Frederick, Virginia and Elizabeth Richardson, daughter of Richard and Mary Richardson, of Frederick Co., Maryland at Richard Richardson's house.

Page 117 - 9 July 1795 - George Drinker, of Town of Alexandria, Virginia, son of Joseph and Hannah Drinker, of the City of Philadelphia, Pennsylvania and Ruth Miller, daughter of Warwick and Elizabeth Miller (deceased) of Chester Co., Pennsylvania (at Alexandria).

Page 124 - 2 May 1798 - Parmenas Lamborn, son of Thomas and Dinah Lamborn, of Chester Co., Pennsylvania and Hannah Williams, daughter of William Williams, of Loudoun Co., Virginia (deceased) and Elizabeth, his wife (since married to Benjamin Purdum) (at Fairfax).

Page 127 - 29 October 1800 - Arthur Paxton, of County of Loudoun, Virginia, son of Jacob Paxton, deceased, of the County of

Hunderton (sic), State of New Jersey, and Mary, his wife, and Pamelia Myers, daughter of Elijah Myers and Mary, his wife, of Loudoun Co., Virginia (at Fairfax).

Page 129 - 1 May 1799 - John Pancoast, of Frederick Co., Maryland and Mary Talbott, of Loudoun Co., Virginia (at Fairfax).

Page 134 - 20 November 1804 - James Russell, of Waterford, Loudoun Co., Virginia, son of John and Hannah Russell, of Frederick Co., Maryland and Susannah Janney, daughter of Joseph (deceased) and Hannah Janney (at Fairfax).

Page 144 - 17 June 1815 - Richard Wood, son of William and Mary Wood, (all of Jefferson Co., Ohio) and Lydia Steer, daughter of Isaac and Phoebe Steer, of Loudoun Co., Virginia (at Fairfax).

Page 145 - 6 April 1814 - William Yeates of Alexandria, D. C. and Sarah Caven, of Waterford, Loudoun Co., Virginia (at Fairfax).

Page 146 - 8 November 1815 - Anthony P. Gover, of Alexandria, D. C. and Sarah Janney, of Loudoun Co., Virginia (at Fairfax).

Page 160 - 26 May 1824 - George Harris, of Waterford, Loudoun Co., Virginia, son of George and Susanna Harris (deceased) of Baltimore, Maryland and Sarah Ann Littler, daughter of John (deceased) and Ann Littler, now Ann Moore, formerly of Wilmington, Delaware.

Page 161 - 21 April 1824 - Joshua Russell, of Frederick Co., Maryland and Rachel Steer, of Loudoun Co., Virginia (at Fairfax).

NOTE: Compiler stopped on page 170 - through 1834.

Charlotte Co., Va. Deed Book 15, page 286 -

10 October 1820 - Indenture between Edmund Cheesman Dubois, of the CITY OF BALTIMORE, MARYLAND of the first part and as attorney in fact for Abraham Dubois of the COUNTY OF SUSQUEHANNA, STATE OF PENNSYLVANIA - Charles C. Eggerton and Jane, his wife - Mary Dubois - James S. Dubois - and Susannah, who was the widow of the late Edward Ireland of the said City of Baltimore and Cornelia Smith of the City of Philadelphia, Pennsylvania - and John Woodhall and Sarah, his wife, of the COUNTY OF MONMOUTH, STATE OF NEW JERSEY of the second part and Samuel Baldwin of the County of Prince Edward, Virginia of the third part - for the sum of $1,700.00 - conveys a certain tract of land in the County of Charlotte, State of Virginia, on the waters of Cubb Creek, containing 368 acres and is the land conveyed by William Hill and wife and Thomas Lorton and wife, to Samuel Cheseman by Deed dated 6 February 1793 etc., and will warrant and defend said title against the claims of their heirs, all other persons, and particularly against all persons claiming as heirs of Samuel Cheseman, deceased.

Certified by various Justices of the various cities and states of residences and in a Power of Attorney, some of the heirs identify Samuel Cheesman, deceased, as late of the Town of Petersburg, Virginia.

 Abraham Dubois, of the City of Philadelphia, residing
in the Township of Great Bend, Susquehanna Co., Pennsylvania,
in his Power of Attorney, identifies Edmund Cheesman Dubois,
of the City of Baltimore as his brother and states further that
he is the descendant and heir at law of Elizabeth, deceased,
late wife of Abraham Dubois, formerly of the City of Philadelphia,
deceased.
 Recorded Charlotte Co., Virginia 4 December 1820.

VIRGINIA
ANCESTORS AND ADVENTURERS, VOL. 2

SECTION 2

EXTRACTS FROM THE FILES OF

THE VIRGINIA GAZETTE

   (a) 1752

   (b) 1752 - 1762

   (c) 1766 - 1767 - 1768

   (d) 1772

EXTRACTS FROM THE FILES OF THE VIRGINIA GAZETTE

Files of 1752: Surry County, February 26, 1752

The Subscriber intends (God willing) for England, by the last of June next. All Persons indebted to me, or that have any Demands against me, are desired to ballance accounts.

-- Samuel Peete

Files of 1752: April 7, 1752

By the Committee of the OHIO Company

The several Members of the said Company, in Virginia and Maryland are desired to meet at Mr. Wetherburn's, in the City of Williamsburg on Thursday the 7th Day of May next.

-- George Mason
-- George Scott
-- John Mercer

Files of 1752: JAMES FORBES, who is suppos'd to have lived some where on the South Side of James River, having an estate left him in Britain, as tis suppos'd very considerable, is hereby acquainted therewith: If he, or, in Case of his Death, any of his family or Relations will apply to the Printer, they shall be in form'd more particularly. Whoever can give Intelligence of him, will very much oblige his Friends, by informing the Printer what they know relating to him.

- April 10, 1752

Files of 1752: To Be SOLD, very reasonable, by the Subscriber, A Tract of Land, containing 1300 Acres, in Pasquatank, North Carolina, joining on a bold navigable River, call'd North-River, and on the main Road that leads through said County from Norfolk to Edenton, about 45 miles from Norfolk, with two Plantations thereon, well wooded and water'd. Quit-rent free, being purchased from an Indian King. For further Particulars enquire of Mr. Thomas Walke, or the Subscriber, living in Princess-Anne County.

-- Francis Clerk

N.B. The Subscriber, being in great Want of Cash, will take 200 Pistoles for it.
-- F. Clerk.

- April 10, 1752

Files of 1752: Being prevented carrying on my Business as usual, by an Arrest for a debt not justly my own, I hereby give Notice that I have taken into Partnership with me Edward Charlton, late from London, who will carry on the Business at my Shop, next Door to the Raleigh Tavern, in Williamsburg. Gentlemen, who please to favour us with their Orders for Wigs, etc. may depend on being well and expeditiously served, and oblige Their very humble Servant

April 16, 1752 -- Richard Gamble.

72

Files of 1752:   To be SOLD, together or in PARCELS
A Tract of Land, in Spotsylvania County, belonging to Mr.
Humphrey Bell, of London, Merchant, containing about 4500 Acres:
For Terms enquire of the Subscriber, living in King & Queen
County.

July 31, 1752   -- Humphrey Hill.

Files of 1752:

NICHOLAS POWELL TAYLOR,
    Is just arriv'd from England, and settled in York Town.
Gentlemen who will favour him with their Commands, may depend
on being faithfully and expeditiously fav'd and in the genteelest
Fashion.

July 31, 1752

Files of 1752:

JOHN WALKER
    Lately arriv'd in Williamsburg from London, and who for
ten Years past has been engag'd in the Education of Youth,
undertakes to instruct young Gentlemen in Reading, Writing,
Arithmetick, the most material Branches of Classical Learning,
and ancient and modern Geography, and History; but, as the
noblest End of Erudition and Human Attainments, he will exert
his principal Endeavors to improve their Morals, in Proportion
to their Progress in Learning, that no Parent may repent his
Choice in trusting him with the Education of his Children.

    Mrs. Walker, likewise, teaches young Ladies all Kinds
of Needle Work; makes Capuchins, Shades, Hats and Bonnets;
and will endeavour to give Satisfaction to those who shall
honour her with their Custom.

    The above-mentioned John Walker and his Wife, live at
Mr. Cobb's new House, next to Mr. Coke's near the Road going
down to the Capitol Landing; where there is also to be sold,
Men's Shoes and Pumps, Turkey Coffee, Edging and Lace for Ladies
Caps and some Gold Rings.

November 6, 1752

Files of 1752:   March 20, 1752

    The Subscriber, who lodges at Mr. Finnie's in
Williamsburg, teaches the Art of Fencing Dancing and the French
tongue; and is ready to begin as soon as he can get a reasonable
Number of Scholars.

                    -- LeChevalier de Poyressy.

Files of 1752-62:   Ran away, on Saturday the 21st of this
Instant, from William Byrd's, Esq; at Westover two Servant Men,
belonging to the Subscriber; they are both Welchmen, by trade

House-Carpenters and Joiners, viz. James Morris, a short well-set Man, of a brown Complexion, with his own short dark colour'd Hair; William Bictlyn, a small springhty Fellow, stoops a little, and wears a black Wig. Had on when they went away, blue Kersey Pea-Jackets, dark-grey Waistcoats, blue Breeches, and coarse Yarn stockings. They are supposed to be gone towards Carolina, and may pretend to be Seafaring Men.

Whoever apprehends and brings them to William Byrd's, Esq. or to the Subscriber, living in King William County, shall have Five Pistoles reward for each, besides what the Law allows.

-- Harry Gaines.

Files of 1752-62: Ran away from the Berry, the 8th of this Instant, vis. John Brown a Scotchman, born at Leith, a well-set smooth fac'd Man and about 24 years.

Samuel McDowell, born at Newport-Glasgow, aged about 32 years; wears his own black hair, and has a large black Beard, talks broad Scotch.

John Charles Stossenburg, a Polander, aged 27 years; a pretty tall Man, talks a little effeminite. They took a Five Oar'd Deal built Yaul, pretty low built forward, with two Oars, Rudder, and Tiller, with Partners for two Masts, painted in the Inside with an Oyster Colour. Whoever stops the said Runaways, and brings them and the Boat to the Berry, at Sheppard's Warehouse, shall have a Guinea Reward, for each of them so taken, besides what the Law allows, paid by

-- James Belcher.

Files of 1766: Elias Booth, who served his time to an eminent woolcomber in the city of Norwich, and about the year 1712 went over to Virginia, where he remained in or near Williamsburg for some years, afterwards came over to England about the year 1726, where he remained about 3 months, then returned to Virginia, and in some small time after his arrival married the daughter of one Mr. Demissy of Williamsburg, by whom he had a son born and christened William, who, if alive is now about 36 or 37 years of age, and may possibly be settled somewhere in or near Williamsburg. If the said Elias Booth, or his son William, or any other of the descendents of the said Elias Booth, will apply to Samuel Metcalfe in King and Queen County, they may hear of something greatly to their advantage; or if any one who has known any of the above mentioned persons, either in Virginia or Maryland, can inform the said Metcalfe where he may send to them, to examine whether they be the persons described and intended as above, to the satisfaction of the said Metcalf, shall in such case receive the sum of 20.1 sterling, as a reward for his discovery.

Files of 1767:

May 14, 1767

Whereas Captain James Esten, of the ship Hanbury, lately advertised that JAMES PARK, Mate of said ship, had run away, and refused to return to his duty, this is to declare that the accusation is false, and that I, the Mate, would never have absented from my duty, had it not been for the ill treatment I received on board from the Boatswain, whose cause the Captain espouses, and refuses to bring him to justice, or be answerable for his good behaviour.

-- James Park.

Files of 1767:   Williamsburg, October 24, 1767

The little regard paid to my former request, and the impossibility of my being able to make personal application to many of my debtors who live at a distance, obliges me once more to take this method, desiring all persons whose accounts are still open on my books to pay their respective balances immediately, or give their notes or bonds, with security for the same, as I am determined to go for England as soon as my affairs can be adjusted.

I will dispose of my stock of drugs, medicines, and shop utensils, on reasonable terms.

-- George Pitt

Files of 1767:   The subscriber from LONDON begs leave to inform the public that he still continues near Market street, in Norfolk, to make and repair all sorts of plain, repeating, and horizontal watches, and all kinds of repeating and musical clocks. Those Gentlemen who will please to favour him with their commands may depend upon the utmost despatch and care from

Their obliged humble servant
-- William Skinker

N.B. Neat enamel dial plates put to watches.

Files of 1767:

MARRIAGES.
WILLIAM RANDOLPH, Esq. to Miss MARY SKIPWITH, a daughter of the late Sir William Skipwith, Bart.

EDWARD LLOYD, of Maryland, to Miss ELIZABETH TAYLOE, a daughter of Hon. John Tayloe, Esq.

Files of 1767:   If a certain THOMAS OSBORNE, who arrived at Charlestown, South Carolina, in a vessel from England, about three or four months ago, will either call upon, or write to, the publisher of this paper, he will hear of something greatly to his advantage; or if any person will give information as above of his being dead, or living, it will be acknowledged by his friends as a singular favor.

N.B. He is about 5 feet 10 inches high, broad set, of a fair complexion, lame of his right arm, letters TO marked on his left wrist with gunpowder, born at Sheffld in Yorkshire, speaks broad English, is about 38 years old, and has served on board his majesty's ships of war. He set out from Charlestown for this province about ten weeks ago.

<u>Files of 1767</u>:   April 2, 1767

    All Persons who have any connexions with me are hereby
to take notice that they are to be brought to an immediate
conclusion, as I am resolved to leave the colony with the utmost
expedition.

                                    -- James Pride.

<u>Files of 1768</u>:

                  LONDON, October 1

    Lately died Miss Elizabeth Gordon, a Maiden Lady, at her
Seat near Harwich, said to have died worth fifty Thousand Pounds,
great part of which she has left to charitable Uses; among the
rest, one Thousand Pounds for erecting an Hospital for the Relief
of indigent Old Maids.

    Amongst the Jewels of an eminent Jeweller of this City is
a Clock of exquisite Workmanship, designed for the Grand Seignior;
the Case is massy Gold finely embossed, overlaid with Diamonds,
some as large as a Guinea, and larger, of the finest Lustre.
Pearls as big as Birds Eggs hand to two Gold enamelled Trees
that grow out of the Gold Rock, on which the Clock stands; as its
Pedestal, a Tree on each Side, the Fruit of which is Pearls, and
Leaves of Emeralds; two great Emeralds as big as Pears, are
fixed on the two Front Pillars; the Characters on the Dial Plate,
which are Turkish are of Diamonds; so are the Hands.

<u>Files of 1772</u>:   New York, August 24.

    Captain Bogart, from Surinam, informs us that a short Time
before he sailed from thence the wild Negroes cut off two Plantations, and killed two white Men on one of them; and that it was
much feared, unless Succours soon arrived there from Holland,
great Damage would be done.

<u>Files of 1772</u>:   London, June 2.

    It is reported, that when the Club of Maccaronies, just
instituted at the Star and Garter, Pall Mall, applied to the
College of Heralds for a set of Arms to be made out for them,
they received for Answer, that, instead of Arms, they had better
apply for Heads.

<u>Files of 1772</u>:   JAMES HALDINE, COPPER SMITH and BRASS FOUNDER
from Philadelphia, in Church Street, near the Church, Norfolk,
Makes and sells all Sorts of COPPER and BRASS WORK, namely,
Stills, Brewing Coppers, Sugar Boilers, Fullers and Hatters
Coppers, Capuchin Plate Warmers, Tea Kitchens, all Sorts of
Ship, Fish and Wash Kettles, Stew Pans, Dutch Ovens, Tea Kettles,
Saucepans, Coffee and Chocolate Pots, Brass Mill Work, Furniture
for Coach and Chair Harness, Fenders, Andirons, Candlesticks,
Cc. at the most reasonable Rates. Also tins and mends all Sorts

of old Copper and Brass Kitchen Work, and gives the best Prices for old Copper, Brass, Pewter or Lead.

All Orders from the Country will be punctually attended to.

N.B. He deals for Cash, or Country Produce.

Those who have old Brass, Copper, Pewter, or Lead, to dispose of, are desired to apply to Mr. Joseph Kidd in Williamsburg or to Mr. McCan, in Hampton, who will receive it for me, and pay them the Value; they will likewise receive old Work to be repaired.

Files of 1772:   Richmond, February 18, 1772

As I intend for England by the 11th of May next, and to return in the Fall, I beg the Favour of all who are indebted to me to have their Accounts settled before my Departure; such as remain unpaid will be left with Mr. James McDowall, Merchant, of this Place, who is properly empowered to collect the same, and pay all just Demands against me. The Shop in Richmond, in Partnership with Ludwick Warrack, will be continued, and properly supplied with fresh Medicines yearly, on the best Terms.

-- James Currie.

Files of 1772:

WILLIAM HOLLIDAY, and Co.
COACHMAKERS.

From LONG-ACRE, LONDON,
Beg Leave to inform the Publick that they have opened a Shop, in the Street leading to the Capitol Landing, next door to Mr. Shepherd's Harness Maker, where those Gentlemen who choose to favor them with their Custom may be supplied with PHAETONS, DOUBLE and SINGLE CHAIRS, made in the neatest and genteelest Manner, and at the most reasonable Rates; also Carriages neatly repaired, with the utmost Expedition. They will undertake all Kinds of JOINERS and CARPENTERS WORK, and HOUSE PAINTING in general.

Williamsburg, April 9, 1772

Files of 1772:   If Mr. DAVID DOIG, late Deputy Provost Marshal of West Florida, will let his Friends in Scotland know where he is to be found, they can inform him of Something very much to his Advantage. For further Particulars, apply to Mr. Hugh McMikin, in Portsmouth.

Files of 1772:   If one Doctor Mariner, and his Son James Mariner who went from Bristol about the Year 1758 to Virginia, are living, they may hear of something to their Advantage by applying at the Post Office in Williamsburg.

Files of 1772:   August 1, 1772

This is to inform MARIA and GOTLIEB DILDEY, of Roppin, in

the Marquistate of Brandenburg, that their Uncle, GEORGE
CHRISTOPHER WHITE, who died in Amelia County, Virginia on the
19th Day of June last, has bequeathed to them his whole Estate,
supposed to be worth fifteen Hundred Pounds, or upwards. He
mentions them as Daughters of his Sister Catherine, by her first
Husband, Peter Dildey. They may be informed farther, by in-
quiring at the Post Office, Williamsburg.

<u>Files of 1772:</u>   Edinburgh, July 2.

Monday fe'nnight passed through Kincardine O'Niel about
ninety Men, Women and Children, all from the Shire of Sutherland
on their way to Glasgow, from whence they are to embark for
America. Not above three in the whole Company could speak English,
and even those very imperfectly.

And we hear from Dundee that last Week arrived there upwards
of one Hundred Emigrants, with about thirty Children, mostly on
the Breast, also from the County of Sutherland, on their Way to
Grennock, to procure Passage to America. They say many more will
follow their Example. They allege the same Reason for their
Conduct as the former Emigrants from Sky, to wit, the enormous
Price of all Sorts of Provisions, and the Oppression of their
Superiors.

<u>Files of 1772:</u>

FIVE POUNDS REWARD

For apprehending JOHN HUTCHINSON, who ran away last Night
from the Subscriber; he is a likely stout Man, about five Feet
ten Inches high, a Blacksmith by Trade, and was born in Yorkshire
in England; his Clothing is a Duroy Coat of a brown Colour lined
with white Durants, the Coat quite new, a white Shirt, and brown
Linen Trousers. He carried with him a brindled Water Dog, which
I expect is still with him, as it was a great Favourite. I
imagine he will procure himself other Clothes, as he has carried
some Cash with him, and also change his Name. The above Reward
will be paid on securing him in any Jail in this Colony, or
delivering him to me, in Lancaster County.

* * * *

CENSUS RECORDS

Lancaster Co., Va.

Graves Co., Ky.

1850 Census, Lancaster Co., Virginia

NOTE BY CHH: Only those families who had members in the household who were born elsewhere than Virginia are listed herewith.

		Age		Birthplace
#23	Lewson Chase	35	Teacher	Massachusetts
	Virginia	24		Virginia
#53	John H. Williams	50	Farmer	Maryland
	Ann	44		Virginia
	John	22		"
	Peter	20		"
	Elizabeth	14		"
	Luther	12		"
	Mary J.	7		"

#125 Richard Sullivan Jr.   11   Tennessee
     (listed as one of the 7 children of Richard and Sally
     Sullivan, all of whom were born in Virginia.)

#128 Oscar D. Shuck   7   China
     (is a "scholar" in the household of Felicia T. Dunaway,
     age 45.)

		Age		Birthplace
#163	Addison Hall	52	Minister	Virginia
	Thomas W. Tobey	30	Minister	Rhode Island
	Isabella	26		Virginia
	Lewis H. Shuck	14	Scholar	China
	Ryland K. Shuck	13	Scholar	China
#170	William Flowers	27	Farmer	Virginia
	Betsy	44		Virginia
	Thomas E. Ward	40	Sailor	Maryland
	Zipporah	18		Virginia
#195	R. S. Nash	29	Minister	New York
	Sarah G.	22		Ohio
	John M.	16		New York

#208 George R. Webb   14   Scholar   Delaware
     (in household of A. Hill Currie, age 28 "teacher".)

		Age		Birthplace
#213	Fayette Ball	24	Farmer	Virginia
	Maria L.	21		Maryland
#224	James A. Holt	35	Farmer	Maryland
	Emeline	40		Virginia

	Emeline Jr.	4		Virginia
	Robert	66		Maryland
#227	William M. Ward	36	Minister	Maryland
	Frances	31		Virginia
	Ellis C.	9		"
	John E.	6		"
	Mary F.	3		"
	Emma	2		"
	Anna	3 months		"
#237	Peter Chase	60	Farmer	Rhode Island
	Ann H.	53		Rhode Island
	William T.	18	Teacher	Virginia
	Eugene	14		Virginia
#242	George S. Lee	64	Teacher	Virginia
	Mary A.	54		Maryland
	Mary C.	12	Scholar	Virginia
#243	Thomas Armstrong	66	Farmer	Ireland
	Ann R.	60		Virginia
	Thomas Jr.	25	Farmer	"
	Ann Beane	13		"
#252	Nancy Carter	38		Maryland
	Jethro	40	Farmer	"
	Isaac	12		"
	Mary	10		"
	John W.	5		Virginia
	Elizabeth A.	2		Virginia
	Maria Catlin	18		Virginia
#256	Peter Francis	45	Seaman	Sweden
	Mary	21		Virginia
	Sarah A.	6		"
	Maria J.	2		"
#258	Georgeanna Nicholas	11	Scholar	Maryland
	(in household of William C. Reaves, age 36, Seaman.)			
#289	John C. Carter	39	Shoemaker	Maryland
	Emeline	33		"

William M. H.	12	Maryland
John W.	10	"
Samuel J.	8	"
Mary E.	3	"
Edward F.	1	Virginia
#304 William Rowe	31 Seaman	Maryland
Sally	24	Virginia
James W.	2	"
Richard Evans	28 Seaman	"
#316 William B. Snead	48 Minister	Virginia
Elizabeth H.	41	"
William S.	21 Physician	Maryland
Victor F.	19 Scholar	Virginia
#335 William Henderson	34 Wood Dealer	Virginia
Isabella	35	Maryland
William Jr.	8 Scholar	Virginia
George	10 Scholar	"
Charles	5	"
Mary A.	27	Maryland
#345 John S. Currell	39 Merchant	Virginia
Margaret	28	Maryland
Elizabeth I.	7 Scholar	Virginia
John S. Jr.	3	Virginia
#393 Thomas Norris Sr.	60 Farmer	Virginia
Eliza	51	Maryland
Mary F.	12 Scholar	Virginia
Ellen	8 Scholar	"
Richard	15	"

1850 Census of Graves Co., Kentucky

(of some former Virginians and their families. Contributed by Mrs. Alice Cavender Cooper, of Naco, Arizona. Thank you very much, Mrs. Cooper.)

848 L. (Ludwig) Overby	43 Farmer	Virginia
Jane (King)	42	"
Mary	19	Kentucky
William	17	"

	John	14		Kentucky
	Robert	12		"
	Edward	7		"
	Ludmill	5		"
	Nancy (Jane)	1		"
849	A. R. Overby	36	Schoolteacher	Virginia
	Sarah	36		"
	William	6		Kentucky
	Charles	4		"
	Sarah	5/12		"
855	R. N. Overby	41	Farmer	Virginia
	Jane	22		Kentucky
	Elizabeth	7		"
	Nancy	5		"
	John	4		"
	Caroline	2		"
	Robert	3/12		"
	J. Moore	18	Farmer	"
466	P. W. Overby	39	Schoolteacher	Virginia
	Elizabeth	25		"
	John	5		"
	E. V.	4		"
	William	1		Kentucky
695	J. (James?) King	45	Farmer	Virginia
	Delila	38		"
	Lafayette	19	Farmer	"
	Mary	16		"
	Sarah	15		"
	James	11		"
	Rice	9		"
	Eliza	4		"
	Munsford	2/12		Kentucky
784	M. King	40	Farmer	Virginia
	Susannah	39		Tennessee
	Mary	20		"
	James	18		"

Eliza	16		Tennessee
Tabitha	14		"
Red	13		"
Joseph	5		Kentucky
Sarah	1		"
Tabitha	94		Virginia

(District No. 2)

775	James M. McCord	25	Farmer	Tennessee
	Tennessee	18		"
	James	6/12		Kentucky
	Elizabeth Overby	65		Virginia
	John	5		Kentucky

* * * *

VIRGINIA
ANCESTORS AND ADVENTURERS, VOL. 2

SECTION 3

(a) Proof of Importations

(b) Contributions by Others

PROOF OF IMPORTATIONS

Henrico Co., Va. Court Orders (1707-1709), page 9 -

10 November 1707 - Upon the pitition of Isaac Lefevre, these are to certifie (sic) there is due unto him one hundred and fifty acres of land for the importation of himself with Ester, his first wife (now deceased) and Magdalane, his second wife, into this Colony. The same being legally proved in open court.

Ibid, page 10 -

1 December 1707 - Upon the petition of John Thomas, these are to certifie (sic) that there is due unto him one hundred acres of land for the importation of himself and Mary, his wife into this Colony. The same being legally proved in open Court.

Ibid, page 18 -

2 February 1707/08 - Upon petition of John Voyer, these are to certifie (sic) that there is due unto him one hundred acres of land for the importation of himself and Jane, his wife, into this Colony.

Ibid, page 34 -

1 May 1708 - Upon the petition of John Forqueran, these are to certifie (sic) that there is due unto him 250 acres for the importation of five persons, to wit: John Forqueson - Elizabeth, his first wife; Jeanne, his 2nd wife; with James Duero and (? Olimp) Duero, his, the said John Forqueran's father and mother-in-law.

Ibid, page 34 -

1 May 1708 - Upon the petition of Peter Massot, these are to certifie (sic) that there is due unto him 350 acres of land for the importation of seven persons into this Colony, whose names are underwritten, the same being legally proved in open Court. To wit:

Peter Massot - Frances, his first wife - Elizabeth, his second wife - John Lozanne, her first husband - Elizabeth Lozanne, his daughter - James Chevair, her 2nd husband. Elizabeth Chevair, his first wife. This is the first certificate, etc.

Ibid, (same date)

Upon the petition of Francis Sasen, these are to certifie (sic) that there is due unto him one hundred acres of land for the importation of himself and Elizabeth, his wife, into this Colony.

Ibid, page 35 -

(same date) - Upon the petition of Henry Cabiness, these

are to certifie (sic) that there is due unto him 200 acres of land for the importation of himself and Mary, his first wife, with Magdalane, his 2nd wife, and Magdalane, her daughter, into this Colony, etc.

Ibid, page 72 -

1 September 1708 - Upon the petition of Peter Sabatie, these are to certifie (sic) that there is due unto him 150 acres of land for the importations of himself with Elizabeth, his wife, and Elizabeth, his daughter, into this Colony.

Ibid, (same date) -

Upon the petition of Jacob Capon, these are to certifie (sic) that there is due unto him 150 acres of land for the importation of himself and in right of Jane, his wife with John Imbert, her first husband, into this Colony. (Legally proved) etc.

Ibid, page 78 -

1 October 1708 - Upon the petition of Peter Goreing, these are to certifie (sic) that there is due unto him 150 acres of land for the importation of himself and John Mary Goring, his wife, with Susan Sellis, his daughter (in all, three) into this Colony. (Legally proven, etc.)

Ibid, page 138 -

2 May 1709 - Upon the petition of John James Fagan (?), these are to certifie (sic) that there is due unto him fifty acres of land for the importation of his own person into this Colony, etc.

Ibid, page 154 -

1 June 1709 - Upon the petition of Mary Gory, relict and executrix of John Gory, deceased, these are to certifie (sic) that there is due unto her (in right of her said husband) one hundred and fifty acres of land for the importation of the said John and Mary with Claudius, their son, into this Colony. (Legally proved, etc.)

Ibid, page 159 -

1 July 1709 - Upon the petition of John Red, these are to certifie (sic) that there is due unto him 100 acres of land for the importation of himself and Ann, his wife, into this Colony. (Legally proved, etc.)

Ibid, page 173 -

1 August 1709 - Upon the petition of Catherine Perue, relict of Peter Perue, deceased, these are to certifie (sic) that there is due unto her, in right of her deceased husband, 150 acres of land for the importation of the said Peter Perue, deceased, with ye said Catharine, his wife, and Peter, his son, into this Colony.

(Legally proved, etc.)

Orange Co., Va. Order Book 2 (1739-1741), page 210 -

    24 July 1740 - William Hutchison came into Court and made oath that he imported himself - John Hutchison Sr. - Margaret Hutchinson - John Hutchinson Jr. and Mary Hutchinson, from Ireland to Philadelphia and from thence into this Colony, at his own charge and this is the first time of his proving his rights in order to obtain land, etc.

Ibid, page 225 -

    25 July 1740 (next day) - George Hutcheson came into Court and made oath that he imported himself; Eleanor, his wife; Jennet - Francis - John - and William Hutchinson and Jacob Carr, from Ireland to Philadelphia and from thence into this Colony, at his own charge, and that this is the first time of his proving his and/or their rights in order to obtain land, etc.

Ibid, page 210 -

    24 July 1740 - George Caldwall (sic) came into Court and made oath that he imported himself, Mary, his wife, William; Mary; John; Jane; David; and Agnes Caldwall, from Ireland to Philadelphia and from thence into this Colony and that this is the first time of his proving his or their rights in order to obtain land, etc.

Ibid, page 211 -

    24 July 1740 - Patrick Crawford came into Court and made oath that he imported himself and Ann, James, George, Margaret and Mary Crawford from Ireland to Philadelphia and from thence into this Colony, and this is the first time of his proving his or their rights in order to obtain land, etc.

Ibid, page 210 -

    24 July 1740 - James Davis came into Court and made oath that he imported himself and Mary, Henry, William and Samuel Davis from Ireland, at his own charge, and this is the first time of his proving his or their rights in order to obtain land, etc.

Ibid, page 210 -

    24 July 1740 - John Maxwell made oath that he imported himself and Margaret, John Jr., Thomas, Mary, and Alexander Maxwell from Ireland to Philadelphia and from thence into this Colony and that this is the first time of his proving his or their rights in order to obtain land, etc.

Ibid, page 210 -

    24 July 1740 - Moses Thompson came into Court and made oath that he imported himself and Jane, William, Robert, and John

Thompson and James Fox from Ireland to Philadelphia and from thence into this Colony and that this is the first time of his proving his or their rights to obtain land, etc.

Caroline Co., Va. Order Book (1755-1758), pp 29-30-31 -

NOTE BY CHH: All of the below listed 15 individuals came into Court and made oath that they (either) imported themselves into this Colony or were imported (all from Great Britain) in the years listed and that this is the first time of proving importation, etc., in order to obtain 50 acres of land. They all sold and/or assigned their rights to James Taylor, Gent. (To Wit:)

William Tate	
Thomas Berry	1715
Robert Robertson	1727
Joseph Sterling	1740
Joshua King	1711
Elizabeth King	1715
William Holmes	1754
Peter Copland	1743
William Gown, Gent.	1733
Thomas Rogers	1752
Benjamin Whithead	1725
John Spalding	1741
Daniel Lefore	1734
John Mitchell	1744
Harbert Price	1732

Norfolk Co., Va. Wills & Deeds "B" (1646-1651), page 141 -

26 March 1650 - A certificate is granted unto Mr. William Moseley, for 550 acres of land, for the transportation of himself, Susanna, his wife, and William and Arthur, his sonnes (sic), Susan Robinson, alias Corker, and six more into this Colony, etc. (Total - 11)

Fairfax Co., Va. Order Book (1772-1774), page 24 -

19 & 20 March 1772 - A letter of attorney from Margaret Savage to Harry Piper executed in the presence of the Right Honorable, the Lord Mayor of the City of Dublin and Certified under his hand and the Seal of the said City, on the motion of the said Harry Piper is admitted to record.

Ibid, page 231 -

22 June 1773 - Harry Piper, in open Court, made oath to the importation of 377 persons into this Colony from Great Britain and Ireland, whose names are mentioned in his Affidavit which is ordered to be certified and the said Harry Piper acknowledged an assignment endorsed on the said certificate to George Mason, Gent., which is also ordered to be certified.

NOTE BY CHH: This transaction would have involved 18,850 acres of land at fifty acres per importation right. It would be very nice if we could learn the names on the cited certificate.

Rappahannock Co., Va. Deeds #7 (1682-88), page 160 -

11 March 1681/2 - James Whitlock, of the COUNTY OF GLOCESTER
(sic), Planter, attorney of Anthony Whitlock, of LAMBETH, in the
COUNTY OF SURRY, in the KINGDOM OF ENGLAND, Husbandman, nephew
and heir of Thomas Whitlock, "the elder", late of Rappahannock
Co. sells (as attorney) to Thomas Swinburne, of the County of
Rappahannock, all the divident of land Thomas Whitlock died
seized of by patent of 1662, etc.
Witnesses: Joseph O'Kean, Francis Horne, Thomas Hutton,
Robert Play.
Recorded 5 April 1682.

Frederick Co., Va. Superior Court Order Book (1843-52), page 435 -

November Term 1851 -

Naturalization Papers -

Robert Hamilton, a native of Ireland, produced a Certificate
of the Corporation Court of Winchester, dated November Term 1844,
in which Robert Hamilton declared his intentions of becoming a
citizen of the U.S. - took the oath of Fidelity to the Commonwealth
of Virginia - proves he has resided in the U.S. for five years
at least and in Virginia one year at least, etc.

Ibid

Patrick Brady, a native of Ireland, produced a Certificate
from County Court of Alleghaney, in State of Maryland, dated
14 October 1839, declaring his intentions to become a citizen, etc.

Ibid

John Murray, a native of Ireland, declares on oath it is
his bona fide intention to become a citizen of the U.S. and to
renounce his allegience to Victoria, Queen of Great Britain, etc.

Ibid, page 443 -

Henry Kenzel, a native of Hope Darmstadt, Germany appeared
in Court and made application to become a citizen of the U. S.,
he having resided in the United States three years next preceeding
his arrival at the age of 21 years and has resided five years
in the U.S. including the three years of his minority.

Ibid, page 458 -

13 May 1852 - James Donaldson, a native of England, this
day declared it his bona fide intention to become a citizen of
the U. S. and to renounce forever his allegience to Victoria,
Queen of Great Britain, etc.

Ibid

5 June 1852 - Andrew McCarty, a native of Ireland, declared
this day it is his bona fide intention to become a citizen of

the U.S., etc. and to renounce former allegience, etc.

Ibid, page 471 -

June Term 1852 - John O'Connor and David Welch, natives of Ireland, this day made oath it is their bona fide intention to become citizens of the U.S. and to renounce former allegience, etc.

Fluvanna Co., Va. Order Book (1860-1867), page 146 -

25 August 1861 - Daniel Cummins, a native of Ireland, this day made oath in open Court that he would support the Constitution of the Confederate States of America; abjures all allegience to Victoria, Queen of the United Kingdom of Great Britain and Ireland whereupon the said Cummins is admitted a citizen of the Confederate States of America.

Ibid, page 147 -

25 August 1861 -
The same entry as above for Michal Buckton of Ireland.
The same entry above for Michael Moran.
The same entry as above for Patrick McCann.
The same entry as above for Timothy Nihan.
The same entry as above for William Divine.
The same entry as above for William J. Campbell, a native of Scotland.

Frederick Co., Va. Order Book 14 (1767-1770)

Aliens took oath of Allegience

Page 9, June 3, 1767	Philip Hoofman Jacob Bowman George Keller
Page 58, July 7, 1767	Christopher Windle Valentine Windle Henry Travett George Maurer Peter Spice Henry Felkner
Page 192, March 2, 1768	John Keplinger Burket Reager
Page 197, March 3, 1768	Henry Seacrist Martin Cryder
Page 301, August 3, 1768	John Limly Christopher Hiskle
Page 311, August14, 1768	Peter Ruffe Christopher Lambert

Page 348, Nov. 1, 1768 Jacob Barnard Sively
           Adolph Iler
           Adam Brewback

Page 508, August 1, 1769 John Newland
           George Merriett
           George Smith
           John Wisecarver
           Adam Moler
           Nicodemus Perksdale
           Peter Lecabough
           Jacob Cackley
           Peter Bedinger

Page 512, August 2, 1769 Simon Linder

Page 561, Sept. 5, 1769 Martin Scotzer
           Alexander Hite
           Jacob Hite

Page 639, May 2, 1770 Peter Chrisman

Page 664, August 17, 1770 William Hanchur (Hancher)

Page 668, August 18, 1770 Fielding Lewis, Gent.
           (Oath of Allegiance - margin)

York Co., Va. Record #5 (1672-1676), page 85 -

10 September 1679 - Certificate is granted to Mr. Martin Gardner for 450 acres of land for the importation of himself five times and Francis Middleton and Henry Talley and John Morritie and Elizabeth (Edy? Ody?) into the Colony.

Ibid

Certificate is granted Mr. Martin Gardner for 700 acres of land for the importation of Mary Gardner - Margery Day - Francisco Mercero - Mary Grose - Henry Holford (?) - Rich Leeker - Alie Adkinson - Grace Deacon - Elizabeth Waterson - Jane Thompson - Elizabeth Smith - John Davis - Califf Currier - Martha Mason - into this Colony.

Brunswick Co., Va. Order Book 3 (1745-1749), page 27 -

3 April 1746 - John Blackwellder made oath that he imported himself; his sons, John and Caleb; his daughters, Elizabeth and Margaret; and his sister, Catherine Blackwellder directly from the Marquiset of Durlock, in Germany into the Province of Pennsylvania and from the said Province into this Colony and that this is the first time of proving such importation, which is ordered to be certified. (He was due 300 acres of land - CHH)

Henings Statutes at Large, Vol. 2, page 308 -   -1673-

On 20 December 1671 - An Act for Naturalization for aliens desiring to make this country a place of their constant residence,

might upon their petition to the Grand Assembly, and taking
the Oaths of Allegiance and Supremacy be admitted to a
naturalization. Whereupon John Peterson - Rowland Anderson -
Michael Vanlandigam - Minor Doodes - Doodes Minor and Herman
Kelderman, aliens, making humble suit as aforesaid - etc.,
enacted etc., their privileges the same (henceforth) as natural
born Englishmen, etc.

COMMENT BY CHH: I have not checked out the above except as to
Minor Doodes, who was a "Dutch" sea captain and that "Doodes"
Minor was his son.

CONTRIBUTIONS BY OTHERS

Hamilton Co., Ohio 1850 Census

NOTE BY CHH: Reference is made to Hamilton Co., Ohio Court
and other Records, Vols. 1 and 2, by Mrs. W. J. (Virginia
Raymond) Cummins, who has kindly and graciously given me permission to extract the names of those residents who were born
in Virginia and settled in Ohio by or before 1850. (Thank you
very, very much Virginia for these "lost links".)

Volume I

Page	Name	Age	Born
133	Thomas Tatersall	78	England
	Nancy Tatersall	65	Virginia
	Charles Tatersall	25	Ohio
	Jacob Tatersall	22	Ohio
138	John Banistor	75	Virginia
140	Abner Garard	49	Virginia
140	George Wilmurth	45	Virginia
143	Roland Vast	40	Virginia
143	Daniel Clay	43	Virginia
144	George W. Martin	38	Virginia
147	Samuel Hendrickson	37	New Jersey
	Zippora Hendrickson	38	Virginia
	Mary Morton	20	New Jersey
	Elizabeth Morton	18	New Jersey
	Zippora Hendrickson	12	New Jersey
	William Hendrickson	10	Ohio
	Julia Ann Hendrickson	8	Ohio
	Catherine Hendrickson	6	Ohio
	George Hendrickson	4	Ohio
	Gideon Hendrickson	4 mos.	Ohio
	Daniel Lantus	25	Virginia
152	William McCash	66	Scotland
	Ann McCash	60	Virginia
	James McCash	22	Ohio
	Parmelia McCash	30	Ohio
	Cordelia McCash	15	Ohio

	William F.	5	Ohio
	John Douberly	26	Maryland
153	Alexander Pendery	68	Virginia
	Mary Pendery	58	Ohio
	Israel Pendery	19	Ohio
	Susan Belle Pendery	15	Ohio
	Alexander Pendery	13	Ohio
	John Gaugh	19	Ireland
	Susan Pendery	25	Ohio
	Catherine Gaugh	16	Ireland
	John Cunningham	19	Ireland
154	John H. Yerkes	31	Virginia
	Elizabeth Yerkes	23	Indiana
	George Yerkes	3	Ohio
	William Yerkes	2	Ohio
156	Eli Meade	33	New York
	Susanna Meade	30	Virginia
	Sarah Meade	4	Ohio
	Mary Meade	1	Ohio
	Sarah Kincaid	50	Virginia
161	Anderson Copeland	33	Virginia
165	Nimrod Price	56	Virginia
	Rachel Price	45	Ohio
	Marcus S. Price	21	Ohio
	Marcus B. Price	19	Ohio
	Amanda A. Price	17	Ohio
	Mahlon F. Price	15	Ohio
	Milton D. Price	12	Ohio
	John N. Price	9	Ohio
	N. S. J. Price	8	Ohio
	Albert P. Price	5	Ohio
	William Price	2	Ohio
166	Thomas Trevillo	42	Pennsylvania
	Maria Trevillo	42	Virginia
	Paul J. Trevillo	18	Ohio
	Elijah Trevillo	16	Ohio
	Martha C. Trevillo	14	Ohio
	James Trevillo	12	Ohio
	Sarah Trevillo	10	Ohio
	William Trevillo	8	Ohio
	Ephraim Trevillo	6	Ohio
	Samuel H. Trevillo	4	Ohio
	Mary E. Trevillo	1	Ohio
167	David Brown	72	Ohio
	Emeline Brown	46	Virginia
	George W. Brown	22	Virginia
	David L. Brown	18	Ohio
	Sarah Brown	16	Ohio
	Thomas M. Brown	10	Ohio
	Emeline Brown	7	Ohio
	Elizabeth Stewart	76	Ohio
	Elizabeth Garner	45	Virginia
	Benjamin Garner	22	Virginia

	John Garner	21	Virginia
	Diana Garner	16	Ohio
	Lucinda Garner	14	Ohio
	Elizabeth Garner	10	Ohio
	Anne Garner	6	Ohio
	Alexander Garner	4	Ohio
168	Aby Buckingham	58	Virginia
	Mary Buckingham	35	Ohio
	Oliver P. Buckingham	19	Ohio
	Alfred Buckingham	17	Ohio
	Isaiah Buckingham	14	Ohio
170	Thomas Cooper	63	Virginia
171	John Gambril	64	Virginia
171	David Kennedy	65	Virginia
172	Sarah Patterson	68	Virginia
172	James Ringlesburg	70	Virginia
173	Elizabeth Wells	66	Virginia
175	John Strickland	35	Virginia

Volume II

Page	Name	Age	Born
168	Thomas Armstrong	74	Virginia
168	J. B. Boland	66	Virginia
168	Eliza Bridges	56	Virginia
168	James Clarke	85	Virginia
168	O. Clarke	66	Virginia
168	Sarah Crosley	62	Virginia
168	John Gerrard	63	Virginia
169	M. Hahn	65	Virginia
169	Henrietta Hill	62	Virginia
169	Comfort Madden	74	Virginia
169	Elizabeth Murdock	69	Virginia
170	Mary Reed	51	Virginia
170	William Shaw	51	Virginia
170	Hannah Webb	67	Virginia
174	Dr. John Bean	28	Virginia
175	Elizabeth Clark	63	Virginia
175	Sarah A. Ewing	65	Virginia
175	Samuel Moar	66	Virginia
176	Kizzia Ashby	76	Virginia
177	John Lodwick	80	Virginia
178	Sarah Harrison	66	Virginia

179	Catharine Bailis	66	Virginia
179	Nancy McDaniel	62	Virginia
—179	Regen Newell	65	Virginia
	Susannah Newell	61	Pennsylvania
182	John Crump	85	Virginia
182	Elizabeth Ligget	70	Virginia
182	Margaret Ruffner	75	Virginia
183	Ellen Barnes	74	Virginia
183	Sarah Compell	78	Virginia
183	Pristy Grigley	86	Virginia
183	Elizabeth McDonald	72	Virginia
184	Catherine Alcoke	81	Virginia
184	Nancy Bascoe	73	Virginia
184	Elizabeth Meyers	81	Virginia
184	Jane Miller	70	Virginia
185	Chris Shettlehue	71	Virginia
185	Jane Branter	75	Virginia
185	Jonas Calvert	75	Virginia
185	Joseph Fassett	75	Virginia
186	Margarett McDonnell	70	Virginia
187	William Burke	80	Virginia
187	Griffin Cox	72	Virginia
187	Emily Troy	76	Virginia
188	Lucy B. Wake	73	Virginia
188	Edward Womable	78	Virginia
190	James Birch	64	Virginia
190	John Boswell	70	Virginia
190	Allen Chumley	60	Virginia
190	Ann Cooper	82	Virginia
190	Solmon Eversoll	61	Virginia
191	Christina Hufman	75	Virginia
191	Catherine Jones	60	Virginia
191	Peter H. Kemper	70	Virginia
192	William Moss	77	Virginia
192	Abraham Ruffener	69	Virginia
192	Martha Ruffener	60	Virginia
193	Eleanor Tucker	70	Virginia
193	Hesekiah Wood	70	Virginia
	Sarah Wood	68	Virginia

193	Philip Younger	60	Virginia
195	Ira Carpenter (Gent)	50	Vermont
	Charlotte Carpenter	41	Pennsylvania
	Cornelius Carpenter	20	Virginia
	Mary Carpenter	18	Virginia
	John Carpenter	16	Virginia
	Victoria Carpenter	9	Ohio
	Isabell Carpenter	6	Ohio
	Susan Carpenter	4	Ohio
203	Jacob R. Roosa	60	New York
	Sarah Roosa	59	Virginia
	Albert Roosa	35	Ohio
	Mathias Roosa	22	Ohio
	Andrew J. Roosa	19	Ohio
	Ester Wasson	22	Ireland
204	Robert Rowan	30	Ohio
	Margaret Rowan	29	Ohio
	John Rowan	3 mos.	Ohio
	Mary Rowan	57	Virginia
	Mary A. Rowan	25	Ohio

The following contributed by Mr. Harley D. Haton, of St. Louis, Missouri. Thank you, Harley!

Frederick Co., Va. Will Book 4, page 129 -

In the Name of God Amen I John Haton of the COUNTY OF FREDERICK and COLONY OF VIRGINIA being of sound Mind & Memory though in a low and declining state of health do make and ordain this my Last Will and Testament -- Imprimis I Give and Recommend my Soul to God my Great Creator (in Hopes of Eternal Life through the Merits of Jesus Christ my Saviour) and my Body to the Earth. Item, I desire and appoint my Lands in HAMPSHIRE COUNTY, (now West Virginia) Consisting of four Tracts and Containing Nine Hundred Acres more or Less which I Purchased from John McCollough and which said McCollugh Purchased of Noah Hampton also one other Tract Situated on Spring Gap Run in said County to be sold as soon as Convenient after my Decease by my Executors to be hereafter Named and the money arising therefrom after deducting the Necessary Fees to the Proprietors Office to be applied to the Payment of my Just debts and the Residue (if any) with the Debts due to me when Collected by my Executors, I Give and Bequeath to John Haton of the COUNTY OF CUMBERLAND IN ENGLAND Son of Thomas Haton and Grandson of my Uncle Thomas Haton. Item, I Constitute and appoint Jacob Hite and Richard Rigg, both of Frederick County, and Joseph Watson, of Fairfax County, Executors of This my Last Will and Testament, hereby Revoking all former Wills and Legacies, ratifying and Confirming this and no other to be my Last Will and Testament in Witness Whereof I have hereunto Set my hand and Seal this twenty first day of July in the year of our Lord one thousand Seven hundred and Seventy one.

Signed Sealed
Published Pronounced
and declared by the said John
Haton as his Last Will and Tes-   JOHN HAYTON   (L.S.)

tament in the Presence of us who
in his Presence and in the Presence
of each other have hereunto Subscribed our Names.

ADAM STEPHEN
JONATHAN SEAMON
REES MORGAN

At a Court Continued and held for Frederick County August 8th. 1771. This Last Will and Testament of John Haton, deceased was Proved by the Oaths of the Witnesses thereto and ordered to be Recorded.

By the Court.

JAMES KEITH C.C.

At a Court continued and held for Frederick County August 7th 1772. Joseph Watson one of the Executors having complied with the Law Certificate is Granted him for obtaining a Probate thereof in due form.

By the Court

Ja. Keith, C. of C.

STATE OF VIRGINIA

COUNTY OF FREDERICK, TO-WIT:

I, Lee N. Whitacre, Clerk of the Circuit Court of Frederick County, Virginia, do hereby certify that the foregoing is a true copy of the Will of John Haton as recorded in Will Book No. 4, at page 129.

Given under my hand and the seal of the Court this 29th day of December, 1952.

(signed) Lee N. Whitacre, CLERK

Hampshire Co. Records by Sage and Jones -

Page 3 - 7 December 1761 - John Hayton is a witness to a Deed of Sale of land by Henry Batton of Hampshire Co. to John McMachan of Frederick Co.

Page 10 - 10 May 1763 - John Hayton witness to Deed from Cornelius Conner (wife Margaret) to Bryan Bruen of Frederick Co.

Page 15 - 3 December 1761 - John Hayton witness to sale of land by Joseph Edwards of Hampshire Co. to Henry Batton of same.

Fluvanna Co., Va. Deed Book 7, page 251 -

THIS INDENTURE made and entered into this 27th day of May in the year of our Lord one thousand eight hundred eighteen between Jesse Hatton of the Town of Mobile and Territory of Alabama of th one part and John R. Perkins, William Pasteur, John Winn, John Johnson Jr. of the County of Fluvannah and State of Virginia of the other part. Witnesseth that the said Jesse Hatton for and

in consideration of the sum of four hundred dollars to me in
hand paid the receipt of which is hereby acknowledged have
bargained, granted, sold, aliened, enfeofed, released and confirm
to the said John R. Perkins, William Pasteur, John Winn, John
Johnson Jr. their heirs and assigns forever all that tract or
parcel of land lying and being in the County of Fluvannah on
Mechunk Creek a water of James River containing three hundred
acres being the same land pattented to James Haggard and devised
by him to his son George Haggard and by said George Haggard
conveyed by Deed bearing date the 6th September 1814 to James
McCally and Reuben Jaes and by said McCally and Jaes by Deed
bearing date the second day of December 1817 to Jesse Hatton
reference being thereto had a description of said land will
more fully appear. To have and to hold the above described land
with the appurtenances to the said John R. Perkins, William
Pasteur, John Winn and John Johnson Jr. their heirs and assigns
to the only proper use and behoof of the said John R. Perkins,
William Pasteur, John Winn and John Johnson Jr. their heirs
and assigns forever and the said Jesse Hatton for himself his
heirs etc. do hereby convenant to and with the said John R.
Perkins, William Pasteur, John Winn and John Johnson Jr. their
heirs and assigns that the said Jesse Hatton the above described
land with the appurtenances to the said John R. Perkins, William
Pasteur, John Winn and John Johnson Jr. their heirs and assigns
shall and will warrant and forever defend against the claim of
all persons whatever. In Testimony whereof the aforesaid Jesse
Hatton has hereunto affixed his hand and seal the day and year
first above written.

Jesse Hatton (SEAL)

In presence of
Thos. W. Glass
Reuben Martin
Absolum Appleberry

Fluvanna County Clerks Office January 25th, 1819.

THIS DEED was this day proved to be the act of Jesse Hatton
a party thereto before me Overton Bernard Deputy Clerk of the
Court of the said County by the oaths of Thomas W. Glass, Reuben
Martin and Absolum Appleberry, the Witnesses thereto and there-
upon admitted to record.

Teste: Overton Bernard, D.C.

A Copy Teste: (signed) Richard F. George Clerk
Fluvanna County Circuit Court

Washington Co., Va. Deed Book 7, page 286 -

This indenture made the 15th day of November in the year of
our Lord one thousand eight hundred and twenty, between James
Reamy of the County of Floyd and State of Kentucky of the one
part, and George Hayton and Margaret Hayton, widow of John
Hayton, deceased, of the other part.

Witnesseth that the said James Reamy for and in consideration
of the sum of three hundred dollars to him in hand paid the

receipt whereof is hereby acknowledged, have this day granted,
bargained, sold and confirmed, and by these presents do grant,
sell and confirm unto the said George Hayton and Margaret Hayton
one certain tract or parcel of land containing 90 acres, be
the same more or less, lying in the County of Washington and on
the north side of the Middle Fork of the Holston River and bounded
as followeth to wit:

Beginning at three white oaks corner to Byars land with a
line of the same South 48, W. 59 poles to two sugar trees and an
ash on the North side of a ridge; N. 80, West 38 poles to a large
Spanish Oak near a clift of rocks; S. 58½, W. 81 poles to a
white oak and Buckeye; thence leaving John Byars land S. 20,
E. 62 poles to a white oak; S. 19, W. 25 poles to a large Spanish
oak corner to Nathaniel Harris's land purchased of the heirs of
John Hayton, deceased, and with lines thereof S. 50, E. 30 poles
to a dogwood in the mouth of a lane; S. 35, East 33 poles to a
white oak on Jacob Wolf's line and with the same N. 26 degrees,
E. 135 poles to two chestnuts on the top of a hill; N. 45, E.
100 poles to a black oak-White oak corner to Jacob Romans land,
with the north 76 W. 34 poles to the first station.

TO HAVE AND TO HOLD the above described tract or parcel of
land with all the appurtenances thereunto belonging or in any
wise appertaining thereunto to them, the said George Hayton and
Margaret Hayton, free and clear from the claim or claims of any
person or persons whatsoever. And the said James Reamy doth
hereby agree and binds hisself, his heirs, executors, administrators and assigns to warrant and forever defend the right and title
to the above described tract or parcel of land, in them, the said
George Hayton and Margaret Hayton for the sole use and behoof
of them, the said George and Margaret Hayton, their heirs,
executors and administrators.

In testimony whereof I have hereunto set my hand and seal
the day and year above written.

Signed: James Reamy (Seal)

Signed, sealed and acknowledged
in the presence of:
James Meek

BETSY HATON - POWER OF ATTORNEY TO GEORGE W. HATON

Know all men by these presents, that I, Betsy Haton, of
the County of Greene, and State of Indiana, have made, ordained,
constituted and appointed and do by these presents make, ordain,
constitute and appoint in my place and stead, put and depute
George W. Haton of Greene County and State of Indiana, my true
and lawful attorney for me and in my name, place and stead to
grant, bargain, sell and convey all that resivoir or tenement
which as I have no need or copy of the Will, I describe as
follows To Wit:

The divided or undivided third of a certain tract or parcel
of land, which by the Last Will and Testiment of the late William
Crabtree of the State of Virginia, deceased, was bequeathed to

the heirs of his daughter, Elizabeth, late the wife of Robert Haton of Greene County and State of Indiana, said land lying and being in what was then called the County of Washington, now the County of Smyth in the State of Virginia as will more fully appear by the said will dully proved and now remaining on file in the clerks office of the proper court of the said County of Smyth formerly Washington.

Now know ye, that I, the said Betsy Haton by these presents ordain, constitute and appoint the above named George W. Haton, my lawful attorney for me and in my name place and stead to grant, bargain and sell and convey the above described premises with the appurtenances and all my Estate, right, title and interest therein unto such person or persons and for such price or prices as he shall think proper and also for me in my name place and stead and as my proper act and deed or deeds of conveyances as shall be necessary for the absolute granting and assureing of the premises to the purchaser or purchasers in fee simple giving and granting to my said attorney all my lawful ways and means in my name for the purposes aforesaid and generally to do and performe all lawful acts and things necessary to be done and performed in and about the premises in my name and as lawfully and amply as I myself might or could do if personally present. And attorney or attorneys under him for the purpose aforesaid to make and constitute and again at pleasure to revoke hereby satisfying, allowing and confirming whatsoever, my said attorney, shall lawfully do in my name in and about the premises, by virtue of these presents -

In Witness whereof I have hereunto set my hand Seal this fifth day of June A.D. Eighteen hundred and forty six.

Signed, Sealed and Delivered
In the presence of:
W. C. Anders (or) Andrews
C. J. Banackman (or) Barrackman

Signed: BETSY X HATON
her mark
(SEAL)

Recorded in the Court Records of Smyth County, State of Virginia, Marion, Virginia in Deed Book #4 at page no. 293-294.

ABSTRACT OF REVOLUTIONARY WAR PENSION APPLICATION
(GSA National Archives # R6663) of

John McCoy

Contributed by Mr. Thomas P. Hughes, Memphis, Tennessee.
Thank you, Tommy.

Hendricks County, State of Indiana - 13 May 1833 -

John McCoy, a resident of aforesaid County and State - aged 68 years (thus born ca 1765) first entered service in the spring of the year 1782 in the month of March as a substitute in the place of Simon Adams ("SI") and served two months. At this time, he was living in Frederick Co., Virginia. He received his discharge at Winchester Barracks from William

Balis, his Captain, and immediately re-enlisted under Major Welsh and Captain Balis. He was later drafted into service in 1786 in Tennessee to fight hostile Indians (his officer, Lt. Edward Mitchell). At this time, he was living in Hawkins Co., Tennessee.

Applicant states that since the Revolutionary War, he has lived 8 years in Tennessee; 25 years in Kentucky; and 7 years in Indiana, (Hendricks Co.). His total service was seven months.

Affidavits of supporting testimony made by Reverend Jacob Reynerson and William Stinson (both of Hendricks Co., Indiana).

26 June 1854 - Power of Attorney from George McCoy, heir at law of John McCoy, to Charles C. Tucker, of Washington City (D.C.) to prosecute the claim of the said John McCoy, etc.
Certified before a Notary Public of Hendricks Co., Indiana, the above date.

This application was rejected by the War Department Pension Office which requested or needed additional evidence.

File # W 11598   Jesse Taylor

Jesse Taylor applied for pension 11 December 1828 in Rutherford Co., Tennessee. Enlisted in Continental Line of State of Virginia for 12 months and was in service at close of war; was orderly Sgt. in Captain Ballard's company in 3rd Regiment under command of Colonel Samuel Meredith.

Declaration made by Mary (Polly) Taylor in Hamilton Co., Illinois 7 April 1845 (age 67); states she was widow of Sgt. Jesse Taylor and that she was married to him latter part of August or 1st of September 1792; that Jesse Taylor died 24 Februa 1832.

Children	Born
Charles Taylor	7/19/1796
Henry	12/4/1798
Lewis	1/10/1801
William	2/25/1803
James	4/21/1805
John	4/ / 1807
Elizabeth	1810

(can't read others - one name born in 1812)

Certificate from Clerk of Warren Co., North Carolina states he cannot find marriage bond of Jesse Taylor to Polly Branton (or Brantley).

Affidavit by Evans Tanner that Jesse Taylor formerly lived in County of Mecklenburg, Virginia and enlisted in Revolutionary War from said county - others support as to service and Mecklenburg Co.

Affidavit made that Jesse Taylor married in 1792 in Mecklenburg Co., Virginia Mary (Polly) Branton who was daughter of James Branton. (Polly Taylor was still living in 1855 in Hamilton Co., Illinois.)

Cumberland Co., Va. Will Book 3, page 288 -

Last Will and Testament of Jesse Thomas dated 29 March 1805 and probated 22 July, 1805.

Directs that the land and plantation on which he resides be sold and a further sum, not exceeding 400 pds., be laid out in land lying within the STATE OF TENNESSEE, which said land so purchased shall be to the use of my wife, Mary Thomas, during her natural life, and at her death, to be equally divided between my sons, John Thomas - Anthony Hoggett Thomas - and Nathaniel Hoggett Thomas (all underage).

The tract of land I purchased of Willis Wilson to be equally divided between my sons, Job Howell Thomas and Phinehas (sic) Thomas.

To my daughter, Betsey Wilkerson, two negroes, Cuff and Judy.

To my daughter, Nancy Scruggs, two negroes, Keziah and Ned.

To my daughter, Nelly Glover, six negroes (named) for her life, then to her children.

To my son, Jesse Wood Thomas - slaves.

To my daughter, Jinney Thomas - slaves

To my daughter, Polly Thomas - slaves.

To my daughter, Porcia Thomas - slaves.

(Also bequeaths slaves to wife and other children already named above.)

Wife is to support his aged mother out of the estate.

Executors: My wife, Mary, and son, Phinehas (sic) Thomas and my son-in-law, Finch Scruggs.
Witnesses: Willis Wilson - James Mathews - Elijah Glover.

CODICIL: 4 May 1805 - further instructions as to his children, Jesse Wood Thomas - Betsey Wilkerson and Nelly Glover.

NOTE BY CHH: This very interesting record was contributed by Mr. Thomas P. Hughes, of Memphis, Tennessee. "Thank you, Tommy."

Following record furnished by Mrs. Charles C. Alexander of Columbia, Tennessee. "Thank you, Mrs. Alexander."

Maury Co., Tenn. Minute Book 8 (1820-1824), pp 185-186 -

January Term 1824. John McCormick aged about seventy years,

106

a resident of Maury Co., appeared in Court applying for
Revolutionary Pension. He enlisted in Buckingham Co., Virginia
in the company commanded by Captain Thomas Paterson, 1st
Regiment, commanded by Colonel Butler, Brigade commanded by
General Mulenburg, etc. His family consisted of himself and
his second wife, aged about twenty-five years, a son named
Charles, aged about fifteen, a son John, age four, and Sarah
Butler, mother-in-law, aged about sixty-five.

Following deposition furnished by Mrs. Bayne P. O'Brien of
Richmond, Virginia. "Thank you, Bayne."

Lancaster Co., Va. Deeds and Wills 11, page 206 -

     The deposition of Mary Rogers of the County of Lancaster
in the Colony of Virginia, widow, aged about 60 years, saith
that about six and twenty years since John Potts of the county
aforesaid together with Ann, his wife, and their three children,
Johanna, John and Anne, went to England. That about twelve
months afterwards the said John Potts, his said wife and heir,
his aforesaid daughters returned (?) leaving their said son
and was reported with his grandfather, John Potts, of the
County of Devon in Great Britton. That the aforesaid named
John Potts' daughter, Anne, dyed here about the age of ten
years and that since then her said father and mother are also
dead without having any more children than aforesaid. That
the Deponant was present at the birth of the aforesaid, Johanna,
now the widow of Thomas Pierce, late of the said county of
Lancaster and which said Johanna is the only surviving child
of her aforesaid father, it being reported that her aforesaid
brother is also dead and furthur she saith not.

May the 2nd 1722   her
                              Mary M Rogers
                                   mark

Following deposition furnished by Mr. James F. Lewis of
Callao, Virginia. "Thank you, Johnny."

Northumberland Co., Va. Loose Chancery Papers, Parker - vs - Beac
File Box 1804 -

     13 April 1804 - Deposition taken at the house of Lewis abb
Lewis Lamkin in Nash Co., North Carolina - 21 April 1803.

     I saw Molly Hatten married to Gabriel Parker for I was
present and gave her away and that the said Molly Parker, as
now is, was the woman that Peter Hatten brought out with him,
which formerly went by the name of Molly Lamkin in Northumberland
Co. and was called the daughter of Lewis Lamkin, deceased, and
that she is now living.

Qu askt by Lewis Lamkin Jun Attorney: was you acquainted in
the house of Lewis Lamkin, deceased, in Northumberland Co. in
Virginia in his life time.

Anr: I was and never heard anything to the contrary but that she was his daughter.

Peter Winstead

Sworn to before us and on the time and at the place above specified.
David Pridger
Abyah Pridger
David Winstead

Contributed by Mr. James F. Lewis of Callao, Virginia. "Thank you Johnny."

Northumberland Co., Va. Record Book 19, pages 537-538 -

20 January 1814 - William Walker and Catherine his wife of Henderson County, Kentucky to Joseph C. Williams of St. Marys Co., Maryland - consideration $411.00 - a tract of land containing thirty four acres, it being our proportional part of the land of the late Jno Cralle Sr., deceased, known by the name of Blincoe field, lying between the lands of Baldwin M. Leland and the heirs of Jno Cralle Jr., deceased.
     Witnesses: Willis W. Hudnall - Edward Downing - Samuel Davis Sr.
     Recorded 14 March 1814.

Northumberland Co., Va. Record Book 21, pages 171-174 -

30 November 1816 - Joseph C. Williams of St. Marys Co., Maryland to Baldwin M. Leland of Northumberland Co. - consideration $1500.00 - all my part of a tract of land called Blenkers - lying in Cherry Point Neck in Northumberland Co. Wife, Priscilla Williams signed deed.
     Witnesses: M. C. Jones - William Dawson.

Ibid, pages 484-487 -

4 February 1818 - William Ficklin and Elizabeth K., his wife (the said Elizabeth being one of the heirs of John Crawley, deceased) of the territory of Missouri and County of Washington - to Baldwin M. Leland of Northumberland Co. - consideration $500.00 - tract of land in Northumberland Co., Virginia on the waters of Coan River - containing 43¼ acres more or less.
     Witnesses: Jno S. Brickey - Shother Covington - B. J. Thompson - John Davis - Benjamin Williams.
     Recorded 14 September 1818.

Northumberland Co., Va. Record Book 22, pages 611-613 -

19 March 1821 - John C. Williams and Henrietta, his wife, of Feliciana Parish in Louisiana to Baldwin M. Leland - consideration $411.00 - all their claim and interest in a tract of land called Blincoe in Cherry Point Northumberland Co., Virginia.
     Witnesses: Thomas Bearhorse - James Holmes.

Ibid, pages 613-614 -

Power of Attorney dated 28 March 1821 - John C. Williams

and Henrietta E., his wife, of Felician Parish in Louisiana to
Joseph C. Williams of St. Marys Co., Maryland -------------
estate of our grandfather John Cralle late of Northumberland
Co., Virginia.
     Witnesses: Frederick Arnel - Joseph Felps.

These cemetery records were contributed by Mrs. George E. Buchner
of Selma, Alabama 36701. "Thank you very much, Mrs. Buchner."

CEMETERY RECORDS

Dallas County, Alabama

Presbyterian Cemetery at Pleasant Hill:

Mary F. Boyd
wife of Thomas B. Sommerville
born in Charlottsville, Va.
March 21, 1830
died March 21, 1898

Thomas B. Sommerville
born in Springfield, Virginia
May 1, 1829
died December 23, 1887

Edward Walker
born Williamsburg, Va.
Sept., 1801
Nov. 1873

Joseph Bell Walker
born Wytheville, Va.
Mar. 19, 1839
died Jackson, Miss.
Mar. 23, 1908

Arch D. Butler
a native of Virginia
born July 27, 1793
died May 25, 1842

Alonzo Vaughan
born near Petersburg, Va.
June 17, 1842
died August 8, 1898
aged 51 years, 2 months

**Pierce Family Cemetery
Old Town, located on the
property of Miles Hardy,
Rt. 1, Tyler, Alabama**

Starting west side:

In memory of
AMY Pierce

consort of
Abram Pierce
born in So. Carolina
and died
March 6th, 1839
aged about
40 years

In memory of
JOHN PIERCE, Sen.
a soldier of the Revolution
born in N. Carolina
moved to Alabama in
1819 and died
August 1840
aged about 89 years
He lived an exemplary
member of the Baptist
Church.

Sacred
to the memory of
JOHN PIERCE,
a native of
South Carolina
who was born
July 28th, 1792
and died
March 7th, 1843
aged 50 years, 7 months
and 9 days

In memory of
ANN PIERCE
consort of
Abram Pierce
born in Virginia
and died
August, 1821
aged about 40 years

In memory of

MRS. ELIZABETH PIERCE
consort of
John Pierce, Sr.
born in Virginia
and died
in Alabama 1819
aged about 73 years.
She was a consistent
member of the Baptist
Church for many years.

In
memory of
ABRAHAM PIERCE
who was born July 1, 1782
and died March 21, 1855
aged 72 years, 8 months
and 17 days.

Underwood Family Cemetery:

James R. Butler
born Halifax Co., Virginia
died in Pleasant Hill, Dallas Co. Ala
August 24, 1868
officer of the Cumberland Presbyterian Church for many years

Sarah F. Butler
wife of James R. Butler
daughter of Samuel and Elizabeth Catts
born in Fairfax Co. Virginia
Dec. 6, 1827, and died at Pleasant
Hill, Ala. Aug. 15, 1852 in the
24th year of her age.

Baptist Cemetery:

Samuel W. Catts
born in Alexandria, Va.
May 8, 1825
died Oct. 18, 1871

Contributed by Mrs. H. A. Knorr of Pine Bluff, Arkansas.
"Thank you, Kitty!"

Lancaster Co., Va. Deeds 21, page 84 -

Power of Attorney dated 20 August 1787, recorded 20 August
1787. Hannah Martin, wodow and administratrix of William Martin,
late of Lancaster Co., deceased, appoints Le Roy Pope, Jr., of
Amherst Co. as her attorney to demand recovery etc. a certain
negro man slave Willoughby, belonging to said decedents estate
which was stolen during his life time and believed to be housed
in the State of North Carolina etc. etc.

Lancaster Co., Va. Marriage Bonds

24 April 1765. Leroy Pope born 21 August 1742, to Elizabeth

110

Mitchell, 22 years of age (dau. of Richard Mitchell)
William Martin gives affidavit as to age of
Leroy Pope, James Tapscott, security.

16 August 1782   William Martin to Hannah Mitchell, James Pinchard,
security.

* * * *

VIRGINIA
ANCESTORS AND ADVENTURERS, VOL. 2

<u>SECTION 4</u>

Index - General   111

ADAMS   24
   Harriett (Jones)   56
   Harris   36
   John   57
   Richard   64
   Robert   35
   Simon   103
   Thomas   57

ADKINS
   Lea   52
   Mary (Gordon)   52

ADKINSON
   Alie   94

AKERS
   Claiborne   25
   Elizabeth (Thompson)   25
   Meredith   25

AKINS
   Joseph   18

ALCOKE
   Catharine   98

ALEXANDER
   Mrs. Charles C.   105

ALIF
   Catharine (Allison)   59
   John   59

ALLEN (ALLIN)
   Drury   39
   Elizabeth   39
   Hartwell   14
   Mary   53

ALLISON
   Catharine   59
   Fanny   59
   Martin   59
   Mary   59
   Nancy   59
   William   59

ALLYN
   Joseph T.   31

ALNUTT
   James   41

ANDERS (?)
   W. C.   103

ANDERSON
   Benjamin   21
   David   47-63
   Henry   61
   Margaret   30
   Mary   61-62
   Rowland   95

ANSILL
   Leonard   19
   Leonard (Sr.)   19
   Walker   19

APPLEBURY
   Abraham   42
   Absolum   101

ARDEN
   Abraham   8

ARMSTRONG
   Ann R.   82
   Thomas   50-82-97
   Thomas Jr.   82

ARNEL
   Frederick   108

ARTHUR
   William   30

ASHBY
   Alcinda   56
   Caroline   56
   Edwin Thomas   57
   Eliza M.   56
   Elizabeth (T)   56
   Frances (Wright)   19
   Henry   56
   Jamison   56
   (Capt) John   55-56
   John Jr.   56-57-58
   Kitty   56
   Kizzia   97
   Lucy S.   56
   Maria   56
   Marshall   56-57
   Martha   56
   Mary   56-57-58
   Mary T.   56
   Mary (Turner)   58
   Nimrod   56-57
   Samuel   56-57
   Susan   56
   Thomson   56-57
   Turner   56-57

ASHBY
  William   56-57
  William C.   56

ASHMORE
  William   15

AUSTINE
  Anne   47

AWBERY
  Francis   51
  Henry   51
  Thomas   51

AYDELOTTE
  Mathias   39

BACKHOUSE
  John   66
  Mary (Sr.)   66
  Mary (Jr.)   66

BACON
  Elizabeth   52
  Lydal   39-52-53
  Mary   52
  Mary (Allen)   53
  Nathaniel   52

BAILEY
  Capt. James   13

BAILIS
  Catharine   98

BALDWIN
  . Samuel   67

BALL
  Fayette   81
  John   60
  Maria L.   81
  Moses   59

BALLARD
  Captain   104
  Mary   23
  William   23

BALIS
  Capt. William   103-104

BALLINGER
  Cassandra (Plummer)   64
  Henry   64

  William   64

BANISTOR
  John   95

BANKS
  Gerard   3

BARKER
  John   24
  Lewis   24
  Thomas   24

BARNARD
  Elizabeth   21
  Francis   21
  Mary   21

BARNES
  Ellen   98
  Francis Jr.   38
  John   43

BARRACKMAN (?)
  C. J.   103

BARRADALL
  Edward   20

BARROW
  Eleazer   45
  Elias   45
  Elizabeth   45
  Ezra   45
  Jane   45
  John   44 (sic)
  John (Jr.)   45
  Randolph   45
  Thomas   45

BASCOE
  Nancy   98

BASS
  Daniel   33

BATTON
  Henry   100

BAYLEY
  John   16

BEALE
  Elizabeth (Hite)   5-6
  Tavener   5-6

BEAN(E)
  Ann   13
  Dr. John   97

BEARHORSE
  Thomas   107

BEATY
  Martin   59

BECK
  Andrew   16
  Moses   16
  Richard B.   35

BEDINGER
  Peter   94

BELCHER
  James   73

BELL
  Humphrey   72

BENTLEY
  William   31

BERNARD
  Overton   101

BERRY
  Aaron   40
  Benjamin   19-41
  David   40
  Henry   41
  Jane   40
  John   40
  Joseph Sr.   39-40
  Joseph Jr.   39-40
  Lydia   40
  Margaret   40
  Patience   40
  Peggy   40
  Sally   40
  Samuel   40
  Thomas   39-40-41-91
  William   39-40

BERRYMAN
  Benjamin   49

BICTLYN
  William   73

BILBRO
  Elizabeth (Noftsinger)49

  Thomas   49

BINFORD
  William   12

BIRCH
  James   98

BLACKLEY
  James   35

BLACKWELDER
  Caleb   94
  Catherine   94
  Elizabeth   94
  John (Sr.)   94
  John (Jr.)   94
  Margaret   94

BLAYDES
  John   32
  Kesiah   32

BOGART
  Captain   75

BOLAND
  J. B.   97

BONDURANT
  Benjamin   32
  Caroline (Smith)   33
  Charles P.   33
  Elizabeth   31-32
  Elizabeth (Davis)   32
  Elliott   32
  George   33
  George W.   32-33
  Jeffrey William   31-32-33
  Joseph   31-32
  Lucinda   33
  Sally (Palmore)   33
  William   33

BONHAM
  John   7
  Juliana (Hoppes)   7

BOOKER
  John   58
  Mary   58

BOOTH
  Elias   73
  William   73

BOSTICK
    Charles   2

BOSWELL
    John   98

BOWMAN
    Amey   11
    Jacob   93
    John   11-18

BOYD
    Mary F.   108

BRADLEY
    Benjamin   12

BRADY
    Patrick   92

BRANTER
    Jane   98

BRANTLEY (?)
    Polly   104

BRANTON (?)
    James   105
    Polly   104

BREWBACK
    Adam   94

BRIAN
    Mort (?)   28

BRICKEY
    John S.   107

BRIDGES
    Eliza   97

BRIZENDINE
    Isaac   39

BROADNAX
    Betty   12
    Edward   12

BROOK (E)(S)
    Artha   2
    Benjamin   3
    Deborah   66
    Hannah (Janny)   64
    James Jr.   64

    Robert   13-45
    Sally   2

BROWN
    Burwell   16-38
    (Census)   96
    Elizabeth
      (Richardson)   66
    Esek   16
    Francis   21
    Isaac   66
    John   66-73
    Margaret   66
    Mary (Barnard)   21
    Nathaniel   21
    Rebecca   38
    Thomas Sr.   27

BRUCE
    John Sr.   21
    Lucy (Gordon)   52

BRUEN
    Bryan   100

BRYANT
    Edmond   34
    Edward   34
    Mary   28
    Morgan   14
    Moses   28

BUCHANAN
    Alexander Pitt   6
    Sarah (Hite)   6

BUCHNER
    Mrs. George E.   108

BUCKANNON
    Elizabeth (Gordon)   52

BUCKINGHAM
    (Census)   97

BUCKTON
    Michal   93

BUFORD
    "Plaintiff"   8

BURCH
    Richard   24

BURKE
    William   98

BURNETT
  Joshua   11
  Mary (Roberts)   11

BURRUS
  Frances   38
  Sarah Ann   38
  Thomas   17-38

BURTON
  Edward   58

BUSHBY
  Mary (Hite)   6
  William   6

BUTLER
  Arch D.   108
  Colonel   106
  James R.   109
  Sarah   106
  Sarah F. (Catts)   109

BYARS
  John   21

BYRAS
  Sarah   59
  Stripling   59

BYRD
  William   72-73

CABINESS
  Henry   88-89
  Magdalene   89
  Magdalene (Jr.)   89
  Mary   89

CACKLEY
  Jacob   94

CALDWELL (COLDWELL)
  Agnes   90
  David   90
  George   90
  Jane   90
  John   17-90
  Mary   90
  Polly (Clyborne)   17
  Robert   48
  William   17-90

CALVERT
  Cornelius Jr.   39
  Jonas   98

(Capt) Max   27

CAMELL
  John   16

CAMPBELL
  Andrew   19
  Eneas   50
  Sarah   51
  Tabitha   51
  Walter   51
  William J.   93

CAPON
  Jacob   89
  Jane (Imbert)   89

CARLOS
  Archelaus   52

CARLTON
  John   50

CARPENTER
  (Census)   99

CARR
  Jacob   90
  Mary (Wilson)   23
  Peter   23

CARRUTH
  John, Esq.   11

CARTER
  Alexander   30
  Barbarie   53
  Charles   31
  Edward F.   83
  Elinor   53
  Elizabeth A.   82
  Emeline   82
  Giles   31
  Isaac   82
  Jacob   12
  Jeduthan   37
  Jethro   82
  John   34
  John C.   82
  John W.   82-83
  Joseph   24-36
  Lucy   33
  Mary   42-82
  Mary E.   83
  Nancy   82
  Robert   42

CARTER
   Robert (Sr.)   31
   Robert (Jr.)   31
   Sally   33
   Samuel J.   83
   Secretary   42
   Thomas   33-42
   William   53
   William M. H.   83

CATLETT
   Peter   26

CATLIN
   Maria   82

CATTS
   Elizabeth   109
   Samuel   109
   Sarah F.   109
   Samuel W.   109

CARTWRIGHT
   Mathew   51

CAVAN (CAVEN)
   Pat   54
   Sarah   67

CHADWELL
   David Sr.   59

CHAMBERS
   William   2

CHANCELLER
   Maria (Ashby)   56

CHANDLER
   Deborah (Brooke) 66
   George   66

CHARLTON
   Edward   71

CHASE
   Ann H.   82
   Eugene   82
   Lewson   81
   Peter   82
   Virginia   81
   William T.   82

CHATTIN
   Elizabeth   36

John   36
John Sr.   36
Joseph   36
Nancy   36
Polly   36
Sally   36
Thomas   36

CHESEMAN
   Samuel   67

CHEVAIR
   Elizabeth   88
   James   88

CHILDERS
   Thomas   12

CHILES
   Henry   24
   John   30

CHINN
   Christopher   46
   Jannett (Scott)   46
   Mary I.   46
   Rawleigh   10
   Thomas   46
   Thomas Jr.   46

CHISOLM
   Rachel (Christmas) 47

CHOCKLEY
   David   55

CHRISMAN
   Peter   94

CHRISTMAS
   Catey   47
   Elizabeth   47
   John   47
   John (Jr.)   47
   Mary   47
   Rachel   47
   Richard   47
   Temperance   47
   Thomas   47
   Thomas (Jr.)   47
   William   47

CHRISUP
   Michael   27

CHUMLEY
   Allen   98

CLARK(E)
   Elizabeth   97
   James   97
   John   64
   John K.   17
   "O"   97
   Thomas H.   36

CLAY
   Daniel   95

CLERK
   Francis   71

CLINE
   David   7

CLYBORNE
   Archibald   17
   James   17
   John   17
   Jonas   17
   Lemuel   17
   Polly   17
   Thomas   17
   William   17

COBB(S)
   Edward   43
   Edward Jr.   43
   Lewis   24
   "Mr."   72

COCKERHAM
   Miner   8

COFFIN
   Christopher   28

COKE
   "Mr'.'   72

COLDWELL
   Henry   7

COLE
   James D.   15

COLEMAN
   Elliott   53
   Gulielmus   53
   Mrs. Margarite   9

COLLINGSWORTH
   Abby   12
   William   12

COLLINS
   Abraham   11
   Susannah (Roberts) 11

COMPELL
   Sarah   98

CONNALLY
   George   34
   John   34

CONNER(S)
   Cornelius   100
   Daniel   19
   Edward   18
   Margaret   18-100
   Mary   18-19
   Robert   18

COOK
   Joseph   30

COOPER
   Mrs. Alice Cavender 83
   Ann   98
   Thomas   97
   William   43

COPELAND
   Anderson   96
   Peter   91

COPLAND
   (See COPELAND)

CORBIN
   Ann   54
   Betty   55
   Elizabeth (Tayloe) 55
   Gawin   55
   Joanna (Tucker)   55
   Mrs. Joanna   54
   Col. Richard   55

CORKER
   Susan (Robinson)   91

COURTNEY
   James   44
   Sarah (Embry)   44

COURTS
  Catharine (Renoe)   15
  Robert H.   15

COVINGTON
  Shother   107

COX
  Coleman   21
  Griffin   98
  Harmon   50
  Jane   50
  Tench   59

CRABTREE
  Abraham   60
  Elizabeth   103
  Job   60
  William   102

CRAFT(S)
  George   25
  Thomas   28

CRAIN
  John Terry   37

CRALLE
  John Jr.   107-108

CRAWFORD
  Ann   90
  George   90
  James   90
  Margaret   90
  Mary   90
  Patrick   90

CRAWLEY
  John   107

CRISP
  Ann (Farmer)   55
  John   55
  John (Jr.)   55
  Mary   55
  Moses   55
  Peter   54
  Samuel   55
  Sarah (Sr.)   54
  Sarah (Jr.)   54

CRITTENDEN   45
  Henry   13

CROCKETT
  Joseph   8

CROSBY
  Susanna (Renoe)   15

CROSLEY
  Sarah   97

CROW
  John   41

CRUMP
  John   98
  Richard M.   25

CRUTCHFIELD
  Major   8

CRYDER
  Martin   93

CULPEPER
  Alexander   26
  Christian   29
  Henry   29
  Henry (Sr.)   29

CUMMINS
  Alexander   8
  Daniel   93

CUNNINGHAM
  John   96

CURLE
  Julius   35

CURRELL
  Elizabeth I.   83
  John S. (Sr.)   83
  John S. (Jr.)   83
  Margaret   83

CURRIE
  A. Hill   81
  James   76

CURRIER
  Califf   94

CUSINS
  Thomas   37

DABBS
William 15-16

DALTON
Anne 17
James 30
Randolph 30
Samuel (Sr.) 17
Timothy 30
William 16-17

DANCY
Francis 12
Francis H. 16

DANIEL(L)
Henry 43
William 27

DARRACOTT
John 47

DARWIN
(Capt) John 49

DAVIS
Benjamin 33
Benjamin T. 32-33
Elizabeth 33
George Sr. 32-33
George Jr. 32-33
Henry 90
James 90
Jeffrey 33
John 94-107
Joseph B. 32-33
Kissey 33
Mary 32-33-90
Samuel 33-90
Samuel Sr. 107
Thomas 51
William 33-90
William T. 15-16

DAWKINS
Frances 10
George 10
Hannah 10
John Sr. 10
John Jr. 10
Joseph 10
Thomas 10
William 10-53

DAWSON
William 107

DAY
Margery 94

DEACON
Grace 94

DE LA SOMET
John 16

DELBRIDGE
Edward 24

DELONG
George 50

DEMISSY
"Mr." 73

DENTON
Abraham 22

DE POYRESSY
Le Chevalier 72

DEWEY
Stephen 52

DICK
"A" 3
Charles 40-41
Patience (Berry) 40

DICKENSON
Ann (Thompson) 27-28
Elisha 39
James 28
John 38
Mary (Dudley) 28
Sarah 27-38
Thomas 27-28

DILDEY
Catharine (White) 77
Gotlieb 76
Maria 76
Peter 77

DILLON
James 23

DIVINE
William 93

DIXON (DIXSON)
Ann 52
Henry 52

John	50-51
Joseph	50-51
Mary	50
Robert	52
Roger	22
Susannah	51
"T"	52
Tilman L.	52

DOBSON
Rev. Thomas 38

DOIG
David 76

DONALD
Robert 55
Thomas 18

DONALDSON
James 92

DOODES
Minor 95

DOUBERLY
John 96

DOUGLAS
Archibald 46
Catharine Sr. 46
Catharine Jr. 46
James 46
Margaret 46

DOWDY
James 7

DOWNING
Edward 107

DRINKER
George 66
Hannah 66
Joseph 66
Ruth (Miller) 66

DUBOIS
Abraham 67-68
Edmund Cheesman 67-68
Elizabeth 68
James S. 67
Mary 67

DUDLEY
Anne Sheldon 28
John 28
Mary (Bryant) 28
William 28

DUERO
James 88
Olimp (?) 88

DUFOUR
Perret 24

DUNAWAY
Felicia T. 81

DUNLAP
Alex 21

DUNLOP
James 38

DUPUY
Bartholomew 31

DYE
William 33

DYER
Fontaine 4
George 4
Joseph F. 4

EARLY
"Defendant" 8
Eaton 11
Jane 11
William 11

EDWARDS
Joseph 100

EDY (?)
Elizabeth 94

EGGERTON
Charles C. 67
Jane 67

ELLIS
Susanna Stokes 53

ELLITT
Cornelius 11

ELLZEY
Col. William   54

EMBRY
Albert G.   44
Anne (Walker)   44
Elizabeth   44
Elizabeth (Homes)   44
John   44
John Thompson   44
Robert   44
Sarah   44
Walker   44
William   44

ENNIS
John   16

ERWIN
Elizabeth   30
Mary   30
Mathew   30

ESTEN
Capt James   73

EVANS
Jesse   60-61
Peggy (Russell)   60-61

EVELICH (?)
Thomas   27

EVERETT
John   64
Rachel   64

EVERSOLL
Solomon   98

EWING
Sarah A.   97

FAIRFAX
Bryan   26
Denny (Martin)   26
Frances   26
Lord   22-23-24-25-26
Robert   26

FAGAN (?)
John James   89

FALLEN
John   44

FAMBROUGH
Hannah (Stewart)   48
Robert   48

FARGUSON
Elizabeth   8
Isaac Sr.   8

FARMER
Anne   55
Catharine (Wygal)   41
Thompson   41

FARQHAR (FARQUHAR)
Ann   65
Elizabeth   65
Mary   65
William   65

FARROW
Isaac   15
Nimrod   57

FASSETT
Joseph   98

FELKNER
Henry   93

FELPS
Joseph   108

FERGUSON
Bryant   15-16-35
Nancy (Moore)   15-16
Robert   54

FERRELL
William   50

FERRIER
William   17

FERRILE
William P.   50

FICKLIN
Elizabeth K.   107
William   107

FINNIE
"Mr."   72

FISHER
Jacob   60
Peter (Sr.)   60

Peter   59-60-61

FLANNAGAN
Whittle   9

FLANNAKEN
John   47

FLEEMAN
Henry   42
Mary (Carter)   42

FLETCHER
Owen M.   12

FLOOD
Joshua   32
Mary   32

FLOWEREE
Daniel   3
French   3

FLOWERS
Betsy   81
William   81

FLOYD
(Gov.) John   55

FONTAINE
Aron   63

FORBES
James   71

FORD
John   43

FORQUERAN   31
Elizabeth   88
Jeanne   88

FOSTER
Catharine   46
Haskew   46

FOX
James   91

FRANCIS
Ann   30
John   30
Maria J.   82
Mary   82
Mary (Erwin)   30

Peter   82
Sarah A.   82
William   30

FREEMAN   37
(See FLEEMAN)

FULTON
James   35
Smith   35

FUNKHOUSER
Christian   22
Christine   22

GAINES
Harry   73

GALLON
Redmond   8

GAMBLE
Richard   71

GAMBRIL
John   97

GANN(S) - (GAN)-
Addam   33-34
Hannah   34
John   34

GARARD
Abner   95

GARDNER
James   43
Martin   94
Mary   94

GARNER
(Census)   96-97

GARROTT
James   2

GAUGH
Catharine   96
John   96

GAY
James   21

GEORGE
Richard F.   101

GERRARD
   John   97

GERMAIN
   James   59
   Nancy (Allison)   59

GILBERT
   Mary   58
   Samuel   58
   William G.   47

GILES
   Ephraim   36
   Nancy (Chattin)   36

GILMAN
   George   9

GIPSON
   Elizabeth (Mrs.)   53
   Gideon   65
   Hannah (Norkles)   65

GLASLEY
   John Jr.   9

GLASS
   Thomas W.   42-101

GLENN (GLEN)
   James   53
   Nathan   53
   Nathaniel   53
   Robert   53
   William   53

GLOVER
   Elijah   105
   Nelly (Thomas)   105

GOLBEE (or GOLDSBY)
   Frances   28-29

GOLDEN
   William F.   35

GOODRIDGE
   William   45

GOREING
   John Mary (sic)   89
   Peter   89
   Susan   89

GORDON   34
   Elizabeth   52-75
   Elizabeth (Bacon)   52
   Jane Allen   52
   Langston B.   52
   Lucy   52
   Lyddal   52
   Martha C.   52
   Mary   52
   Richard   52
   Roderick   52
   Sarah   52
   Susannah (Ellis)   53
   Thomas   52
   William   52

GORY
   Claudius   89
   John   89
   Mary   89

GOVER
   Anthony P.   67
   Sarah (Janney)   67

GOWER   24

GOWN
   William   91

GRAHAM
   David   42

GRANT
   Edward   39

GRANTHAM
   Mary (Ashby)   56

GRAVATT
   Richard   40-41

GRAVES
   Esom   2

GREGG
   Rebeckah (Janney)   65
   Thomas   65

GRIFFITH
   Abraham   66
   Isaac   66
   Rachel (Taylor)   66

GRIGLEY
    Pristy   98

GRIGSBY
    Lewis   3
    Sharlott (sic) 3

GRISSOM
    Ann   18
    Robert   18

GROSE
    Mary   94

HADDEN
    David   21
    William   21

HADEN
    Anthony   58-64
    John   58-64

HAGGARD
    George   101
    James   101

HAHN
    "M"   97

HALDINE
    James   75

HALL
    Addison   81

HAMILTON
    John   9
    Robert   92

HAMLET(T)
    Fanny   15
    "Heirs"   15
    James   14

HAMLIN
    Charles H. 38
    Sarah   28
    Thomas   28

HAMPTON
    Frankie   24
    George   23
    Mary (Ballard) 23
    Noah   99
    Susanna   24

HANCHER
    William   94

HARDING
    Hopkins   45

HARDYMAN
    Stith   16

HARRIS   24
    Allen Howard 9
    Benjamin   9
    Francis   43-44
    Francis E. 43
    George (Sr.) 67
    George (Jr.) 67
    (Col) John 44
    John F.   43
    Jordan   44
    Joseph   9
    Joseph Sr. 9
    Nathaniel 21-102
    Robert   17
    Sarah Ann (Littler) 67
    Susannah 67

HARRISON
    Benjamin 20
    Charles   26
    John P.   38
    Sarah   97

HART
    John M.   14

HARTSHONE
    Rebecca   66
    Susannah 66
    William   66

HARVIE
    J. D.   18

HASKINS
    Christopher 42

HATCHER
    Henry   7
    James   55

HATFIELD
    Abner   59

HATON (HAYTON)
    Betsy   102-103
    Elizabeth (Crabtree)103

George   21-101-102
George W.   102-103
Harley D.   99
John   21-99-100-101-102
John (Jr.)   99
Margaret   21-101-102
Robert   103
Thomas   99
Thomas (Jr.)   99

HATTEN (HATTON)
    Jesse   41-42-100-101
    Molly   106
    Peter   106

HAUPMAN
    John D.   5

HAWKINS
    John   63

HAYDON
    Charles   45
    Ezekiel   45

HAYNES
    Anthony   11
    Jane (Eaton)   11

HAYNIE
    Stephen   45

HEADLY
    Ann (Pugh)   5
    Henry   4-5

HEDRICK
    Elizabeth (Hoppes)   7
    John   7

HEILY
    Martin   28

HENDERSON
    Alexander   18-46
    Archibald   46
    Charles   83
    George   83
    Isabella   83
    Mary A.   83
    William (Sr.)   83
    William (Jr.)   83

HENDRICK
    John   31

HENDRICKSON
    (Census)   95

HENNEN
    James   38

HESTHER
    Charles   63
    Rachel (Tait)   63

HICKMAN
    John   57
    Margaret   42
    William P.   42

HIGGASON
    Catey (Christmas)   47
    John   47
    Richard   47

HIGGINS
    Aron   9

HIGHT
    Sarah   12

HILL
    Elijah   60-61
    Henrietta   97
    Humphrey   72
    William   67

HINTON
    Christopher   34

HISKLE
    Christopher   93

HITE
    Alexander   5-94
    Catharine   6
    Deborah   6
    Elizabeth   5
    Frances   6
    George   5-6
    Hans Yost   6
    Jacob   5-6-94-99
    James   6
    John   6-26
    Mary   6
    Sarah   6
    Thomas   6

HOBSON
    Samuel   43

HOG
Peter 26

HOGAN
William 8

HOGE
John 42
John M. 42
Moses H. 42
Nancy R. 42
Rebecca 42

HOGG
Sarah (Campbell) 51

HOLFORD (?)
Henry 94

HOLLIDAY
William 76

HOLMAN
Tandy 64

HOLME
William 12

HOLMES
James 107
William 91

HOLT
Emeline 81
Emeline (Jr.) 81
James A. 81
Robert 82
Timothy 2
William 36

HOMES
Edmund 44
Elizabeth 44

HOOFMAN (HUFMAN)
Philip 93

HOOK
Isaac 23
Mary 23

HOPKINS
Elizabeth 39-66
Hannah (Janney) 66
James 8

John 39-66
Samuel 31
Thomas 8

HOPPES (or HOPPER?)
Barbara 7
Catharine 7
Elizabeth 7
Henry Sr. 7
Henry Jr. 7
Juliana 7
Margaret 7
Mary 7
Polly 7

HOPSON
Sarah (Gordon) 52

HORNE
Francis 92

HOUGH
Burnett 54

HOWARD
Elizabeth 49
Samuel Noftsinger 49

HOWE
William H. 42

HOY
Thomas 58

HUBBARD
Richard 19-49

HUDNALL
Willis W. 107

HUFMAN
Christina 98

HUGHES (HUGHS)
Betty (Jones) 56
Constantine 65
Elizabeth 65
Elizabeth (Nickols) 65
Matthew 65
Thomas P. 10-103-105

HUME
James 22
Sarah 22
William 22

HUMPHREY
David   38

HUNTER
James   41

HUTCHINSON
John   77

HUTCHISON
Eleanor   90
Francis   90
George   90
Jennet   90
John   90
John Sr.   90
John Jr.   90
Margaret   90
Mary   90
William   90

HUTSON
Shadrick   58

HUTTON
Thomas   92

HYRICK
Owen   12

ILER
Adolph   94

IMBERT
Jane   89
John   89

IRBY
Francis   12
John   16

IRELAND
Edward   67
Susannah   67

IRWIN
James   9
John   9

JACKSON
(?Nat)   52
Thomas   52

JAES
Reuben   101

JAMISON
Milley (Renoe)   15

JANNEY (JANNY)
Elizabeth   65-66
Hannah   64-66-67
Jacob   65
Joseph   66-67
Mahlon   64
Rebeccah   65
Sarah   67
Sarah (Plummer)   64
Susannah   67
William   23-65-66

JEFFRESS
Jennings M.   38

JENKINS
Jacob   40
John   40

JETT
Thomas   38

JOHN (Sic)
Thomas   50

JOHNSON
Daniel   31-35
James   12
John (Sr.)   42
John Jr.   42-100-101
Orphans   31-42

JOHNSTON
John   7
Margaret (Hoppes)   7
Capt. Thomas   49

JOLLY
Edward   12
John   12
Thomas   12

JONES
Abraham   24
Benjamin   5
Betty   56
Charles   17
Catharine   98
David   53
Dolly (Ashby)   56-57
Elizabeth (Pugh)   5
Francis Slaughter   56

Gabriel 26-56
Harriett 56
James 47
John 11-21
John A. 56
Juliett 56
Lewis 53
M. C. 107
Mary 47
Owen 53
Paul 12
Polly 56
Robert 56
Roger 12
Stephen 17
William 12
Wood 11

JUSTICE
William 12

JUSTIS(S)
John 13
Mark 13

KEATON
William Jr. 17

KEITH
Prof. Arthur L. 19
James 100

KELDERMAN
Herman 95

KELLER
George 93

KELLY
Dennis 18

KEMPER
Peter H. 98

KENNEDY
David 97

KENNON
Fanny 40
Sally (Berry) 40
William 39-40

KENZEL
Henry 92

KEPLINGER
John 93

KERCHEVAL
Jane (Berry) 40
John 40
Lewis C. 40
Matilda 40
Thomas B. 40

KERN
Elizabeth 22
James 9

KERR
James 27
James (Sr.) 27
(Sgt.) Robert 26
Samuel 27

KERSHAVELL
Barbary 53
Samuel 53

KIDD
Andrew 28
James 31
Joseph 76

KINCAID
Sarah 96

KING
Delila 84
Eliza 84-85
Elizabeth 91
"J" 84
James 13-84
Joseph 85
Joshua 91
Lafayette 84
"M" 84
Mary 84
Munsford 84
Peggy 13
Red 85
Rice 84
Sarah 84-85
Susannah 84
Tabitha (Sr.) 85
Tabitha (Jr.) 85

KNIGHT
Samuel 27

KNORR
  Katherine (Kitty)   109

LAGARDE
  John   26

LAMBERT
  Christopher   93

LAMBORN
  Dinah   66
  Hannah (Williams)   66
  Parmenas   66
  Thomas   66

LAMKIN
  Abb Lewis   106
  James   8
  Lewis (Jr.)   106
  Molly   106

LAMOTT
  William   18

LANDERS
  Abraham   37

LANDMAN
  Elizabeth (Pugh)   5
  William   4-5

LANGDON
  Samuel   25

LANGFORD
  Curly   43

LANTUS
  Daniel   95

LEAN
  Abraham   27

LEARY
  William   28

LECABOUGH
  Peter   94

LEE
  Catharine (Hite)   6
  George S.   82
  Mary A.   82
  Mary C.   82
  Theodrick   5-6
  William   34

LEEKER
  Rich   94

LEFEVRE
  Ester   88
  Isaac   88
  Magdalene   88

LEFORE
  Daniel   91

LEFTWICH
  John   8

LE GRAND
  Elizabeth   31
  Jacque   31
  James   31
  John   31

LELAND
  Baldwin M.   107

LEVEREAU
  Moses   31

LEWELLIN
  Lyson   13
  Sally   13

LEWIS   9
  Elizabeth   32
  Fielding   94
  Capt "J"   30
  James F.   106-107
  John   19-34

LIGGET(T)
  Elizabeth   98
  William   9

LIGHTFOOT
  Polly (Jones)   56

LIMLY
  John   93

LINDER
  Simon   94

LINDSAY
  Reuben   9

LINK
  Jesse   2
  John Sr.   2

Thomas   2

LITTLE
Charles   34
David   34

LITTLER
Ann   67
John   67
Sarah Ann   67

LLOYD
Edward   74
Elizabeth (Tayloe)   74
Matilda   42
Moses B.   42
Thomas   14

LODWICK
John   97

LOGAN
David   48
John   48
William   48

LONG
Edward   25
Edward Sr.   25
Eliza A.   42
George   25
James   20
John   36
Richard   25
Thomas   20
William   25

LORTON
Thomas   67

LOVELL (?)
William   62

LOXAM
Capt.   5

LOYD
William   20

LOZANNE
Elizabeth   88
John   88

LUCAS
Samuel   13

LUCK
George F.   24

McADAM
Arch: 18

McALISTER
Abigail (Tate)   62

McCALLY
James   42-101

McCANALTY
Fanny (Allison)   59
John   59

McCAN(N)
"Mr."   76
Patrick   93

McCARTY
Andrew   92

McCASH
(Census)   95-96

McCOLLOUGH
John   99

McCORD
James   85
James M.   85
Tennessee   85

McCORMICK
Charles   106
John   105-106
John (Jr.)   106

McCOY
George   104
John   103-104

McDANIEL
Nancy   98

McDONALD
Angus   26
Elizabeth   98

McDONNELL
Margaret   98

McDOWALL (McDOWELL)
James   76
Samuel   73

McGREW
James ... 64
Mary (Ridgeway) ... 65

McINTYRE
Alexander ... 53-54
Alexander Jr. ... 54
Catharine ... 54
Charles ... 54
Daniel ... 54
(Rev.) Dugald ... 42
Elizabeth ... 54
Jane ... 53-54
John ... 54
Patrick ... 54
Rebecca S. (Hoge) ... 42
Robert ... 54
William ... 54

McLEAN
Hugh ... 18

McLELAND
Malcolm ... 55

McMACHAN
John ... 100

McMICKIN
Hugh ... 76

McNEELY
Thomas ... 37

MACE
Peter ... 49
Polly (Noftsinger) ... 49

MACKAY
Angus ... 20

MACKFERESON
Ann ... 28-29

MACKY
Robert ... 26

MACLIN
James ... 24

MACON
John ... 53

MADDEN
Comfort ... 97

MANN
Elizabeth ... 3
George Sr. ... 3
George Jr. ... 3
Hannah ... 3
James ... 35

MANNING
Caleb ... 12
Malachy ... 39
Mathew ... 39
William ... 38-39

MAPLES
Josiah ... 25-36
Peter ... 25
William ... 35
William (Jr.) ... 36

MARINER
Doctor ... 76
James ... 76

MARLOW
John ... 22

MARSHALL
Colonel ... 49
David ... 59
Humphrey ... 25
John ... 56
Rebeccah ... 59
Thomas ... 25

MARTIN
Andrew ... 39
Ann Susannah ... 26
Anna (or Amey?) ... 11
(Rev.) Denny ... 26
Eunity (Unity) ... 11
Frances ... 26
George W. ... 95
Hannah (Mitchell) ... 109-110
John ... 11
John Sr. ... 11
Mrs. John ... 28-29
Philip ... 26
Rebecca ... 11
Reuben ... 42-101
Sybella ... 26
Thomas ... 11
Thomas Bryan ... 26
William ... 109-110

MARTINDALE
John 58

MASON
George 19-48-71-91
Martha 94

MASSEY
Lee 20

MASSOT
Elizabeth 88
Frances 88
Peter 88

MATHEWS
Ann 19
James 105
Margaret 20
William 19-20

MAUPIN
Gabriel 17

MAURER
George 93

MAXEY
Edward 30
Nancy 13
Thomas Jefferson 13
William 32

MAXWELL
Alexander 90
John 28
John (Sr.) 90
John (Jr.) 90
Margaret 90
Mary 90
Thomas 90
William 28

MEADE
(Census) 96

MEARS
John 51

MEEK
James 21-102

MELCAR (?)
Richard 8

MERCER
Colonel 49
(Col.) George 40-41
John 71

MERCERO
Francisco 94

MEREDITH
Col. Samuel 104

MERRIETT
George 94

METCALFE
Elizabeth 38
Samuel 73
William 38

MEYERS
Elizabeth 98

MICHELL
Archelaus 64

MIDDLETON
Francis 94

MILLER
Elizabeth 66
George 32
James 41
Jane 98
Mordecai 66
Peggy (Wygal) 41
Rebecca (Hartshorne) 66
Ruth 66
Simon 53
Warwick 66

MINOR
Doodes 95
Garrett 62-63

MIRE
Henry 22

MITCHELL
Andrew 46
(Lt.) Edward 104
Elizabeth 109-110
Hannah 110
John 16-17-91
Richard 110

MOAR
  Samuel   97

MOLER
  Adam   94

MONNELL
  William   21

MOOR(E)
  Mrs. Ann (Littler)   67
  George   15-16-35
  John   12-19
  Joseph   8-35
  Mathew   36
  Nancy   15-16
  Sarah   15
  Thomas   20

MORAN
  Michael   93

MORE
  Jesse   34
  Lydia (Renoe)   15
  Valentine   34
  William   34

MORGAN
  Henrietta   60
  Rees   100

MORRIS
  James   73

MORRITIE
  John   94

MORTON
  Elizabeth   95
  Joseph   34
  Mary   95

MOSELEY
  Arthur   91
  Benjamin   13-24-45
  Isaac   24
  "L"   43
  Robert   13-43-45
  Susanna   91
  Thomas   24
  William   45
  William Sr.   45-91
  William Jr.   13-91

MOSS
  (Capt.) Henry   31
  John   51
  William   98

MULENBURG
  General (Peter)   106

MULHOLLAND
  Charles   33

MUNFORD
  Betty (Broadnax)   12
  Edward   12

MUNSAY (MUNDAY?)
  Jesse   21

MURDEN
  Edward   39
  Elizabeth (Hopkins)   39
  Jeremiah   39
  John   39

MURDOCK
  Elizabeth   97
  James   54
  Jeremiah   21

MURPHY
  Ezekiel   35

MURRAY
  John   92

MYARS
  Joseph   6

MYERS
  Elijah   67
  Mary   67
  Pamelia   67

MYRES
  Esther   65

NANCE
  Philip   59

NASH
  John M.   81
  R. S.   81
  Sarah G.   81

NEAL
    Eliza M. (Ashby)   56

NELME
    Thomas   27

NELSON
    Ambrose   36
    Basil (Sr.)   36
    Bazel (Jr.)   36
    Elizabeth (Chattin)   36
    James   36-37
    Samuel   37
    Susanna (Shelton)   37
    William B. A.   37

NEWELL
    Regen   98
    Susannah   98

NEWLAND
    John   94

NEWTON
    Burton   31
    Robert B.   42

NICHOLAS
    Georgeanna   82
    Nathaniel   3

NICKOLS
    Elizabeth   65
    Ruth   65
    Thomas   65

NIDA
    John   7
    Sally   7

NIHAN
    Timothy   93

NISWANGER
    Elizabeth (Kern)   22
    John   22
    Solomon   22

NOFTSINGER
    Abraham   49-50
    Elizabeth   49
    Isaac   49-50
    Polly   49
    Samuel   49
    Sarah (Sally)   50

NOLAND
    Philip   19

NORKLES
    Hannah   65

NORRIS
    Eliza   83
    Ellen   83
    Mary F.   83
    Richard   83
    Thomas Sr.   83

NUGENT
    Ann   4

O'BRIEN
    Mrs. Bayne P.   106

O'CONNOR
    John   93

ODELL
    Caleb   22

ODEN
    Leonard   48
    Ruth   48

O'KEAN
    Joseph   92

OLIVER
    Elizabeth   29
    Mary   29
    Thomas   29

ORR
    Alexander   60-61
    Faith (Russell)   60-61

OSBORN(E)
    John   55
    Thomas   74

OURAM
    Thomas   23

OVERBY
    A. R.   84
    Caroline   84
    Charles   84
    Edward   84
    Elizabeth   84-85
    E. V.   84

Jane   84
Jane (King)   83
John   84-85
Ludmill(?)   84
Ludwig   83
Mary   83
Nancy   84
Nancy (Jane)   84
P. W.   84
R. N.   84
Robert   84
Sarah (Sr.)   84
Sarah (Jr.)   84
William   83-84

OWNES
    Joshua   38

PACE
    Catharine   8
    John   8

PAIN(E)
    John   8
    Robert   53

PALMORE
    Charles   33
    John R.   33
    Sarah (Sally)   33
    Thomas   22-23

PANCOAST
    John   65-67
    Mary (Talbott)   67
    Ruth (Nickols)   65

PANNILL
    Elizabeth   34
    Pierce B.   34

PARISH
    Timothy   24

PARK
    James   74

PARKER
    Gabriel   106
    Kedar   52
    Molly (Hatten)   106

PARROTT
    Elijah   2
    Elizabeth   2
    James   2

John   2
John (Jr.)   2
Judith   2
Ledford   2
Mourning   2
Nancy   2
Penelope   2
Ruth   2
Sally   2
Susannah   2

PASTEUR
    William   42-100-101

PAT(T)ERSON
    Sarah   97
    Capt. Thomas   106

PAULETT
    Elizabeth (Christmas)47

PAVEY
    Ann (Nugent)   4
    Sarah (Tock)   4
    Sibella   4
    Walter   4
    Webley   4

PAXTON
    Arthur   66
    Jacob   66
    Mary   67
    Pamelia (Myers)   67

PAYNE
    Frances   35
    Jesse   35
    Col. John   59
    John   10-35-47
    John C.   35
    Josiah Jr.   10
    Richard   46
    William   47
    William G.   35

PEARSON
    Joseph   14
    William   15

PECK
    Adam   17
    Elizabeth   17
    Joseph   17

PEERSON
    Charles   14

Elizabeth 14
Jesse A. 14
Joe 13-14
Mastin 14
Richmond 13-14
Sherwood 13-14
Thomas 14
William 14

PEETE
Samuel 71

PENDERY
(Census) 96

PENNELL
Joseph 8
Pierce Butler 35

PERKINS
John R. 42-100-101

PERKSDALE
Nicodemus 94

PERUE
Catharine 89
Peter 89
Peter (Jr.) 89

PETER
Capt. Thomas 13

PETERMAN
Jane R. 42
John 42

PETERSON
John 95

PEYTON
Henry 10
Timothy 10

PHILLIPS
James Jr. 50
Jenkins 9
Ruth 50

PIDGION
Charles 64
Rachel(Everett) 64
William 64

PIERCE
Johanna (Potts) 106
Thomas 106

PIERPONT
Esther (Myres) 65
Francis 64
Mary 64
Obed 65

PIGGOTT
John 23

PINCHARD
James 110

PIPER
Benjamin 58
Harry 91
John 9

PITT
George 74

PLAY
Robert 92

PLEASANTS
Robert 12
Robert Jr. 12

PLUMMER
Cassandra 64
Elener (Poultney) 64
Joseph 65
Joseph West 65
Mary (Taylor) 65
Mary (Tucker) 65
Samuel 64-65
Samuel Sr. 65
Sarah 64-65
Sarah (Jr.) 64
Susannah 65
Thomas 64

POLLEY
Henry 25

POOL
Joseph 23

POPE
Elizabeth
(Mitchell) 109-110

LeRoy Jr.   109-110
Worden   41

POTTS
   Ann   106
   Anne   106
   Edward   66
   Johanna   106
   John   106
   John (Jr.)   106
   Mary (Backhouse)   66

POULTNEY
   Elener   64

POWELL
   Nicholas   72
   Peyton   43

POYTHRESS
   William   27

PRESTON
   Robert   59

PRICE
   Ann (Grissom)   18
   (Census)   96
   Harbert   91
   Henry   18
   Prentiss   5

PRIDDY
   Robert   35

PRIDE
   James   75

PRIDGER
   Abyah   107
   David   107

PRIDHAM
   Christopher   4

PUGH
   Ann   4-5
   David   4-5
   David Sr.   5
   Elizabeth   5
   Elizabeth (Barrow)   45 (sic)
   Henry   4-5
   John   5
   Lewis   4-5
   Lewis Sr.   4-5

   Robert   45 (sic)
   Willoughby   4-5

PURDUM
   Benjamin   66
   Mrs. Elizabeth
         Williams   66

PURLEY
   Francis   27

PUTNEY
   Benjamin   13
   Richard   12

QUARLES
   William   62

QUEEN
   Hugh   11
   Jean (Roberts)   11

RADDELL
   Lewis   17

RADFORD
   Rebecca   32
   Richard Sr.   32

RAINS
   Heartwell   12
   Mary (Wygal)   41
   Meredith   41

RAMSAY
   Anne   51
   William   51

RANDOLPH
   Mary (Skipwith)   74
   William   74

RANKINS
   Peggy (Berry)   40
   Col. Robert   40

RAPHELL
   Halbert   53

READ
   Clement   11

REAGER
   Burket   93

REAMY
   James   21-101-102

REAVES
   William C.   82

RED(D)
   Ann   89
   John   15-89

REED
   Mary   97

REES (?)
   David   40

RENOE
   Baylis   15
   Catharine   15
   Dolley   15
   Enoch   15
   Fanny   15
   Francis Sr.   15
   Francis Jr.   15
   George   15
   Jane   15
   Lewis   15
   Lidia   15
   Milley   15
   Nancy   15
   Susanna   15
   Thomas   15

RENOLDS
   Bernard   24

REYLYE
   James   34

REYNERSON
   Rev. Jacob   (?)

REYNOLDS
   Mary   29

RHODES
   John   22

RICE
   Joseph   38

RICHARDSON
   Elizabeth   66
   Mary   66
   Mary (Pierpont) 64

   Richard   66
   Richard Sr.   64
   Richard Jr.   64

RICKETTS
   Mary   7

RIDENOUR
   Joanna   8
   Thomas J.   7-8

RIDGEWAY
   Mary   65

RIGG
   Richard   26-99

RIGHT
   (see Wright)

RIGHTON
   McCully   27

RINGLESBURG
   James   97

RITTER
   Catharine (Hoppes) 7
   Gasper   7

ROACH
   Hannah   65
   Mary   65
   Richard   65

ROBERSON
   Aley   47
   John   46-47
   Polley   46
   Richard   46-47
   Thomas   46-47

ROBERTS
   Edward   21
   Esther   11
   Eunity (Martin) 11
   Jean   11
   John   11-66
   Joshua   11
   Martin   11
   Mary   11-66
   Maurice   11
   Morris   11
   Rebecca   11
   Rebeckah (Scott) 66

Richard   66
Susannah   11
Thomas   11

ROBERTSON
    Henry   38
    James   14
    John   47
    Robert   91
    Thompson   37
    William   47
    William (Sr.)   47

ROBINSON
    Susan (Corker)   91

ROBISON
    Ann   58
    Elizabeth   58
    John   58
    William   58

RODGER
    William   18

ROGERS
    Henry   24
    John   24
    Mary   106
    Mary (Roach)   65
    Mildred   38
    Oliven   65
    Rhodam   38
    Rhodam Jr.   38
    Stephen   24
    Thomas   91

ROMAN
    Jacob   21-102

ROOSA
    (Census)   99

ROUNTREE
    John   59
    Lottishea   59
    Thomas   59

ROWAN
    (Census)   99

ROWE
    James W.   83
    Sally   83
    William   83

ROWNTREE
    James   10
    Randol   9-10
    Richardson   9-10
    Thomas   10
    Turner   10
    William   10
    Woodson   10

ROWZEE
    John   13

RUDDER
    Alexander   37-38
    Edward   37
    Rebecca (Brown)   38
    Samuel   37-38

RUFFE
    Peter   93

RUFFENER
    Abraham   98
    Martha   98

RUFFNER
    Margaret   98

RUSSELL
    Ezekiel   37
    Faith   60-61
    Hannah   67
    James   67
    John   8-67
    John Sr.   60-61
    Joshua   67
    Peggy   60-61
    Rachel (Steer)   67
    Richard   43
    Ruth   60-61
    Susannah (Janney)   67

RUTTER
    John   29

SABATIE
    Elizabeth (Sr.)   89
    Elizabeth (Jr.)   89
    Peter   89

SALLE
    Abraham   31

SANDERS
    John   47

Mary	47
Nancy	47
Rietter	47

SANDIES
Elizabeth (Robison) 58

SARGANT
Jane 20
William 20

SASEN
Elizabeth 88
Francis 88

SAVAGE
Margaret 91

SAWYER
James Sr. 37

SCHENCK
Ralph 50

SCOTT
Charles Robert 46
Elizabeth 66
George 71
Heirs of Robert 46
Jacob 66
Jannett 46
Rebeckah 66
Robert 46
William 46

SCOTZER
Martin 94

SCRUGGS
Finch 105
Nancy (Thomas) 105

SEACRIST
Henry 93

SEAMON
Jonathan 100

SEED
Elizabeth (Barnard) 21
Thomas 21

SELLIS
Susan (Goreing) 89

SHARP
John D. 60-61
Solomon 18
Thomas 43

SHAW
William 97

SHEPHERD
Andrew 16-17
"Mr." 76

SHETTLEHUE
Chris (sic) 98

SHILTON (SHELTON)
Benjamin 37
Susanna 37
Wesley 36

SHORT
Cornelius 48
Thomas 20

SHUCK
Lewis H. 81
Oscar D. 81
Ryland K. 81

SIES
William 53

SIMES
Arthur L. 58

SIMMS
Elizabeth 47

SIMORE
Larkin 21

SIMS
Nathaniel 34

SIVELY
Jacob Barnard 94

SKINKER
William 74

SKIPWITH
Mary 74
Sir William 74

SLAUGHTER
  Francis Sr.   53

SMALLWOOD
  Ann   19
  Bayne   19
  Elizabeth   19-49
  Family   19
  Hester   19
  Col. James   19
  Prior   19-48-49
  William   19

SMITH
  Ann   33
  Caroline   33
  Carnelia   67
  Edward W.   35
  Elizabeth   94
  Francis   9
  George   20-30-94
  Henry   66
  Jabez   14
  James   33
  James M.   4
  John Jr.   2
  Capt. John   30
  Joseph   20
  Joseph Blackwell   59
  Mahlon   23
  Mary   23
  Nicholas   20
  Robert   15
  Samuel   8
  Sarah   66
  Thomas   21

SMITHERS
  Thomas   26

SNEAD
  Elizabeth H.   83
  Micajah   33
  Victor F.   83
  William B.   83
  William S.   83

SNELL
  John   46
  John (Sr.)   46
  Philemon   46
  Robert   46

SNELSON
  Charles   61-62-63
  Mary (Tait)   61-62-63

SOMMERVILLE
  Mary F. (Boyd)   108
  Thomas B.   108

SORRELL
  Thomas   51
  William   62

SPALDING
  John   91

SPARRILL
  Samuel   37

SPENCER
  Robert   24
  Thomas   24

SPICE
  Peter   93

STANARD
  Larkin   3

STANDLEY
  Barbara (Walker)   65
  Micajah   65

STANFIELD
  Thomas   2

STANLEY
  Jesse   58

STEER
  Isaac   67
  Lydia   67
  Phoebe   67
  Rachel   67

STEPHEN(S)
  Adam   100
  Thomas   31

STEPP
  Stephen   18

STERLING
  Joseph   91

STEWART
  Agnes   48
  Charles   48
  Charles (Jr.)   48
  Elinor   48
  Elizabeth   96

Hannah	48
James	48
John	48
Rachel	48
Rebeckah	48
Robert	48
Robert W.	48
Ruth	48
Thomas	48

STINSON
William	104

STOKES
Allen	39
Col. David	14
Col. John	14
Richmond	14

STOSSENBURG
John Charles	73

STREET
Anthony	39
David	14
John Tate	62
Joseph	61-62-63
Sarah (Tait)	61-62

STRICKLAND
John	97

STRIPLING
Elizabeth (Wright)	19

STRONG
William	58

STROTHER
Robert	53
William	20

STUART
Charles	48
James	48
John	48

SULLIVAN
Richard Sr.	81
Richard Jr.	81
Sally	81

SUMMERELL
Thomas	43

SUTTON
James	45

SWANN
Mary (Ricketts)	7
Robert	7

SWINBURNE
Thomas	92

TABSCOTT
Polly	50

TACKETT
Fanny (Renoe)	15

TAIT(E) (TATE)
Abigail	62-64
Abigail (Jr.)	62
Alice	64
Anderson	61-62
Anthony	61-62
Caswell	61-62
Cisley	64
Elizabeth	64
Enos	63-64
Fanny	61-62
Hannah	61-62
James	63-64
James Jr.	64
John	61-62-63
John Jr.	61-62-63
Joseph	64
Margaret	62
Mary	61-62-63
Nathan	63
Peggy	64
Rachel	63
Richard	61-62
Robert	62-64
Sally	61-62
Sarah	61-62-63
Uphan	61-62-63
Uriah	64
Waddy	61-62-63
Zacharias	61-62-63
Zachius	61-62-63
Zedekiah	61-62-63
Zenas	62-63
Zephaniah	61-62-63

TALBOT(T)
John	58
Mary	67

144

TALIAFERRO
William   19-49

TALLEY
Henry   94

TANNER
Evans   104
Jonathan   42

TAPP
Newton H.   24

TAPSCOTT
James   110

TATE (see TAIT(E)
William   91

TATERSALL
(Census)   95

TAYLOE
Elizabeth   55-74
John   74

TAYLOR
Bernard   66
Caleb   65
Charles   104
Elizabeth   104
Henry   104
James   91-104
(Sgt.) Jesse   104
John   40-47-104
Lewis   104
Mary (Polly)   65-104-105
Rachel   66
Robert   53
Sarah (Smith)   66
Timothy   66
Thomas   65-66
William   104

TERRELL
Chiles   43-44
William   62

THACKER
Pleasant   14

THOMAS
Anthony Hoggett   105
Benjamin   35
Betsy   105
Jesse   105

Jesse Wood   105
Jinney   105
Job Howell   105
John   13-88
John Thomas   105
Mary   88-105
Nancy   105
Nathaniel Hoggett   105
Nelly   105
Phinehas   105
Polly   105
Porcia   105
William   18

THOMPSON
Ann   28
B. J.   107
Edward   23
Elizabeth   25
George   25
Jane   90-94
Jane (Barrow)   45
John   25-90
Joseph   25
Moses   90
Robert   27-90
Waddy   63
William   44-90-91

THOMSON
Mrs. Ann (Mathews) 19

THRIFT
Nathaniel   12
William   12

TOBEY
Isabella   81
Thomas W.   81

TOCK
Sarah   4

TOLER
Zachariah   35

TOWLES
"P"   3

TRABUE
Anthony   31
Daniel   11

TREVILLO
(Census)   96

TRIBLE
  (Rev.) Andrew   38
  Sarah Ann Burrus 38

TROY
  Emily   98

TUCKER
  Charles C.   104
  Eleanor   98
  Jane Allen (Gordon) 52
  Joanna   55
  Joanna (Corbin) 55
  Joseph   40
  Lydia   65
  Margaret (Berry) 40
  Martha C. (Gordon) 52
  Mary   65
  Robert   65
  Col. Robert   55

TUNSTALL
  Will   36

TURBEVILLE
  Betty Tayloe (Corbin) 54-55
  George Lee   54

TURNER
  James   55-58
  John   43
  Mary   58
  Ranson   2

TUTT
  Elizabeth (Ashby) 56-57
  John   56-57
  Kitty   56
  Mary   53

TWEDEL
  Abigail   37
  Benjamin   36-37
  John   37
  Silas   37
  William   37

UPDEGRAFF
  Nathan   23

VADEN
  Polly (Chattin) 36
  Silvanus A.   36

VANLANDIGAM
  Michail   95

VAST
  Roland   95

VAUGHAN
  Alonzo   108
  William   52

VICTORIA
  Queen   92

VOYER
  Jane   88
  John   88

WADE
  Ann (Robison) 58
  John   35

WAGHILL
  (See WIGLE-WYGAL)

WAKE
  Lucy B.   98

WALKE
  Thomas   71

WALKER
  Anne   44
  Barbara   65
  Benjamin   14
  Catharine   107
  Edward   108
  John   72
  Joseph Bell   108
  Mrs.   72
  Solomon   44
  Dr. Thomas   9
  William   107

WALL
  John   51

WALLACE
  (Rev.) John H. 42

WALLER
  Richard   59
  William   39

WALTER
    Isaac   51

WALTON
    George (Sr.)   14
    George (Jr.)   14
    Robert   14
    Sarah   14

WANECK (?)
    John   21

WARD
    Anna   82
    Ellis C.   82
    Emma   82
    Frances   82
    John E.   82
    Mary F.   82
    Thomas E.   81
    William M.   82
    Zipporah   81

WARE
    Edward   54

WARING
    Thomas   20

WARRACK
    Ludwick   76

WARREN
    William   2

WARRINGTON
    Francis   28-29
    Mrs. Francis   28-29

WASHINGTON
    George   40
    Lawrence Augustine   44
    Mary Dorcas   44

WASSON
    Ester   99

WATERS
    Artrage   65
    Samuel Sr.   65
    Samuel Jr.   65
    Susanna (Plummer)   65

WATERSON
    Elizabeth   94

WATKINS
    Joel   15
    John   15
    Sarah (Walton)   14
    Thomas   2-14

WATSON
    Benjamin   32
    Joseph   99-100
    William H.   32

WEADON
    Colonel   49

WEBB
    George R.   81
    Hannah   97
    William   21

WEEKS
    James   38
    Thomas   38

WEISEL
    Frederick   20

WELCH (WELSH)
    Chloe   58
    David   93
    Isham   58
    James   58
    John   58
    John (Sr.)   58
    John (Jr.)   58
    Major   104
    Mary (Gilbert)   58
    Samuel   58

WELLS
    Elizabeth   97

WESSON
    John   12

WEST
    James   15
    Lynn   15

WETHERBURN
    "Mr."   71

WHARTON
    Samuel   53

WHITACRE
    Lee N.   100

WHITE
    Frances (Golbee)   29
    George Christopher   77
    Thomas   29

WHITHEAD
    Benjamin   91

WHITLEDGE
    Nancy (Renoe)   15
    Robert   15

WHITLOCK
    Anthony   92
    Charles   47
    James   47-92
    Nathaniel   47
    Thomas   47-92

WHITT
    (Rev.) Richard   25

WIGLE (WYGAL)
    Adam   41
    Anne Christina   41
    Barbary   41
    Catharine   41
    John   41
    Mary   41
    Peggy   41
    Sebastian   41

WILEY (WYLIE)
    Anne Christina (Wygal)41

WILKERSON
    Betsey (Thomas)   105

WILKINS
    Richard   30
    Robert   8

WILLIAMS
    Ann   81
    Benjamin   107
    Daniel   21
    Elisha   41
    Elizabeth   66-81
    Hannah   66
    Henrietta(e)   107-108
    John   29-46-81
    John C.   107

John H.   81
Joseph C.   107-108
Luther   81
Mary J.   81
Nathaniel   30
Peter   81
Phebe   29
Priscilla   107
Sally (Chattin)   36
Sarah   29
Thomas   29
William   36-66

WILLIAMSON
    Elizabeth   53
    Henry   53
    James Sr.   7
    James Jr.   7
    Jane   53
    Leonard H.   7

WILLIS
    George D.   47
    Henry   3
    John Whitaker   3
    Lewis   3

WILMURTH
    George   95

WILSON
    Henry Lawrence   23
    Hezekiah   23
    John   23
    John Jefferson   23
    Kezia   23
    Maria   23
    Mary   23
    Peter   8
    William   40
    Willis   105

WINDLE
    Christopher   93
    Valentine   93

WINN
    Dorothy (Wright)   19
    John   42-100-101

WINSTEAD
    David   107
    Peter   107

WINSTON
    Anthony   61-62-63

John Tate — 62
Uphan (Tait) — 61-62

WISECARVER
  John — 94

WITHERS
  Eliza — 57
  Jannett (Chinn) — 46
  Martha — 57
  Martha (Ashby) — 56-57
  Mary — 57
  Samuel — 57
  William — 57

WOLF
  Jacob — 21-102

WOMABLE
  Edward — 98

WOMACK
  Nathan — 53
  Richard — 31

WOOD
  Hesekiah — 98
  Lydia (Steer) — 67
  Mary — 67
  Richard — 67
  Sarah — 98
  William — 67

WOODCOCK
  John S. — 26

WOODFIN
  Samuel — 13

WOODHALL
  John — 67
  Sarah — 67

WOODSON
  Benjamin — 10
  Tucker (Sr.) — 14

WOOLDRIDGE
  Robert — 11
  Thomas — 11

WROUGHTON
  Mary — 40-41

WRIGHT
  Dorothy — 19

Elizabeth — 19-65
Elizabeth
    (Farquhar) — 65
Frances — 19
Francis — 19
Joel — 65
John — 65
Joseph — 65
Mary (Farquhar) — 65
Robert — 37-43
Thomas — 53
"W" — 37

WYNN
  David — 7
  Mary (Hoppes) — 7
  Robert — 12
  Robert W. — 60
  Sarah — 12

YATES
  William C. — 21

YEARY
  Adam — 60
  Benedict M. — 60
  Henrietta — 60
  Henry — 60-61
  Henry Sr. — 61
  Matilda — 60-61
  Ruth (Russell) — 60-61
  Susannah — 61

YEATES (YEATS)
  Sarah — 4
  Sarah (Caven) — 67
  William — 67

YERBY
  Betsey — 45
  Charles — 45
  John — 45
  Judith — 45
  Mary — 45
  Thomas — 45

YERKES
  (Census) — 96

YOUNG
  J. R. — 3
  John D. — 15
  Robert — 3

YOUNGER
  Philip — 99

VIRGINIA
ANCESTORS
AND ADVENTURERS

Volume 3

VIRGINIA

ANCESTORS AND ADVENTURERS, VOL. 3

TABLE OF CONTENTS

Dedication.. i

Preface.. ii

Introduction....................................... iii

SECTION ONE

County Abstracts................................... 1

Marriage Records.................................. 48

Depositions....................................... 56

SECTION TWO

Naturalization of French Huguenots............... 58

Proof of Importations............................ 60

SECTION THREE

Revolutionary War Pensions....................... 64

SECTION FOUR

A Virginia Ancestor Adventurer................... 82

SECTION FIVE

General Index.................................... 108

DEDICATION

To my tried and true blue friend,
Mr. Thomas P. Hughes III, of
Memphis, Tennessee. A very fine
genealogist in his own right.

PREFACE

     Mr Giles, the translator of the William of
Malmesbury (died ca 1143) Chronicle, Gesta Regum
Anglorum, says in his preface to that work that
"a desire to be acquainted with the transactions
of their ancestors seems natural to men in every
stage of society, however rude or barbarous."

     Edward Gibbon (1737-1794) says in his inim-
itable autobiography "A lively desire of knowing
and of recording our ancestors so generally pre-
vails that it must depend on the influence of
some common principle in the minds of men".

     To these profound observations, this writer
can only add his belief that the possible answer
may be that it is very hard to explore the records of our ancestors without coming face to face
with ourselves.

INTRODUCTION

As in our previous five books, this genealogical researcher and editor continues his passionate pursuit for the migration records of our durable and sometimes redoubtable Virginia ancestors. More often than not, these records, when discovered, also provide direct proof of identity and relationship to others.

As we have indicated and stated before, we are primarily concerned with records establishing a "link" proving the origin of an individual or a family from somewhere settling in Virginia or of a Virginian removing and settling somewhere else. Citation to source or authority is given for each item so found.

In order to test our reader's reaction and/or possible attraction for more of the same, we have included a new feature in Section Four of this volume, which is a chapter on an early Virginia colonist, Colonel George Mason, who was the ancestor of Colonel George Mason "of Gunston Hall", a distinguished Revolutionary War patriot and the author of the "Bill of Rights".

This is an account of a previously unproven collateral branch of the family and is rendered verbatim from three reports found necessary to establish and document the pedigree of a valued client.

It is hoped that our readers will notice and comment on the style in which the reports are presented and the progressive procedure involved, from one clue or lead to the next. This method is opposed to the present prevailing narrative type, which is annotated with innumerable footnotes or sometimes with none at all.

This writer confesses that he long ago became allergic to "footnotes" as they generally consist of extremely long lines denoting source, author, book and page (or "ibid") and nothing concerning content or context. In addition, they are usually very difficult of access.

It is also hoped and believed that the records found herein may encourage others not to be discouraged and will point their way to the types of primary sources necessary to search for "Happy Hunting" and rich rewards.

Charles Hughes Hamlin
Route 2, Box C-44
Powhatan, Virginia 23139

SECTION I

(a)-County Abstracts

1.

<u>NORTHUMBERLAND COUNTY, VA. RECORD BOOK-(1652-1658)-PAGE 106.</u>

29 October 1656 - Know all men by these presents that I, William Barker of Ratclift in the County of Middlesex, Marriner; for divers good & valuable causes & considerations me thereunto moving have made, constituted, ordained, affirmed, deputed, authorized, appointed & putt; by these presents do make, constitute, ordain, assign, depute, authorize & appoint & put my very loving friend Thomas Smith, of Limehouse, in the aforesaid County of Middlesex, Marriner, now bound outwards on a voyage to Virginia in the parts beyond the seas my true & lawful deputy & attorney for me & in my name to my onely & proper use to (?) receive by order of law compound or otherwise howsoever all & every of any person or persons whatsoever in Virginia aforesaid all & every or any sum & sums of money or moneys worth, goods, chattles, remedies, merchandizes due & demands what so ever which now is or are or which at any time hereafter shall become due, oweing payable (?) or belonging to me - etc. - etc.
Witnesses: Robert Carter (?) - John Parker - John Carter.
Recorded 4 May 1657.

2 May 1657 - These presents witnesseth that I, Thomas Smith, being the lawful attorney of Capt. William Barker do acquitt & discharge Francis Clay, his Executors or assigns of and from all bonds, bills, accounts & all demands whatsoever from the beginning of the world unto this present day - etc. 4 May 1657 - Recorded.
Witnesses: Walter Brodhurst - Richard Wright.

<u>CAMPBELL COUNTY, VA. - DEED BOOK 4, PAGE 79.</u>

22 November 1796 - Robert Willson, of Campbell County, Virginia, appoints Messers David and John Graham, "Merchants", of the Philadelphia, his true and lawful attornies, to sell 2500 acres of land in Montgomery County, Virginia, on Bush Creek and the Waters of Blue Stone, which land he had purchased of Archibald Curle, etc.
Witnesses: William Alexander - John Patrick. Acknowledged by Robert Willson, December Court, 1796 and ordered to be recorded.

<u>CAMPBELL COUNTY, VA. - DEED BOOK 5, PAGE 505.</u>

27 January 1801 - Thomas Arthur and Sarah, his wife, of the County of Knox, State of Kentucky, appoint Thomas Gooch, of Campbell County, Virginia, their true and lawful attorney,

2.

to secure legacy that is coming to my wife, Sarah, in the
hands of John Clark, of Campbell County, who was appointed
by the Court of Campbell County, executor of the estate of
William Arthur, deceased, etc. Acknowledged and certified
same day by the Clerk of Court of Knox County, Kentucky.
Recorded Campbell County, Virginia, June 14, 1802.

CAMPBELL COUNTY, VA. - DEED BOOK 5, PAGE 531.

23 January 1802 - State of Georgia, County of Wilkes:-
William Arthur, of the County of Wilkes, and State aforesaid,
appoints his friend, Robert Hughes of the same place, his true
and lawful attorney in fact to act upon a relinquishment he
has from all the heirs of Barnard Arthur to his estate, etc.
Acknowledged by William Arthur before the Clerk of Wilkes County, Georgia, the same day and recorded Campbell County, Virginia, June 15, 1802.

CAMPBELL COUNTY, VA. - DEED BOOK 6, PAGE 8.

4 November 1799 - Wilkes County, Georgia. John and Jean
Routen, James and Lucy McKelroy, Martha Arthur Senior and
Martha Arthur Junior - All of the State and County aforesaid-
also Matthew Arthur, of the aforesaid State, County of Franklin and Talbot Arthur, of the aforesaid State, County of Jackson - each and severally relinquish unto William Arthur of the
said State and County - all our interest and claim, title and
demand in the Estate of Barnabas Arthur, deceased, formerly
of the State of Virginia and County of Campbell, whose legal
heirs we do hold ourselves to be, etc. Acknowledged same day
before Clerk of Court of Wilkes County, Georgia by all the
above parties and recorded Campbell County, Virginia December
13, 1802.

LOUDOUN COUNTY, VA. - DEED BOOK "D" -(1763-1765)- PAGES 7-9.

14th and 15th August 1763 - Patrick Lafferty, of the County of Craven, Province of South Carolina, and Prudence, his
wife, the surviving daughter and sole heiress of Jacob Binks,
late of the County of Stafford (now Loudoun) in the Colony of
Virginia, sell to John Neavill, of the County of Frederick,
Colony of Virginia, for (lease 5 shill-Release £50) a tract of

land in Loudoun County, on the Northwest side of Goose Creek,
on a branch called Tuscarora, alias Sicotin's Branch, contain-
ing 145 acres of land, etc.
Witnesses: James Lindsey - Joseph Pierce - John Lindsey, Jr.-
Kezia Pennington - William Cannon.
Proved and recorded October 11, 1763.

ibid - pages 3-5.

25th and 26th July, 1763 - Abraham Lindsey, of the County
of Craven, Province of South Carolina sells to John Neavill,
of the County of Frederick, Colony of Virginia, for (Lease 5
shill-Release ₺50) a certain tract of land now in Loudoun (formerly Stafford) on Goose Creek, adjoining land of Landon Carter
and Jacob Bink, containing 76 acres, etc.
(Same witnesses as above) - Proved and recorded October 11, 1763.

BEDFORD COUNTY, VA. - DEED BOOK 5 -(1773-1778) - PAGE 523.

25 October 1777 - Indenture in which Nathaniel Williams of
North Carolina, Guilford County, sells to Francis Dickerson, of
Bedford County, Colony of Virginia --- for ₺50 --- a tract of
land in Bedford County containing 200 acres being part of a
tract of 4000 acres granted by patent to ye said Nathaniel
Williams on the waters of Goose Creek, etc.
Witnesses: Charles Moorman - John Dickenson - Thomas Preston-
Eusebeous Stone - Henry Stratton. Proved and recorded 24 Nov-
ember 1777.

BEDFORD COUNTY, VA. - DEED BOOK 8 -(1787-1791)- PAGE 484.

2 May 1791 - Indenture in which Robert Williams, Attorney
in fact for Nathaniel Williams, of North Carolina, County of
Rockingham, sells to Elisha Hurt of Bedford County, Virginia,
for ₺40, a tract of land in Bedford County, Virginia, on Goose
Creek, containing 100 acres, etc.
Witnesses: Henry Haynes - Byrom Ballard - William Ballard.
Recorded 25 July 1791.

BEDFORD COUNTY, VA. - DEED BOOK 10 -(1795-1798)- PAGE 83.

31 August 17__ - Indenture in which Dodson Thorp, of the
County of Madison, State of Kentucky, sells to Charles Reynolds, of Bedford County, Virginia for ₺30 - a tract of land in

4.

the County of Bedford, Virginia, on the Headwaters of Elk
Creek on the East side of No Business Mountain - containing
217 acres, etc. (The deed is signed "Dodson Thorpe Senior").
Witnesses: Benjamin Gaddy - John Kerr - Benjamin Edins.
Recorded 26th, October 1795.

WESTMORELAND COUNTY, VA. RECORDS & INVENTORIES #2 - PAGE 131[a].

31 July 1750 - The deposition of William Davis, aged 42
years or thereabouts (thus born ca 1708) sayeth that he knows
and is acquainted with William Blackmore and knows him to be
the son of Samuel Blackmore of the County of St. Mary -(?) -
in the County of Devon and to be the same person mentioned in
the will of George Blackmore, late of the County of Westmoreland, in the Colony of Virginia, deceased, etc.
Recorded 11, August 1750.

(NOTE BY CHH: - The will of George Blackmore of Westmoreland
County, was dated 10 October 1745; proved 25 February 1746;
and his legatees were (1) his wife (not named) - (2) Lovel
White, land bought of his father, John White; - (3) William,
son of my brother, Samuel Blackmore of the Parish of St. Mary
OTTRY, County of Devon in Great Brittain; - (4) To Cousin
(i.e. nephew) Samuel, son of my brother, Samuel; and to Gideon
Blackmore, my Cozen (i.e. nephew) son of Gideon Blackmore.
(Bk. X).

WESTMORELAND COUNTY, VA. RECORDS AND INVENTORIES #4, PAGE 222[a].

(no date) - Samuel Griffith, of Dorchester County, in the
Province of Maryland, give power of attorney to "my trusty and
loving friend, Samuel RUST", of Westmoreland County, Colony of
Virginia to collect money due him by David Boyd, George Hull,
Richard Lowe and/or any others. Recorded 30 September 1766.

ibid, page 224[a].

2 October 1766 - Power of Attorney from Francis Gilbert,
of Prince George County, Province of Maryland, to Vincent
Smith Baley, of the Parish of Cople, County of Westmoreland,
Colony of Virginia, etc., etc. Recorded same day.
The witnesses were John Baley - James Baley - and William
Gilbert.

5.

NORTHUMBERLAND COUNTY, VA.,"ORDERS #4", PAGE 291.

16 September 1685 - Petition of Samuel Sanford who intermarried with Elizabeth, executrix of Edward Elliott-----Pro-
bate is granted him on the oath of Francis BOON that he did see
the testator (Edward Elliott) sign, seal and deliver ye said
will as doth appear under ye hand of William Hatton, one of ye
Lord Justices of ye Peace for ye County of St. Marys in ye Province of Maryland dated 24 June 1681. The other witness, William Hooke, is deceased. (ibid-same day-Samuel Sanford married
Elizabeth Keen, executrix of Edward Elliott, deceased.)

MONTGOMERY COUNTY, VA. - DEEDS AND WILLS -(1773-1779)- PAGE 197.

27 June 1795 - Indenture in which Henry Dewees, of Burk
County, North Carolina, sells to John Kelly, of Franklin County,
Virginia -- for ₤35, a tract of land in Montgomery County, Vir-
ginia, containing 128 acres on the branches of Black and Little
River, etc., etc.
Witnesses: Jesse Dewees - Thomas Dewees - William Dewees.
Proven and recorded August Court 1795.

MONTGOMERY COUNTY, VA. -DEED BOOK "E"- (1810-1815) - PAGE 293.

1 February 1811 - Indenture in which Jesse Deweese, of
Cumberland County, State of Kentucky, sells to Frederick Pickle,
of the County of Montgomery, State of Virginia -- for $100.00,
a tract of land in the County of Montgomery, Virginia, containing 100 acres, adjoining the land of John Long and Stephen Reed,
on the waters of Little River, on a ridge near the old field of
Hannah Deweese, up the Laurel Branch, etc.
Witnesses: John Long - Jonathan Conner - Stephen Reed. Proven
June Court 1811. Recorded August Court 1812.

COMMENT: - The above Jesse Deweese was named as one of his sons
by William Deweese in his will proven in October Court 1807 and
acted as his executor in the sale of some of his lands. "The
old field of Hannah Deweese" may have referred to the widow of
Paul Deweese, formerly of Botetourt County in 1789, when he made
his will and recorded in Montgomery County, Virginia in March
Court 1797. Jesse Deweese married Mary Lowder, daughter of
Jacob Lowder, of Montgomery County, Virginia 1 November 1896.
(Worrell p. 15)-

PATRICK COUNTY, VA. - DEED BOOK 1 - (1791-1801) - PAGE 452.

28 April 1797 - Power of Attorney from Humphrey Smith of Patrick County. Executor of the will of Cornelius DEVEESE, deceased, appointing David Morgan of the same County, his true and lawful attorney, to receive from all and every person in North Carolina all such monies, debts, etc. due or payable to the estate of Cornelius DeVeese, deceased, aforesaid and also to recover all lands or titles or entries for land to sell and convey titles thereon in the State of North Carolina, etc., etc.

NOTE BY CHH: Cornelius Deweese died testate in Patrick County, Virginia before May 1794 and left a legacy to his wife (not named and his three children, William, Bartley and Mary.

SOUTHAMPTON COUNTY, VA. - WILL BOOK 1 - PAGE 66.

Last will and testament of John Person, dated 31 August 1752; proven 13 February 1752/3. No wife named or mentioned.

SONS: John - Henry - Thomas and William Person.

DAUGHTERS: Hannah - Priscilla - Sarah - Mary - Rebecca - Elizabeth.

GRANDSON: John, son of my son, John Person.

Names again, my ten children-------------
In addition to land in Virginia, he bequeaths 490 acres of land in Northampton County, North Carolina, where Benjamin Person now lives; 600 acres of land in Granville County, North Carolina (in two tracts of 300 acres). Two other tracts of 200 acres and 244 acres in Granville County, North Carolina, mentions and bequeaths 80 acres of land he recovered in General Court from the executors of Edward Jacquelin, deceased.
Names his sons, John and Henry, executors. Witnesses: Arthur Garris - Francis Sharp - John Inman, Sr. - William Bowen.

OF INTEREST: In Southampton County, Virginia, marriages by Knorr page 84, is recorded the marriage of Benjamin Person of Bute County, North Carolina, on 12 May 1768 (bond) to Lucretia Browne, daughter of Jesse Browne. (Dr. Jesse Browne, in his will dated November 1770, left land in Hertford County, North Carolina, and named his son-in-law, Benjamin PARSONS (sic), as one of his executors. (Will Book 2, page 357).

SOUTHAMPTON COUNTY, VA. - WILL BOOK 2, PAGE 193.

Last Will and Testament of John Person, dated 10 February 1767; proven 9 April 1767.

Wife, Dorcas - (see note below)

To sons, Presley - Phillip - Colin and Turner Person, all lands belonging to me in North Carolina and South Carolina to be divided when Turner becomes age 21 years.

Executors: - Wife, Dorcas - brother, William Person, and cousin, Benjamin Person, of Bute County, North Carolina.

Witnesses: Allen Jones - Willie Jones - E. Haynes.

NOTE BY CHH: The will of Simon Turner, dated 7 July 1761; proven 10 December 1762; (Southampton County, Virginia Will Book 1, page 410) names among his other children and legatees, his daughter, Dorcas Person, wife of John Person, and a legacy to Turner Person. He leaves several large tracts of land in Johnson County, North Carolina to his other various sons.

SOUTHAMPTON COUNTY, VA. - WILL BOOK 2, PAGE 267.

Last Will and Testament of William Person; dated 17 October 1768, proven 8 October 1768 (sic).

Wife, Mary Person -

Sons, John, Anthony and William Person (under 21.):

All lands belonging to me in North Carolina. Executors: Wife, Mary Person, and Day Ridley of Hertford County, North Carolina.

Witnesses: Thomas Person - William Blunt - James Jones - Peterson Thorpe - John Dawson.

NOTE BY CHH: Southampton County, Virginia, marriages by Knorr, page 84, records the marriage of William Person to Mary Thorpe on 10 November 1757 (bond) Surety, Timothy Thorpe.

ibid, WILL BOOK 3, PAGE 69.

Last Will and Testament of John Person, dated 20 July 1773, proven 9 September 1773.

Bequeaths his entire estate to William Blunt, Senior, including 2100 acres of land in Orange and Granville Counties, North Carolina and 500 acres in Bute County, North Carolina. Executors, William Blunt, Sr. and John Blunt - (Priscilla Blunt is one of the witnesses) -

OF INTEREST: Southampton County, Virginia marriages by Knorr, page 14, 24 February 1756 - William Blunt and (MRS.) Mary Person, widow. Surety, Henry Thomas.

PATRICK COUNTY, VA. - DEED BOOK 2 -(1801-1806)- PAGE 247.

1 January 1803 - Thomas P. Jordan of the County of Buncombe, State of North Carolina, sells to Elijah Dehart of the County of Patrick, State of Virginia, for ₤15, a tract of land in the County of Patrick, on the mountain called Blue Ridge, containing 130 acres, etc. Witnesses: Joseph Reynolds - Richard Reynolds - Ben Kinzey. Acknowledged and recorded September Court 1803.

ibid - PAGE 422.

8 November 1804 - Benjamin Kinzey of Buncombe County, North Carolina, sells to Elijah Dehart, 395 acres of land adjoining the land of William Elexander (sic). Recorded April Court 1805.

PATRICK COUNTY, VA. - DEED BOOK 12 -(1844-1847)- PAGE 588.

7 June 1847 - Power of Attorney in which John S. Dehart of Howard County, State of Missouri, appoints Zephaniah Dehart of Patrick County, State of Virginia, his lawful attorney in fact to collect and receive his share of the estate of Elijah Dehart, Senior, deceased, late of the said County of Patrick, Virginia. Signed - John Dehart. Recorded July Court 1847.

LUNENBURG COUNTY, VA. - DEED BOOK 5 -(1757-1760)- PAGE 311.

20 March 1758 - Robert Allen of Amelia County, sells to Benjamin Jones of the County of Northampton in the Province of North Carolina - for ₤26, 17 shillings and sixpence - 200 acres of land in Lunenburg County, Virginia - on head branches of Tucker's Creek. Being part of a patent of land granted the said Robert Allen 10 September 1755, etc. Witnesses: William Stokes- Isaac Farguson - Allen Stokes - Hugh Bragg. Recorded 1 August 1758.

NOTE BY CHH: - ibid, page 350 - 27 May 1758, Robert Allen of Amelia County sells to Joseph Sullivan of Lunenburg County, 157 acres of land in Lunenburg County, Virginia. (Recorded 5 December 1758).

9.

ibid - PAGE 443 -

7 August 1759 - Indenture in which Drury Allen of the Pro-
vince of North Carolina, sells to Tyree Glenn of the Colony of
Virginia - for ₤15, a tract of land containing 400 acres in the
County of Lunenburg, Virginia, etc. Recorded Lunenburg County
Court same day and Elizabeth, wife of Drury Allen, relinquished
her right of dower.

LUNENBURG COUNTY, VA. - DEED BOOK 5 -(1757-1760)- PAGE 489.

1 October 1759 - Indenture in which David Allen of the
County of Johnson, Province of North Carolina and Allen Gentry
of the County of Lunenburg, Virginia, of one part, sell to
Richard Haggard of Lunenburg County - for ₤30 - a tract of land
containing 100 acres in the County of Lunenburg, on Crooked
Creek, etc. Witnesses: John Hanna Smith - John COLVIN - Elisha
Brooks. Recorded 2 October 1759.

ibid - PAGE 558.

13 December 1759 - Indenture in which John McDonal of
Johnson County, Province of North Carolina, sells to William
Allen of Lunenburg County, Virginia - for and in consideration
of a tract of land in Johnson County, North Carolina, delivered
to him by the said William Allen and for which he, the said John
McDonal, conveys to the said William Allen a tract of land in
Lunenburg County, Virginia, on the south side of Meherrin River
containing 200 acres, etc. Recorded 5 February 1760.

ibid - PAGE 348.

(?) July 1760 - Indenture in which Francis Ray, of Johnson
County, Province of North Carolina, sells to William Allen of
the County of Lunenburg, Colony of Virginia, a tract of land in
Lunenburg County, containing 50 acres, etc. Witnesses: William
Gentry - David Gentry - John Brooks - Allen Gentry. Recorded 3
February 1761.

LUNENBURG COUNTY, VA. - DEED BOOK 11 -(1767-1771)- PAGE 124.

7 March 1768 - Indenture in which Drury Allen, of the
County of Granville, Province of North Carolina, sells to Isaac
Brizendene of the County of Lunenburg, Government of Virginia -

10.

for ₤70, a tract of land in Lunenburg County, Virginia, on the head branches of Tucking Creek, containing 300 acres, etc. Witnesses: Lydall Bacon - Allen Stokes - Anthony Street. Recorded 11 March 1768 and Elizabeth, wife of Drury Allen, relinquished her right of dower.

HALIFAX COUNTY, VA. - DEED BOOK 55 -(1853-1855)- PAGE 453.

14 January 1853 - Indenture in which Beverley E. Whitehead and Mary Jane, his wife, of the County of Polk, State of Georgia, sell to Rebon and Robert Adams, of the County of Halifax, State of Virginia, for $600.00, 2 tracts of land in said County of Halifax, one tract containing 9-5/8 acres - another tract containing 28½ acres, etc.
(Certified by Justices of Polk County, Georgia and recorded in Halifax County, Virginia 22 May 1854.)

POWHATAN COUNTY, VA. - DEED BOOK 7, PAGE 399.

1 November 1820 - Deed of Trust between Jesse Tucker of County of Powhatan, State of Virginia and James Tucker and Hartwell Tucker of County of Limestone, State of Alabama - gives, grants, etc. one negro girl named Louisa, about 13 or 14 years old, bed furniture, etc., to said James and Hartwell Tucker as trustees for the exclusive use and benefit of Nancy Tucker, wife of Burwell Tucker, and her children. Certified by Clerk of the Court, 4 November 1820 and recorded. (margin-Clerk's note: delivered original deed to Hartwell Tucker 4 November 1820.)

LUNENBURG COUNTY, VA. - DEED BOOK 18 -(1797-1801)- PAGE 109A.

16 February 1799 - Indenture in which Robert Beasley of Oglethorpe County, State of Georgia, and William Beasley of the County of Chesterfield, State of Virginia, (of one part) sell to James Knott of Lunenburg County, Virginia - for ₤211, a tract of land in the County of Lunenburg containing 370 acres, etc. Witnesses: Francis Smithson - George Clarke - John Hudson - Richard Knott. Proved and recorded 11 April 1799.

LUNENBURG COUNTY, VA. - DEED BOOK 16 -(1790-1795)- PAGE 245.

13 September 1792 - Robert (x) Beasley and Betty (x), his wife, of Lunenburg County, Virginia, sell Seth Farley of the same County, 65½ acres of land in said County on the north side of Springfield Creek. Recorded same day.

ibid - PAGE 257.

11 May 1792 - John Glenn of Lunenburg County, State of Virginia, sells to Robert Beasley of the same County, for ₤50, one negro girl, about 12 years old, named Hannah, which property is now in the State of Georgia - Nevertheless, the above is only as security for a debt for the said John Glenn, etc. - and to keep said Beasley harmless, etc. Recorded 11 October 1792.

CUMBERLAND COUNTY, VA. - DEED BOOK 9, PAGE 425.

10 February 1804 - William Wright, son and heir and administrator of Henry Wright of the State of Georgia, Archibald Wright, Gabriel Wright and William Gills and Mary, his wife, of the County of Buckingham, State of Virginia, legatees of George Wright, the elder, deceased, of one part, sell to William Wright and Henry Ransone of the County of Cumberland, for 287 pounds, 200 acres of land devised by the said George Wright, the elder, to be sold by his executors - being the same land whereon Elizabeth Armstrong formerly lived and whereon George Wright formerly lived, etc. Recorded 27 August 1804.

GOOCHLAND COUNTY, VA. - DEED BOOK 20 -(1807-1810)- PAGE 280.

25 November 1808 - Anderson Page and Fanny, his wife, of Spartanburg District, State of South Carolina, sell to William Page of Goochland County, Virginia - for ₤42 - all that part of the land that they may be entitled to by will of our deceased father, James Page, which is the ¼ part of a tract of land containing 81½ acres on which the said James Page, deceased, formerly lived --- in Goochland County on the waters of Lickinghole Creek, etc. Witnesses: Daniel McKee - Major Hancock (Carolina) Josiah Leake - John M. Leake - Johnson Hodges. Recorded 19 December 1808.

12.

Note: Major Hancock married Mary Page, daughter of William Page, 14 April 1794.

Note: Anderson Page married Fanny Williams, 10 October 1789, Goochland County, Virginia, Deed Book 15, page 318.

GOOCHLAND COUNTY, VA. - DEED BOOK 22 -(1815-1817)- PAGE 28.

8 May 1815 - Power of Attorney by Pleasant Page, of the County of Logan, State of Kentucky, appointing "my brother, Samuel L. Page", of the same place, his lawful attorney, to receive what may be due him in the County of Goochland, Virginia, and to sell his share and interest in the land held by the heirs of Jesse Page, deceased, etc. Witness: John Breathett. Certified by Clerk of Logan County, Kentucky, the same day. Recorded in Goochland County, Virginia 17 July 1815.

Note: Pleasant Page married Janey Page, daughter of Leonard Page, 12 March 1811, Goochland County, Virginia, Marriages, page 70. (Will of John Page, proved 1804, named Pleasant and Samuel as sons of his son, Jesse Page.)

PITTSYLVANIA COUNTY, VA. - DEED BOOK 5, PAGE 172.

1 December 1778 - Thomas Henderson, of the State of North Carolina, sells to George Allen, of Pittsylvania County, Virginia, for 150 pounds, a tract of land containing 354 acres in Pittsylvania County, on both sides of Allens Creek, etc. Witnesses: Ben Lankford - James George - John George - John Buchley - James Fares - Joel Short. Recorded 15 June 1779.

PITTSYLVANIA COUNTY, VA. - DEED BOOK 6, PAGE 255.

15 January 1782 - David Hall of the County of Pittsylvania, State of Virginia, and Judith, his wife, sell to Abraham Allen of Orange County, State of North Carolina, for 100 pounds specie a tract of land containing 240 acres in Pittsylvania County, on both sides of the head branch of Banister River adjoining land of William Deven-Emmorson-William Cook, etc. Witnesses: Joseph Akin - Moses Hodges - William Hopwood - Sam Parks.

FLUVANNA COUNTY, VA. - DEED BOOK 11 -(1835-1838)- PAGE 253.

23 September 1835 - Richard Kerby and Ann, his wife, of Rockcastle County, Kentucky, sell to Doctor A. Herndon of Pittsylvania County, Virginia, for $40.00, all their right, title and interest in the lands of Joseph Herndon, deceased, of Fluvanna County, Virginia, as heirs of the said Joseph Herndon, deceased, - on the waters of Hardware River, etc. Certified by Justices of Rockcastle County, Kentucky, same day and recorded in Fluvanna County, Virginia 26 September 1836.

PRINCE EDWARD COUNTY, VA. - DEED BOOK 8 -(1788-1790)- PAGE 188.

3 August 1789 - Jesse Lewelling of the County of Wake, State of North Carolina, sells to Richard Phillips of the County of Prince Edward, State of Virginia - for ₺25 - 70 acres of land in Prince Edward County, Virginia, adjoining land of said Richard Phillips, etc. Recorded 19 October 1789.

COMMENT: The above 70 acres of land was formerly in Amelia County and was sold by William Craddock, 24 May 1753, to Susannah Lewelling for life, and at her death, to her son Jesse Lewelling. (Amelia County, Virginia Deed Book 4, page 549). Susannah must have been the widow of Thomas Lewelling, whose estate was inventoried, appraised and returned to Amelia Court by William Craddock, his administrator (Amelia County, Va. Will Book 1, page 87). Recorded 25 June 1752.

FREDERICK COUNTY, VA. - SUPREME COURT DEED BOOK 3 -(1796-1799)-
PAGE 31.
27 September 1796 - Know all men by these presents - whereas Stephen Holzenbell (or Hotzenbella), deceased, did by his last will and testament, dated 2 April 1776, devise a certain plantation, whereon he then lived, unto Barbara, his wife, during her natural life and then to be sold by his executors (viz.) his son-in-law, Valentine Switzer and his son, Jacob Hotzenbella. The said Barbara being now dead, said plantation sold to Joseph Lucky of Frederick County. Jacob Hotzenbella gives his power of attorney to Valentine Switzer to make a sufficient deed, etc. Recorded 6 October 1796.

ibid - PAGE 45.

3 October 1796 - Valentine Switzer of the County of Hampshire and Jacob Hotzenpeller of the County of Bath, Virginia, executors of Stephen Hotzenpeller, deceased, late of the County of

Frederick, sell to Joseph Lucky of County of Frederick, for ₺1060 a tract of land on the west side of Opeckon Creek in County of Frederick, containing 347 acres - being a part of a large tract of 450 acres granted by Jacob Hite to Stephen Hotzenpeller by deed dated 23 March 1736, signed by Valentine Switzer in unreadable German script. Recorded 6 October 1796.

FREDERICK COUNTY, VA. - DEED BOOK 48 -(1823-1824)- PAGE 296.

2 March 1822 - Phillip Switzer and Elizabeth, his wife, late Elizabeth Wolf, daughter and heir of Jacob and (Geo.?) Wolf of Hampshire County, sell to Joseph Snap, a tract of land in the Counties of Frederick and Shenandoah, on both sides of Cedar Creek, which is their one-third part or share, etc., being the same land George and Jacob Wolf bought of David Briggs, containing 183 acres, etc. Certified by Justices of Hardy County same day. Recorded in Frederick County 6 April 1824.

FREDERICK COUNTY, VA. - DEED BOOK 67 -(1838-1839)- PAGE 148.

14 November 1837 - Indenture in which Joshua WALN, of Highland County, State of Ohio, sells to Jacob Switzer of Alleghany County, State of Maryland, for $900.00, eight-ninths of a tract of land that Joseph WALN Senior, deceased, died seized of in Frederick County, Virginia on the Warm Spring and Packhorse road, containing 197½ acres, being all the interest the said Joshua Waln, one of the heirs of the said Joseph Waln, deceased, and the interest of the following heirs, to-wit: Henry Waln and Elizabeth, his wife - Nancy, wife of John (Groves ?) - William Waln and Mary, his wife - Joseph Waln and Elenor, his wife - Elizabeth, wife of Randal Lockhart - Mary, wife of Leonard Kendrick - John Waln and Martha, his wife and all the claim and title of Mary Waln, relict of Joseph Waln, deceased, etc. - etc. Certified by Justices of Frederick County, Virginia and recorded 7 November 1838.

(Note) - This deed is followed (page 150) by a Deed of Trust from Jacob Switzer of Frederick County, Virginia, who is indebted to Joshua Waln of Highland County, Ohio, in the sum of $500.00, gives a mortgage on 197½ acres of land in Frederick County, Virginia, etc. Recorded 7 November 1838.

15.

BEDFORD COUNTY, VA. - DEED BOOK 2 -(1761-1766)- PAGE 523.

18 February 1765 - Power of attorney from James Cole, of
the County of Craven, Province of South Carolina Gent., appointing James Rentfro, Jr., of the County of Halifax, Colony of Virginia - to transact all business, etc. - Witnesses: Joseph
Woffard - Edward Keefe - William Rentfro.
Recorded, Bedford County, Virginia 26 March 1765.

ibid - page 525.

26 March 1765 - James Cole of Craven County in the Govern-
ment of South Carolina, sells to William Rentfro, of Bedford
County, Virginia - for ₺30 - a tract of land containing 215
acres in Bedford County on Little Creek, a branch of Blackwater
River, etc. Acknowledged by James Rentfro, Jr., attorney for
James Cole and recorded the same day.

(NOTE: - the same day, William Rentfro sold 107 acres of the
above tract to Benjamin Richardson, etc.)

FRANKLIN COUNTY, VA. - DEED BOOK 3 - (1793-1800) - PAGE 611.

24 September 1798 - Indenture in which Moses Rentfro of
Garrett County, State of Kentucky, sells to Jacob NAVE, of the
County of Franklin, State of Virginia, for ₺110 - 140 acres of
land in the County of Franklin on the branches of Hatchet Run
and Blackwater, etc. Acknowledged October Court 1798 and recorded.

FRANKLIN COUNTY, VA. - DEED BOOK 3 - (1793-1800) - PAGE 297.

12 March 1787 - William Rentfro of Franklin County, Virginia, gives bond in sum of ₺1000 to James Rentfro of Fayette
County (now Kentucky), the condition being the said William
Rentfro is to make a good and lawful conveyance of a tract of
land on the waters of Cumberland River, State of North Carolina
containing 640 acres, if the said William Rentfro should obtain
a right to the above said land, etc. Witnesses: - Joseph Rentfro -Daniel French - Isham Jarrold - Jacob Webb. (Note: September 21 1795 - James Rentfro assigns his right and title of the
within bond to Joseph Rentfro - Teste Absalom Rentfro.) Recorded 7 March 1796.

MADISON COUNTY, VA. - DEED BOOK 11 - (1830-1833) - PAGE 198.

28 September 1832 - Alice T. Johnson, William Johnson and Mary, his wife, Thornton F. Johnson and Margaret, his wife, Henry Streshly and Elizabeth, his wife, Benjamin Johnson and Philip Johnson sell to Thompson Cockrell - Whereas William Johnson, late of the County of Madison, sold to said Cockrell 270 acres - now to fulfill the wishes of their deceased Father, etc. Acknowledged 2 October 1832 in Madison County by Alice Johnson, Henry Streshly and Elizabeth, his wife, (formerly Johnson) Benjamin Johnson. Acknowledged 30 October 1832 in Scott County, Kentucky by Thornton F. Johnson and Margaret, his wife, and Philip B. Johnson. Acknowledged 26 November 1832 in Henrico County, Virginia by William Johnson and Mary, his wife.

BEDFORD COUNTY, VA. - DEED BOOK 1 - (1754-1762) - PAGE 159.

(not dated) - Power of attorney from Nicholas and Ruth Haile to William Meadason (Madison) to make William Renphro (sic) a right and deed to land on which he lives but for which he has not as yet received a patent containing 350 acres, etc.
Recorded 27 March ___?___. (see below)

ibid - page 160.

27 July 1757 - Nicholas Haile and Ruth, his wife, of Roan County in (NORTH) Carolina, sell to William Renfro of the County of Bedford, Colony of Virginia - for ₺50 - 350 acres of land on the Waggon Road, called Rentfro Road, on a branch called Indian Run, in Bedford County, etc. -----
27 March 1758 - Acknowledged in Court by the attorney for Nicholas Haile and Ruth, his wife, and ordered to be recorded.

BEDFORD COUNTY, VA. - DEED BOOK 3 - (1766-1771) - PAGE 176.

11 March 1768 - Nicholas Hayle of the Province of Maryland, sells to William Heath of the County of Bedford - for ₺20 - 400 acres of land in Bedford County on Linwell's Creek, etc. Witnesses: John Talbot - John Quarles - Robert Baber. Recorded 22 March 1768.
(Note: ibid, page 180 - Nicholas Hayle gives bond for ₺100 that his wife Ruth Hayle, will relinquish her right of dower in the above tract.)

17.

WESTMORELAND COUNTY, VA. - RECORDS AND INVENTORIES #4 - PAGE 222ᴬ

Recorded 30 September 1766 - Power of attorney from Samuel
Griffith of Dorchester County, Province of Maryland, to his trusty
and loving friend, Samuel RUST, of Westmoreland County, Colony
of Virginia, to collect sums of money due him by David Boyd,
George Hall, Richard Lowe or any others, etc. Witnesses: John
Rust - Gerrard Ball - Julius Augt Jackson.

ibid - page 224ᴬ

2 October 1766 - Power of attorney from Francis Gilbert of
Prince George County, Province of Maryland, to Vincent Smith
Baley, of the Parish of Cople, County of Westmoreland, Colony of
Virginia, etc. Witnesses: John Baley - William Gilbert - James
Baley. Recorded same day.

BEDFORD COUNTY, VA. - DEED BOOK 1, PAGE 70.

Indenture dated 12 January 1756 in which Rice Price of
Anson County in North Carolina, sells to William Auther (ARTHUR)
of Bedford County, Virginia - for ₤100 - a tract of land in Bedford County, containing 223 acres on both sides of Flatt Creek
adjoining land of James Johnson, etc. Witnesses: Matthew Talbot
- Isham Talbot - Barnabas Arthur. Recorded 26 January 1756.

AMHERST COUNTY, VA. - DEED BOOK "D" - PAGE 341.

10 June 1775 - Carter Braxton Esq. and Elizabeth, his wife,
of the County of King William, sell to Samuel Allen of the County
of Amherst, at the special instance and request of James Higginbotham, attorney for the heirs of Thomas Higginbotham, deceased,
late of the Province of Georgia, and for ₤54, 12 shillings, 5
pence, which was due the said Carter Braxton from the said Thomas Higginbotham, in hand paid by the said Samuel Allen - a tract
of land containing 475 acres in the County of Amherst on the
North branch of Buffalo River, etc. Witnesses: Gabriel Penn -
William Cabell - Richard Harvie. Recorded 5 February 1776.

18.

FAUQUIER COUNTY, VA.- DEED BOOK 14 - (1798-1801) - PAGE 856.

22 November 1800 - Indenture in which John Winn Smith of the County of Columbia, State of Georgia, sells to Joseph Allen, of the County of Fauquier, State of Virginia - for ₤35 - a tract of land in the County of Fauquier, on the waters of the Marsh Run - containing 31 acres, etc. Witnesses: James Allen, Jr.- John Tyler Allen - Peter Conway. Recorded 22nd December 1800.

Note by CHH: - Mathew Smith married Martha Winn of Fauquier County, 25 November 1771 - (page 112ᴮ) and therefore the middle name of John Smith (above) may be significient - Mathew Smith was a son of Augustine Smith of Westmoreland and Fauquier Counties.

BOTETOURT COUNTY, VA. - DEED BOOK 4, PAGE 379.

3 January 1792 - George Graham of the District of West Carolina, sells to Thomas Madison of Botetourt County, Virginia- for ₤1100 - 400 acres in the County of Botetourt, on Tinkers Creek - which formerly belonged to William Graham, purchased in Augusta County in 1750 and devised by him to his wife, Priscilla Graham and son, the said George Graham. Recorded August Court 1792.

CAMPBELL COUNTY, VA. - DEED BOOK 2, PAGE 3.

30 July 1784 - Indenture in which William Stearman of Guilford County, State of North Carolina, sells to Thomas RAFFETY for ₤60, a tract of land containing 240 acres in the County of Campbell, State of Virginia on the north side of Falling River, etc. Witnesses: John Raffeth - Thomas Sturman - Harry Terrell- Joel Terrell. Recorded 4 November 1784.

Note by CHH: - I do not find William Stearman (Sturman) listed in the 1790 census of North Carolina.

CAMPBELL COUNTY, VA. - DEED BOOK 3, PAGE 352.

15 March 1793 - Indenture in which Daniel Mitchell and
Judith Mitchell, formerly Judith Prewit, wife of the said Daniel Mitchell, of the County of Fayette in Kentucky, sell to
Absalom Watkins of the County of Campbell, Virginia for £100,
all their right, title, interest, etc. in a tract of land in
the County of Campbell, Virginia, containing 700 acres on Falling River, being the lands where Thomas Watkins, deceased, formerly lived and died and which he devised to the said Judith on
condition of her continuing unmarryed, etc., also their title
and interest in certain negro slaves in the will of the said
Thomas Watkins, on conditions aforesaid, etc. Certified by the
Clerk of County Court of Lincoln County, Kentucky, 30 March
1793. Recorded Campbell County, Virginia, September 5, 1793.

CAMPBELL COUNTY, VA. - DEED BOOK 3, PAGE 499.

25 December 1793 - Indenture in which Thomas Sturman of
North Carolina sells to Thomas Hancks of Campbell County, Vir-
ginia, for £60, a tract of land containing 220 acres in the
County of Campbell, on both sides of Hatt Creek, bounded on
lands of William Sturman, Abram Hancks, James Hancks, William
Dodson, his own lands, Thomas Mackey, etc. Witnesses: Charles
Walker - Valentine Sturman - Peter Bass - William Sturman -
James Hancks, (sic) - Recorded July 3, 1794.

WESTMORELAND COUNTY, VA. - DEEDS AND WILLS # 19, PAGE 227.

28 September 1796 - Thomas Sturman of the County of Gilford
(sic) (Guilford), State of North Carolina - sells to Alexander
Parker and Charles Muse of the County of Westmoreland, State of
Virginia, for £25, a tract of land in Westmoreland County, con-
taining 80½ acres,- adjoining the lands of Youel Rust and Thomas
Shadrick, deceased, etc. Witnesses: Benjamin Hackney - James
Hackney - W. Hurst - John Mullins. Recorded 28 November 1796.

20.

MONTGOMERY COUNTY, VA. - DEED BOOK "A", PAGE 273.

2 September 1782 - Michael Dougherty of the County of Montgomery, sells to Robert Graham of the County of Mecklenburg, State of North Carolina - for ₤300 - 93 acres of land in the County of Montgomery, Virginia, on Reed Creek, a branch of New River, etc. Recorded November 5, 1782.

LUNENBURG COUNTY, VA. - DEED BOOK 24, PAGE 185.

24 February 1816 - Articles of Agreement between James Farmer, Guardian of Lodowich Moon, orphan of Abner H. Moon, deceased, of the one part and Thomas Farmer of the other part-leases a lot of land, etc. Thomas Farmer agrees to educate Lodowich Moon, etc. Recorded 15 November 1816.

LUNENBURG COUNTY, VA. - DEED BOOK 24, PAGE 432.

10 June 1818 - in which Jesse Moon and Permelia, his wife, of the State of South Carolina, sell to Samuel G. Williams of the County of Nottoway, Va. - for $300.00 - 55 acres of land on North Meherrin River, County of Lunenburg, bounded by lands of Samuel G. Williams, formerly Narcissa Moon's - Julia Moon - James Smith - etc. (Permelia Moon relinquished her dower rights in an affidavit signed in Greenville District, South Carolina, 27 July 1818).

LUNENBURG COUNTY, VA. - DEED BOOK 28, PAGE 91.

24 April 1828 - Jesse Moon of Greenville District, South Carolina to Thomas Cheatham of the County of Lunenburg, Virginia for $60.00, his right, title and interest in land held by his Mother, Juliana Moon, as her dower of the land belonging to the Estate of her late husband, Abner H. Moon, deceased.

Note by CHH: - Jesse Moon married Permelia Farmer November 25, 1814 in Lunenburg County, Virginia. His mother was Juliana Farmer as proven by the will of her mother, Sarah Farmer in 1788.

LUNENBURG COUNTY, VA. - DEED BOOK 29, PAGE 68.

(?) January 1826 - in which Alexander B. Moon of the County of Lunenburg and John Moon, of the State of South Carolina - for $155.00 paid to our father in his life time by William Parrott as is proved to us by his receipt shown us - etc., (70 acres of land), etc.

Note by CHH: - (This land was given by Deed of Gift from Gideon Moon to his son, John.) 1789 - Deed Book 16, page 57.

LUNENBURG COUNTY, VA. - DEED BOOK 28, PAGE 159.

3 December 1831 -(?)- Jesse Moon, acting under a Power of Attorney from Pleasant Moon of Greenville District, South Carolina, of one part and Thomas Cheatham of Lunenburg County, Virginia, of the other part - sells for $55.00, all right, title and interest, which the said Pleasant Moon has in a certain tract of land held by his mother, Juliana Moon, as her dower of land belonging to the Estate of her late husband, Abner H. Moon, deceased. Signed by Jesse Moon as agent for Pleasant Moon.

LUNENBURG COUNTY, VA. - DEED BOOK 29, PAGE 160.

20 September 1828 - State of South Carolina, Greenville District - Pleasant Moon nominates and appoints Jesse Moon of Greenville District and State aforesaid (South Carolina), his true and lawful attorney to sell his interest in certain property in Virginia and County of Lunenburg, as one of the heirs at law of Abner H. Moon, deceased, and also to sell his interest in a tract of land he purchased from William R. Geers, who married Sarah, another of the heirs at law of the said Abner H. Moon, deceased, etc. Recorded December Court 1831.

LUNENBURG COUNTY, VA. - DEED BOOK 30, PAGE 511.

Know all men that I, Alexander B. Moon, of the County of Bedford and State of Tennessee, guardian of Ann B. Brown and Mary I. Brown, two of the minor heirs of John and Ermine Brown, deceased, nominate and appoint Robert R. Wilson of the County of Lunenburg, Virginia, my true and lawful attorney to receive certain lands and negroes of the estate of John Brown, deceased, etc. Dated 22 December 1836.

BOTETOURT COUNTY, VA. - DEED BOOK 5,- (1793-1796) - PAGE 64.

10 October 1793 - William Scott and Mary, his wife, of Woodford County, State of Kentucky - sell to John Wright of the County of Botetourt, State of Virginia - for ₤30 - a tract of land containing 42 acres in Botetourt County on Potts Creek, a branch of the James River, etc. Recorded February Court 1794.

SUSSEX COUNTY, VA. - DEED BOOK "O" - (1823-1826) - PAGE 179.

29 July 1824 - Power of Attorney from Peter Tatum of the County of Madison, State of Tennessee, appointing Joseph Clanton of the County of Sussex, State of Virginia, his true and lawful attorney to receive his portion of the estate of Thomas and John Tatum, deceased, that he is entitled to by their last will or by law as their heirs, etc. Recorded 7 October 1824.

LOUISA COUNTY, VA. - DEED BOOK "I", PAGE 362.

7 November 1797 - Power of Attorney from George Johnson of the State of Kentucky, to his brother, Henry Johnson of the State of Virginia, to convey by deed, a tract of land in the County of Louisa to Thomas Meriwether of the same State (Virginia), being a tract of land he had of his father, Major Thomas Johnson, etc. Certified by a Justice of Harrison County, Kentucky, same day and recorded in Louisa County, Virginia 11 December 1797.

SPOTSYLVANIA COUNTY, VA. - WILL BOOK "E" - (1772-1798) -PAGE 944.

Last Will and Testament of (Mrs.) Ann Cunningham, dated 23 April 1789; Executors Bond dated 6 August 1789.

SONS	DAUGHTERS	BROTHER
James	Elizabeth	Edward Elley
Henry	Ann	
George	Nelly	
William		

Bequeaths land in the County of Fayette, on the Kentucky River as by patent bearing date 17 August 1786, to be equally divided among her above listed children.
Executors: My brother, Edward Elley - friend, James Lewis and son, James Cunningham.
Witnesses: Elisha Hall - John Chew - Jesse Haydon.

ibid, page 947.

Last Will and Testament of Stapleton Crutchfield, dated 17 June 1788. Executors Bond dated 1 September 1789. Wife, Sarah Crutchfield.

SONS	DAUGHTERS	SONS-IN-LAW
John	Jane Lipscomb	Samuel Woodfork
Robert	Agatha Woodfork	Richard Noel
Stapleton	Mary Noel	Edward Herndon
Thomas		(son of Joseph
Achilles		Herndon)

Bequeaths land he holds by 2 patents in the District of Kentucky, County of Fayette.

SPOTSYLVANIA COUNTY, VA. - WILL BOOK "E" -(1772-1798)- PAGE 964.

Last Will and Testament of Daniel Barksdale, dated 23 April 1789; Executors Bond dated 1 December 1789.
To son, Joseph Barksdale, land in Kentucky, located by Captain Hays --- To Grandsons, Daniel Basil White and Anthony Bartlet, land in Kentucky located by James Howard --- To daughter, ____(?)____ Bartlet --- to daughter, Katy Gains --- Son, Daniel Barksdale --- daughter, Polly White ---
Executors: Captain John White - Captain Francis Coleman and Mr. Thomas Lipscomb. Witnesses: Joseph Willoughby - Mary White-Richard JARILSONES.

ibid, page 1293.

Last Will and Testament of Beverley Winslow, dated 22 February 1793; Executors Bond dated 3 September 1793.

SONS	DAUGHTERS	NEPHEW
Thomas	Elizabeth Winslow	Richard Parker
William	Mary Chew	
	Catherine Robinson Winslow	
	Agatha Beverley Nelson, wife	
	of John Nelson	
	Susanna, wife of William Parker	

LEGATEE
Robert Johnson of Kentucky

Bequeaths land in Orange County, Virginia and in Fayette County, Kentucky. Executors: Sons, Thomas and William Winslow. Witnesses: Benjamin Robinson - Henry Winslow - Robert S. Coleman - Christopher Daniel.

BOTETOURT COUNTY, VA. - WILL BOOK "G" - (1843-1849) - PAGE 350.

Will of Robert Wiley dated 24 October 1845. Proven July Court 1847.
To my son, F. M. Wiley, land in addition to what I have already deeded him.
The residue of all my land in the Valley of Sinking Creek, in Botetourt County, I give and bequeath to my 4 sons - RO:MAY - Byron S. - Oscar and Benton and their heirs forever to be equally divided.
To my 2 saughters - Lucy Ann and Van Buren, 2 tracts of land.
To my 4 sons (named above) - the house and lot in Fincastle where Dr. Williams now resides and rents.
To my daughters, Lucy Ann and Van Buren, my house and lot in Fincastle, known by the name of "SOLITUDE" - and also the bank stock of Farmer's of Virginia.
To son Benton (underage) -(to receive as good an education as his brother, Robert May) - Refers to my 6 children of my last marriage.
Slaves to my daughter Elvera, and the tract of land deeded to her husband, known as "Highland Grove", also the house and lots deeded to her in Fincastle and her husband, O'Callaghan. (Note: He is Oliver Callaghan).
All the negroes I got by my last marriage with my wife I give to my 6 children by her -(viz) Ro:May - Byron S. - Lucy Ann- Oscar - Van Buren and Benton.
The negroes I claim in my own right to my 5 sons, Ferdinand M. - Robert M. - Byron S. - Oscar and Benton and my 2 daughters, Lucy Ann and Van Buren.
Some years ago, I gave Oliver Callaghan a Power of Attorney respecting my wife's lands in the State of Kentucky, which I now revoke and make null and void.
To my son, Robert May, my patent lever silver watch and to my son Byron S., one common silver watch.

To my son, Benton, my cane marked James L. Woodville, which
I value highly through my respect to the donor.

ibid, page 397.

Note: Inventory and appraisal of his estate itemized - Total
$21,092.84 plus notes due the estate of $5,394.51.

BOTETOURT COUNTY, VA. - WILL BOOK "B" - (1801-1815) - PAGE 183.

Will of James Mason, Gent., 2 March 1803, proven May Court
1808.
All debts and demands due me by James McKeachey, either as
executions of my father or otherwise, be fully discharged in
case his son Andrew should survive me.
To my nephew, William Crawford, 126 acres, also 3 tracts
of land adjoining - 185 plus 140 plus 119 acres (total 444).
To my nephew, Samuel Crawford, Jr., 206 acres.
To my nephew, Mason Crawford, land.
Land to be sold and proceeds divided between Jane Pate,
Eleanor Jenneys, Margaret Crawford and Sarah Crawford, daughters
of Samuel Crawford and Jenet Crawford, his wife,,(my sister), of
the State of Kentucky.
To Mary Pate, wife of Edward Pate, another daughter of said
Samuel and Jenet Crawford.-
To my sister, Janet, my best friend, land in Montgomery
County, -VA.)- Kentucky - Botetourt - land in dispute with Nathan
Scott, etc.
Land to the children of my deceased brother, William Mason,
late of State of Kentucky.
The children of my deceased sister, Mary Edgar, late the
wife of James Edgar of Bedford County - The children of my sister
Margaret Snodgrass, wife of Joseph Snodgrass of Tennessee State.
To my brother, Joseph Mason of Kentucky State - about 1400
acres, chiefly in Franklin County.
Executors: My trusty friends, Joseph Mason - Samuel Craw-
ford and John Pate of the County of Breckenridge, State of Ken-
tucky and Major Elijah McClanahan of Botetourt, Virginia.
(No witnesses listed)

COMMENT: In the Inventory and appraisal of his estate, he is designated as "Major" James Mason.

26.

MADISON COUNTY, VA. - WILL BOOK 4, PAGE 369.

Will of John Ford of Madison County, dated 10 February
1825 - Proved 28 April 1825.
Land and plantation I now live on to my beloved wife,
Rosanna Ford, containing between 300 to 400 acres on the north
side of Main road from Thomas B. Wayland's Mill to Pratt's line,
for her natural life; also slaves (names 4) - also Winny and
her children (4)- also cows, sheep, horses, etc.
To son, James Ford, the same land after the death of my
wife providing he conveys the land he now lives on to my son-in-
law, Nathaniel Tatum.
To son, William Pannell Ford, the remainder of my land in
Madison and Culpeper Counties, providing that he pays the sum
of $452.00 to my 3 grandchildren, William Fontaine Tucker -
James Monroe Tucker and John Thompson Tucker, as they respect-
ively arrive to the age of 21 years - also slaves to him, my
said son.
To my son Benjamin Ford's children -
To my daughter, Nancy Ford of Kentucky - a slave.
To my son, John Ford, $1.00, having already given to him
his share of my estate.
To my grandson, John Thompson Tucker, a negro boy named
Stephen and a horse, bridle and saddle -
To my grandson, James Monroe Tucker, a horse of the value
of $60.00 cash..
To Janny Myrtle, daughter of my first wife, born after my
marriage with her mother, $1.00.
Executors: Son, James Ford, and son-in-law, Nathaniel
Tatum. Witnesses: Wesley Fry - William Bickers - John Massey -
Simeon B. Wayland.

CULPEPER COUNTY, VA. - DEED BOOK "N" - (1785-1787) - PAGE 208.

19 April 1786 - Indenture in which Reginal Burdyne and
John Grisson and Barbara, his wife, of the State of South Car-
olina, County of Abbeville, and Samuel Burdyne and Nathaniel
Burdyne, of the State of North Carolina, County of Wilkes,
parties of the one part, sell to William Chapman, of the County
of Culpeper, State of Virginia - for five shillings, a tract of
land in Culpeper County, containing 165 acres, on the Roberson
River, adjoining the land of John Burdyne, etc.
Witnesses: Ephriam Dicken - John Thomas - Joseph Snider.
Proved and recorded 16th May 1786.

27.

CULPEPER COUNTY, VA. - WILL BOOK "C" - (1783-1791)

Will of John Burdyne - dated 28 March 1786. Proved
April 1786.

Wife, Betty, - land in Cantuckey (sic)

SONS   DAUGHTERS
Benjamin   Susanna Burdyne
Amos   Catharine Burdyne   (ALL
              Sarah Burdyne
              Betty Burdyne   MINORS)
              Nancy Burdyne
              Agnes Burdyne

£30 in trust to William Chapman for support of his mother,
Catharine Burdyne -

Executors: Betty Burdyne - John Dicken - Joseph Dicken -
Witnesses: William Chapman, (and others).

CULPEPER COUNTY, VA. - DEED BOOK "H" - (1775-1778) - PAGE 1.

19 July 1774 - Deed of Gift from Constant Chapman, of
Charles County, Province of Maryland, widow and relict of Nathaniel Chapman, of the same place, deceased, to George Chapman,
son of the said Constant and Nathaniel, of the same place - for
natural love and affection for her said son, 865 acres of land
in the County of Culpeper, Virginia - in Dark Run in the Robinson fork, it being the land granted to the said Constant Chapman
by the Rt. Hon. Thomas, Lord Fairfax, 27 November 1772, in Liber
P folio 170. Proved and recorded 15 May 1775.

PRINCESS ANNE COUNTY, VA. - D & W #3 -(1714-1724)- PAGE 298.

21 January 1719 - Power of Attorney from Robert Bond of
North Carolina, appointing his trusty and well beloved friend,
Thomas Walke, to appear in Court in Princess Anne County, Vir-
ginia, to acknowledge all those deeds by me made, etc.
Witnesses: Hillary Moseley - Thomas Haynes - John Smythe -
Recorded 3 February 1719.

ibid - 20 January 1719 - Indenture in which Robert Bond, of North Carolina, sells to John Lovett of Parish of Linhaven, County of Princess Anne, a tract of land containing 100 acres on the eastern shore, which was formerly the land of Francis Bond, and is out of that tract of land of 250 acres which Lewis Purvine sold to the said Robert and Francis Bond, by his deed dated 1 March 1698/9 - Signed by Thomas Walke, Gent., Attorney of Robert Bond- (Witnesses, same as above.)

NOTE: (Other records prove Robert and Francis were brothers.)

ibid - page 9 - 3 December 1714 - Robert Bond of Princess Anne County, sells 95 acres of this same 250 original acre tract to John Lovett - etc. (NOTE: in another deed, Robert Bond and John Lovett exchange land and John is designated as a son of Lancaster Lovett.) - (ibid - page 48) - and Ezabella, wife of John Lovett, relinquished her right of dower.

PRINCE EDWARD COUNTY, VA. - DEED BOOK 14 - (1806-1812) - PAGE 312.

(-----) 1809 - Daniel Moseley and Martha, his wife, of Buckingham County, Virginia, Reizen Porter and Mary, his wife, William Cook and Elizabeth, his wife, Jane Pettus and Rebecca Pettus, of Prince Edward County, of one part, sell to John Pettus of Prince Edward County - for ₤300 - 261 acres of land in Prince Edward County, near or on Vaughan's Creek, being part of the land whereon the late Stephen Pettus lived and was conveyed by him in his last will to his above named daughters to be equally divided, etc. Recorded 16 October 1809.

ibid - page 313 - 5 August 1809 - Stephen Pettus of the State of Tennessee, sells to James Watt, of the County of Buckingham, State of Virginia, for ₤439, a tract of land containing 237 acres in Prince Edward County, it being part of the land on which the late Stephen Pettus lived and was conveyed by him in his last will to the aforesaid Stephen Pettus (party to this deed), etc. Witnesses: Thomas C. Martin - Samuel Shepherd - William Preston- John C. Owens. Recorded 16 October 1809.

ISLE OF WIGHT COUNTY, VA. - DEED BOOK 4 - (1729-1736) - PAGE 14.

(----) June 1728 - Barnaby Machinne, of the upper Parish of Bartee Precinct in the County of Albemarle, in North Carolina, sells ro Henry Flowers, of the County of Isle of Wight, in Virginia - for ₺10 - 150 acres of land on the south side of the main Blackwater Swamp in said County of Isle of Wight, being part of 490 acres granted to said Barnaby, 16 June 1714. Recorded 25 May 1730.

ibid - DEED BOOK 6 - (1741-1744) - PAGE 125.

21 October 1741 - Edward Flowers and Elizabeth, his wife, of Carolina, sell to Arthur Edwards of Isle of Wight County in Virginia, for ₺40, a tract of land in Isle of Wight County, containing 110 acres, being part of a patent granted to Edward Goodson and Mathew Rushon, dated 16 June 1714, etc.
Teste - Benjamin Johnson, Jr. - Jacob Barnes - Jacob Flowers. Acknowledged and recorded 26 July 1742.

ISLE OF WIGHT COUNTY, VA. - DEED BOOK 6 - (1741-1744) - PAGE 179.

30 December 1742 - Edward Flowers and Henry Flowers, of North Carolina, of the one part, sell to Richard Johnson of Isle of Wight County, Virginia, for ₺15, 120 acres of land in Isle of Wight County, on the north side of Nottoway Swamp, etc. Witness: Jacob Flowers - William Wotten - Joshua Barnes. Recorded 21 January 1742. (sic)

SUSSEX COUNTY, VA. - DEED BOOK "A" - (1754-1759) - PAGE 304.

21 April 1758 - William (W) Avent, of Northampton County, Province of North Carolina, and Sarah, his wife, sell to David Mason, Gent., of County of Sussex, Colony of Virginia, for ₺310, a tract of land in the County of Sussex, Colony of Virginia, on Otterdam Swamp, adjoining the land of John Avent, son of John Avent, Gent., containing 1400 (?) acres - it being all the land belonging to the said William Avent, devised to him by his father, Thomas Avent, Gent., by his last will, etc.
Acknowledged and recorded same day.

30.

SUSSEX COUNTY, VA. - DEED BOOK "B" - (1759-1763) - PAGE 13.

22 October 1760 - William Avent of North Carolina and Thomas Vinson of Brunswick County, Colony of Virginia, Executors of Thomas Avent, Gent., deceased, sell to John Dillard of the Parish of Albemarle in the County of Sussex, for ₺8.5, 200 acres of land in Sussex, on the east side of the great Swamp, adjoining Peter Avent --- directed by will to be sold, etc. Witnesses: William Joseph and John Doby. Proved and recorded 21 November 1760.

BRUNSWICK COUNTY, VA. - DEED BOOK 8 - (1765-1767) - PAGE 54.

26 February 1765 - Peter Avent of Orange County, North Carolina, sells to Gilbert Hay of Albemarle Parish, Sussex County, Virginia, for ₺60, 488 acres of land in Brunswick, Meherrin Parish, being the land that said Peter Avent purchased of John Cumbo and Joseph Studart, (sic) 26 September 1760 - Rest of patent to Joseph Right, 1 August 1745. Witnesses: James Stewart, Thomas Avent, Henry Mason, David Mason, James Mason. Proved 25 March 1765.

BRUNSWICK COUNTY, VA. - DEED BOOK 9 - (1767-1770) - PAGE 472.

31 October 1768 - Isham Avant of Roan (Rowan) County, North Carolina, sells to Thomas Moss of Brunswick County, Colony of Virginia, for ₺30, 200 acres of land in Brunswick, Meherrin Parish, part of Simon Lane's survey. Witnesses: John Doby, William Avant, William Robinson. Proved 24 April 1769 and recorded 26 June 1769.

BRUNSWICK COUNTY, VA. - DEED BOOK 12 - (1776-1777) - PAGE 259.

10 February 1777 - Peter Avant of Cumberland County, North Carolina to Mrs. Mary Tomlinson of Brunswick County, Virginia, Marriage Contract - for ₺300, she releases any claim to his estate. Witnesses: William (x) Sheehorn, William Rives, James Young. Proved 25 August 1777.

ROANOKE COUNTY, VA. - DEED BOOK "G" - (1863-1869) - PAGE 42.

25 March 1863 - Thomas G. Godwin and Martha M., his wife;
John Godwin and Sarah, his wife; Harriet Snyder, formerly Harriet
Godwin; William J. Alexander and Sarah, his wife, formerly Sarah
Godwin; Frederick Rhodes and Eliza, his wife, formerly Eliza
Godwin; Lewis Whitten and Charlotte, his wife, formerly Charlotte
Godwin; and Isaac F. Renn, executor of John Renn, deceased, who
represent the interest of James C. Huff and Jane, his wife, form-
erly Jane Godwin, of the first part, sell to George P. Terrell,
of the second part - whereas James Godwin, Sr., late of Roanoke
County, died intestate, leaving the parties of the first part,
his heirs at law, (besides James Godwin, Jr., who is now in the
State of Missouri and owing to the condition of the country (i.e.
Civil War) cannot unite in the present conveyance), and whereas
the said James Godwin owned at his death a certain house and lot
in the Town of Salem (#42), now for the sum of (--), paid to each
of the 7 heirs of James Godwin, Sr. (leaving out James, Jr.) All
sign by own signatures. Certified before Justices - as to:
    Thomas G. Godwin &
    Martha M. Godwin of Botetourt County, Virginia

    Lewis Whitten &
    Charlotte Whitten of Monroe County, Virginia

    John M. Godwin &
    Sarah J. Godwin of Albemarle County, Virginia

    W. J. Alexander & Sarah of Roanoke County, Virginia

    Frederick Rhodes & Eliza of Roanoke County, Virginia

    Harriet Snyder of Roanoke County, Virginia

Recorded 2 April 1863.

ROANOKE COUNTY, VA. - DEED BOOK "G" - (1863-1869) - PAGE 466.

28 July 1868 - James A. Godwin and Rebecca R. Jane Godwin,
his wife, of Grundy County, State of Missouri, sell to Jacob
Bonsack and Daniel C. KISER of Roanoke County, Virginia, all
their right, title and interest in and to a certain lot of land
on Main Street, in the Town of Salem, County of Roanoke, Virginia
(#42), which lot descended from the late James Godwin, Sr. upon
his 8 heirs at law of whom the grantor, the said James A. Godwin
is one. Certified by Justice of Grundy County, Missouri, same
day and recorded in Roanoke County, Virginia 7 August 1868.

32.

TAZEWELL COUNTY, VA. - DEED BOOK 11 - (1853-1855) - PAGE 186.

15 September 1853 - Power of Attorney from Andrew D. Brown and Jane, his wife, of the County of Grundy, State of Missouri, appointing Samuel K. Witten of the same County and State, our attorney to take possession of and/or to dispose of all property due us in the County of Tazewell, State of Virginia - to perform everything that is necessary, etc. Certified by Justice of Grundy County, Missouri, 16 September 1853. Recorded 30 March 1854, Tazewell County, Virginia.

FAIRFAX COUNTY, VA. - DEED BOOK "D-3" - PAGE 360.

7 October 1837, Eliab C. Butler of Nashville, Tennessee, Power of Attorney to Nathaniel B. Butler of Nashville, to receive from Charles F. Ford of Fairfax County, Virginia, Administrator of my late Father, John Butler, deceased, late of Fairfax County, Virginia, my portion of his estate. Acknowledged in Davidson County, Tennessee, 7 October 1837. Recorded in Fairfax County, Virginia 21 December 1837.

ibid - page 361 - 7 October 1837, Eliab C. Butler of Nashville, Tennessee, guardian of James W. Butler and Eugenia Butler. Power of Attorney to Nathaniel B. Butler to receive from Charles F. Ford of Fairfax County, Virginia. Executor or Administrator of James Turley, Sr., deceased, late of Fairfax, the distributive share coming to my said wards. Acknowledged and recorded as above.

ibid - page 363 - 7 October 1837, Eliab C. Butler Power of Attorney to Nathaniel B. Butler to receive from Daniel B. Kinchloe of Fairfax - Executor or administrator of William C. B. Butler, late of Fairfax, whatever is coming to me. Acknowledged and recorded as above.

FAIRFAX COUNTY, VA. - DEED BOOK "F-3" - (1839-1841) - PAGE 175.

30 July 1840 - Elisha Jenkins of Vicksburg, Mississippi, sells to William H. Butler of Fairfax County, Virginia for $150.0 135 acres of land (Lot #8) in division of Elisha Jenkins, decease also undivided interest in Lot #9, allotted to Anna Jenkins and said Anna Jenkins dying intestate, the 11th part fell to said Elisha. Acknowledged in Fairfax County, 30 July 1840.

FAIRFAX COUNTY, VA. - DEED BOOK "G-3" - (1841-1842) - PAGE 152.

23 August 1841 - Nathaniel B. Butler and Susan M., his wife, of Nashville, Tennessee; William H. Butler and Frances, his wife; Henry G. Butler, Fanny Butler, John Butler and Elizabeth, his wife, of Fairfax County, Virginia, sell to John Ish of Loudoun County, Virginia, for $429.00, 143¼ acres of land in Fairfax on Bull Run, purchased of the executors of Alexander Henderson of Prince William. Acknowledged in Davidson County, Tennessee, 16 October 1841 and in Fairfax County, 17 December 1841.

FAIRFAX COUNTY, VA. - DEED BOOK "B-3" - (1833-1835) - PAGE 148.

28 September 1833 - Lewis Jenkins, Travis Jenkins, Richard H. Jenkins, Benjamin Jenkins and Susan Jenkins of Fayette County, Kentucky, to William H. Butler of same, for $75.00, undivided (-?-) of land in Fairfax, where Anna Jenkins, late of said County died, being Lot #9, in division of Elisha Jenkins. Acknowledged in Kentucky, 28 September 1833.

FAIRFAX COUNTY, VA. - DEED BOOK "D-3" - (1836-1838) - PAGE 295.

6 July 1837, Eliah Cooper Butler of the Town of Nashville, State of Tennessee, to William E. Beckwith of Fairfax, for $500.00, 207 acres of land allotted to William C. B. Butler, deceased, in the division of the estate of his father, John Butler, deceased, and willed to said Eliah Cooper Butler by his brother, William C. Butler. Acknowledged 6 July 1837, Davidson County, Tennessee. Recorded 13 September 1837, in Fairfax County, Virginia.

PITTSYLVANIA COUNTY, VA. - DEED BOOK 3 - (1772-1774)

ibid - page 415 - 25 December 1773 - Power of Attorney from John Anderson of the County of Orange, Province of North Carolina, to Thomas Owen of the County of Guilford (sic), Province of North Carolina, to receive all the estate, negroes, money, etc. due him in the County of Hanover, Virginia and elsewhere, chiefly now in the hands of Mr. Nelson Anderson, of Hanover County, it being in heirship which falls to me of the estate of John Anderson, Sr. and Sarah, his wife. Witnesses: John Owen, Sr. - John Thompson - James Mitchell - Benjamin Williams. Recorded 24 February 1774.

34.

NOTE BY CHH: The following deed to the above deed on page 416, specifies that John Anderson of Orange County, North Carolina, was the <u>son</u> of ALEANAH Anderson, deceased. (I do not know whether this is a male or female name.)

PRINCE WILLIAM COUNTY, VA. - DEED BOOK "E" - (1740-1741) - PG.238.

27 October 1740 - John Hancock of the Province of North Carolina and County of Bladen, conveys to his eldest son, Scarlet Hancock, of Hamilton Parish, Prince William County, Virginia, for natural love and affection, and ₤100, all my lands and personal estate in Virginia. Witnesses: Moses Linton, William (x) Davis, William (X) Bland, Elizabeth (X) Cole. Proved 27 April 1741.

PRINCE WILLIAM COUNTY, VA.- WILL BOOK "C" - (1734-1744) - PG. 272.

Will of Scarlet Hancock (undated). Wife Anne, land called Old Field. Daughter, Anne Hancock; son, John Hancock, land where I now live in the Neck on Morumsco Creek and 400 acres left to me by will of Richard Brett. Executors: Wife, Anne; John Gregg, Marmaduke Lawson, Moses Linton. Proved 23 March 1740/41.

NOTE BY CHH: (see Hening, Vol. 8, pages 635-637 - February 1772- "To dock the entail of land of John Hancock".)

PRINCE WILLIAM COUNTY, VA. - DEED BOOK "R" - (1768-1771) -PG.143.

22 February 1770 - Henry Brett of Charles County, Maryland, "Yeoman" and Tabitha, his wife, sell to Cuthbert Bullitt of Prince William County, Gent., for ₤20, land in Prince William, on the Potomac River, which George Brett, late of the same County, Gent., deceased, by his last will and testament, devised to the said Henry Brett, until he should enjoy or possess the lands descended to him from his <u>Mother, Sarah More</u>, then lately deceased. Witnesses: Evan Williams, Robert Wickliff, Gustavus B. Wallace. Proved 6 August 1770.

PRINCE WILLIAM COUNTY, VA. - DEED BOOK "R" - (1768-1771) -PG.224.

19 July 1770 - Henry Brett of Charles County, Maryland, quit-claims to John Brett of Prince William County, as well on his own account as that of being Executor of the last will and testament of George Brett, deceased, all claims against said John Brett. Witnesses: Henry Peyton, Mary Peyton. Proved 1 October 1770.

STAFFORD COUNTY, VA. - DEED BOOK "NN" - (1842-1845) - PAGE 410.

10 February 1844 - ANN N. TACKETT, OF STAFFORD COUNTY, VIRGINIA , IN HER OWN RIGHT - WILLIAM BARBER AND SARAH, HIS WIFE, of Stafford County, ELIAS BARBER, of Jackson County, Alabama, for himself and as attorney in fact for MARGARET E ., his wife - JOHN B. FANT, of Marshall County, Mississippi and JANE, HIS WIFE (who was JANE BARBER) - by WILLIAM BARBER, their attorney in fact- ENOCH BARBER and PAMELA, HIS WIFE, of Fauquier County, Virginia and BERNARD BARBER AND SARAH, HIS WIFE, of Stafford County, Virginia, (all) "HEIRS AND DISTRIBUTEES OF EDWARD BARBER, DECEASED" sell to Sanford Humphrey of Fauquier County, for $795.50 - 250 acres of land in Stafford County, according to a survey made in 1801, except 35 acres taken by SARAH DUFFEY, ANOTHER DISTRIBUTEE, as her portion, on Aquia Run. Recorded January 1845.

COMMENT BY CHH: There seems to be no doubt or contention that ANN N. TACKETT, widow and relict of CHARLES TACKETT, had the maiden name of "BARBER". She must have been in her late 50's or 60's at this time and so it would take some other research to determine if the above heirs of EDWARD BARBER were his children or his siblings.

STAFFORD COUNTY, VA. - WILL BOOK "Z" - (1699-1709) - PAGE 2.

19 October 1699 - Anne (x) Carmalt, late of Maryland, widow, but now of Stafford County, Virginia, binds as a servant to my loving friend, Edward Barton, of Stafford County, my son, John Carmalt, he being now eleven years of age ---- in this my great want and necessity. Witnesses: Thomas (x) Chapman, Thomas (x) Chapman, Jr., G. Mason (Church Warden). Recorded 9 November 1699.

STAFFORD COUNTY, VA. - WILL BOOK "Z" - (1699-1709) - PAGE 3.

19 October 1699 - Anne (x) Carmalt binds Henry Carmalt, age 5, and Bridget Carmalt, age 7, to Burr Harrison.

PATRICK COUNTY, VA. - DEED BOOK 1 - (1791-1801) - PAGE 236.

24 November 1794 - Joshua Hudson of the County of Stokes, State of North Carolina, sells to Edward Tatum of the County of Patrick, State of Virginia, for ₤30, 100 acres of land, being part of 355 acres granted by Patent, to said Joshua Hudson, assignee of Ralph Shelton in Patrick County, formerly Henry County, on Read branches of Russell's Creek, etc. Witnesses: Hall Hudson - Jesse Tatum, Jr. - David Hanby, Jr. Recorded 27 November 1794.

PATRICK COUNTY, VA. - DEED BOOK 1 - (1791-1801) - PAGE 257.

22 December 1794 - Joshua Hudson of the County of Stokes, State of North Carolina, sells to Robert Hall, of the County of Patrick, State of Virginia, for ₤150, 200 acres of land in the County of Patrick, on the headwaters of Russell's Creek, etc. Witnesses: Harvey Fitzgerald - John Hall - Jacob Lawson. Recorded 25 December 1794.

NOTE: ibid, page 258 -(same day) Joshua Hudson (for ₤10) sells to (?) Golden Davison of Patrick County, 55 acres of land in Patrick County, on headwaters of Russell's Creek. Same witnesses.

PATRICK COUNTY, VA. - DEED BOOK 1 - (1791-1801) - PAGE 372.

8 June 1795 - Abner Eckhols (Echols), of the State of Georgia and County of Franklin, Power of Attorney to my trusty friend, William Fuson of the State of Virginia and County of Patrick, to sell land in Stokes County, North Carolina, bought of Joseph Goin (Goan) on Peters Creek. Proved 28 January, 1796 and 31 March 1796.

37.

FAUQUIER COUNTY, VA. - DEED BOOK 9 - (1785-1787) - PAGE 182.

25 September 1785 - George Neavell of the County of Davison in the State of North Carolina, gives his Power of Attorney "to my trusty and well beloved friends, Martin Pickett and John Moffett, Gent., of Fauquier County", to convey to Roley Smith and John Smith (who are assignees of Joseph Smith), 270 acres of land at the Pig Nutt Ridge in Fauquier County, etc. Witnesses: Richard Jackman - Enocj Bradford - Joshua Burditt. Proved 25 September 1786 in Fauquier County by Enoch Bradford and recorded.

AUGUSTA COUNTY, VA. - DEED BOOK 36 - (1810-1811) - PAGE 148.

8 March 1810 - Indenture in which Ann Frame, widow and relict of John Frame, deceased, and Archibald Frame, Ann Frame, Elizabeth Frame, John Allison and Polly, his wife, late Polly Frame, of Augusta County, Virginia - John Robertson and Margaret, his wife (late Margaret Frame) of Montgomery County, Virginia, and Joseph Shields and Rachel, his wife, late Rachel Frame, of Washington County, Tennessee, heirs a law of said decedent, sell to Valentine Fawver (also spelled Fawber), of Rockingham County, Virginia, for ₤300, 350 acres of land in Augusta County, on a branch of the South river near the South Mountain, conveyed by William Graham and Ann, his wife, to John Frame, 15 October 1782. Witnesses: Uriah Phillips, John Cofer, Joseph Bell, Joseph (x) Fawver. Acknowledged 7 May 1810, in Washington County, Tennessee, by the Shields; 3 July 1810, in Montgomery County, Virginia, by the Robertsons; 31 August 1810, in Augusta and recorded.

COMMENT: Chalkley's Augusta County, Virginia Records, Vol 2, pages 344 and 358, lists the marriage bond (24 November 1800) of Joseph Shields, "widower" to Rachel FREAM (sic), daughter of John FREAM (sic), who consents. Married 27 November 1800 by Rev. John McCue, who says "to Rachel FRAME" (sic).

CHARLOTTE COUNTY, VA. - DEED BOOK 17 - (1823-1827) - PAGE 117.

10 September 1824 - Power of Attorney from Sabra Hazzlewood, John Hazzlewood, William Hazzlewood, Joshua Hazzlewood, Jeremiah Russell and Elizabeth, his wife, (formerly Hazzlewood), Abram Hill and Patsy, his wife, (formerly Hazzlewood), Fleming Hazzlewood, of the Counties of Bedford and Williamson, State of Tennessee, appointing Dr. F. Fuquia, of the County of Williamson,

38.

Tennessee, our true and lawful attorney to receive from Zacheus
Carwile of Charlotte County, Virginia, who was executor of the
estate of Sabra Morris, deceased, etc.
Certified by Justices of State of Tennessee, Williamson County.
Recorded in Charlotte County, Virginia 19 January 1825.

GREENSVILLE COUNTY, VA. - DEED BOOK 5 - (1816-1824) - PAGE 401.

4 February 1822 - Power of Attorney from James Allen, of
the County of Limestone, State of Alabama, appointing William
Holt, of the same County, his lawful attorney, to transact all
his business in the County of Greensville,State of Virginia, and
to convey to Francis Hill, all his right, title and interest to
a tract of land in Greensville County, Virginia, which was sold
by Benjamin Allen to said Francis Hill on the condition I made a
right for same on 11 October 1814.

GREENSVILLE COUNTY, VA. - DEED BOOK 5 - PAGE 403.

7 October 1822 - James Allen, of the County of Limestone,
State of Alabama, by William Holt of said County and State, his
lawful attorney, sells to Patrick H. Hill - Miles Cary in right
of his wife Anna (Arind) (late Hill) - Harriott Hill - Bassett
M. Calvert in right of his wife, Francis (late Hill) - all of
the County of Warwick, State of Virginia - devisees of the last
will and testament of the Reverend Francis Hill, deceased, for
$354.10, a tract of land containing 63¼ acres in the County of
Greensville, it being the land which descended to the said James
Allen by the death of his father, Aaron Allen, deceased, reserving unto Sally Hill, widow and relict of Francis Hill, deceased,
profits of same, etc., for her natural life - etc.
Recorded 7 October 1822.

AMELIA COUNTY, VA. - DEED BOOK 11 - (1769-1772) - PAGE 365.

17 February 1772 - Indenture in which Thornton Pryor, of the
Province of North Carolina, sells to John Thweat, of the County
of Prince George, Colony of Virginia, for £130, a tract of land
in the County of Amelia, Colony of Virginia, containing 347 acres

etc., it being all that tract of land the aforesaid Thornton Pryor purchased of John and Elizabeth Ellis, 23 November 1758, excepting 100 acres sold to Chrispen Shelton, etc. (has six witnesses) - Proved and recorded 27 February 1772.

ibid - page 451.

22 June 1772 - Deed of Gift from Richard Dennis Senior of the County of Amelia to John Pryor, of the same County, for natural love, good will and affection and as the husband of my daughter (not named) - 150 acres of land in the County of Amelia, Parish of Nottoway, on Cellar Creek. Acknowledged and recorded 25 June 1772.

GRAYSON COUNTY, VA. - DEED BOOK 4 - (1818-1824) - PAGE 46.

4 December 1818 - Indenture in which Elisha Bedwell and Mary, his wife, of the County of White, State of Tennessee, sells to William Cornutt, of the County of Grayson (Va.), for $150.00, a tract of land in Grayson County, containing 59 acres, on Elk Creek, also one other tract containing 125 acres on Elk Creek, adjoining the before mentioned tract, etc. (Signed Elisha Bedwell, by John CORNUTT, attorney in fact). Recorded 26 January 1819.

NOTE BY CHH: The attorney, John Cornutt, had married Mourning Bedwell, June 23, 1814. (MR # 1, page 9.)

GRAYSON COUNTY, VA. - DEED BOOK 1 - (1793-1803) - PAGE 11.

23 November 1793 - Indenture in which William Norton and Jamima, his wife, of the County of Pendleton, State of South Carolina, sell to William Bradley, of the County of Grayson, State of Virginia, for ₤50, a tract of land in Grayson County, Virginia, containing 93 acres, more or less, on Crooked Creek, a branch of New River, etc. Witnesses: Edward Norton, Gideon Norton, Jesse Harris. Proven by the witnesses and recorded 17 December 1793.

ibid - page 204.

27 October 1799 - Indenture in which Jacob Cummins, of the State of Kentucky, sells to Elisha BEDSAL (sic), of Grayson

County, Virginia, for $50.00, a tract of land in Grayson County,
on the waters of Chestnut Creek, containing by survey 100 acres,
etc. Witnesses: Flower Swift, Elisha Bedsaul, George Jones.
Recorded March Court 1800.

GRAYSON COUNTY, VA. - DEED BOOK 2 - (1803-1811) - PAGE 116.

22 December 1804 - Indenture in which George Currin of Grayson County, Virginia, sells to George Martin of Grainger County,
Tennessee, for $71.88, a tract of land in Grayson County, on both
sides of Chestnut Creek, a branch of New River, containing 640
acres in different tracts, so as to include Bedsals old improve-
ments, it being my legacy of the estate of Elisha Bedsall, decease
due me, which is the fourth part of all Elisha'Bedsall's lands,
etc.
Signed by George Martin and Amey (x) Martin, his wife. Witnesses: Amos Ballard - Elisha Bedsall - John Martin. Recorded
March Court, 1805.

AMELIA COUNTY, VA. - DEED BOOK 19 - (1789-1794) - PAGE 294.

16 November 1793 - Indenture in which Daniel Farley and
Martha, his wife, of the County of Shelby, State of Kentucky,
sell to Matthew Farley, of the County of Amelia, State of Virgini
for ₤178, 15 shillings - a tract of land in Amelia County, containing 130 acres, etc. Witnesses: P. Roberts - Joshua Hundley
John Robert - William Farley. Proved and recorded 26 December,
1793.

NOTE BY CHH: (ibid, page 296) - Mary Farley, widow of Joseph
Farley, remarried to Joshua Hundley in 1786 and for natural love
and affection for her son, (the above Daniel Farley), relinquishe
her right in the above cited land, which Daniel then reassigned
to the above Mathew Farley. (The will of Joseph Farley was prove
23rd May 1782 and recorded in Amelia County Will Book 3, page 97.

HENRY COUNTY, VA. - DEED BOOK 11, PAGE 556.

6 October 1835 - Power of Attorney from James Rea and Polly
Taylor, of the County of Giles, State of Tennessee, both being

children of James Rea, deceased, late of the County of Henry,
State of Virginia - (the said Polly Taylor being the widow of
John Taylor, deceased, late of Giles County, Tennessee.) - appointing John Rea of the County of Giles, State of Tennessee,
our true and lawful attorney, to transact all business with the
other heirs and legatees of the said James Rea, deceased, etc.
(both signed by their "x") - Certified in Giles County, Tennessee,
by the Clerk and recorded in Henry County, Virginia, 11 January
1836.

COMMENT: See Will of Andrew Rea of Henry County, who named his
son, James, among other children - (Henry County Will Book 2,
page 155. Proven 26 January 1807.)

NORTHUMBERLAND COUNTY, VA. - RECORD BOOK 16 - (1799-1803) -PAGE 279.

10 September 1801 - Indenture in which Zachariah Barr (attorney for Jane Easton) of the State of Kentucky, sells to George
Haydon, of the County of Northumberland, State of Virginia, for
$264.00, that tract of land which fell to Zachariah Barr by the
death of John Barr, which said Zachariah Barr sold to John Easton
whose orphan, Jean (sic) Easton hath empowered him to sell, situated in the County of Northumberland, Virginia, containing 88
acres, more or less, etc. Witnesses: Hopkins Harding - William
Blackerby - Cyrus Harding - Seth Lumford. Acknowledged and recorded 14 September 1801.

ibid - page 443. -

4 August 1802 - William Blackerby and Caty, his wife, sell to
George Haydon, for $480.83, that tract of land on which the said
George Haydon now lives on, which was purchased by me from Zachariah Barr, containing 94¼ acres, etc. Recorded 13 September,
1802.

FREDERICK COUNTY, VA. - Will BOOK 4 - (1770-1783) - PAGE 129.

Will of John Haton, dated 21 July 1771, proven 8 August 1771,
desires his land in Hampshire County (4 tracts, 900 acres) purchased of John McCollough, who purchased it from Noah Hampton and
one other tract on Spring Gap Run in said County, to be sold.

Balance of my estate to John Haton of the County of Cumberland in England, son of Thomas Haton, and grandson of my uncle, Thomas Haton. Executors: Jacob Hite and Richard Rigg of Frederick Count and Joseph Watson of Fairfax County.

(Signed - John Hayton)

Witnesses: Adam Stephen
Jonathan Seamon
Rees Morgan

August 7, 1772 - Joseph Watson qualified as executor.

FREDERICK COUNTY, VA. - DEED BOOK 1 - (1743-1749) - PAGE 481.

17 March 1748 - Power of Attorney from Robert Heaton of Nort ampton in the County of Bucks, Province of Pennsylvania - appoint ing his trusty and loving friends James Carter and George Holling worth, both of Frederick County, Virginia, to transact all busi- ness, recover all debts due, etc. and to sell and convey all my property to that tract of land on Back Creek, whereon John Frost now lives, etc. Witnesses: David Nance - William Green - John Milburn - William Glover.

(Signed Robert Heaton - SEAL)

Proved and recorded 4 April 1749.

FREDERICK COUNTY, VA. - DEED BOOK 49 - (1824-1825) - PAGE 232.

(---) November 1823 - Power of Attorney from Hannah Heaton the County of Greene, Pennsylvania, appointing her two sons-in-l Thomas Colver of the County of Greene, Pennsylvania and Isaac Buckingham of the County of Washington, Pennsylvania - whereas, brother, John Bowen, deceased, late of Frederick County, Virgini died intestate, possessed of considerable real and personal pro- perty, etc. (Rees Hill, Esq., his administrator) - etc. Witnes Samuel Black - Hiram Heaton - H. B. Heaton. Recorded 4 January 1825.

43.

FREDERICK COUNTY, VA. - DEED BOOK 62 - (1833-1834) - PAGE 27.

5 September 1833 - Indenture in which Jacob B. Heaton and Rachel, his wife, of the County of Fayette, State of Pennsylvania, sell to John Buckingham of the County of Washington, Pennsylvania, whereas,Jacob Bowen and John Bowen, brothers, deceased, died possessed of property in the County of Frederick, Virginia - on Apple Pye Ridge, whereon Rees Hill resides, and Jacob Bowen died intestate, without children, leaving the said John Bowen, Priscilla Hill, Hannah Heaton, Ann Carter, Margaret Bowl (?) and Jane Fitzpatrick, his brother and sisters, his heirs at law and personal representatives and distributees of his estate, etc., do sell their right, title and interest to the said John Buckingham, for the sum of $200.00, etc. Recorded 2 October 1833. Witnesses: Robert Rogers and Francis Worester.

BEDFORD COUNTY, VA. - ORDER BOOK 10 - (1790-1795) - PAGE 261.

23 September 1793 - The Last Will and Testament of William Thornhill, deceased, late of Bedford County, was produced in Court. And it appearing by the Certificate of Thomas Henderson, Chief Justice of Hawkins County, Tennessee, in the territory of the United States, South of the River Ohio, returned to this Court agreeable as a writ for that purpose to him directed that the same was proven according to law. It is ordered that the same be admitted to record. And on the motion of Sarah Thornhill, widow and relict of the said decedent, who comes into Court and refuses to accept of the provisions made for her in her said husband's will. It is ordered that Thomas Leftwich, Christopher Clark and Charles Moorman do lay off and allot unto her, her thirds of her deceased husband's estate according to law and make return thereof to Court.

BEDFORD COUNTY, VA. - WILL BOOK 2 - (1788-1803) - PAGE 118.

Will of William Thornhill of Bedford County, Virginia, dated 30 November 1789.

To Wife Sarah Thornhill, all estate for life. At her death or marriage, to son William Thornhill, land where I live.

To son, Ezekle Thornhill, 100 acres.

To daughter, Rachel Thornhill, a sorrell mare.

44.

To all the rest of my children that is not married -

My wife, Sarah and William Thornhill, Executors. John Payne and
Rawly (x) Dodson, Witnesses. Proved September Sessions 1790,
Hawkins County, North Carolina by John Payne and Rawley Dodson.
Thomas Hutchings, C.H.C.

Commission to Thomas Henderson, Gent., presiding Judge or
Chief Magistrate of County Court of Hawkins, in the State of
North Carolina. Whereas the witnesses to said will are out of the
jurisdiction of this Court. - 31 August 1790.

10 September 1793 - Thomas Henderson - P.J.H.C. Proved by
John Payne, who saw Rawleigh Dodson sign.

10 September 1793 - Certificate of Richard Mitchell, Clerk,
that Thomas Henderson is J. P. and Chairman of the Court of Hawkins County.

23 September 1793 - Recorded in Bedford County, Virginia.

ALBEMARLE COUNTY, VA. - DEED BOOK 10 - PAGE 176.

14 March 1791 - Power of Attorney from Joseph H. Morrison
of the County of Amherst, being about to move out of this state,
to the State of Georgia, do herewith constitute and appoint Samuel Higgenbotham, of Amherst County, and James Books (or Booth?)
of the County of Albemarle, my lawful attornies - to sell two
tracts of land on the waters of Rockfish Creek, in the County of
Amherst. (1) containing 190 acres by patent dated 25 September
1762 and (2) containing 200 acres by patent dated 20 September
1768, etc. Recorded June Court 1791.

AMHERST COUNTY, VA. - MARRIAGE REGISTER - (1763-1852) - PAGE 112

October 7, 1796 - Joseph Higgenbotham Morrison married to
(Mrs.) Mary Walker, widow. James Higgenbotham Sec and W. L.
Crawford, Witnesses.

45.

FREDERICK COUNTY, VA. - DEED BOOK 27 - PAGE 157.

Power of Attorney from Jacob Niswanger and Susanna Niswanger, of the District of Laurens, State of South Carolina, appointing Moses Madden of the same District and State, their true and lawful attorney to make good and sufficient title to 349 acres of land in Frederick County, State of Virginia, on Stephen's Run - to one Thomas Steele of Frederick County, Virginia, which land was purchased from us some years past by the said Thomas Steele, as will appear by a bond given by the said Jacob Niswanger with John McGinnis security, - dated (blank) 1800. Certified by Justice of Quorum, John A. Elmore of Lauren District, South Carolina, 27 November 1800. Recorded Frederick County, Virginia, 6 April 1801.

NOTE BY CHH: Moses Madden sold the above land 1st January 1801 to Thomas Steele and therein identified Susanna as wife of Jacob Niswanger, and further identified her as the daughter of George Wright, who willed the 349 acres which he had patented 20 July 1765, (Book "M", page 425) and states further that the said George Wright dated his will 11 June 1787 and died in 96 District, South Carolina, with reference to the will at the County of Lawrence Register Office.(Laurens??)

SHENANDOAH COUNTY, VA. - DEED BOOK "C" - PAGES 476-477.

23 April 1782 - Jacob Niswanger and wife, Elizabeth, of the County of Shenandoah, sell to Michael Wine (see note) of the State of Maryland, (lease 5 sh Rel 550 pd) a tract of land in the said County adjoining the land of George Brock - Mary Wells - Reuben Moor, containing 228 acres, etc.

*(note: The deed of lease us signed by John (sic) Niswanger and the deed of release states that the land is sold by John and wife, Elizabeth - (The lease states 228 acres, the release, 288 acres.)

Recorded 30 May 1782.

*(further note) - This is NOT Michael Wise, but IS Wine.

CHANCERY COURT OF RICHMOND, VA. - DEED BOOK 193C - PAGE 388.

27 May 1893 - James A. Gresham (census: b. 1843) and Emma F., his wife, of the City of Kansas City, State of Missouri, and Joseph D. Gresham and Lida V., his wife, of Birmingham, State of

Alabama - parties of the first part and Richard Hugh Gresham,
(census: b. 1845) of the County of Henrico, State of Virginia -
parties of the second part.

In consideration of the sum of $833.33 to each of the parties
of the first part, do grant to the said Richard Hugh Gresham, all
their right, title and interest in and to that lot of land in the
City of Richmond, on the west side of 25th Street, between Clay and
Leigh Streets, and is the same lot partitioned to <u>Mary E. Gresham</u>
(census: b. 1819) by a decree of the <u>Circuit Court of Henrico
County</u>, 5 May 1892, in the suit of Gresham vs Gresham and of which
the said Mary E. Gresham died seized and possessed and which descended to the parties hereto and Mary E. Gresham, the mother of
the said Joseph A. (should be James A.), Joseph D. and Richard
Hugh Gresham, having died intestate, and <u>leaving no other issue or
descendants of any other</u>, which interests hereby conveyed consists
of two undivided thirds thereof, etc.

Acknowledged before and certified by Notary Public of Kansas
City, Missouri as to James A. and Emma F. and by Notary Public of
Jefferson County, Alabama, as to Joseph D. and Loda V.

Recorded in Richmond Chancery Court, 4 June 1907.
(Margin by Clerk - Del. to R. H. Gresham, July 13, 1908.)

BEDFORD COUNTY, VA. - DEED BOOK 25 - PAGE 293.

25 January 1836 - Marriage agreement between Thomas Stewart
of the County of Christian, State of Kentucky and Charlotte Carter
of the County of Bedford, State of Virginia - said Stewart re-
nounces all claim to all property of said Charlotte Carter by
right as her husband, etc.

LANCASTER COUNTY, VA. - DEED BOOK 41 - (1849-1855) - PAGE 151.

11 November 1850 - Indenture in which Edward F. Smallwood and
Margaret S., his wife, of the County of Craven, State of North
Carolina, sell to Archibald L. Stott of Lancaster County, Virginia
for $423.00, a tract of land in Lancaster County, containing 82
acres and 26 poles - in Fleets Island, being a portion of John
Fleets estate allotted to Lucy Smallwood, one of the heirs of John
Fleet, deceased, etc. (Signatures of both) Certified by Justices
of Craven County, North Carolina. Recorded in Lancaster County
Court, 20 January 1851.

47.

FAIRFAX COUNTY, VA. - LAND CAUSES - (1812-1832) - PAGE 13.

10 May 1742 - Indenture in which Thomas Brooke, of St. Mary County, Province of Maryland, Gent., sells to Robert Boggess, of Prince William County, Province of Virginia - for (lease 5 shillings - release £71) - a tract of land on the southwest side of Pohick Run, in the County of Prince William, containing 320 acres, being part of a larger tract containing 2550 acres, granted by patent to Richard Normansel, of the County of Stafford, Gent., and sold by him to Martin Scarlet, who sold the aforementioned 320 acres unto Michael Valandigan, of the County of Stafford, 6 February 1692, bounding upon one Morety of the said patent formerly sold by the said Martin Scarlet to Captain George Mason, 10 March 1690/91 - and the said Michael Valandigan afterward sold the said 320 acres to the said George Mason and the said George Mason, afterward, by his last will and testament, dated 29 January 1715, did devise the said 320 acres to his son, Thomas Mason, which said Thomas Mason, being since dead without any heirs begotten of his body or making any will - and the said 320 acres is now legally descended to Sarah, the wife of the above mentioned Thomas Brooke, the only surviving sister and heir of the whole blood to the said Thomas Mason, etc. Witnesses: Henry Threlkeld - Richard Osborne- Baxter Davis. Recorded 24 May 1742, in Prince William County Court.

SECTION I - (b)

Marriage Records

48.

LOUDON COUNTY, VIRGINIA MARRIAGE RECORDS, FAIRFAX MONTHLY MEETING

(1751 - 1892)

N.B. - This is a continuation of the records transcribed in
Virginia Ancestors and Adventurers, Vol. 2, pages 64 - 67. The
records exhibited herewith are selected from among many others
and are the ones which indicate residence in another state than
Virginia by either the bride or the groom.

(Continue)

Page 171 - Benjamin E. Norris, of Frederick Co., Maryland and
Sarah Ann Stone, daughter of Daniel and Sarah Stone, of Loudoun
Co., Va. Married this 18th day, 11th month, 1835.

Page 172 - Richard Luke, of Baltimore Co., Maryland and Hannah
M. Lupton, daughter of Isaac and TAMSON Lupton, deceased.
Married 17th day, 3rd month, 1836 at Fairfax.

Page 175 - Edward J. Mathews, of Baltimore County, Maryland,
son of Mordecai and Ruth Mathews, of the County and State aforesaid, (both deceased) and Sarah H. Gover, daughter of Jesse and
Miriam Gover, of Loudoun Co., Va. Married this 14th day, 10th
month, 1841 at a public meeting held in Waterford, Va.

Page 176 - Joshua Wood, of Redstone, County of Fayette, State
of Pennsylvania and Eleanor H. Stone, of Fairfax, Loudoun Co.,
Va. Married this 17th day of 11th month, 1842 at Fairfax.

Page 182 - Eli M. Price, of Baltimore County, Maryland, son of
John and Susan M. Price, of the County and state aforesaid, and
Eliza Ann Schooley, daughter of Mahlon and Elizabeth Schooley
(the latter deceased) of Loudoun Co., Va. Married 16th day, 4th
month, 1851 at Fairfax.

Page 191 - Joseph M. DUNLOP, of Johnson County, Indiana, son of
James and Ann Dunlop, of the same place and Lizzie S. Dutton,
daughter of John B. and Emma S. Dutton, of Loudoun Co., Va.
Married this 17th day, 1st month, 1882.

N.B. - of special interest are the following selected marriage
records - (same source)

Page 4 - William Standly, of the County of Hanover, Colony of
Virginia, and Elizabeth Walker, daughter of William Walker, deceased, and Sarah Walker, his widow, of Loudoun Co., Va. Married this (? 14th) day of 11 month, 1758 at Fairfax.

Page 12 - Thomas Dodd, of Loudoun Co., Va. and Sarah Sample, of the same County, married 29th day of 7th month, 1760 at Fairfax.

Page 14 - Joseph Hutton, of Loudoun Co., Va. and Sarah Janney, of the same place, married 16th day, 9th month, 1761 at Fairfax.

Page 17 - Thomas Gregg, of Loudoun Co., Colony of Va., and Amey Gregg, of the same County and Colony, married 3rd day, 12th month, 1766 at Fairfax.

Page 20 - Lewis Neale, of Frederick Co., Va. son of Lewis Neale, of the same place, and Rachel Janney, daughter of ABEL Janney, of Loudoun Co., Va. married 15th day, 6th month, 1774 at Fairfax.

Page 21 - Jonathan Connard, son of Sarah Connard, of Loudoun Co., Va., yeoman, and Jane Potts, daughter of David Potts, of Loudoun Co., Va., married 18th day, 4th month, 1764 at Gap Meeting House.

Page 22 - William Barker, of Loudoun Co., Va. and Mary Janney, of said County, married 17th day, 4th month, 1765.

Page 23 - Joseph Parker, of Loudoun County, Va., son of Nicholas Parker, deceased, and Martha, his widow, and Eliza Eblen, (daughter of John Eblen and Mary, his wife of the County and Colony aforesaid) married 23rd day, 4th month, 1765.

Page 23 - John Smith and Sarah Myers, both of Loudoun Co., married 14th day, 5th month, 1766 at Fairfax.

Page 25 - William Gregg, of Loudoun Co. and Rebeckah Gregg, of same place, married 4th day, 11th month, 1767 at Fairfax.

Page 26 - Isaac Nichols and Rebeckah Gibson, both of Loudoun Co., Va., married 10th day, 12th month, 1767.

50.

Page 27 - Aaron Hackney, of Frederick Co., Va., and Hannah
Gregg, of Loudoun Co., married 31st day, 3rd month, 1768 at
Fairfax.

Page 29 - William Williams and Elizabeth Everett, both of
Loudoun Co., married 6th day, 9th month, 1769.

Page 30 - Samuel Canby and Elizabeth Hough, both of Loudoun
Co., married 28th day, 2nd month, 1770.

Page 31 - James Ball and Mary Brown, both of Loudoun Co.,
married 8th day, 8th month, 1770.

Page 32 - Jonathan Nutt and Elizabeth TREBBE, both of Loudoun
Co., married 28th day, 11th month, 1770.

Page 34 - Abel Janney and Mary Janney, both of Loudoun County,
married 3rd day, 4th month, 1771.

Page 36 - Benjamin Burson, son of George Burson and Sarah, his
wife, of Loudoun Co., and Hannah Young, daughter of Hercules
Young and Sarah, his wife, of the same County, married 8th day,
1st month, 1772 at the Fourth Fork Meeting House.

Page 37 - John Hough, Jr. and Lydia Hollingsworth, both of Loudoun County, married 29th day, 4th month, 1772.

Page 38 - William Harris and Elizabeth Holmes, both of Loudoun
Co., married 22nd day, 10th month, 1772.

Page 40 - Thomas Hatcher and Rebeckah Nickols, both of Loudoun
Co., married 14th day, 4th month, 1773 at Goose Creek.

Page 41 - Isreal Janney, son of Jacob and Hannah Janney, and Pleasant HAGUE, daughter of Francis Hague, all of Loudoun Co., married 5th day, 5th month, called May, 1773.

Page 42 - Stephen Morlan, son of William Morlan, and Mary Rhodes, daughter of Mary Rhodes, all of Loudoun Co., married 20th day, 10th month, 1773.

Page 44 - Samuel Hague and Jane SHUARD, both of Loudoun Co., married 23rd day, 12th month, 1773.

Page 45 - Benjamin STEER and Anna Everitt, both of Loudoun Co., married 7th day, 9th month, 1774.

Page 47 - Moses Gibson and Lydia Leonard, both of Loudoun Co., married 15th day, 2nd month, 1775 at South Fork.

Page 48 - John Brown and (Mrs.) Mary Rhodes, widow, both of Loudoun Co., married 8th day, 2nd month, 1775 at Fairfax.

Page 49 - Elisha Gregg, son of George and Elizabeth Gregg, and Martha Lovett, daughter of Daniel Lovett, all of Loudoun County, married 1st day, 3rd month, 1775 at Fairfax.

Page 50 - Thomas HOGUE, son of Francis Hogue, and Sarah Wilkinson all of Loudoun Co., married 2nd day, 5th month, 1775.

Page 51 - John Gregg and Hannah Steer, both of Loudoun Co., married 7th day, 9th month, 1775 at Goose Creek.

Page 53 - James Daniel, son of William Daniel, and Hannah SEYBOLD, daughter of Jasper Seybold, all of Loudoun County, married 15th day, 4th month, 1778 at South Fork.

52.

Page 54 - Stacy Janney and Hannah Brown, both of Loudoun County, married 10th day, 4th month, 1776.

Page 55 - John Brown, son of Henry and Esther Brown, and Martha Ball, all of Loudoun Co., married 10th day, 4th month, 1776 at Fairfax.

Page 56 - Samuel Smith and Mary Daniel, both of Loudoun Co., married 11th day, 4th month, 1776 at Goose Creek.

Page 57 - Caleb Whitacre and Phebe GORE, both of Loudoun Co., married 31st day, 10th month, 1776 at Goose Creek.

Page 58 - George Hatcher and Prudence Woodward, both of Loudoun Co., married 28th day, 5th month, 1778.

Page 59 - Joseph Janney, Jr. and Mary Holmes, both of Loudoun Co., married 4th day, 6th month, 1778 at Goose Creek.

Page 60 - Israel Thompson and Sarah Hogue, daughter of Francis Hogue, all of Loudoun Co., married 2nd day, 7th month, 1778 at Fairfax.

Page 61 - Elijah Myers, son of Jonathan and Mary Myers, and Mary Ball, daughter of William Ball, all of Loudoun Co., married 18th day, 12th month, 1778.

Page 62 - Thomas Hughes, son of Matthew and Elizabeth Hughes, deceased, and Sarah Schooley, daughter of John and Mary Schooley, all of Loudoun Co., married 13th day, 1st month, 1779 at Fairfax.

Page 63 - John Nickols and Margaret Spencer, both of Loudoun Co., married 18th day, 2nd month, 1779 at Goose Creek.

Page 64 - William Hatcher, Jr. and Mary McGray, both of Loudoun Co., married 27th day, 5th month, 1779 at Goose Creek.

Page 65 - James Roach and Elizabeth Gregg, both of Loudoun Co., married 2nd day, 6th month, 1779 at Fairfax.

Page 66 - Samuel Canby and Ann Shene, both of Loudoun Co., married 1st day, 9th month, 1779 at Fairfax.

Page 68 - Elisha Schooley, son of John and Mary Schooley, and Rachel Holmes, daughter of William and Mary Holmes, married 16th day, 12th month, 1779 at Goose Creek.

Page 69 - Abner Gregg, son of John Gregg and Sarah Smith, daughter of William Smith, all of Loudoun County, married 39th day 12th month, 1779 at Goose Creek.

Page 71 - Isaiah Myers and Alice Yates, Jr., both of Loudoun Co., married 15th day, 10th month, 1777 at South Fork.

Page 72 - WITHAM Schooley and Hannah Brown, both of Loudoun Co., married 15th day, 11th month, 1780.

Page 74 - Owen Rogers (Rodgers) of Hamoshire Co., Va., and Mary Roach, daughter of Richard and Hannah Roach, of Loudoun County, Va., married 29th day, 11th month, 1780 at Fairfax. (note: This is a correction from Va. Anc. & Adv., Vol. 2, page 65.)

Page 75 - George Gregg and Margaret Todhunter, both of Loudoun Co., married 27th day, 12th month, 1780.

Page 76 - James Moore, son of Thomas and Elizabeth Moore, and Phebe Myers, daughter of Joseph and Phebe Myers, all of Loudoun County, married 9th day, 1st month, 1782 at Fairfax.

54.

Page 78 - MAHLON Hough, son of John Hough, of Loudoun County, and Mary Stabler, daughter of Edward Stabler, of Dinwiddie Co., Va., married 6th day, 3rd month, 1782 at Fairfax.

Page 79 - John Long, of Loudoun Co., and Mary Clarke, of Farquier Co., Va., married 39th day, 10th month, 1782 at South Fork Meeting House.

Page 80 - Samuel Hough, son of John Hough, of Loudoun Co., and Ann Stabler, daughter of Edward Stabler, of Dinwiddie Co., Va., married 30th day, 4th month, 1783.

Page 81 - Robert Whitacre, son of John and Naomi Whitacre, and Sarah Roach, daughter of Richard and Hannah Roach, all of Loudoun Co., married 28th day, 5th month, 1783.

Page 83 - Simeon Haines and Elizabeth Randall, both of Loudoun Co., married 27th day, 11th month, 1783 at Goose Creek.

Page 84 - John Smith and Sarah HIRST, both of Loudoun Co., married 6th day, 5th month, 1784 at Goose Creek.

Page 85 - Isaac HOGE, son of Solomon and Ann HOGE, and Elizabeth Nichols, all of Loudoun Co., married 29th day, 4th month, 1784 at Goose Creek.

Page 86 - Isaac Brown, Jr. and Sarah BURSON, both of Loudoun Co., married 26th day, 5th month, 1784 at South Fork.

Page 87 - John Seybold, son of Jasper Seybold and Hannah Crammer, daughter of ANDRES Crammer, all of Loudoun Co., married 30th day, 6th month, 1784.

Page 88 - John Coffee, and Rachel PIDGEON, Jr., both of Loudoun Co., married 8th day, 12th month, 1784.

Page 89 - Samuel GOVER and Sarah Janney, both of Loudoun Co., married 16th day, 12th month, 1784 at Goose Creek.

Page 90 - Thomas CADWALADER and Jane Daniel, both of Loudoun Co., married 31st day, 3rd month, 1785 at Goose Creek.

SECTION I - (c)

Depositions

CHARLES CITY COUNTY, VIRGINIA - ORDER BOOK - (1676-1679)

Ages of some residents from Depositions,
Court Judgments, etc. - Please note that
residents were set "Levy Free", upon their
request, when age 60 years or over - Age is
figured from the date of the deposition.

Page 165 - 4 June 1677   William Lambert   18 years old

Page 168 - 4 June 1677   George Guillman   13 years old

Page 177 - 3 August 1677   Abraham Underwood   13 years old

Page 178 - 17 July 1676   Francis South (nearly)12 years old

Page 182 - 3 August 1677   Capt. Nicholas Wyatt   30 years old

Page 190 - 13 Sept. 1677   Richard Jackson   23 years old

Page 191 - 13 Sept. 1677   John Finly   24 years old

Page 199 - 6 July 1677   William Melton   30 years old

Page 199 - 10 July 1677   Richard Withers   40 years old

Page 199 - 10 July 1677   John Pleasant   30 years old

Page 200 - 8 June 1677   Francis Eppes   49 years old

Page 200 - 27 April 1676   Walter Vannham   50 years old
                                                    or upward
Page 208 - 14 Sept. 1677   Allen Jenkins   40 years old

Page 211 - 15 Sept. 1677   Joan Strong, dau. of   13 years old
                            Thomas
Page 231 - 19 Nov. 1677   John Bridges   14 years old

Page 231 - 19 Nov. 1677   Charles Hill   14 years old

Page 264 - 4 Feb. 1677/8   William Johns   14 years old

Page 264 - 4 Feb. 1677/8   Richard Allen   14 years old

Page 267 - 4 Feb. 1677/8   Mark Harker   14 years old

Page 270 - 14 Feb. 1677/8 John Daniell   14 years old

Page 291 - 16 April 1678   Robert Dennis-Levy Free-60 years?plus

Page 316 - 5 Aug. 1678   John Miles   23 years old

57.

Page 329 - 16 Aug. 1678	Ralph Rotchell-Levy Free-60 years?plus	
Page 329 - 16 Aug. 1678	Edward Ross-(soldier-Levy-60 yrs.?plus	
Page 332 - 3 Oct. 1678	John Fisher	Free) 13 years old
Page 353 - 17 Feb. 1678/9	John Snudge	11 years old
Page 353 - 17 Feb. 1678/9	John Vandevan	11 years old
Page 355 - 17 Feb. 1678/9	Martha Cordell	21 years old
Page 376 - 4 April 1679	Jethrow Barker	over 14-under 21 years old
Page 378 - 4 April 1679	Francis Slead	10 years old

SECTION 2

1. Naturalization of French Huguenots.....58.

2. Proof of Importations.................60.

SPECIAL NOTE:

The list of names of the French Huguenots on
the next two pages are in alphabetical order
and are not included in the general index.

58.

An Act for Naturalization of Claud Phillipe de Richebourg,
Francis Ribot, Peter Faure, John Joanny, James Champagne, and
others.

COMMENT BY CHH: This "Act of Naturalization" of the French
Huguenots of Manakin was listed by title only in Hening's
Statutes, Vol. 3, page 228 (as above rendered) and was signed
12 May 1705. It was rendered in it's full context, including
the names of 148 individuals in Laws of Virginia Supplement
(1700-1750) by Waverly K. Winfree, pages 39-41, published
1971 by The Virginia State Library.
The names have been re-arranged and alphabetized by this
compiler and writer as listed below.

Amonet, Jacob
Aubry, Andrew

Belivet, James
Bering, Francis
Bernard, David
Blovet, Daniel
Bocard, Peter
Bondurant, John Peter
Bossard, John
Bradonneau, Henry
Brok, Moses
Brousse, James

Cabany, Henry
Callot, Joseph
Calvet, John
Cambel, John
Cantepie, Michel
Capon, Jacob
Castige, Paul
Chambon, Gedeon
Champagne, James
Chastain, Stephen
Chataigmer, Peter
Chatain, Peter
Chermeson, Joseph
Clapier, Francis
Claud, Philipe
Cocke, Andreas

Decoppet, John Francis
Delaune, Jean
Delony, Jacob
Delony, John
Dep, John
DeRichebourg, Claud Phillipe
DeRosseaux, Theodore
DeVesaz, Paul

Duchemin, Daniel
DuClos, John Oger
DuFertre, Lewis
DuFoy, Peter
DuMass, Jeremiah
DuPre, John
DuPre, Thomas
Dupuy, Barthlemy

Farey, John
Fauire, Daniel
Faure, Peter
Fellon, Peter
Figuier, Isaac
Flournois, Jacob
Flournoy, Francois
Flournoy, Jaques
Fonjall, Peter
Fonvielle, John
Forquerand, John

Gaudoven, Isaac
Gevandon, Anthony
Gori, John
Gori, Peter
Guerant, John
Guerin, John
Guil, John
Guil, Joseph
Guil, Stephen

Hungaute, Simon
Hungazel, Samuel

Imbert, John

Joanny, John

Korner, Gaspard

Korneau, John

LaCaze, Jaimes
LaFite, Isaac
LaForie, Rene Massomeau
LaGrand, James
Langlade, Daniel
LaPierre, Charles
LeFebure, Isaac
LeVillam, John
Livreau, Moses
Lorange, John
Lovis, Stephen
Lucadon, John

Macant, Peter
Mallard, John
Mallard, Peter
Mallet, Stephen
Mariott, John
Martin, John
Massau, Peter
Matton, Anthony
Maupin, Gabriel
Mazeres, John
Mebins, Daniel
Menetries, David
MerVeil, David
Michaux, Abraham
Michel, Michel
Minot, Abraham
Miromon, Francis
Morell, Timothy
Morissatt, Peter
Moulins, Abraham
Mouluner, Joseph

Oger, Mathieu
Oliver, Joseph
Orange, Lewis

Panetier, John
Parentos, Isaac
Parmentier, John
Pasteur, Jean
Peru, Peter
Petit, Joshua
Phaisant, John James
Pinson, James
Pommier, Francis
Prevot, Peter

Rapine, Anthony
Rebant, Daniel
Remy, Abraham
Rey, John Guy
Ribbeau, James
Ribot, Francis
Robert, John
Roger, John
Rosset, John
Roux, James
Roux, Timothy

Sabbatier, Peter
Sarazen, Stephen
Sassin, Francis
Say, John
Serjanton, John
Simon, Augustin
Soblet, Abraham
Soblet, James
Soblet, Peter
Sobrih, Gasper
Sollaegre, John
Soville, John

Thilbeaurt, Jean
Thomas, John
Tournein, Stephen
Trabueq, Anthony

Valton, John
Vignes, Adam
Vitte, Peter
Voyer, John

Waldenborg, Charles

60.

PROOF OF IMPORTATIONS

SURRY COUNTY, VA. - ORDER BOOK - (1691-1713) - PAGE 352.

November 7, 1710 -

Certificate granted to Nicholas Smith for 50 acres of land for importation of himself into this Colony, having been in above 15 years and was a servant when he came in.

Certificate granted to Ann Smith for 50 acres of land for importation of herself into this Colony, having been in above 20 years and was a servant when she came in.

Certificate granted to William Bensen for 50 acres of land for importation of himself into this Colony, having been in above nine years and was a servant when he came in.

Certificate granted to James Rayle for 50 acres of land for importation of himself into this Colony, having been in ten years and was a servant when he came in.

Certificate granted to Samuel Walton for 50 acres of land for importation of himself into this Colony, having been in 35 years and was a servant when he came in.

• Certificate granted to John Mills for 50 acres of land for importation of himself into this Colony, having been in ten years and was a servant when he came in.

Certificate granted to Nicholas Sessoms for 50 acres of land for importation of himself into this Colony, having been in 44 years and was a servant when he came in.

Certificate granted to Margaret Dikes for 50 acres of land for importation of herself into this Colony, having been in 34 years and was a servant when she came in.

Certificate granted to John Doyle for 50 acres of land for importation of himself into this Colony, having been in 12 years and was a servant when he came in.

Certificate granted to Elizabeth Doyle for 50 acres of land for importation of herself into this Colony, having been in 10 years and was a servant when she came in.

PAGE 353 - November 7, 1710.

Certificate granted to Daniel Mack Daniel for 50 acres of land for importation of himself into this Colony, having been in 10 years and was a servant when he came in.

Certificate granted to Evan Humphrey for 50 acres of land for importation of himself into this Colony, having been in 30 years and was a servant when he came in.

Certificate granted to John Brown for 50 acres of land for importation of himself into this Colony, having been in 28 years and was a servant when he came in.

Certificate granted to Samuel Ward for 50 acres of land for importation of himself into this Colony, having been in 11 years and was a servant when he came in.

Certificate granted to Charles (?Sledge?) for 50 acres of land for importation of himself into this Colony, having been in 24 years and was a servant when he came in.

NORTHUMBERLAND COUNTY, VA. - ORDER BOOK - (1652-1665) -PAGE 3.

20 September 1652 - According to sufficient proof made before this Court, there is due to Thomas Youlle, 200 acres of land for the transportation of these persons following into this Colony - to:wit, John Wilson - Marga(ret) POSLEY - John CAMMELL- and John CHEOWS (?).

ibid:- page 8 -
20 January 1652/3 - According to sufficient proofs made before this Court, there is due to John Bennett, carpenter, 50 acres of land for the transportation of William SPENSE into this Colony.

WESTMORELAND COUNTY, VA. - RECORDS AND INVENTORIES #2 - PAGE 132ª

31 July 1750 - Deposition of William Davis, age 42 years (b ca 1708) or thereabouts, that he knows William Blackmore and knows him to be the son of Samuel Blackmore, of Saint Mary (?) in the

62.

County of Devon and to be the same person mentioned in the
will of George Blackmore, late of the County of Westmoreland,
in the Colony of Virginia, deceased.
Recorded 11 August 1750.

CHARLES CITY COUNTY, VA. - ORDER BOOK - (1676-1679)

Page 166-

3 May 1677 - Power of attorney from John POWD, of the Parish
of St. Bartolf's, without Aldgate, London "Cooper" to his beloved friends and kinsman, William POWD, of Wilmington Parish,
in Virginia to recover from John Drayton, Jr., of Westover,
1800 lbs. of tobacco.
Recorded 16 June 1677.

Page 233-

19 November 1677 - Mr. John Drayton proves the importation of
20 persons into this Colony on the oath of Mr. Thomas Grendon,
(as listed) - Peter Wyke, John KEBSSALL, Ann Presthood, Margaret Drownwell, John Walton, John Browne, William Ethridge,
Christopher Crisp, Ann CHUEGE, Epher Coomes, John Shaw, John
Smith, Susanna Raye, John Byrd, Isaac Baites, Rachell Baites,
John Hedgepath, John King, Ann Walton, and David, (these being
assigned by said Grendon to said Drayton). John Drayton has
also proved 3 more rights on oath of Edward Richards, Viz:
Robert Athorne, John Brocks and William Lewis.

Page 234-

John Turner has proved rights for importation of six per-
sons assigned him by Captain Thomas Mallory, Viz: Christian
Addams, William Lambert, Joseph Perry, Margaret Case, John
Stanley and Thomas Mallory.

Page 289-

15 April 1678 - Rowland Place, Esquire, proves right for 750
acres of land for the importation of Francis Bacon, William
White, Ann Dawson, Mathew Perry, Elizabeth Smith, Richard Pulem,
Abraham Bayley, Jonathan Gladen, Thomas Place, SIBRAN Johnson,
William Hills, Henry Cabell, Isabella Dobson and Isaac, a negro.

63.

Page 334-

3 October 1678 - Suit of Lidra Norvell, plaintiff, versus Edward Jordan, defendant, he having gone to Maryland, Mr. Crabb offers security for the defendants appearance at next Court.

Page 335-

3 October 1678 - Complaint of William Frost, apprentice of John Harrison, taylor, that he was beaten by his fellow "prentices" and not taught the trade by his master and also that he has been sent for by his mother in Ireland and wishes to be released. The neighbors, denying any ill-treatment, the Court calls it a childish complaint; redraws his indenture; and charges that the art of tailor be carefully taught and at the end of his indenture, his master to give said Frost one good gun, two suits of apparel, linen and woolen from top to toe and one cow and calf.

Page 339-

3 December 1678 - Henry Newcombe proves right to 200 acres of land for the importation of William Fintch - William Strong - Thomas Burcher - Ann Graunt - William Strong - but one not proved.

Page 351-

17 February 1678/9 - Mrs. Sarah Bland proved in Court her letter of attorney from her husband, Mr. John Bland, of London.

Page 360-

18 February 1678/9 - Thomas Bottom, plaintiff, brings suit against Ralph Pool, defendant, the said Thomas Bottom contracted to work for said Pool as a shoemaker in Virginia for 4 years for which the said Pool was to pay 450 pounds of tobacco per year for the support of said Bottom's wife and children in England, etc.

NORTHUMBERLAND COUNTY, VA. - ORDER BOOK #2 - PAGE 8.

20 January 1652/3 - According to sufficient proof made before this Court, there is due to John Bennett, "carpenter", 50 acres of land for transporting William Spense into this Colony.

SECTION 3

Revolutionary War Pension Applications*........64.

*These applications were abstracted by the writer from Xerox copies from the files of the National Archives, of Washington, D. C., furnished him by various clients. In general, only pertinent genealogical details were extracted. For those who may have further interest in one of these specific soldiers, other details of a historical or biographical nature may be found included in their files.

64.

REVOLUTIONARY WAR PENSION APPLICATIONS

PREAMBLE BY C. H. HAMLIN

The papers in the Pension Application File of Augustine Smith will be summarized later. The name was noticed as being possibly significant in connection with WILLIAM SMITH, "OF GEORGIA" for whom genealogical research is now underway.

On numerous occasions all genealogists receive from clients and correspondents various records and references to records adorned and embellished with graffites in the margins such as.....Who is he?.....How does he fit in?.....He is not mine.....Why do we want this?.....etc......I was particularly amused by Colonel David Avant's marginal comment in re the subject....."If this Augustine Smith is mine, I descend from a long line of batchelors."

The answer is simple. We sometimes need records to DIS-PROVE RELATIONSHIP as well as to PROVE RELATIONSHIP. Especially when we are involved with such a numerous "Clan" as "SMITH". These Pension Applications very often include such vital information as place born; date of birth; residences in various states and counties; names of siblings; children; parents; copies of Wills; Bible Records; etc. From the evidence sometimes found therein we can very often work-out many historical details as well as biographical and genealogical details.

As far as our present project is concerned our results here are 'negative' but they can very well be used as an example to illustrate the fact that he is "DISPROVEN" and "eliminated from further consideration" as well as an example affording possibilities for extended research and amplification, if warranted. (Not only for the soldier, himself, but of others mentioned by him.)

REVOLUTIONARY WAR PENSION APPLICATION (VA. #23911 - S 1946)

AUGUSTINE SMITH (Private, Virginia) Application dated 1 November 1832 in Nelson County, Virginia......(Received pension $80.00 per annum)

Enlisted in 7th Virginia Regiment for two years under Captain Samuel Cabell (and Lieutenant Benjamin Toliver) and believes his commanding officer was Colonel Taylor. Place of enlistment was Amherst County, Virginia.....promoted to 'Sergeant'.....was placed on recruiting service and enlisted four men among whose names was an AUSTIN SMITH.....gives details of service and experiences.....received a severe injury in his back and was given a furlough to recover but could not walk or get out of bed for several years.....On his way home he was met "BY MY BROTHER, JOHN SMITH" and Joel Shropshire, both of whom are now dead.....

States further that he is about 80 years of age (thus born ca 1752) and was born in Westmoreland County, Virginia and that his parents removed to Amherst County when he was a small boy.....That he has resided the whole time since the Revolutionary War in that part of Amherst that became Nelson County.....Supporting affidavits filed by Joseph Fox (age 67) of Amherst County; by SARAH LOWE, of Amherst; and Littleberry N. Ligon, J.P. of Amherst.....

Affidavit dated 26 May 1835 by MARY SMITH, executrix of the Will of Augustine Smith, that he died (testate) 1 December 1832 without wife or surviving children and that he was never married (undoubtedly by reason of his broken back).....

Included in the File is EXHIBIT "A" The Last Will and Testament of AUGUSTINE SMITH, of Nelson County, Virginia, dated 26 February 1830; proved 24 December 1832.....(continue.....) in which he leaves his land and property to his "SISTER, MARY SMITH" (and names her as his executrix) for the natural life of his other two sisters, SALLY LOWE and JUDITH SMITH..... disqualifies his brother in law, WILLIAM LOWE, husband of his sister, SALLY, "who has long been absent", from any benefit.... Witnesses: John B. Spiece, John Rudisell and Richard Fox....

Without any extreme effort or noteworthy endeavor, we have found the following items of interest concerning the subject, if our continued interest had been warranted.

66.

(1)..<u>WESTMORELAND COUNTY WILLS - (1655-1794) - by CROZIER, PG. 73</u>.

Will of JOHN SMITH, dated 22 November 1777; proved 24 November 1778.....Legatees: - Wife, ELIZABETH.....SONS, JOHN SMITH and AUGUSTINE SMITH.....SON, LEWIS SMITH....."my small children"....."my daughters" (not named or numbered).....

(2)..TAX PAYERS.....AMHERST COUNTY, VIRGINIA.....1785.....

AUGUSTINE SMITH - 4 white souls.....1 dwelling place.....

(3)..NELSON COUNTY, VIRGINIA formed from AMHERST COUNTY, 1807-8.

(4)..<u>AMHERST COUNTY in the REVOLUTION, by Sweeny, page 16</u>.

Muster Roll of CAPTAIN SAMUEL JORDAN CABELL'S COMPANY of the 6th VIRGINIA REGIMENT OF FOOT under command of Lt. Col. James Hendricks for the months of May and June 1777.....BENJAMIN TALIAFERRO, FIRST LIEUTENANT.....#13 AUSTIN SMITH..... <u>#58 AUGUSTINE SMITH</u> - "<u>LEFT SICK, VIRGINIA</u>"..... (Austin Smith, who was recruited by Augustine, appears on several later payrolls).....

(5)..Captain Samuel Jordan Cabell's Company was detached as a Rifle Company 1st August 1777 to the <u>7th</u> Virginia Regiment under the command of Colonel Daniel Morgan.....In December 1777, Benjamin Taliaferro was promoted to Captain and given the Company and Captain Samuel Cabell was promoted to Lieutenant-Colonel in the 7th Virginia Regiment of 1778 and was among those captured at Charleston, South Carolina 12 May 1780.....

(6)..D.A.R. Patriot Index, page 624 has listed an "AUSTIN SMITH" (Cpl., Va.) born October 1760; died 11/27/1810; married Elizabeth Hubbard.....

Quod Erat Demonstradum.....

Charles H. Hamlin, C. G

CHH/

28 September 1972

REVOLUTIONARY WAR PENSION APPLICATION

WILLIAM SMITH - (Private, South Carolina) File #S-31973 (and
W-590).....

NOTE BY CHH: We have noted this file prior to this but had
only an abstract to work with.....This abstract is from a complete xerox file now to hand.....SEE COMMENTS LATER.....

FRANKLIN COUNTY, GEORGIA - Application and Declaration
dated 10 September 1832.....by WILLIAM SMITH, age 69 years
(thus born ca 1763).....entered South Carolina Militia service in Ninety-Six District, South Carolina in November 1780...
substituted for William Flanagan......other enlistments as a
volunteer described.....mentions a widowed sister named POLLY
PATTASON, living in Jackson County, Georgia.....

Declares further that he was born 26 February 1763 in
Moore County, North Carolina.....see our previous comment that
he must have meant CUMBERLAND COUNTY, NORTH CAROLINA, FROM WHICH
MOORE COUNTY WAS FORMED AS A NEW COUNTY IN 1784.....that he
was living in Ninety-Six District, South Carolina when he enlisted (1780).....that after the war he lived three years in
Moore and Montgomery Counties, North Carolina and removed from
there to Elbert County, Georgia and has lived for the last 42
years at his present address (i.e., in Franklin County, Georgia
since 1790).....

Supporting affidavits by John Williams - Rev. Matthew
Vandiver - and Jesse Smith (all of Franklin County, Georgia)...

COMMENT: Reference is made to the abstract of the File of
William Smith # S-31976 which, in addition to other records,
contains a final pension payment to the William Smith of the
above abstract (# S-31973) stating that he died in FRANKLIN
COUNTY, GEORGIA 9th July 1833, leaving a widow, "SARAH SMITH"..
this record should be transferred back from # S-31976 to File
S-31973.....In addition to this mixture of the two above cited
files, there seems to be a further mixture of another William
Smith, "OF COWETA COUNTY, GEORGIA".....Supposed to be in File
S-16940.....This William Smith has a wife named MEREDY SMITH,
two sons and a daughter.....As far as I can advise, these two
files have records of THREE WILLIAM SMITHS and their records
should be studied and segregated into THREE piles as follows:

1...William Smith (South Carolina) died 1833 in Franklin County, Georgia.

2...William Smith (Virginia) died 1836 in Clarke County, Georgia.

3...William Smith (?) died 1852 in Coweta County, Georgia.

WILLIAM SMITH -(VIRGINIA SERVICE) - FILE # 31976 -

Pension application dated 7 January 1833.....Now a resident of Clarke County, Georgia.....States he was born 22 April 1754 in Sussex County, Virginia; enlisted for service 1 March 1781 in Henry County, Virginia; Served two tours of duty under Captain David Lanier (General Greene's army).....Lived in Sussex County, Virginia 10 years; in Brunswick County, Virginia 11 years; Henry County, Virginia 12 years; moved to York County, South Carolina and lived there 19 years; moved to Clarke County Georgia where he now lives.....no family data.....

NOTE: Mrs. Frances Wynd (Genealogist) states his Will is to be found in Clarke County, Georgia Will Book "B", dated 28 June 1831; proved 26 January 1836, naming the following legatees (no wife named or mentioned...presumed deceased).....Son, Vines Smith.....Grandsons, William E. and Thomas V. (sons of Vines) and daughters, Lucy Ezzel - Elizabeth Stodgen - Sally Foster - and Susannah Gregory.

FURTHER NOTE: Mr. Joseph Coulter (Genealogist) states in a letter dated 29 March 1972 that under File # S-31976 (supra) that a final pension payment was made to the above soldier in 1833 and THAT HE DIED IN FRANKLIN COUNTY, GEORGIA 9 JULY 1833 LEAVING A WIDOW, SARAH SMITH.....

There is clearly an error somewhere as these two records cannot be reconciled. It is this writer's opinion that Mrs. Wynd is correct in her abstract and identification and that the above information from Mr. Coulter should be re-checked by him. IT SEEMS MUCH MORE LIKELY THAT THIS INFORMATION REFERS TO WILLIAM SMITH, FILE # S-31973, WHO MADE APPLICATION FOR PENSION IN FRANKLIN COUNTY, GEORGIA, 10 SEPTEMBER 1832 AND OF WHOM WE HAVE JUST FINISHED TREATING OF. THIS LATTER WILLIAM SMITH HAS NOW BECOME OF EXTREME IMPORTANCE FOR FURTHER RESEARCH AS HE SEEMS TO BE OUR MOST LIKELY CANDIDATE AS CLIENT'S ANCESTOR AT THE PRESENT TIME.....

<u>WILLIAM SMITH</u> - (? SERVICE) - FILE # 16940 ? - (not found)-

Application for arrears in pension payments dated 4th of September 1848.....<u>Now residing in Coweta County, Georgia</u> for the past 16 years (i.e., since 1832).....before which he lived <u>in DeKalb County, Georgia</u>.....States that his Pension Certificate is number 16940 (which he exhibits) which was dated 16th October 1833, retroactive to 4 March 1831 in the amount of $80.00 per annum.....Charles L. Henry, Esquire, of Chatham County, Georgia is his attorney.....

Mr. Joseph S. Coulter, of Alexandria, Virginia, (Genealogist) states his original File # 16940 has not been found, as yet, in the National Archives but he has found other documents in connection in the file of his widow in her application for pension which discloses that her husband, William Smith, of Coweta County, Georgia (formerly of DeKalb County, Georgia) received a Pension of $80.00 per year (which agrees with his application of 1848 supra) and that he died 7 May 1852 leaving as his heirs:

> MEREDY SMITH (the widow)
>
> AMERICUS SMITH (son)
>
> LAFAYETTE SMITH (son)
>
> EVIRA JACKSON SMITH (daughter)

(It is this writer's guess that File # 16940 is very probably mixed in with the papers of some other File # and will eventually be found).....(I do not find it in Hoyt's Index of Revolutionary War Pension Applications).....

<u>MRS. MOURNING SMITH</u> - (Widow of <u>WILLIAM SMITH</u>-Captain, South Carolina) - FILE # W-22272 -

26 September 1832 - Declaration of MAJOR WILLIAM SMITH, age 81 years (born ca 1751).....That he entered service in the Fall of 1775 from Spartanburg County, South Carolina as a "Lieutenant".....describes several tours of duty.....names of officers, etc.....promoted to "Captain".....states further that he was born in Bucks County, Pennsylvania, 20 September 1751.....(Widow states that he died in Spartanburg District, South Carolina, 22 June 1837).....

9 February 1839, Spartanburg District, South Carolina,
Declaration of MOURNING SMITH, age 75 years on the 15th of June,
last (1838), that she was married to her husband in 1779.....
Exhibits a family Bible record stating that she,

"MOURNING BEARDEN, DAUGHTER OF JOHN AND LETTICE BEARDEN,
was born 15 June 1763.....that her eldest son was born 12 January 1781 (named AARON SMITH).....her daughter, LETTICE SMITH,
was born 6 June 1783.....her son, ISAAC SMITH, was born 31 October 1784 and that EBER SMITH, their son, was born the 12th day
of (blank) 1787.....other children are proven later.....By records in the file, MOURNING (BEARDEN) SMITH died 2 October 1842..

3 April 1855 - Certification that DR. J(OHN) WINSMITH,
(name changed from SMITH) and ELIHU P. SMITH are the "Executors" of the estate of MAJOR WILLIAM SMITH, late of Spartanburg
District, South Carolina, who died 23rd (sic) June 1837 and of
MOURNING SMITH, his widow, who died 2 October 1842.....names the
surviving children and heirs as DR. J. WINSMITH - ISAAC SMITH -
RALPH SMITH - WILLIAM SMITH - ELIPHAS SMITH and ELIHU SMITH....

Statement that at one time, MAJOR WILLIAM SMITH was a representative in the United States Congress (from South Carolina).

In 1832 WILLIAM SMITH referred to a sister but did not
state her name or residence or give any other details concerning her.....

This is an extremely large and complex file and among other
records therein are several receipts by the State of South Carolina to MR. WILLIAM SMITH - CAPTAIN WILLIAM SMITH, "of SPART-
ANBURG DISTRICT, SOUTH CAROLINA" and to MAJOR WILLIAM SMITH....
etc.....There seems to be identical copies of these same records in the file of MRS. CELIA SMITH, File #R-9701½, widow of
another CAPTAIN WILLIAM SMITH.....

(MRS.) CELIA SMITH (widow of CAPTAIN WILLIAM SMITH)-(South Car-
     olina and Georgia Services) - FILE # R-9701½ -

Application and Declaration made 15 July 1843 at Tallapoosa
County, Alabama by Mrs. Celia Smith, age 98 years (born ca 1745)

States that her husband, CAPTAIN WILLIAM SMITH, served as a
Captain of a mounted Indian Spy Company against both Indians and
Tories.....gives details of his services.....that he built sev-
eral forts in Georgia (ONE IS IN WILKES COUNTY CALLED SMITH"S
FORT ON THE OPECHEE).....that she was married to her husband in
CUMBERLAND COUNTY, NORTH CAROLINA about two years before the
War.....

Supporting affidavits as to his Revolutionary War services;
as to the marriage in Cumberland County, North Carolina, and that
CAPTAIN WILLIAM SMITH died 27 November 1824 in CLARK COUNTY,
ALABAMA.....

Power of Attorney dated 14 June 1852 by Elijah Jorden, of
Tallapoosa County, Alabama, "Administrator" of the estate of
CELIA SMITH, DECEASED, late of the County of Tallapoosa, Ala-
bama, who was the widow of WILLIAM SMITH, DECEASED, "late of the
County of Munroe, State of Alabama".....states that William
Smith died in Munroe County, Alabama in 1822 (sic).....that
Celia Smith died 20 October 1849, leaving FIVE children (to-wit)-

JAMES SMITH (now residing in Texas) - THOMAS SMITH (of Pike County, Alabama) - SARAH McBURNET - CELIA JOURDAN - and RUTH BUCE
(all of Tallapoosa County, Alabama) and that they are the only
"SURVIVING" children.....etc.....names the children again as:

                    THOMAS SMITH...........age 70 years

                    RUTH BUCE..............age 75 years

                    JAMES SMITH

                    CELIA JOURDAIN (JORDAN)

                    SARAH McBURNET

To this list of children, RUTH BUCE makes an affidavit
dated 24 April 1846, Tallapoosa County, Alabama, "now in her
68th year (born ca 1778).....that she is the daughter of CAP-
TAIN WILLIAM and CELIA SMITH, who had four children older than
she.....to-wit: MARY, now deceased, who would be age 75, if
living.....NICHOLAS SMITH, now dead, who would be 74 years old,
if living.....THOMAS SMITH, now living in his 73rd year.....
ACHAIL, now in her 71st year.....

72.

This file has copies of several receipts by the State of
South Carolina for sums of money paid to MR. WILLIAM SMITH, JR.
for Militia Service.....for services as a private and as a Lieu-
tenant.....as a Captain of the 96th District, South Carolina and
for duty as a Major in 1780.....THESE SEEM TO BE IDENTICAL COPIES
OF THE SAME RECORDS THAT ARE ALSO FOUND IN THE FILES OF MRS.
MOURNING SMITH, FILE # W-22272 - WIDOW OF ANOTHER CAPTAIN WILLIAM
SMITH.....

4 April 1855 - Affidavit of Edward L. Canida of Tallapoosa
County, Alabama, that he is "Administrator" of the estate of
MRS. CELIA SMITH, DECEASED.....

WILLIAM SMITH - (Private, Maryland) - FILE # R-9876 -

Application and Declaration by WILLIAM SMITH, (age 74 years)
(thus born ca 1761).....now a resident of Boone County, Missouri,
(interlined "Carrol County, Missouri").....dated 5 October 1835..

States that he entered service 1 April 1777 in Charles County, State of Maryland, and was then in the 16th year of his
age.....that he served not less than ten tours of service from
1½ to 3½ months each tour.....describes his services.....offic-
ers.....etc.....

States that he moved from Charles County, Maryland to Prince
William County, Virginia and from there to Fauquier and Culpeper
Counties, Virginia.....from there, he removed to Madison County,
Kentucky and from there to Boone County, Missouri.....that re-
cently, in the last few months, he has moved to Carrol County,
Missouri, a new County in the State, and is 60 or 70 miles dis-
tant from Boone County.....Supporting statements that the appli-
cant has lived in Boone County, Missouri for 12 or 15 years past

2 November 1854 - WILLIAM J. SMITH, son of WILLIAM SMITH,
DECEASED, of Boone County, Missouri, gives a power of attorney to
prosecute the claim of the said William Smith...etc.....

COMMENT: This file seems to have records of another WILLIAM
SMITH mixed in with this file. This other WILLIAM SMITH had
North Carolina Service and an application and Power of Attorney
was made by the children and heirs in 1853 and 1854 at Thomas-

ville, County of Oregon, State of Missouri, stating that he died
in 1832; his widow died in 1848 (1849).....that they were married in North Carolina in 1778 (1779) and that her maiden name
was Charity Lee.....children were: RICHARD D. G. SMITH - ANDREW
SMITH - a daughter (not named) who removed to Texas.....

WILLIAM SMITH - (NORTH CAROLINA SERVICE) - FILE # R-9878 -

Application and Declaration made 5 November 1838 in the
County of Giles, State of Tennessee, by WILLIAM SMITH (age 76
years-thus born ca 1762).....served as a waggoner and as a substitute for his brother, SAMUEL SMITH.....

The applicant states further that he was born in County
Derry, Ireland; that he was living in Mecklenburg County, North
Carolina when he served in the Revolutionary War.....that he was
married in this country.....describes his services.....names of
officers.....etc.....

After his marriage, he removed from Mecklenburg County,
North Carolina to Green County, Georgia and from there to Madison
County, Alabama, where he lived for about ten years.....from
there, he removed to Giles County, Tennessee, his present residence, where he has lived to the present time.....No further
family data.....

WILLIAM SMITH - (SERGEANT-VIRGINIA SERVICE) - FILE # S-452 -

1823 - Has drawn an Invalid (disability) pension for his
services in the Revolutionary War from 1 January 1803.....
Served in the Company of Captain John Webb in the Regiment of
Colonel Alexander McClannahan.....removed from Virginia to
North Carolina and in 1818, removed to Lincoln County, Tennessee,
where he now resides.....Amount of pension, $8.00 per month
($96.00 per annum).....

No family data in file.....(This abstract is evidently not from his original pension application which no doubt would be much more complete in essential details).....D A R Patriot Index, page 630, lists a William Smith (Sergeant, Virginia) born in 1759; died after 2 January 1830; married Mary Smith.....(who may or may not be this William Smith (supra).....Colonel Alexander McClannahan was Commander of the 7th Virginia Regiment from 7 October 1776 until 13 May 1778 when the Regiment was redesignated the 5th Virginia Regiment.....In the re-organization, the soldiers were assigned to two divisions (Companys) and most of them were captured at Charleston and made prisoners.....

WILLIAM SMITH - (VIRGINIA SERVICE) - FILE # W-4806 -

Pension application dated 30 January 1834 - Now a resident of Nelson County, Virginia.....states he was born 19 May 1755 in Albemarle County, Virginia and was living there before and after his war service.....he removed to Amherst County, Virginia and now resides in Nelson County, Virginia.....he was a militiaman and was first drafted in 1776.....he hired a substitute for this tour and also for his second draft in 1777.....on his third tour, he served under Captain James Garland and was stationed in 1778 at Albemarle Barracks.....other tours of duty described....supporting affidavits by Charles Rodes and Claudius Buster who served with him.....also testimony that William Smith married a daughter of Charles Massey.....and had a son, Charles Smith....

29 December 1836, affidavit by Charles A. Smith, of Nelson County, Virginia, that he is 61 years of age and is the eldest son of William and Elizabeth Smith.....

15 February 1837 - Affidavit of Elizabeth Smith of Nelson County, Virginia, age 78 years on the 10th of March next (thus born 10 March 1759).....that she is the widow of William Smith, a Revolutionary War pensioner and that they were married 22 December 1775.....her husband died 29 December 1836.....

19 February 1837 - Affidavit by Jane Martin (age 78 years) widow of Hudson Martin, that she married in 1778 and that "Betsy (Elizabeth) Massey married William Smith before her marriage and had a son named Charles Smith.....

WILLIAM C. SMITH - (NORTH CAROLINA and GEORGIA SERVICES)-FILE
#S-3924-

Pension application dated 18 April 1833 - Now a resident of
Lincoln County, Tennessee (age 71 years).....was born 4th of
March 1762 in Mecklenburg County, Virginia.....First entered service May 1779 at Hillsboro, North Carolina under Captain (later
Colonel) Lewis Bledsoe.....gives description of service, experiences, officers, etc.....(a long account covering several pages.
was living in Wake County, North Carolina at time of first enlistment.....was living in Wilks County, Georgia in 1789 when he
re-enlisted for twelve months to fight the Indians.....under Captain Charles Williamson.....served six months of this and was
then honorably discharged.....After the enlistment, he removed
to Pendleton District, South Carolina where he lived until about
sixteen years ago (1817).....From there he removed to Lincoln
County, Tennessee where he now lives.....no family data.....

WILLIAM SMITH - (NORTH CAROLINA SERVICE) - FILE # S-1723 -

Pension application dated 16 October 1832.....Now a resident of Lincoln County, Tennessee and is age 70 years.....states
he was born 17th of February 1762 in Lunenburg County, Virginia..
He was living in Washington County, North Carolina in that part
which later became Tennessee in a settlement on the Watauga River
when he first volunteered as a lad of fourteen years of age in
the year 1776 and at that time was living with his widowed
mother.....Describes several tours of duty and his experiences...
His first officer was Captain (later Colonel) John Sevier.....
He was promoted to "ensign" in March 1781 under Captain Valentine Sevier.....was later "Lieutenant" and on an expedition in
September 1782 was appointed "Captain" by Colonel John Sevier...
Relates how they rescued a white woman named Jane Ireland who had
been taken captive on Roan's Creek, Washington County, North Carolina, and also a white man named Samuel Martin who had been captured by the Indians at Nashville.....his present residence is
300 to 400 miles from Carter County, Tennessee which was the part
of Washington County, North Carolina in which he lived during
the periods of his enlistments.....From Washington County, North
Carolina, he removed to what is now Davidson County, Tennessee in
1789 and lived there and in Rutherford County, Tennessee to the
year 1807 and from there removed to Lincoln County, Tennessee....
No family data except mention of a son-in-law (and daughter) who
receive mail in Fayetteville, Tennessee in 1833 and whose name
is Isaac Southworth.....

76.

WILLIAM SMITH - (Virginia and North Carolina Service)-FILE #S-4853

        Pension application dated 17 November 1832.....Now a resi-
dent of Robertson County, Tennessee.....States he was born in
1764 in Amelia County, Virginia and was living in Brunswick County, Virginia in 1779 when he first enlisted.....Since the War,
he has resided several years in the counties of Northampton and
Anson, in North Carolina and from Anson County, North Carolina
he removed to Robertson County, Tennessee and has lived there
many years.....Served four enlistments.....gives details of his
services, names his officers, etc.....In his last three enlistments he volunteered in Halifax County and in Northampton Counties, North Carolina.....No family data.....

WILLIAM SMITH - (South Carolina Service) -(age 86)- FILE #S-4855 -

        Pension application dated 2 October 1832.....Resident of
Jefferson County, Tennessee.....States he was born 16th of January 1746 on Christy's Creek, a branch of the Shenandoah River,
in Virginia.....(NOTE: This river is in the north central portion of Virginia).....He removed with his father to South Carolina and was living in the District of 'Ninety-Six' in South Carolina, on the Saluda River in 1776 when he first volunteered...
Since the war he has lived on the Tyger River in South Carolina
and about 14 years ago (1818), he removed to East Tennessee,
where he now lives in Jefferson County.....He volunteered three
times and was drafted once and also had several shorter periods
of service.....gives details of his services, experiences, and
officers.....No family data.....

REVOLUTIONARY WAR PENSION APPLICATION MADE BY JOHN JEFFRIES -
UNDER FILE # S-16888 -

        Application made 11 October 1832, in Tippicanoe County, Ind-
iana, at age 72 years on the 7th day of February 1760.....

        He enlisted from Essex County, Virginia, in the year 1777
under Captain William Gatewood, Colonel Holt Richardson and
General Nelson.....also gives his other tours of duty and enlistments.....Was at Yorktown when Cornwallis surrendered.....

States that he has resided part of the time in the State of Virginia, part in the State of North Carolina, part in the State of Ohio and of late, in the State of Indiana.....under remarks, is the statement that there is no data on file as to his family.

DELILAH JEFFREYS -(also spelled JEFFERS - JEFFRIES)- FILE #W-26,158-

Application of the widow of JOHN JEFFREYS for land bounty warrant, dated 11 April 1855, in Alamance County, North Carolina in which she states that she is now 80 years of age and a pensioner of the United States.....Her husband died 15 April 1845, in the aforesaid State and County.....Applicant was issued BLWT-26840-160-55.....The file also contains a certified copy of her marriage bond issued in Orange County, North Carolina, 8 December 1824, to John Jeffers (sic) to marry Dilly Ballard..... Securitees on bond were: Andrew Jeffers and Eaton Jeffers.....

The file also includes a copy of the application of JOHN JEFFREYS for pension, dated Orange County, North Carolina, 26th November 1832.....at which time he was 67 years old (born ca 1765).....He enlisted in the summer of 1780 in Brunswick County, Virginia in the Company of Captain Thomas Threadgill...etc..... gives record of his service...etc.....States he lived in Brunswick County, Virginia until 1808, at which time he removed to Orange County, North Carolina, where he has resided ever since.

JOHN JEFFREYS - FILE # S-8754 -

Received pension in Orange County, North Carolina.....proved service as a private in the Virginia Militia, in the Company commanded by Captain Threadgill, Colonel Glenn and General Stephens.

Declaration made by Thomas Jeffreys, son and only heir at law of his father, JOHN JEFFREYS, SENIOR, deceased, also a resident of Orange County, North Carolina.

States that his father was born in Halifax County, Virginia and lived in that County until December, 1832, when this declarant moved his father to this County, as his father was very infirmed and blind. His father was born in the year 1733 and was 101 years old when he died on December 4th, 1834. He left no widow surviving.

COMMENT: Halifax County, Virginia was not formed as a County until 1752. In 1733, when John was born, it was a part of Brunswick County, Virginia.

REUBEN JEFFRIES - (WIFE, ANNE) - FILE # W-20178 -

REUBEN JEFFRIES, a resident of Rappahannock County, Virginia, made application for pension 5 August 1833 and stated he was 70 years of age the 25th day of January past. (Thus born 25 January 1762).

States that he was drafted in the early Spring of 1781 in the Militia from Culpeper County, Virginia in the Company of Captain John Waugh, Regiment of Colonel Slaughter. Testifies as to other tours of duty and enlistments.

States further that he can prove his services by living witnesses, to-wit: John Jeffries, Alexander Jeffries and Reuben Sims. His answers to questions are as follows:

(1) - Born 25 January 1762 in Stafford County, Virginia.

(2) - Was living in Culpeper County, Virginia when called into service - in that part which was formed into Rappahannock County, Virginia.

11 October 1841 - Francis M. Jeffries gives bond in the sum of $200.00 as administrator of the estate of Ann Jeffries, deceased.

Reuben Jeffries died 26 June 1837 in Rappahannock County, Virginia, leaving a widow, Ann Jeffries, who died 20 May 1841, and children: William, Reuben, Nancy Jeffries and Celia Jones, the wife of Rodham Jones, who are all and only heirs at law, etc.

This file contains a certified copy of the marriage record in Stafford County, Virginia of Reuben Jeffries, of Culpeper County, Virginia to Anne Hore, daughter of Edward Hore of Brunswick Parish, Stafford County, Virginia, dated 22 January 1787.

REVOLUTIONARY WAR PENSION APPLICATION MADE BY MARY PEARSON,
widow of PARRIS PEARSON, (died 1832) who was a pensioner inscribed on the Roll of North Carolina. - FILE # W-4761 -

    5 August 1844 - Orange County, North Carolina, (Mrs.) Mary
Pearson applied for widow's pension; declares on oath that she
is the widow of Paris Pearson, who was a soldier in the Revolution.....describes tours of enlistment; names of officers. etc.
States she was married to her husband in the County of Wake,
North Carolina, in the year 1785 and that some years after, they
migrated to the County of Orange, North Carolina, where she has
resided ever since.....States her husband, Paris Pearson, died
in 1832 and was 71 years of age when he departed this life (thus
born ca 1761).....She, herself, is now 75 years of age (thus born
ca 1769).....and that her maiden name was Mary Gilmore.....
Certified by Noah Trice, J.P. and John Taylor, Clerk of Orange
County, North Carolina, 25 November 1844.

    16 December 1844 - Wake County, North Carolina, affidavit
of William Pope (now in his 74th year of his age), that he was
born and raised in the County of Wake, North Carolina and was
well acquainted with Paris Pearson, who married Mary Gilmore,
and was a soldier in the Revolutionary War.....He was not a soldier himself, but was a near neighbor...etc.....Certified by
Jordan Womble, a magistrate of Wake County, North Carolina and
James T. Marriott, Clerk of the Court of Wake County, North Carolina, 16 December 1844.....

21 August 1844 - Johnston County, North Carolina, affidavit of
James Stephenson, who states he is now 85 years of age (thus born
ca 1759),that he was born in the State of Virginia and that his
father migrated to the above County and State when he was about
seven years of age (thus, about 1766/7).....that he was well acquainted with Paris Pearson, who married Mary Gilmore, who was
a soldier in the Revolutionary War.....that they served in the
same regiment.....Certified by Amos Couts, (J.P.)

REVOLUTIONARY WAR PENSION APPLICATION OF WILLIAM WALKER STURMAN,
FILE # W-8768 - and also application of MARY STEERMAN (STURMAN)
his widow and relict.

    Soldiers application dated 25 August 1832, in Green County,
Kentucky (age 77 years), signed as William Walker Steerman.....
entered service in Campbell County, Virginia, in the 5th Virginia
Regiment, under Captain Henry Terrell, commanded by Colonel Josiah Parker.

States he was born in Westmoreland County, Virginia, 9th October 1755 (widow's application proves he died 9 November 1841).....Gives experiences and details of service for two enlistments.....total of 2 years of service.....

States that he removed from Campbell County, Virginia, after the war to Mercer County, Kentucky, where he resided about six years and from there to Green County, Kentucky, where he has resided ever since.

His widow, Mary Steerman made her application 27 January 1842, in Green County, Kentucky (87 years of age), and states further that she was born in Bedford County, Virginia, 23 January 1755; married the said William Walker Steerman in Campbell County, Virginia, 17 December 1779 and that they removed in the year 1786 from Virginia to Kentucky.

REVOLUTIONARY WAR PENSION APPLICATION OF ELLIS ADKISSON - FILE # S-12904 -

Ellis Adkisson - 27 August 1832 (thus born ca 1762) of Madison County, Kentucky.....Declares that he served from Bedford County, Virginia in 1777 as a substitute for Caleb Compton for 6 months.....Marched to Prince Edward County Courthouse and served under Lieutenant Nathaniel Rice.....to Richmond, Virginia and placed under Captain Ewell.....Discharged March 1782 and given his discharge by Captain Newell.....

He was born in Amelia County, Virginia and moved from there to Bedford County, Virginia and has lived in Madison County, Kentucky for 24 years (thus, since ca 1808).

Received pension of $20.00 per annum and was of Estell County, Kentucky at this time.....Certificate 7501 issued 21 April 1833.

COMMENT: D A R Patriot Index, page 5, has listed "Ellis Adkisson (Private, Virginia), born 1760; died post 1832; married Nancy Prather."

REVOLUTIONARY WAR PENSION APPLICATION BY JONATHAN SWAN -
FILE # R-10332 -

23 November 1832 - Jonathan Swan, a resident of Gwinnette
County, Georgia.....States that he is 80 years old and was born
in Prince George County, Maryland in 1752.

He first enlisted in Henry County, Virginia under Captain
Thomas Handby and Lieutenant William Watkins, under General
Greene and served as a Militia Man.....(Gives details of his
service).....States that there is no one he can prove his service by, but Basel Neal.

At the close of the War, he settled in Henry County, Virginia and removed from there to Pendleton District, South Carolina and from thence to Columbia County, Georgia and from there
to Gwinnette County, Georgia, where he now resides.....(Signed
by his mark "X").

SECTION 4

A Virginia Ancestor Adventurer..........82.

Colonel George Mason

For some time, this writer has contemplated including a chapter in one of his books of an early Colonial Virginia Ancestor, whose decendants he has been able to trace to the present day.

He can think of no better example than the following "Genealogical Report" of Colonel George Mason, the first of his name to arrive in Virginia, through his grandson, French Mason (Senior), whose decendants have never been traced heretofore.

It is thought that many readers might enjoy this present account if rendered in typical report form as found by this researcher and presented to his client, Mrs. Arthur N. Littlefield, of Knoxville, Tennessee, who has given her gracious permission to reprint here.

W I L E Y
F A M I L Y
R E C O R D S

R E P O R T

NO. I

C O M P I L E D   B Y

Charles Hughes Hamlin C.G.
Certified Genealogist
Route 2, Box C-44
Powhatan, Virginia 23139

82.

W I L E Y   A N D   A L L I E D   F A M I L I E S

GENEALOGICAL
RESEARCH
REPORT NO. I

<u>RESEARCHER</u>: Charles H. Hamlin, Certified Genealogist, Powhatan, Virginia.

<u>ASSIGNMENT</u>: Twelve hours; complied with, herewith.

    Mrs. Arthur N. Littlefield (nee Florence Gammon) of Knoxville, Tennessee (hereafter called client) has furnished the following information which is rendered here in Chart form for easier comprehension.

$$FRENCH\ MASON\ ^5\ m\ \ Mary\ Ann\ Major$$

FRENCH MASON ^{5} m Mary Ann Major

CATHARINE MASON m WILLIAM SCOTT ^{4}

MARY ANN SCOTT m ROBERT MAY WILEY ^{3}
(1828-1895)   (1825-1884)

SARAH CATHARINE WILEY m MATHEW HAYNES GAMMO ^{2}
(died 1932)   (died 1926)

FLORENCE GAMMON m ARTHUR NELSON LITTLEFIELD ^{1}
(client)

<u>COMMENT</u>:

    This is a most remarkable assignment in that client does not have prima facie proof of an acceptable nature for any of the above statements or allegations and is basing the premise on family tradition and heresay evidence. The remarkable fact is that all of the above has been found to be true and factual and the proper evidence to support the pedigree has been found and is herewith submitted within this report. The Virginia records commence with her grandparents cited above.

ROBERT MAY WILEY   (THIRD GENERATION)..........

Virginia Military Institute - Register of Former Cadets (1939) -
CLASS OF 1845 -

WILEY, ROBERT MAY - Fincastle, Virginia, (County Seat of Botetourt County) - 3 years; Graduated 10 (i.e., 10th in Class) -
Farmer and merchant; Colonel on Governor's Staff during Civil
War; Member of Virginia Legislature (both houses) continuously
from 1846 to 1865; died July 16, 1884. (Client has changed this
to 1882)..........

COMMENT:

      This is a very valuable record and was furnished by client.
Colonel Robert May Wiley is stated to have married MARY ANN SCOTT
and a search was made in the counties of Botetourt and Alleghany
for the record but it was not found. We do have proof of the
marriage in the records of her father, WILLIAM SCOTT, (of which
more later). The parentage of Colonel Robert May Wiley will be
proven next.........Please note that all of the records within
this report are planned to be separated by name and generation
in order that other or later evidence found can be inserted in
chronological order, in the allied families. It is recommended
that the census records of 1850-1860-1870 and 1880 be searched
for additional evidence as to this subject and his family.

             ROBERT WILEY   (FOURTH GENERATION)...........

BOTETOURT COUNTY, VIRGINIA RECORDS:

MARRIAGE RECORDS (1770-1853) page 299 -

25 August 1824 - ROBERT WILEY AND MRS. LUCY ANN LUCK.   WILLIAM
SCOTT, Security.

page 246 - 8 July 1817 - William H. Luck and LUCY ANN BOTT,
DAUGHTER OF JOEL BOTT. David Shanke, Jr., Security. Married
15 July 1817 by James McCan, minister.

84.

COMMENT: All of the above are new ancestors of whom client was
not aware and of whom more later. In a search of the tax records
of Botetourt County from 1819 thru 1824 it seems that ROBERT WILEY
came into the county as a resident in the year 1821 from somewhere else or else he became age 21 in this year. The latter
seems more probable and if correct, he would have been born circa
1799 or thereabouts. Earlier tax records should be searched to
prove or disprove this allegation.

WILL BOOK "G" - (1843-1849) - page 350 -

Last Will and Testament of ROBERT WILEY, dated 24 October 1845;
proved July Court 1847..........

    To my son, F. M. WILEY, (this is for Ferdinand M. Wiley by
other records)..........land in addition to what I have already
deeded him.

    The residue of all my land in the Valley of Sinking Creek,
in Botetourt County, I give and bequeath to my four sons: RO:MAY-
BYRON S. - OSCAR and BENTON and their heirs forever to be equally
divided..........

    To my two daughters, LUCY ANN and VAN BUREN.....two tracts
of land..........

    To my four sons (named above), the house and lot in Fin-
castle where Dr. Williams now resides and rents..........

    To my daughters, LUCY ANN and VAN BUREN, my house and lot
in Fincastle, known by the name of "Solitude" and also my Bank
Stock of Farmers of Virginia..........

    My son, BENTON, (underage) is to receive as good an education
as his brother, ROBERT MAY WILEY..........

Refers to "MY SIX CHILDREN BY MY LAST MARRIAGE".....(I have not
found his first marriage as yet but it would seem that FERDINAND
M. WILEY was the only issue of the first marriage..........I am
wrong, see the following bequest..........

    Leaves slaves to his daughter, ELVIRA and the tract of land
deeded to her husband, known as "Highland Grove".....also the
house and lot deeded to her in Fincastle and her husband, O'CALL-
AGHAN..........

    All the negroes I got by my last marriage with my wife I give
to my six children by her, (viz) ROBERT MAY - BYRON S. - LUCY ANN
OSCAR - VAN BUREN and BENTON..........

The negroes I claim in my own right to my five sons, FERDI-NAND M. - ROBERT M. - BYRON S. - OSCAR and BENTON and my two daughters, LUCY ANN and VAN BUREN..........

Some years ago I gave OLIVER CALLAGHAN a power of attorney respecting my wife's lands in the State of Kentucky, which I now revoke and make null and void..........

To my son, ROBERT MAY, my patent lever silver watch and to my son, BYRON S.. one common silver watch..........

To my son, BENTON, my cane marked James L. Woodville, which I value highly through respect to the doner.....(I wonder if this could be a "clue" as to his former wife???)

Ibid, page 397-

Inventory and Appraisal of the Personal Estate of ROBERT WILEY, DECEASED.....itemized and valued.....Total $21,092.84.....plus notes due the estate of $5,394.51.....

COMMENT:

This is the Will of an extremely wealthy man. There are many more records in this county pertaining to him which could not be obtained within this first attempt..........

WILLIAM SCOTT - (FOURTH GENERATION)............

BOTETOURT COUNTY MARRIAGES - (1770-1853) - page 294 -

6 November 1823 - WILLIAM SCOTT AND CATHARINE MASON. Security, Matthew Petticrew.....

COMMENT:

Alleghany County was formed as a new county in 1822 and the land on which William Scott resided must have fallen in the county when it was formed.

86.

<u>ALLEGHANY COUNTY WILLS and INVENTORIES # 3-(1849-1876)-page 504</u>-

Last Will and Testament of WILLIAM SCOTT; dated 7 April 1871;
proved 17 August 1874..........

   To my dearly beloved wife, CATHARINE M. SCOTT, my plantation
for her life and all my personal property..........

   My executor to rent out all my town property including the
lots between the depot and Covington..........

   My property to be divided into four equal parts as follows:
one-fourth to my son-in-law, BENTON WILEY, to be held by him in
trust for the children of my son, WILLIAM M. SCOTT..........

   One-fourth part to my daughter, <u>MARY A. E. WILEY, WIFE OF
ROBERT M. WILEY</u>.....(here is the proof!)

   One-fourth part to my daughter, SALLIE C. WILEY, WIFE OF
BENTON WILEY.....(this is the youngest brother of your Robert
May)..........

   One-fourth part to my daughter, EMMA HAMMOND..........

   My plantation and lands to be divided also into four equal
parts as above.....Executors, my friend Robert L. Parrish and
my son-in-law, BENTON WILEY..........

<u>CODICIL - 14 November 1873</u> -

   <u>My beloved wife having departed this life</u>.....makes further
provisions for his daughter,, EMMA HAMMOND and her children and
for the children of his son, WILLIAM M. SCOTT, who are to be
maintained for a period of five years after his death..........

The Executor's Bond was $15,000.00 (a very tidy sum in the Re-
construction Period after the Civil War).....R. L. Parrish qualified as Executor..........

<u>Ibid, page 513</u> -

Inventory and Appraisal of the Personal Estate of WILLIAM SCOTT,
DECEASED,.....itemized and valued.....included 150 volumes of
books.....etc.....Total $6,069.93.....Recorded 3 October 1874...

COMMENT:

Proof of the parentage of CATHARINE MASON, wife of WILLIAM
SCOTT, could not be proven in Botetourt and Alleghany County
records, so as a last resort, we went into Fairfax County, where
we knew of an older FRENCH MASON and Colonel George Mason. We
were successful and her parentage will be proven in the records
of her father, FRENCH MASON (a younger one). Incidently, I may
mention that in the early Colonial period, the designation,
"COUSIN" more often meant "NEPHEW" or NIECE than it did "COUSIN".
The degree of relationship of an actual "COUSIN" was designated
as "KINSMAN". This will resolve your problem as to this referred
to in your letters.

FRENCH MASON (FIFTH GENERATION)..........

FAIRFAX COUNTY, VIRGINIA RECORDS:

Liber "Y-2" - page 217 -

26 September 1828 - Indenture in which WILLIAM SCOTT AND CATHARINE
M. SCOTT, HIS WIFE, FORMERLY CATHARINE M. MASON, OF THE COUNTY
OF ALLEGHANY, VIRGINIA, sell to Peter Coulter, of the County of
Fairfax.....for $700.00.....a tract of land in Fairfax County,
at the Falls of Pohick.....adjoining the lands of and alloted
to AMINTA GRIMES (formerly AMINTA MASON) and the heirs of MARY
MASON, DECEASED.....containing 168¼ acres.....it being one-third
part of a tract of land belonging to the heirs of FRENCH MASON
which was laid off and alloted to the said CATHARINE M. SCOTT
as her portion thereof.....Certified by the Justices of Alleghany
County and recorded in Fairfax County 18th of May 1829.........

COMMENT:

I believe this one record is the only record now in existance which will prove that CATHARINE M. MASON, wife of William
Scott, was the daughter and heir of French Mason of Fairfax County.
There was no time left to check the records of this county for
further evidence as to French Mason beyond the fact that the index
does not indicate a Will or Inventory by him. We did discover
that the above cited AMINTA and MARY MASON, who had adjoining
land to CATHARINE, were daughters of a GEORGE MASON and were not
her sisters as we first suspected. It seems possible that they
may have been "cousins".

M A S O N
F A M I L Y
R E C O R D S

R E P O R T
N O   2

C O M P I L E D   B Y

Charles Hughes Hamlin
Certified Genealogist
Route 2, Box C-44
Powhatan, Virginia 23139

FRENCH MASON (FIFTH GENERATION)..........

<u>REVIEW</u>:

In our first report we cited proof that CATHARINE M. MASON, only child of FRENCH MASON, of Fairfax County, Virginia, married WILLIAM SCOTT, 6 November 1832 in Botetourt County, Virginia.

Of primary importance is the record in the first report in which WILLIAM SCOTT and CATHARINE, his wife, (stated therein to have been formerly CATHARINE M. MASON) sold land in Fairfax County, Virginia, (28 September 1828) which was stated to be a ONE-THIRD PORTION ALLOTED TO HER AS THE HEIR OF FRENCH MASON AND WHICH LAND WAS LOCATED "AT THE FALLS OF POHICK ADJOINING THE LANDS OF TWO OF THE DAUGHTERS OF GEORGE MASON, WHOSE NAMES WERE AMINTA AND MARY.

In all records, this GEORGE MASON is always described as "GEORGE MASON OF POHICK" to distinguish him from "COLONEL GEORGE MASON OF GUNSTON HALL" and another "COLONEL GEORGE MASON OF AQUIA" I now have records and notes proving the children of both these two latter named "GEORGE MASONS".

Although many of the records of Fairfax County are now lost or destroyed, there can be no doubt that your ancestor (FRENCH MASON) was the only son of GEORGE MASON "OF POHICK" and the brother of AMINTA and MARY MASON and who died as a very young man in the year 1801 shortly after the death of his father. There is now no record of the division of the land of GEORGE MASON "OF POHICK" but it is evident that CATHARINE received her one-third portion as the daughter of FRENCH MASON and that her two aunts (AMINTA and MARY) received the other two shares (of which more later.)

<u>BUREAU OF VITAL STATISTICS - DEATH RECORD - LINE NO. 13 -</u>

CATHARINE MYER SCOTT, age 75, died 12 November 1873 (thus born ca 1798) in Alleghany County, Virginia, "near Covington"; Information by WILLIAM M. SCOTT, "SON" -

<u>COMMENT</u>: The informant stated further that she was born in Alleghany County, Virginia, but this is obviously in error as Alleghany County was not formed until the year 1822. Actually, by evidence now to hand, she must have been born in Fairfax County, Virginia.

FAIRFAX COUNTY - LIBER "Y-2" - (1828-1830) - PAGE 14 -

3 April 1801 - Indenture in which William Dulany and Nancy, his wife, of the County of Alexandria, sell to CATHARINE MASON, ONLY CHILD AND HEIR OF FRENCH MASON, LATE OF FAIRFAX COUNTY, DECEASED. for $200.00 PAID BY FRENCH MASON IN HIS LIFETIME - a tract of land in Fairfax County.....on the turnpike from Alexandria to Leesburg.....containing 7 acres.....etc.....Recorded 23 September 1801.....

COMMENT: This record is further proof that CATHARINE was the ONLY child of FRENCH MASON and that he died before the above date of 3rd April 1801. Catharine must have been about age three at this time.

Ibid, page 194-

19 March 1829 - It appearing to the satisfaction of the Court that CATHARINE MASON does not reside within this Commonwealth and has no guardian or agent known and that she owns a tract of land in Fairfax County through which the Middle Turnpike Company desires to lay out a new road.....Commissioners appointed to assess the damages to the land.....26 March 1829, damages assessed at one cent..........

FAIRFAX COUNTY, VIRGINIA RECORDS:

PERSONAL PROPERTY TAX LISTS - (original records) -

These records were studied, each year, from 1782 (when they commence) to 1805. FRENCH MASON appears as a white male adult resident of the county for the first time in the year 1799, proving he was born circa 1778 or thereabouts. He is taxed on himself; one slave; and 8 horses in the years 1800 and 1801. He does not appear after these years and we have already proven that he died before 3 April 1801 (supra). He was therefore only 23 years of age when he died. By Virginia Law, it was necessary for fathers of sons to report them as tithable when they became age 16 and until they became age 21 years. In the year 1793, GEORGE MASON "OF POHICK", reported himself only and two slaves as tithable. In the years 1794 and 1795, he reports himself and one other white tithe of age 16 but under age 21, who is evidently his son, FRENCH MASON. This evidence proves again that French was born circa 1778 or thereabouts.

Of much interest is the fact that since both George "of Pohick" and French had died by or before 1801, that the two daughters of George - "AMINTA AND MARY MASON" are taxed on two slaves in the year 1803. They would not have been taxed in their names if there had been a white male adult in their family.

90.

Apart from the fact that Fairfax County has lost most of its records, it is very doubtful that FRENCH MASON would have been of sufficient age to have made any records in his own right and responsibility until after he attained his majority and before he died.

GEORGE MASON "OF POHICK" (SIXTH GENERATION).........

FAIRFAX COUNTY, VIRGINIA RECORDS:

PERSONAL PROPERTY TAX RECORDS AND LAND TAX RECORDS:

These records were examined from the year 1782 thru the year 1805 and each year (until 1800), the name of GEORGE MASON (always described as "OF POHICK") is taxed on one or two slaves and himself. In 1785 he is taxed on two whites whom I believe must have been himself and his nephew, FRANCIS MASON, son of his brother FRENCH MASON, for whom he must have named his own son. The records of this nephew, FRANCIS MASON, have proven to be most valuable as by them we can prove his lineage (and the lineage of his uncle, George "of Pohick") back to the original emigrant to Virginia.

In the Land Tax Records, we find in the years 1782 thru 1787, that GEORGE MASON "OF POHICK" is taxed on 496 acres. In 1788 and through 1795, he has two tracts of 496 acres and 50 acres stated by the clerk in 1788 to have been acquired from FRANCIS MASON. In 1796, his land is reduced to 477 acres and 50 acres or a total of 527 acres. In 1796 the clerk has noted that 16½ acres was altered from George Mason to Robert Speck. George Mason "of Pohick" is still taxed on 527 acres at the time of his death in 1799 or 1800. We believe this land must have gained in acreage by a new survey after his death when his land was divided into three parts as we know that Catharine received 168½ acres as her portion and it will be proven later that her two aunts had 400 acres between them. Of interest is the land tax record of 1782 in which 531 acres are taxed to FRENCH MASON (brother of your George "of Pohick") as will be more amply proven later, and which should have properly been cited by the clerk as French Mason ESTATE. This land is later disposed of by FRANCIS MASON, son of the above cited FRENCH MASON.

FAIRFAX COUNTY, VIRGINIA RECORDS:

Liber "Y-2" - page 225 (old number, page 226) -

5 March 1827 - Indenture in which Doddridge Pitt Chichester, of
Fairfax County, sells to George Chichester, of the same County....
WHEREAS: AMINTA MASON AND MARY MASON, to secure Daniel McCarty
Chichester for being their security for their administration on
the estate of their father, GEORGE MASON, did convey by deed (of
Trust) dated 19 August 1803, a tract of land in Fairfax County
heired by them, the said AMINTA AND MARY, from their father,
GEORGE MASON "OF POHICK", containing 400 acres.....in trust.....
unless a default occurred.....the default having occurred.....
notice having been given.....the land was sold at public auction
5 March 1827.....and George Chichester being the highest bidder
for $600.00.....etc.....Recorded 29 May 1829.....

Liber "O-1" - (1785-1788) - page 444 -

10 March 1787 - GEORGE MASON "OF POHICK" of Fairfax County, Virginia gives bond in the sum of ₤500 to FRANCIS MASON, of the
same County,.....The condition being that the said GEORGE MASON
AND FRANCIS MASON hath a certain tract of land on Pohick Run,
on the west side, known BY THE NAME OF NORMANSELS, to be divided
between them and to prevent future disputes.....have mutually
agreed.....etc.....Witnesses: John Coffer - French Simpson -
Gilbert Simpson.....Recorded 17 July 1787.....

Liber "P-1" - (1784-1785) - page 474 -

13 June 1785 - FRANCIS MASON, OF FAIRFAX COUNTY, VIRGINIA, GRANDSON
OF FRENCH MASON, LATE OF SAID COUNTY, DECEASED, sells to Daniel
McCarty, Jr......The said FRENCH MASON, DECEASED, being possessed
of a tract of land on the upper side of POHICK CREEK, known as
Shop-Point, being so seized on the 10th February 1734, did farm,
rent and lease unto Thomas Monteith, late of the County of King
George, for his life and the life of Phillis Monteith, his wife,
the said tract of land containing 200 acres.....etc.....(the rest
of this document is torn and destroyed.....)

Liber "S-1" - (1789-1790) - page 411 -

23 March 1790 - FRANCIS MASON, of Fairfax County, Virginia, sells
to John Cofer, of the same County, for ₤160, all that part of a
tract of land granted to Richard Normansel and Martin Scarlet,
which (now) belongs to the said FRANCIS MASON.....on Pohick Run

92.

.....ADJOINING THE LAND OF GEORGE MASON "OF POHICK" AND THE
SAID FRANCIS MASON.....containing 244 acres EXCEPTING THE DOWER
OF ANN DONALDSON, MOTHER OF THE SAID FRANCIS MASON.....etc.....
Recorded 19 July 1790.....

ibid, page 462 -

13 February 1790 - FRANCIS MASON, OF FAIRFAX COUNTY, VIRGINIA,
"GRANDSON OF FRENCH MASON SENIOR", deceased, sells to French
Simpson, of the same County, for ₤100 specie, a tract of 200
acres of land on the upper side or northeast side of Pohick
Creek, known as Shotes (?) or Shop-Point, BEING PART OF A TRACT
OF LAND PURCHASED BY CAPTAIN GEORGE MASON, SENIOR, from Thomas
James, BY DEED DATED 9 SEPTEMBER 1690 and which is recorded in
Stafford County.....then devised BY WILL OF THE SAID GEORGE
MASON TO HIS SON, FRENCH MASON, WHICH WILL WAS DATED 29 JANUARY
1715 IN THE RECORDS OF STAFFORD COUNTY, AND THEN DEVISED BY WILL
OF THE SAID FRENCH MASON TO HIS SON, FRENCH MASON, which will
was dated 15 November 1748 in the records of Fairfax County and
then at the death of the said FRENCH MASON, IT DESCENDED TO HIS
LAWFUL SON AND HEIR, FRANCIS MASON, PARTY TO THESE PRESENTS.....
the said FRANCIS MASON, did by lease dated 13 June 1785, rented
and leased the same to Daniel McCarty, Jr......Witnesses: W.
Donaldson - ANN DONALDSON - Robert Speak - William Reardon.....
Acknowledged and recorded 19 July 1790.....

COMMENT:

        This is one of the most beautiful genealogical records I
have ever seen.   It proves four full generations in one record.
This is also your line for three generations, of which much more.

Liber "T-1" - (1790-1792) - page 234 et seq -

February Court 1791 - On the motion of ANN DONALDSON, Commissioners are appointed to set apart the dower of the said ANN in the
lands of her late husband, FRENCH MASON, DECEASED, and report to
the next Court.....this is followed by a surveyor's plat of the
land divided into 244 acres - 82 acres (widow's dower) - and
21 7/8 acres.....

In their summary, the Commissioners state that Mr. William Donald
son is the husband of Mrs. Ann Donaldson, late widow of FRENCH
MASON and that FRANCIS MASON is his son and heir at law.....

.....a further record charges 1/3 part of the rents to William
Donaldson "in right of his wife" for a twelve year period dating
from 1778 (which must have been from the time of their marriage)
and there is further charge for 1/3 part of the tenement occupied
by Mr. Robert Boggess AS BY THE DEPOSITION OF GEORGE MASON, ES-
QUIRE, "OF GUNSTON HALL" RESPECTING AN AGREEMENT BETWEEN GEORGE
MASON, JR. "OF POHICK" AND HIS BROTHER, FRENCH MASON.....FURTHER
.....has relation to a possible dispute as to the boundary line
BETWEEN GEORGE MASON "OF POHICK" AND HIS NEPHEW (SIC) FRANCIS
MASON.....and thus we have prima facie proof of the relationship
and the lineage of each.

FRENCH MASON, SENIOR (SEVENTH GENERATION)..........

FAIRFAX COUNTY, VIRGINIA RECORDS:

Will Book "A-1" - (1742-1752) - page 256 -

Last Will and Testament of FRENCH MASON, "GENT.", (not dated)-
proven and recorded 18 November 1748.....

   To my daughter, ROSANNA, the plantation I live on and 100
   acres adjoining..........

   To my daughter, LUCRETIA, the plantation on which Charles
   Christmas now lives and 100 acres adjoining..........

   TO MY ELDEST SON, GEORGE MASON (YOUR ANCESTOR, "LATER CALLED
   "OF POHICK") one half of my land remaining..........

   To my youngest son (not named here but we now know he was
   FRENCH MASON, JUNIOR) the remaining half of my land including the plantation rented to Thomas Monteith and that rented to Mr. Ben Grayson on which the mill now is..........

   Having formerly given my daughter, LEANNA TALBOT, what I
   intended.....etc.....(signs by his mark "F" Mason).....

Witnesses: (Rev) Charles Green - Jeremiah Bronaugh.....
Executors Bond - ₤500 sterling given by GEORGE MASON with Jeremiah Bronaugh, his security.....(This George Mason, the executor
of the Will, was named in the Will as "MY COUSIN, GEORGE MASON"),
(NEPHEW?????)

94.

<u>REGISTER OF OVERWHARTON PARISH - STAFFORD COUNTY, VIRGINIA -</u>
<u>King, page 151</u> -

"<u>A QUIT RENT ROLL FOR 1723</u>"

COLONEL GEORGE MASON - 18,807 acres (brother of your French Mason)

FRENCH MASON   - 1,455 acres (your ancestor).....

<u>Ibid, pages 184-185</u> -

    Under "JUSTICES OF THE PEACE for 1726 and 1729", is listed
FRENCH MASON.....(This is Colonial Societies eligibility).....

NOTE BY CHH: Fairfax County, Virginia was formed in 1742 from
Prince William County, which was formed in 1730/1 from King George
and Stafford Counties. There should therefore be many interesting records in these older Counties of your ancestors. They
have not been examined as yet. From the records we have exhibited in this report, we can now present our evidence in CHART form
for easier comprehension (Viz).........

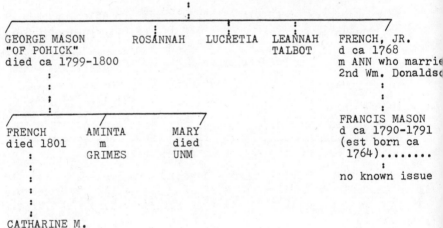

```
              COLONEL GEORGE MASON (died testate 1716) (more later)
                        :
              FRENCH MASON, SENIOR (died testate 1748)
                        :
                        :
 /━━━━━━━━━━━━━━━━━━━━┯━━━━━━━┯━━━━━━━┯━━━━━━━━━━━━━━━━━/
GEORGE MASON        ROSANNAH  LUCRETIA  LEANNAH   FRENCH, JR.
"OF POHICK"                             TALBOT    d ca 1768
died ca 1799-1800                                 m ANN who marrie
  :                                               2nd Wm. Donaldso
  :                                                 :
  ;                                                 :
  :                                               FRANCIS MASON
/━━━━━━━━━━━┯━━━━━━━━━/                            d ca 1790-1791
FRENCH       AMINTA    MARY                        (est born ca
died 1801    m         died                          1764)........
  :          GRIMES    UNM                            :
  :                                               no known issue
  :
  :
  :
CATHARINE M.
born 1798
died 12 Nov. 1873
married 6 Nov. 1823
WILLIAM SCOTT
```

OF INTEREST:

 Reference is now made to the copy of the very interesting
letter of GEORGE MASON, in 1758, to Colonel George Washington
seeking an officers commission for his relative "FRENCH MASON"...
We can now identify him as FRENCH MASON, JUNIOR, son of French,
Senior and brother of your GEORGE MASON "OF POHICK",,,,,,,,,,

COLONEL GEORGE MASON (2nd) (EIGHTH GENERATION)..........

VIRGINIA STATE LIBRARY ACCESSION # 20487 - "JOHN MERCER LAND BOOK"
(1728-1765) - page 248.т........

Last Will and Testament of COLONEL GEORGE MASON, SENIOR, "GENT",
of the County of Stafford, Colony of Virginia.....dated 29 January 1715/16.....Proven 14 November 1716.....

 ALL THE LAND I BOUGHT OF MARTIN SCARLET AND THOMAS JAMES
TO MY SON, FRENCH MASON.....ALSO BEQUEATHS HIM SEVERAL SLAVES,
(named).....

To my son, NICHOLSON MASON.....land and slaves.....

To my son, FRANCIS MASON.....land and slaves.....

To my son, THOMAS MASON.....land and slaves.....

To my dear wife, SARAH MASON, two slaves, Stafford and Nicholas.

To my daughters, ELIZABETH MASON - SIMPHER ROSE MASON - and
CATHARINE MASON.....to each land and slaves.....

To my son, GEORGE MASON, two silver candlesticks, snuffer
and snuff dish.....the rest of my silver plate to my wife
and son, NICHOLSON.....(Note by CHH: this son, GEORGE MASON
is COLONEL GEORGE MASON, the father of COLONEL GEORGE MASON
"OF GUNSTON HALL".....)

To my daughter, SARAH MASON.....

Mentions "MY BROTHER-IN-LAW, JOSEPH WAUGH" and "MY SONS-IN-
LAW, WILLIAM DARRELL AND GEORGE FITZHUGH".....

Bequeaths 200 acres of land to John Hudman (no relationship
stated.....)

Executors: My sons, GEORGE MASON and NICHOLSON MASON.....(NOTE:
in the probate in 1716, the son, NICHOLSON MASON, had also departed this life and GEORGE MASON qualified as sole executor)....

GEORGE MASON to GEORGE WASHINGTON

Race Ground at Bogges 1/8
Sat. 6th May 1758-5 P.M.o'-
clock

Dear Sir -

The bearer, French Mason, a relative of mine, has an incl-
ination to serve his country upon the intended expedition. I
recommend him to the President for a lieutenancy in the regiment
now raising, but unfortunately, before he reached Williamsburg,
every commission was disposed of, otherwise he was sure of succ-
eeding, as the President would have done him any service in his
power. As there are some vacancies in your regiment, his honor
has been so kind to give him a letter of recommendation to you.
Had I known of these vacancies, I should have taken the liberty
of _____ to you sooner on his behalf, for as he proposes to
continue longer in the service than this campaign and persue his
fortune in that way of life, he would prefer a commission in your
regiment, and it would give me great satisfaction that he was
under the immediate command of a gentleman for whom I have so
high an esteem. You may be assured, sir, that I would not recommend a person to your favor whom I did not from my own knowledge believe to be a young fellow of spirit and integrity. He
has lived a good while with me, and, if I am not greatly deceived
he has personal bravery that will carry him thru any danger with

reputation, and this opinion I am the more confirmed in as he never was a flashy fellow.

He has been but little in company and has not that address which is requisite to set a man in an advantageous light at first, but he is a very modest lad and does not want parts, and I am confident will endeavor to deserve your good opinion, as well as to support the character I have given him. He, this moment, came up from Williamsburg and found me here, and as I thought there was no time to be lost, advised him to set off instantly for Winchester, as soon as I could procure this scrap of paper and find a place in the crowd to sit down and write.

If he fails of a commission, he has thoughts of going out as a volunteer, but as he has but a small fortune, I advised against it.

Whatever you are so kind to do for him on this occasion, I shall always regard it as a particular obligation for me. I beg you will excuse this trouble and believe me on all occasions.

Very sincerely,

Dear Sir

Your most obedient

humble servant

G. Mason

98.

Fairfax County
Dogues Neck, 16th May,1758

Dr Sir

I am favored with yours of the 8th inst per French Mason and am
perfectly satisfied with the justice of your reasons for not providing for him in your regiment at this time - I am convinced
from your state of the case, that it would not well have been
done without prejudicing the service. He tells me you were kind
enough to promise him a commission the next vacancy that happens.
I should have been very glad his fortune would have supported
him as a volunteer. Both he and I were very fond of his enter-
ing as such in your regiment, but I really did not think it ad-
visable that he would run his own little estate in debt upon the
occasion.
          ****

The copy of above ends abruptly. Where these excerpts of letters
were copied from I have no way of knowing. The following is interesting for I always understood that French Mason was George
Mason's nephew and not his cousin.

Dogues Neck, Fairfax Count
4th January 1758

Dear Sir
                    (i.e.,"nephew")
     The bearer, (my cousin French Mason) waits on you with an

account I received from Capt. Trent, amounting to ₺165-12-24.

     As I have an immediate call for a pretty large sum, you wil
particularly oblige me in sending the cash per this bearer who

will give a receipt for what he recs. If you happen not to have

the cash at home, I must beg the favor of you to order---------

COLONEL GEORGE MASON (2nd) (EIGHTH GENERATION)...........

GENEALOGICAL
RESEARCH
REPORT NO 3

RESEARCHER: Charles Hughes Hamlin, Powhatan, Virginia

ASSIGNMENT: Twelve hours; complied with, herewith.

TAPESTRY :

  A review of our first two reports reveals that we have been successful in tracing client's ancestry to COLONEL GEORGE MASON[2] (16?? - 1716) thru his son, FRENCH MASON, SENIOR, (died testate 1748) who was of the seventh generation removed from client. As far as we can determine this specific branch has never before been traced or published.

  From certain evidence to hand we had also determined that Colonel George Mason[2] had been thrice married and had issue by each wife. In his Will he named five sons; four daughters; and two sons-in-law who had married two other daughters (not named).

  It was therefore deemed necessary to first find proof of the three wives, from authentic sources, and (secondly) to prove the names of the children of each wife. This proved to be easier than we had thought as we found that the second wife had only one child and the third wife had three. The other children, named and proven by the Will, were therefore necessarily of the first wife. While we found no specific account or chart rendered in this fashion (exhibited later) we were greatly helped by various notes found in The Overwharton Parish Register (Stafford County) by George H. S. King, FASG; FNGS, etc., of Fredericksburg, Virginia, whose sources and interpretations were checked and found to be authentic and authoritative.

PROOF OF THE NAMES OF THE THREE WIVES OF COLONEL GEORGE MASON[2].....

NOTE BY CHH: Annotations to proof of the above are quoted from The Register of Overwharton Parish, Stafford County, Virginia, 1723-1758) by George H. S. King whose sources to authority were records in the Public Domain; Virginia Genealogies, by Rev. Horace E. Hayden; and adventurers of Purse and person by Jester and Hiden. This source is hereafter quoted as "OPR"..........

100.

OPR, page 220 -

Major Benjamin Strother (ca1700-1765) married (1st) ca 1726 MARY (MASON) FITZHUGH, widow of George Fitzhugh, Gent.,(169?-1722) and DAUGHTER OF COLONEL GEORGE MASON (16..-1716) AND MARY FOWKE. HIS FIRST WIFE.....etc.....

OPR, page 226 -

Thomas Fitzhugh, Gent., (ca 1689-1719) married ANNE FOWKE (MASON) DARRELL, DAUGHTER OF COLONEL GEORGE MASON AND MARY (FOWKE) MASON, and widow of William Darrell (16..-1715).....she married (3rdly) Thomas Smith (d 1764)..........

OPR, page 248 -

ELIZABETH WAUGH, younger daughter of Rev. Mr. John and Elizabeth Waugh, MARRIED COLONEL GEORGE MASON (16..-1716), WIDOWER OF MARY FOWKE. She died shortly after the birth of her only child, CATH-ERINE MASON, (born 21 June 1707; died 15 June 1750) who married John Mercer, Esq., COLONEL GEORGE MASON MARRIED (THIRDLY) SARAH TALIAFERRO (16..-1716), DAUGHTER OF FRANCIS TALIAFERRO AND ELIZA-BETH CATLETT, HIS WIFE.....(We will quote her will later, which names her three children.....CHH)

OPR, page 217 -

Biographical sketch of John Mercer, Gent., (born 6 February 1704, died 14 October 1768) who married (1st) on 10 June 1725 CATHARIN MASON (b. 21 June 1707 - died 15 June 1750) ONLY CHILD OF COLONE GEORGE MASON (16..-1716) and HIS SECOND WIFE, ELIZABETH WAUGH, daughter of Rev. Mr. John Waugh.....John Mercer married (2ndly) on 10 November 1750, ANN ROY (17..-1770) daughter of Dr. Mungo Roy, of Essex County, Virginia.

JOHN MERCER LAND BOOK (1728-1765) - Virginia State Library Acces # 20487 - page 252 -

Last Will and Testament of MRS. SARAH MASON, dated 13th Feb ruary 1715/16 - proved 14 November 1716.....

"Of the Parish of Overwharton, County of Stafford"

To my loving daughter, SARAH MASON, two slaves named Staff-ord and Nicholson.....

To my loving sons, FRANCIS AND THOMAS MASON, the silver
plate left to me by my deceased husband.....etc........

To my THREE CHILDREN, FRANCIS - THOMAS and SARAH MASON.....

Executor: MR. GEORGE MASON and NICHOLSON MASON, GENTS......

COMMENT: We observe that Colonel George Mason; his wife, SARAH;
and his son NICHOLSON MASON, all died about the same time......
We now have the names of his three wives and the children of
his last two wives from the above cited records.....As stated
(supra) the other children named in his Will (which see) were
therefore necessarily of his first wife.

CHART OF THE FAMILY OF COLONEL GEORGE MASON^2

COLONEL GEORGE MASON^2 (COL GEORGE^1)-(born ca 16..- died testate
1716)-married:.....

1. MARY FOWKE, daughter of Colonel Gerard Fowke and Anne
   Thorowgood, his wife (Ref: Va. Gen. by Hayden, pp 156-
   534 and Adv. of Purse and Person, Jester and Hiden, p.
   331 (of whom more later).

2. ELIZABETH WAUGH, daughter of Rev. John and Elizabeth
   Waugh.....

3. SARAH TALIAFERRO, daughter of Francis Taliaferro and
   Elizabeth Catlett, his wife.....

   CHILDREN OF FIRST WIFE: (not necessarily in order) -

- ANNE FOWKE MASON   m (1st) William Darrell-(2nd) Thomas
                        (3rd) Thomas Smith....   Fitzhugh

- MARY MASON   m (1st) George Fitzhugh-(2nd) Major
                                                 Benjamin
                                                 Strother

- COLONEL GEORGE MASON^3 (1690-1735) removed to Maryland.....

- NICHOLSON MASON   died 1716.....dsp.....

- FRENCH MASON, SR.   died testate 1748.....client's ancestor..

6.	ELIZABETH MASON	no data.....

7. SEMPHER ROSE MASON   (1703-1761) m (1st) Major John Dinwiddi
                                      (2nd) Col. Jeremiah Brono
                                                            Jr

CHILD OF SECOND WIFE:

8. CATHARINE MASON   (1707-1750) m John Mercer, Esq.
                                    (10 children)

CHILDREN OF THIRD WIFE:

9. FRANCIS MASON   dsp

10. THOMAS MASON   dsp

11. SARAH MASON   m Thomas Brooke "of Maryland".....

2
COLONEL GEORGE MASON (EIGHTH GENERATION)..........

Fairfax County, Virginia Land Causes # 1 -(1812-1832)-page 13 et

10 May 1742 - Indenture in which Thomas Brooke, of St. Mary's
County, Maryland, Gent., sells to Robert Boggess, of Prince
William County, Province (sic) of Virginia.....for (lease 5 sh;
release ₤71).....a tract of land on the southwest side of POHICK
RUN, in the County of Prince William....containing 320 acres,
being part of a larger tract containing 2,550 acres granted by
patent to Richard Normansel, of the County of Stafford, Gent.,
and sold by him to Martin Scarlet, who sold the aforementioned
320 acres to Michael Vanlandigan, of the County of Stafford on
the 6th of February 1692, bounded upon one moiety of the said
patent formerly sold by the said Martin Scarlet to CAPTAIN GEORG
MASON 10 March 1690/1.....and the said Michael Vanlandigan (sic)
afterwards sold the said 320 acres to the said GEORGE MASON, whi
the said GEORGE MASON, afterwards, by his last Will and Testamer
dated 29 January 1715, did devise the said 320 acres to his son,
THOMAS MASON, which said Thomas Mason, being since then dead,
without any heirs begotten of his body or making any Will and th
said 320 acres is now legally descended to SARAH, the wife of
the above mentioned Thomas Brooke, the only surviving sister and
heir OF THE WHOLE BLOOD to the said Thomas Mason.....Witnesses:
Henry Threlkeld - Richard Osborne - Baxter Davis.....Recorded
24 May 1742 in Prince William County Court.....

VIRGINIA COLONIAL MILITIA, by Crozier, page 106 -

    VIRGINIA MILITIA OFFICERS - 1699

GEORGE MASON - Lieutenant-Colonel and Commander in Chief.....
           Stafford County, Virginia.....

COLONIAL VIRGINIA REGISTER, by W. G. Stanard, pp 91,94,95,102,103-

    MEMBERS OF THE HOUSE OF BURGESSES - STAFFORD COUNTY

        1696 - GEORGE MASON

        1701-02 - GEORGE MASON

OPR by King, pages 180-181.

9 March 1692 - George Mason, High Sheriff of Stafford County......

1698 - Militia Officers of Stafford County....Major George Mason..

19 October 1699 - GEORGE MASON, Churchwarden of Stafford Parish...

1702-1703 - Justices of Stafford County....COLONEL GEORGE MASON...

17 June 1703 - List of Militia for Stafford County, Virginia,
           certified to Her Majesty, Queen Anne, among the
           field officers named........"COLONEL GEORGE MASON".

Ibid, page 178 -

Notation that Captain Martin Scarlett and COLONEL GEORGE MASON
16..-1716) were members of the House of Burgesses in 1691 for
Stafford County and again in 1695.....

THE VIRGINIA GENEALOGIST, Vol. 3 - (1959) - page 58 -

This is an account of Major John Dinwiddie, by George H. S. King
In which is stated that COLONEL GEORGE MASON (died 1716) married

(1st) MARY FOWKE, DAUGHTER OF COLONEL GERARD FOWKE AND ANNE
THOROWGOOD, HIS WIFE and quotes as his references (1) Virginia
Genealogies by Horace E. Hayden, pp 156, 534 and (2) Adventurers
of Purse and Person, by Jester and Hiden (1956), page 331.......

FOWKE - THOROWGOOD EXCURSUS:

Life of George Mason (1725-1792) by Kate Mason Rowland (N.Y.1892)
(2 vols).....Vol. 1, pages 2, 3...........(brief excerpts)........

  COLONEL GERARD FOWKE, the emigrant, is stated to have been
"of Brewood Hall and Gunston" in Staffordshire, England. The
account contains much of earlier interest of the family to about
1403 A.D. and has many footnote references. Volume 2, page 475
(Appendix) has the description of the coat-of-arms of FOWKES OF
GUNSTON, STAFFORDSHIRE and also of MASON OF STRATFORD-UPON-AVON,
WARWICKSHIRE.

Ibid, page 29 -
                2
  States that COLONEL GEORGE MASON [2] (d 1716) married (1st)
MARY FOWKE, prior to 1694, WHO WAS THE DAUGHTER OF GERARD FOWKE,
THE SECOND OF THE NAME IN VIRGINIA, who removed and settled in
Charles County, Maryland where he built a substantial mansion
which he called "Gunston Hall". The children of this marriage
are named as in our chart (supra) and states further that "of the
sons of Colonel George Mason, only two, George and French Mason[3]
married and left descendants".

  Adventurers of Purse and Person (1956) by Jester and Hiden,
page 329 et seq, has an authoritative account of the descendants
of CAPTAIN ADAM THOROWGOOD[1] (d 1640) who came to Virginia 1621
in "The Charles" which includes his daughter, ANNE THOROWGOOD[2]
who married (1st) Job Chandler, of Portoback (Port Tobacco) Maryland and (2ndly) GERARD FOWKE, OF CHARLES COUNTY, MARYLAND. Another well written and well documented account of the descendants of Captain Adam Thorowgood has recently appeared in the Virginia Genealogist, Vol 16 (1972) written by Mrs. Phyllis W. Fran
cis, of Williamsburg, Virginia, which this writer extols and re-
commends.

  The only copy of the Will of Captain Adam Thorowgood[1] (now
lost) appeared in the Richmond Standard, 26 November 1881 and wa
dated 17 February 1639/40 and ordered to record 17th April 1640.

His wife, SARAH, and his children are briefly rendered here as:

1. ADAM (underage) m. ca 1655 - Frances Yeardley, daughter of Argall.

2. ANN (under 16) m. (1) Job Chandler; (2) GERARD FOWKES

3. SARAH (under 16) m. Simon Oversee

4. ELIZABETH (under 16) m. Captain John Michaels

His wife was appointed by him "sole executrix and guardian" and he named as "overseers" of his will, his well beloved friends, Captain Thomas Willoughbie and Mr. Henry Seawell here in Virginia and "MY DEARLY BELOVED BROTHER, SIR JOHN THOROWGOOD, OF KINSINGTON, NEAR LONDON" and MR. ALEXANDER HARRIS, "MY WIFE'S UNCLE" LIVING ON TOWER HILL. This account continues with the evidence that his widow, (NEE OFFLEY) married (2ndly) by 2 May 1641, Captain John Gookins, Gent., (d 1643) and (3rdly) Colonel Francis Yeardley. She died August 1657 (tombstone record).

The children of ANNE THOROWGOOD[2] (Chandler-Fowke) are listed as: WILLIAM CHANDLER   GERARD FOWKE

RICHARD CHANDLER   MARY FOWKE

ANNE CHANDLER   ELIZABETH FOWKE

Reference should also be made to the several patents in Cavaliers and Pioneers, by Neil Nugent, the first being to THOMAS FOWKES, GENT., who names himself and GERARD FOWKES in his list of headrights. This land was later re-patented or renewed by GERARD FOWKES "HEIR OF THOMAS FOWKES" but whether as "son" - "brother" or "nephew" is not known to this writer.

[1]
COLONEL GEORGE MASON (NINTH GENERATION)..........

Life of George Mason (1725-1792) by Kate Mason Rowland (N.Y.1892) 2 volumes....."E 302 6 M45 R8".....Vol. 1, pages indexed........

This source is, of course, concerned primarily with "GEORGE MASON OF GUNSTON HALL", author of The Bill of Rights and one of our greatest Revolutionary War patriots.

There is entirely too much in this account concerning COL-
ONEL GEORGE MASON[1], his emigrant ancestor, to be able to trans-
cribe at this time and so we will touch lightly upon only the
essential and most noteworthy details or items. (pages 1 thru 16)

There is mention of a copy of an old (family) paper dated
1793 by George Mason "of Lexington" concerning the subject emigrant which states that he was a royalist refugee who commanded
a troop of horse at the Battle of Worcester and escaping from
this fatal field, disguised himself and was concealed until he
could find embarquation to America. The account states further
that he was born in Staffordshire and was of the family of
"MASONS" of Stratford-Upon-Avon, in Warwickshire. The account
continues that his first record in Virginia is a patent he received (for 950 acres) in Westmoreland County (later fell in
Northumberland County) dated March 1655. In a deed of Sale of
Land in 1658, his wife, MARY, gave her consent and her maiden
name is thought to have been "FRENCH" but is not proven.

In this earliest period he was generally called "Captain"...
in 1670 he is called "Major" and held the office of Sheriff of
Stafford County, Virginia.....he was Clerk of Court of Stafford
County in 1673 and County Lieutenant of Stafford 1673-1675 which
is the highest office in the County and entitled him to the rank
of Colonel of Militia and a seat on the Council.....he was electe
Burgess for Stafford County in 1675 and probably died in 1686 as
a Will of this date was in Stafford County as late as 1840 but
is now lost or destroyed.

VIRGINIA COLONIAL MILITIA, by Crozier, page 105 -

MILITARY OFFICERS IN VIRGINIA - 1680

COLONEL GEORGE MASON = STAFFORD COUNTY

COLONIAL VIRGINIA REGISTER, by W. G. Stanard, page 81 -

MEMBERS OF HOUSE OF BURGESSES

1676 - GEORGE MASON - STAFFORD COUNTY

RECOMMENDED READING:

OPR by King, page 171 - "A HISTORICAL SKETCH" - 23 March 1662 -

Concerns a charge of high treason and murder against Wahanganoche, King of the Potomac Indians (which was dismissed).....
evidence found in the trial that Captain Giles Brent - COLONEL GERRARD FOWKE - CAPTAIN GEORGE MASON - Mr. John Lord had done the King of the Potomacs many injustices, injuries and affronts and they were ordered to pay him various tributes and to give bond for their good behavior.....etc.....The original trouble seems to have been caused by the murder of several Englishmen by the Indians.....etc.....The Indian King died on his way home from the trial and shortly thereafter all the Potomac tribe of Indians seem to have vanished.....This "Historical Sketch" continues with an account of Colonel George Mason[1] (1628-1686) who was among the "Cavaliers" who settled in Stafford County, Virginia and which contains interesting details concerning him and his son, Colonel George Mason[2] (died 1716).....

SECTION FIVE

General Index............................... page 108

SPECIAL NOTE:
        The following index does _not_ include the
list of French Huguenots in Section Two, pages 58 and
59, which have been exhibited in alphabetical order.

108.

GENERAL INDEX

ADAMS
Rebon 10
Robert 10

ADDAMS
Christian 62

ADKISSON
Ellis 80
Nancy (Prather) 80

AKIN
Joseph 12

ALABAMA 10,35,38,46
70,71,72,73
ALEXANDER
Sarah (Godwin) 31
William 1,8
William J. 31

ALLEN
Aaron 38
Abraham 12
Benjamin 38
David 9
Drury 9,10
Elizabeth 9,10
George 12
James 38
James, Jr. 18
John Tyler 18
Joseph 18
Richard 56
Robert 8
Samuel 17
William 9

ALLISON
John 37
Polly (Frame) 37

ANDERSON
Aleanah 34
John 33,34
John, Sr. 33
Nelson 33
Sarah 33

ARMSTRONG
Elizabeth 11

ARTHUR
Barnabas 2,17
Barnard 2
Martha, Sr. 2
Martha, Jr. 2
Matthew 2
Sarah 1,2
Talbot 2
Thomas 1
William 2,17

ATHORNE
Robert 62

AVANT (AVENT)
Col. David A. 64
Isham 30
John, Jr. 29
John, Sr. 29
Peter 30
Sarah 29
Thomas 29,30
Thomas, Jr. 30
William 29,30

BABER
Robert 16

BACON
Francis 62
Lydall 10

BAITES
Isaac 62
Rachell 62

BALL
Gerrard 17
James 50
Martha 52
Mary 52
Mary (Brown) 50
William 52

BALEY (see BAYLEY)
James 4,17
John 4,17
Vincent Smith 4,17

BALLARD
  Amos   40
  Byrom   3
  Delilah (Dilly)   77
  William   3

BARBER
  Ann N.   35
  Bernard   35
  Edward   35
  Elias   35
  Enoch   35
  Jane   35
  Margaret E.   35
  Pamela   35
  Sarah   35
  William   35

BARKER
  Jethrow   57
  Mary (Janney)   49
  William   1,49

BARKSDALE
  Daniel, Jr.   23
  Daniel, Sr.   23
  (Daughter)   23
  Joseph   23
  Katy   23
  Polly   23

BARNES
  Jacob   29
  Joshua   29

BARR
  John   41
  Zachariah   41

BARTLET
  Anthony   23
  Barksdale   23

BARTON
  Edward   36

BASS
  Peter   19

BAYLEY (see BALEY)
  Abraham   62

BEARDEN
  John   70
  Lettice   70
  Mourning   70

BEASLEY
  Betty   11
  Robert   10,11
  William   11

BECKWITH
  William E.   33

BEDSAL(L) - (BEDSAUL)
  Elisha   39,40

BEDWELL
  Elisha   39
  Mary   39
  Mourning   39

BELL
  Joseph   37

BENNETT
  John   61,63

BENSON
  William   60

BICKERS
  William   26

BINKS
  Jacob   2,3

BLACK
  Samuel   42

BLACKMORE
  George   4,62
  Gideon, Sr.   4
  Gideon, Jr.   4
  Mrs.   4
  Samuel   4,61
  William   4,61
  William, Jr.   4

BLACKERBY
  Caty   41
  William   41

BLAND
  John   63
  Mrs. Sarah   63
  William   34

BLEDSOE
  Col. Lewis   75

BLUNT
  John   7
  Mary (Person)   7
  Priscilla   7
  William   7
  William, Sr.   7

BOGGESS
  Robert   47,93,102

BOND
  Francis   28
  Robert   27,28

BOOKS
  James   44

BONSACK
  Jacob   31

BOON
  Francis   5

BOTT
  Joel   83
  Lucy Ann   83

BOTTOM
  Thomas   63

BOWEN
  Hannah   42
  Jacob   43
  Jane   43
  John   42,43
  Margaret   43
  Priscilla   43
  William   6

BOWL (?)
  Margaret (Bowen)   43

BOYD
  David   4,17

BRADFORD
  Enoch   37

BRADLEY
  William   39

BRAGG
  Hugh   8

BRAXTON
  Carter   17
  Elizabeth   17

BREATHETT
  John   12

BRENT
  Capt. Giles   107

BRETT
  George   34,35
  Henry   34,35
  John   35
  Richard   34
  Sarah   34
  Tabitha   34

BRIDGES
  John   56

BRIGGS
  David   14

BRIZENDINE
  Isaac   9

BROCK(S)
  George   45
  John   62

BRODHURST
  Walter   1

BRONAUGH
  Jeremiah   93
  Col. Jeremiah   102
  Sempher Rose   102

BROOKE(S)
  Elisha   9
  John   9
  Sarah (Mason)   47,102
  Thomas   47,102

BROWN(E)
  Andrew D.   32
  Ann B.   21
  Ermine   21

BROWN(E)-con't.
Esther	52
Hannah	52,53
Henry	52
Isaac, Jr.	54
Jane	32
Dr. Jesse	6
John	21,22,51,52,61,62
Lucretia	6
Martha (Ball)	52
Mary	50
Mary I.	21
Mrs. Mary R.	51
Sarah B.	54

BUCE
Ruth (Smith)	71

BUCHLEY
John	12

BUCKINGHAM
Isaac	42
John	43

BULLITT
Cuthbert	34

BURCHER
Thomas	63

BURDETT
Joshua	37

BURDYNE
Agnes	27
Amos	27
Benjamin	27
Betty	27
Catharine	27
John	26,27
Nancy	27
Nathaniel	26
Reginal	26
Samuel	26
Sarah	27
Susanna	27

BURSON
Benjamin	50
George	50
Hannah Y.	50
Sarah	50,54

BUSTER
Claudius	74

BUTLER
Eliab C.	32
Eliah Cooper	33
Elizabeth	33
Eugenia	32
Fanny	33
Frances	33
Henry G.	33
James W.	32
John	32,33
Nathaniel B.	32,33
Susan M.	33
William C. B.	32,33
William H.	32,33

BYRD
John	62

CABELL
Henry	62
Capt. Samuel	65,66
William	17

CADWALADER
Jane D.	55

CALLAGHAN
Elvera (Wiley)	24,84
Oliver	24,84,85

CALVERT
Bassett M.	38
Frances (Hill)	38

CAMMELL
John	61

CANBY
Ann S.	53
Elizabeth H.	50
Samuel	50,53

CANIDA
Edward L.	72

112.

CANNON
    William   3

CARMALT
    Mrs. Anne   35,36
    Bridget   36
    Henry   36
    John   35

CARTER
    Ann (Bowen)   43
    Charlotte   46
    James   42
    John   1
    Landon   3
    Robert   1

CARWILE
    Zacheus   38

CARY
    Anna (Hill)   38
    Miles   38

CASE
    Margaret   62

CATLETT
    Elizabeth   100,101

CHANDLER
    Anne   104,105
    Anne (Thorowgood)
         104,105
    Job   104
    Richard   105
    William   105

CHAPMAN
    Catharine B.   27
    Constant   27
    George   27
    Nathaniel   27
    Thomas   36
    Thomas, Jr.   36
    William   26,27

CHEATHAM
    Thomas   20,21

CHEOWS (?)
    John   61

CHEW
    John   23
    Mary (Winslow)   24

CHICHESTER
    Daniel McCarty   91
    Doddridge Pitt   91
    George   91

CHUEGE
    Ann   62

CLANTON
    Joseph   22

CLARK(E)
    Christopher   43
    George   10
    John   2
    Mary   54

CLAY
    Francis   1

COCKRELL
    Thompson   16

COFFEE
    John   54
    Rachel P.   54

COFFER (COFER)
    John   37,91

COIN (COAN)
    Joseph   36

COLE
    Elizabeth   34
    James   15

COLEMAN
    Capt. Francis   23
    Robert S.   24

COLVER
    Thomas   42

COLVIN
    John   9

COMPTON
    Caleb   80

CONNARD
Jane (Potts) 49
Jonathan 49
Sarah 49

CONNER
Jonathan 5

CONWAY
Peter 18

COOK
Elizabeth P. 28
William 12,28

COOMES
Epher 62

CORDELL
Martha 57

CORNUTT
John 39
Mourning B. 39
William 39

CORNWALLIS
Lord 76

COULTER
Joseph S. 68,69

COUTS
Amos 79

CRABB
Mr. 63

CRADDOCK
William 13

CRAMMER
Andres 54
Hannah 54

CRAWFORD
Eleanor 25
Jane 25
Jenet (Mason) 25
Margaret 25
Mary 25
Mason 25

CRAWFORD (con't.)
Samuel, Sr. 25
Samuel, Jr. 25
Sarah 25
W. L. 44
William 25

CRISP
Christopher 62

CRUTCHFIELD
Achilles 23
Agatha 23
Jane 23
John 23
Mary 23
Robert 23
Stapleton 23
Stapleton, Jr. 23
Sarah 23
Thomas 23

CUMBO
John 30

CUMMINS
Jacob 39

CUNNINGHAM
Ann 23
Mrs. Ann (Elley) 22
Elizabeth 23
George 23
Henry 23
James 23
Nelly 23
William 23

CURLE
Archibald 1

CURRIN
George 40

DANIEL(L)
Christopher 24
Daniel Mack 61
Hannah S. 51
James 51
Jane 55
John 56
Mary 52
William 51

DARRELL
Anne F. (Mason)100,101
William 95,100,101

DAVIS
Baxter 47,102
William 4,34,61

DAVISON
Golden 36

DAWSON
Ann 62
John 7

DeHART
Elijah 8
John 8
John S. 8
Zephaniah 8

DENNIS
(Daughter?) 39
Richard, Sr. 39
Robert 56

DeVEESE
Bartley 6
Cornelius 6
Mrs. 6
Mary 6
William 6

DEVEN
William 12

DeWEESE
Hannah 5
Henry 5
Jesse 5
Mary (Lowder) 5
Paul 5
Thomas 5
William 5

DICKEN
Ephraim 26
John 27
Joseph 27

DICKENSON
John 3

DICKERSON
Francis 3

DIKES
Margaret 60

DILLARD
John 30

DINWIDDIE
Maj. John 102,103
Sempher Rose 102

DOBSON
Isabella 62

DOBY
John 30

DODD
Sarah (Sample) 49
Thomas 49

DODSON
Rawley 44
William 19

DONALDSON
Mrs. Ann (Mason) 92,94
William 92,93,94

DOUGHERTY
Michael 20

DOYLE
Elizabeth 60
John 60

DRAYTON
John 62
John, Jr. 62

DROWNWELL
Margaret 62

DUFFEY
Sarah 35

DULANY
    Nancy   89
    William   89

DUNLOP
    Ann   48
    James   48
    Joseph M. 48
    Lizzie S. 48

DUTTON
    Emma S.   48
    John B.   48
    Lizzie S. 48

EASTON
    Jean   41
    John   41

EBLEN
    Eliza   49
    John   49
    Mary   49

ECHOLS
    Abner   36

EDGAR
    James   25
    Mary (Mason) 25

EDINS
    Benjamin   4

ELEXANDER
    (see ALEXANDER)

ELLEY
    Ann   23
    Edward   23

ELLIOTT
    Edward   5
    Elizabeth 5

ELMORE
    John A.   45

EMMORSON
    (?)   12

ENGLAND
    ·   1,4,42,62,63
    104,105,106

EPPES
    Francis   56

ETHRIDGE
    William   62

EVERETT
    Elizabeth 50

EVERITT
    Anna   51

EWELL
    Captain   80

EZZEL
    Lucy (Smith) 68

FAIRFAX
    Lord Thomas 27

FANT
    Jane (Barber) 35
    John B.   35

FARES
    James   12

FARGUSON
    Isaac   8

FARLEY
    Daniel   40
    Joseph   40
    Martha   40
    Mary   40
    Mathew   40
    Seth   11
    William 40

FARMER
    James   20
    Permelia 20
    Sarah   20
    Thomas   20

FAWVER (FAWBER)
    Joseph   37
    Valentine 37

FINLY
    John   56

FINTCH
    William 63

FISHER
  John   57

FITZGERALD
  Harvey   36

FITZHUGH
  Anne F. (Mason)100,101
  George   95,101
  Mary (Mason)   100,101
  Thomas   100,101

FITZPATRICK
  Jane (Bowen)   43

FLANAGAN
  William   67

FLEET
  John   46
  Lucy   46

FLOWERS
  Arthur   29
  Edward   29
  Elizabeth   29
  Henry   29
  Jacob   29

FORD
  Benjamin   26
  Charles F.   32
  James   26
  John   26
  John, Jr.   26
  Nancy   26
  Rosanna   26
  William Pannell   26

FOSTER
  Sally (Smith)   68

FOWKE
  Anne (Thorowgood) 101
                 104,105
  Elizabeth   105
  Col. Gerard   101,104
                 105,107
  Mary   101,104,105
  Thomas   105

FOX
  Joseph   65
  Richard   65

FRAME (FREAM)
  Ann   37
  Mrs. Ann   37
  Archibald   37
  Elizabeth   37
  John   37
  Margaret   37
  Polly   37
  Rachel   37

FRANCIS
  Phyllis W.   104

FRENCH
  Daniel   15

FRENCH HUGUENOTS
                           58,59

FROST
  John   42
  William   63

FRY
  Wesley   26

FUQUIA
  Dr. F.   37

FUSON
  William   36

GADDY
  Benjamin   4

GAINS
  Katy (Barksdale)   23

GAMMON
  Florence   82
  Mathew H.   82
  Sarah C. W.   82

GARLAND
  Capt. James   74

GARRIS
  Arthur   6

GATEWOOD
  Capt. William   76

GEERS
Sarah (Moon) 21
William H. 21

GENTRY
Allen 9
David 9
William 9

GEORGE
James 12
John 12

GEORGIA 2,10,11,17,18
36,44,64,67,68
69,71,73,75,81

GIBSON
Lydia L. 51
Moses 51
Rebeckah 49

GILBERT
Francis 4,17
William 4,17

GILLS
Mary 11
William 11

GILMORE
Mary 79

GLADEN
Jonathan 62

GLENN
Colonel 77
John 11
Tyree 9

GLOVER
William 42

GODWIN
Charlotte 31
Eliza 31
Harriet 31
James, Sr. 31
James, Jr. 31
James A. 31
Jane 31

GODWIN (con't.)
John 31
John M. 31
Martha M. 31
Rebecca R. Jane 31
Sarah J. 31
Thomas G. 31

GOOCH
Thomas 1

GOODSON
Edward 29

GOOKINS
Capt. John 105
Sarah (Offley) 105

GORE
Phebe 52

GOVER
Jesse 48
Miriam 48
Samuel 55
Sarah H. 48
Sarah J. 55

GRAHAM
Ann 37
David 1
George 18
John 1
Priscilla 18
Robert 20
William 18,37

GRAUNT
Ann 63

GRAYSON
Ben 93

GREEN(E)
Rev. Charles 93
General 68,81
William 42

GREGG
Abner 53
Amey 49
Elisha 51

118.

GREGG (con't.)
Elizabeth	51,53
George	51,53
Hannah	50
Hannah S.	51
John	34,51,53
Margaret T.	53
Martha L.	51
Rebeckah	49
Sarah S.	53
Thomas	49
William	49

GREGORY
| Susannah (Smith) | 68 |

GRENDON
| Thomas | 62 |

GRESHAM
Emma F.	45,46
James A.	45,46
Joseph D.	45,46
Lida V.	45,46
Mary E.	46
Richard Hugh	46

GRIFFITH
| Samuel | 4,17 |

GRIMES
| Aminta (Mason) | 87,94 |

GRISSON
| Barbara | 26 |
| John | 26 |

GROVES (?)
| John | 14 |
| Mary (Waln) | 14 |

GUILIMAN
| George | 56 |

HACKNEY
Aaron	50
Benjamin	19
Hannah (Gregg)	50
James	19

HAGGARD
| Richard | 9 |

HAGUE
Francis	51
Jane S.	51
Pleasant	51
Samuel	51
(See HOGUE)

HAILE (HAYLE)
| Nicholas | 16 |
| Ruth | 16 |

HAINES
| Elizabeth R. | 54 |
| Simeon | 54 |

HALL
David	12
Elisha	23
George	17
John	36
Judith	12
Robert	36

HAMMOND
| Emma (Scott) | 86 |

HAMPTON
| Noah | 41 |

HANBY
| David, Jr. | 36 |

HANCKS
Abram	19
James	19
Thomas	19

HANCOCK
Anne	34
Anne (Jr.)	34
John	34
John, Jr.	34
Major	11,12
Mary (page)	12
Scarlet	34

HANDBY
| Capt. Thomas | 81 |

HARDING		
Cyrus	41	
Hopkins	41	
HARKER		
Mark	56	
HARRIS		
Alexander	105	
Elizabeth H.	50	
Jesse	39	
William	50	
HARRISON		
John	63	
HARVIE		
Richard	17	
HATCHER		
George	52	
Mary (McGray)	53	
Prudence W.	52	
Rebeckah N.	50	
Thomas	50	
William, Jr.	53	
HATON (HAYTON)		
John	41,42	
Thomas	42	
HATTON		
William	5	
HAYDEN (HAYDON)		
George	41	
Rev. Horace E.	99,101 104	
Jesse	23	
HAYNES		
"E"	7	
Henry	3	
Thomas	27	
HAY(S)		
Captain	23	
Gilbert	30	
HAZZLEWOOD		
Elizabeth	37	
Fleming	37	
John	37	

HAZZLEWOOD (con't.)		
Joshua	37	
Patsy	37	
Sabra	37	
William	37	
HEATH		
William	16	
HEATON		
Hannah (Bowen)	42,43	
H. B.	42	
Hiram	42	
Jacob B.	43	
Rachel	43	
Robert	42	
HEDGEPATH		
John	62	
HENDERSON		
Alexander	33	
Thomas	12,43,44	
HENDRICKS		
Lt. Col. James	66	
HENRY		
Charles L.	69	
HERNDON		
Doctor A.	13	
Edward	23	
Joseph	13,23	
HIGGENBOTHAM		
James	17,44	
Samuel	44	
Thomas	17	
HILL(S)		
Abram	37	
Anna	38	
Charles	56	
Frances	38	
Francis	38	
Rev. Francis	38	
Harriott	38	
Patrick H.	38	
Patsy H.	37	
Priscilla B.	43	
Rees	42,43	
Mrs. Sally	38	
William	62	

HIRST (HURST)
   Sarah   54

HITE
   Jacob   14,42

HODGES
   Johnson   11
   Moses   12

HOGE
   Mrs. Ann   54
   Elizabeth N.   54
   Isaac   54
   Solomon   54

HOGUE
   Francis   51,52
   Sarah   52
   Sarah W.   51
   Thomas   51
(See HAGUE)

HOLLINGSWORTH
   George   42
   Lydia   50

HOLMES
   Elizabeth   50
   Mary   52,53
   Rachel   53
   William   53

HOLT
   William   38

HOOKE
   William   5

HOPWOOD
   William   12

HORE
   Ann   78
   Edward   78

HOTZENBELLA
   Barbara   13
   Jacob   13
   Stephen   13,14

HOUGH
   Ann S.   54
   Elizabeth   50
   John   54
   John, Jr.   50

HOUGH (con't.)
   Lydia H.   50
   Mahlon   54
   Mary S.   54
   Samuel   54

HOWARD
   James   23

HUBBARD
   Elizabeth   66

HUDMAN
   John   95

HUDSON
   Hall   36
   John   10
   Joshua   36

HUFF
   James C.   31
   Jane (Godwin)   31

HUGHES
   Elizabeth   52
   Matthew   52
   Robert   2
   Sarah S.   52
   Thomas   52

HUGUENOTS
   French   58,59

HULL
   George   4

HEMPHREY
   Evan   61
   Sanford   35

HUNDLEY
   Joshua   40
   Mary (Farley)   40

HURST
   "W"   19

HURT
   Elisha   3

HUTTON
   Joseph   49
   Sarah (Janney)   49

INDIANA
48,76,77

INMAN
John, Sr.   6

IRELAND
63,73

IRELAND
Jane   75

ISH
John   33

JACKMAN
Richard   37

JACKSON
Julius Augt   17
Richard   56

JAMES
Thomas   92,95

JANNEY
Abel   49,50
Hannah   51
Hannah (Brown)   52
Isreal   51
Jacob   51
Joseph, Jr.   52
Mary   49,50
Mary (Holmes)   52
Pleasant H.   51
Rachel   49
Sarah   49,55
Stacy   52

JARILSONES
Richard   23

JARROLD
Isham   15

JEFFERS
(See Jeffries)

JEFFRIES (JEFFREYS)
Alexander   78
Andrew   77
Anne (Hore)   78
Celia   78
Delilah (Ballard) 77
Eaton   77

JEFFRIES (con't.)
Francis M.   78
John   76,77,78
Nancy   78
Reuben   78
Thomas   77
William   78

JENKINS
Allen   56
Anna   32,33
Benjamin   33
Elisha, Sr.   32,33
Elisha, Jr.   32
Lewis   33
Richard H.   33
Susan   33
Travis   33

JOHNS
William   56

JOHNSON
Alice T.   16
Benjamin   16
Benjamin, Jr.   29
Elizabeth   16
George   22
Henry   22
James   17
Margaret   16
Mary   16
Philip B.   16
Richard   29
Sibran   62
Major Thomas   22
Thornton F.   16
William   16

JONES
Allen   7
Benjamin   8
Celia (Jeffries) 78
George   40
James   7
Rodham   78
Willie   7

JORDAN (JORDEN)
Edward   63
Elijah   71
Thomas P.   8
(See JOURDAN)

122.

JOSEPH
    William   30

JOURDAN
    Celia (Smith)   71

KEBSSALL
    John   62

KEEFE
    Edward   15

KEEN
    Elizabeth   5

KELLY
    John   5

KENDRICK
    Leonard   14
    Mary (Waln)   14

KENTUCKY
    1,3,5,12,13,15,16,19
    22,23,24,25,26,27,33
    39,40,41,46,72,79,80
    85

KERBY
    Ann   13
    Richard   13

KERR
    John   4

KINCHLOE
    Daniel B.   32

KING
    George H. S.99,103,107
    John   62

KINZEY
    Ben   8
    Benjamin   8

KISER
    Daniel C.   31

KNOTT
    James   10
    Richard   10

LAFFERTY
    Patrick   2
    Prudence (Binks)   2

LAMBERT
    William   56,62

LANE
    Simon   30

LANIER
    Capt. David   68

LANKFORD
    Ben   12

LAWSON
    Jacob   36
    Marmaduke   34

LEAKE
    John M.   11
    Josiah   11

LEE
    Charity   73

LEFTWICH
    Thomas   43

LEONARD
    Lydia   51

LEWELLING
    Jesse   13
    Susannah   13
    Thomas   13

LEWIS
    James   23
    William   62

LIGON
    Littleberry N.   65

LINDSEY
    Abraham   3
    James   3
    John, Jr.   3

LINTON
    Moses   34

LIPSCOMB
    Jane (Crutchfield)   23
    Thomas   23

LITTLEFIELD
 Mr. Arthur Nelson 82
 Mrs. Arthur Nelson 82

LOCKHART
 Elizabeth (Waln) 14
 Randal 14

LONG
 John 5,54
 Mary C. 54

LORD
 John 107

LOVETT
 Daniel 51
 Ezabella 28
 John 28
 Lancaster 28
 Martha 51

LOWDER
 Jacob 5
 Mary 5

LOWE
 Richard 4,17
 Sarah (Smith) 65
 William 65

LUCK
 Mrs. Lucy Ann 83
 William H. 83

LUCKY
 Joseph 13

LUKE
 Hannah M. (Lupton) 48
 Richard 48

LUMFORD
 Seth 41

LUPTON
 Hannah M. 48
 Isaac 48
 Tamson 48

McBURNET
 Sarah (Smith) 71

McCAN
 Rev. James 83

McCARTY
 Daniel, Jr. 92

McCLANAHAN
 Col. Alexander 73,74
 Maj. Elijah 25

McCOLLOUGH
 John 41

McCUE
 Rev. John 37

McDANIEL
 (See DANIEL)

McDONAL
 John 9

McGINNIS
 John 45

McGRAY
 Mary 53

McKEACHEY
 Andrew 25
 James 25

McKEE
 Daniel 11

McKELROY
 James 2
 Lucy 2

MACHINNE
 Barnaby 28,29

MACKEY
 Thomas 19

MADDEN
 Moses 45

MADISON
 Thomas 18
 William 16

MAJOR
 Mary Ann 82

MALLORY
  Thomas   62
  Capt. Thomas   62

MARRIOTT
  James T.   79

MARTIN
  Amey   40
  George   40
  Hudson   74
  Jane   74
  John   40
  Samuel   75
  Thomas C.   28

MARYLAND
  4,5,14,16,17,27,34,35
  45,47,48,63,72,81,101
  102,104

MASON
  Aminta   87,88,89,91,94
  Ann D.   91,94
  Ann Fowke   100,101
  Catharine   82,85,87,88
            90,94,95,100
  David   29,30
  Elizabeth   95,102
  Elizabeth (Waugh)   100
  Francis 90,91,92,93,94
            95,101,102
  French 82,87,88,89,90
          91,92,93,94,95
          96,98,99,101,104
  French, Jr.87,88,89,90
            92,93,94,95
  George 36,87,88,89,90
          91,92,93,94,95
          96,101,102,104,106
  Capt. George 47,92,102
                106,107
  Col. George   82,87,88
          94,95,96,97,99,100
          101,102,103,104,105
                106,107
  Henry   30
  James   30
  Maj. James   25
  Janet   25
  Joseph   25
  Leanna   93,94
  Lucretia   93,94
  Mary   25,87,88,89,91
              94,100

MASON (con't.)
  Mary Ann Major   82
  Mary (Fowke)   100,101
  Margaret   25
  Nicholson   95,96,101
  Rosanna   93,94
  Sarah   47,95,100,101
                    102
  Simpher Rose   95,102
  Thomas   47,95,101,102
  William   25

MASSEY
  Charles   74
  Elizabeth   74
  John   26

MATHEWS
  Edward J.   48
  Mordecai   48
  Ruth   48
  Sarah H. (Gover) 48

MEADASON
  (See MADISON)

MELTON
  William   56

MERCER
  Ann (Roy)   100
  Catharine (Mason) 100
                    102
  John   95,100,102

MERIWETHER
  Thomas   22

MICHAELS
  Elizabeth T.   105
  Capt. John   105

MILBURN
  John   42

MILES
  John   56

MILLS
  John   60

MISSISSIPPI
                  32,35

MISSOURI
  8,31,32,45,46,72,73

MITCHELL
  Daniel   19
  James   33
  Judith (Prewit)   19
  Richard   44

MOFFETT
  John   37

MONTEITH
  Phillis   91
  Thomas   91,93

MOON
  Abner H.   20,21
  Alexander B.   21
  Gideon   21
  Jesse   20,21
  John   21
  Julia   20
  Juliana   20,21
  Lodowick   20
  Narcissa   20
  Permelia   20
  Pleasant   21
  Sarah   21

MOOR(E)
  Elizabeth   53
  James   53
  Phebe M.   53
  Reuben   45
  Thomas   53

MOORMAN
  Charles   3,43

MORE
  Sarah   34

MORGAN
  Col. Daniel   66
  David   6
  Rees   42

MORLAN
  Mary (Rhodes)   51
  Stephen   51
  William   51

MORRIS
  Sabra   38

MORRISON
  Joseph H.   44
  Mary (Walker)   44

MOSELEY
  Daniel   28
  Hillary   27
  Martha (Pettus)   28

MOSS
  Thomas   30

MULLINS
  John   19

MUSE
  Charles   19

MYERS
  Alice (Yates)   53
  Elijah   52
  Isaiah   53
  Jonathan   52
  Joseph   53
  Mary   52
  Mary (Ball)   52
  Phebe   53
  Sarah   49

MYRTLE
  Janny   26

NANCE
  David   42

NAVE
  Jacob   15

NEAL(E)
  Basel   81
  Lewis   49
  Lewis, Sr.   49
  Rachel (Janney)   49

NEAVILL
  George   37
  John   2,3

NELSON
  Agatha B. (Winslow)   24
  General   76

NELSON (con't.)
John   24

NEWCOMBE
Henry   63

NEWELL
Captain   80

NICHOLS (NICKOLS)
Elizabeth   54
Isaac   49
John   52
Margaret S.   52
Rebeckah   50
Rebeckah G.   49

NISWANGER
Elizabeth   45
Jacob   45
John   45
Susannah W.   45

NOEL
Mary (Crutchfield)   23
Richard   23

NORMANSEL
Richard   47,91,102

NORRIS
Benjamin E.   48
Sarah Ann (Stone)   48

NORTON
Edward   39
Gideon   39
Jamima   39
William   39

NORTH CAROLINA
3,5,6,7,8,9,12,13,15
16,17,18,19,20,26,27
28,29,30,33,34,36,37
38,44,46,67,71,72,73
75,76,77,79

NORVELL
Lidra   63

NUGENT
Nell   105

NUTT
Elizabeth T.   50
Jonathan   50

OFFLEY
Sarah   105

OHIO
                             14,77

OSBORNE
Richard   47,102

OVERSEE
Sarah T.   105
Simon   105

OWEN(S)
John C.   28
John, Sr.   33
Thomas   33

PAGE
Anderson   11,12
Fanny   11
Fanny (Williams)   12
James   11
Janey   12
Jesse   12
John   12
Leonard   12
Mary   12
Pleasant   12
Samuel   12
Samuel L.   12
William   11,12

PARKER
Alexander   19
Eliza (Eblen)   49
John   1
Joseph   49
Col. Josiah   79
Martha   49
Nicholas   49
Richard   24
Susanna (Winslow)   24
William   24

PARKS
Sam   12

PARRISH
Robert L.   86

PARROTT
  William   21

PARSONS
  (See Persons)

PATTASON
  Polly (Smith)   67

PATE
  Edward   25
  John   25
  Mary (Crawford) 25

PATRICK
  John   1

PAYNE
  John   44

PEARSON
  Mary (Gilmore) 79
  Parris   79

PENN
  Gabriel   17

PENNINGTON
  Kezia   3

PENNSYLVANIA
      1,42,43,48,69

PERSON
  Anthony   7
  Benjamin   6,7
  Colin   7
  Dorcas (Turner) 7
  Elizabeth   6
  Hannah   6
  Henry   6
  John   6,7
  John, Jr.   6,7
  Lucretia B.   6
  Mary   6,7
  Mary (Thorpe) 7
  Philip   7
  Presley   7
  Priscilla   6
  Sarah   6
  Thomas   6,7
  Turner   7
  William   6,7

PERRY
  Joseph   62
  Mathew   62

PETTICREW
  Matthew   85

PETTUS
  Elizabeth   28
  Jane   28
  John   28
  Martha   28
  Mary   28
  Rebecca   28
  Stephen   28
  Stephen, Jr. 28

PEYTON
  Henry   35
  Mary   35

PHILIPS
  Richard   13
  Uriah   37

PICKETT
  Martin   37

PICKLE
  Frederick 5

PIDGEON
  Rachel, Jr. 54

PIERCE
  Joseph   3

PLACE
  Rowland 62
  Thomas   62

PLEASANT
  John   56

POOL
  Ralph   63

POPE
  William 79

PORTER
  Mary (Pettus) 28
  Reizen   28

POSLEY
    Margaret   61

POTTS
    David   49
    Jane   49

POWD
    John   62
    William   62

PRATHER
    Nancy   80

PRATT'S   26

PRESTHOOD
    Ann   62

PRESTON
    Thomas   3
    William   28

PREWIT
    Judith   19

PRICE
    Eli M.   48
    Eliza Ann   48
    John   48
    Rice   17
    Susan M.   48

PRYOR
    Mrs. (?) (Dennis)   39
    John   39
    Thornton   38,39

PULEM
    Richard   62

PURVINE
    Lewis   28

QUARLES
    John   16

RAFFETH
    (See Rafferty)

RAFFERTY
    John   18
    Thomas   18

RAFFETY
    (See Rafferty)

RANDALL
    Elizabeth   54

RANSONE
    Henry   11

RAY(E)
    Francis   9
    Susanna   62

RAYLE
    James   60

REA
    Andrew   41
    James   40,41
    James, Sr.   41
    John   41
    Polly   40,41

REARDON
    William   92

REED
    Stephen   5

RENFRO (RENPHRO)
    (See Rentfro)

RENN
    Isaac F.   31
    John   31

RENTFRO
    Absalom   15
    James   15
    James, Jr.   15
    Joseph   15
    Moses   15
    William   15,16

REYNOLDS
    Charles   3
    Joseph   8
    Richard   8

RHODES (See Rodes)
Eliza (Godwin) 31
Frederick 31
Mary 51
Mrs. Mary 51

RICE
Lt. Nathaniel 80

RICHARDS
Edward 62

RICHARDSON
Benjamin 15
Col. Holt 76

RIDLEY
Day 7

RIGG
Richard 42

RIGHT (See Wright)
Joseph 30

RIVES
William 30

ROACH
Elizabeth G. 53
Hannah 53,54
James 53
Mary 53
Richard 53,54
Sarah 54

ROBERTS
John 40
"P" 40

ROBERTSON
John 37
Margaret (Frame) 37

ROBINSON
Benjamin 24
William 30

RODES (See Rhodes)
Charles

ROGERS
Mary R. 53
Owen 53

ROSS
Edward 57

ROTCHELL
Ralph 57

ROUTEN
Jean 2
John 2

ROWLAND
Kate Mason 104,105

ROY
Ann 100
Dr. Mungo 100

RUDISELL
John 65

RUSHON
Mathew 29

RUSSELL
Elizabeth 37
Jeremiah 37

RUST
John 17
Samuel 4,17
Youel 19

SAMPLE
Sarah 49

SANFORD
Elizabeth 5
Samuel 5

SCARLET(T)
Martin 47,91,95,102
Capt. Martin 103

SCHOOLEY
Elisha 53
Eliza Ann 48
Elizabeth 48
Hannah B. 53
John 52,53
Mahlon 48

SCHOOLEY (con't.)
Mary   52,53
Rachel H.   53
Sarah   52
Witham   53

SCOTT
Catharine   82,85,86
               87,88,94
Emma   86
Mary   22
Mary Ann   82,86
Sally C.   86
William   22,82,83,85
            86,87,88,94
William M.   86,88

SEAMON
Jonathan   42

SEAWELL
Henry   105

SESSOMS
Nicholas   60

SEVIER
Col. John   75
Capt. Valentine   75

SEYBOLD
Hannah   51,54
Jasper   51,54
John   54

SHADRICK
Thomas   19

SHANKE
David, Jr.   83

SHARP
Francis   6

SHAW
John   62

SHEEHORN
William   30

SHELTON
Ralph   36

SHENE
Ann   53

SHEPHERD
Samuel   28

SHIELDS
Joseph   37
Rachel (Frame)   37

SHORT
Joel   12

SHROPSHIRE
Joel   65

SHUARD
Jane   51

SIMPSON
French   91,92
Gilbert   91

SIMS
Reuben   78

SLAUGHTER
Colonel   78

SLEAD
Francis   57

SLEDGE
Charles   61

SMALLWOOD
Edward F.   46
Lucy (Fleet)   46
Margaret S.   46

SMITH
Aaron   70
Americus   69
Andrew   73
Ann   60
Anne F. (Mason) 100,101
Augustine   18,64,65,66
Austin   65,66
Celia   70,71,72
Charity (Lee)   73
Charles A.   74
Eber   70

131.

SMITH (con't.)

Elihu P.	70
Eliphas	70
Elizabeth	62,66
Elizabeth H.	66
Elizabeth S.	68
Elizabeth (Massey)	74
Evira (Jackson)	69
Humphrey	6
Isaac	70
James	20,71
Jesse	67
John	27,37,49,54
	62,65,66
John, Jr.	66
John Hannah	9
Dr. John Winn	18,70
Joseph	37
Judith	65
Lafayette	69
Lettice	70
Lewis	66
Lucy E.	68
Martha (Winn)	18
Mary	65,71
Mary (Daniel)	52
Mathew	18
Meredy	67,69
Mourning (Mrs.)	67,70
	72
Nicholas	60,71
Polly	67
Rachail	71
Ralph	70
Richard D. G.	73
Roley	37
Ruth	71
Sally	65,68
Samuel	52,73
Sarah	53,54,67,68,71
Sarah (Myers)	49
Susannah G.	68
Thomas	1,71,100,101
Thomas V.	68
Vines	68
William	53,64,67,68
	69,70,71,72
	73,74,75,76
William C.	75
William E.	68
William J.	72
William, Jr.	72
Capt. William	71,72
Maj. William	70,72

SMITHSON
Francis 10

SNAP
Joseph 14

SNIDER
Joseph 26

SNODGRASS
Joseph 25
Margaret (Mason) 25

SNUDGE
John 57

SNYDER
Harriet G. 31

SOUTH
Francis 56

SOUTH CAROLINA 2,3,7
11,15,20,21,26,39,45
67,68,69,70,74,75,76,81

SOUTHWORTH
Isaac 75

SPEAK
Robert 92

SPECK
Robert 90

SPENCER
Margaret 52

SPENSE
William 61,63

SPIECE
John B. 65

STABLER
Ann 54
Edward 54
Mary 54

STANDLEY
Elizabeth 48
William 48

STANLEY
    John   62

STEARMAN
    Thomas   18,19
    Valentine   19
    William   18,19

STEELE
    Thomas   45

STEER
    Anna E.   51
    Benjamin   51
    Hannah   51

STEPHEN(S)
    Adam   42
    General   77

STEPHENSON
    James   79

SREWART
    Charlotte (Carter)   46
    James   30
    Thomas   46

STODGEN
    Elizabeth (Smith)   68

STOKES
    Allen   8,10
    William   8

STONE
    Daniel   48
    Eleanor H.   48
    Eusebeous   3
    Sarah   48
    Sarah Ann   48

STOTT
    Archibald L.   46

STRATTON
    Henry   3

STREET
    Anthony   10

STRESHLY
    Elizabeth   16
    Henry   16

STRONG
    Joan   56
    Thomas   56
    William   63

STROTHER
    Maj. Benjamin   100,101
    Mary (Mason)   100,101

STUDART
    Joseph   30

STURMAN
    Mary   79,80
    William Walker   79,80

SULLIVAN
    Joseph   8

SWAN
    Jonathan   81

SWIFT
    Flower   40

SWITZER
    Elizabeth (Wolf)   14
    Jacob   14
    Philip   14
    Valentine   13,14

TACKETT
    Ann N. (Barber)   35
    Charles   35

TALBOT
    Isham   17
    John   16
    Leanna (Mason)   93,94
    Matthew   17

TALIAFERRO
    Lt. Benjamin   66
    Elizabeth (Catlett)
        100,101
    Francis   100,101
    Sarah   100,101

TATUM
    Edward   36

ATUM (con't.)
Jesse, Jr. 36
John 22
Nathaniel 26
Peter 22
Thomas 22

AYLOR
Colonel 65
John 41,79
Polly (Rea) 40,41

ENNESSEE 21,22,25
28,32,33,37,38,39,40
41,43,44,73,75,76,82

ERRELL
George P. 31
Harry 18
Capt. Henry 79
Joel 18

EXAS 73

HOMAS
Henry 7
John 26

HOMPSON
Israel 52
John 33
Sarah H. 52

HORP(E)
Dodson, Sr. 3,4
Mary 7
Peterson 7
Timothy 7

HORNHILL
Ezekle 43
Rachel 43
Sarah 43,44
William 43
William, Jr. 43,44

HOROWGOOD
Capt. Adam 104
Adam, Jr. 105
Ann(e) 101,104,105
Elizabeth 105
Frances Y. 105
Sarah (Offley) 105
Sir John 105

THREADGILL
Capt. Thomas 77

THRELKELD
Henry 47,102

THWEAT
John 38

TODHUNTER
Margaret 53

TOLIVER
Lt. Benjamin 65

TOMLINSON
Mrs. Mary 30

TREBBE
Elizabeth 50

TRENT
Captain 98

TRICE
Noah 79

TUCKER
Burwell 10
Hartwell 10
James 10
James Monroe 26
Jesse 10
John Thompson 26
Nancy 10
William Fontaine 26

TURLEY
James, Sr. 32

Turner
Dorcas 7
John 62
Simon 7

UNDERWOOD
Abraham 56

VANDEVAN
 John 57

VANDIVER
 Rev. Mathew 67

VANLANDIGAN
 Michael 47,102

VANNHAM
 Walter 56

VINSON
 Thomas 30

WAHANGANOCHE 107

WALKE
 Thomas 27,28

WALKER
 Charles 19
 Elizabeth 48
 Sarah 48
 William 48

WALLACE
 Gustavus B. 34

WALN
 Elenor 14
 Elizabeth 14
 Henry 14
 John 14
 Joseph 14
 Joshua 14
 Martha 14
 Mary 14
 Mrs. Mary 14
 Nancy 14
 William 14

WALTON
 Ann 62
 John 62
 Samuel 60

WARD
 Samuel 61

WASHINGTON
 Col. George 95,96

WATKINS
 Absalom 19
 Thomas 19
 Lt. William 81

WATSON
 Joseph 42

WATT
 James 28

WAUGH
 Elizabeth 100,101
 Capt. John 78
 Rev. John 100,101
 Joseph 95

WAYLAND
 Simeon B. 26
 Thomas B. 26

WEBB
 Jacob 15
 Capt. John 73

WELLOUGHBIE
 Capt. Thomas 105

WELLS
 Mary 45

WEST VIRGINIA-13,14,41,53

WHITACRE
 Caleb 52
 John 54
 Naomi 54
 Phebe (Gore) 52
 Robert 54
 Sarah R. 54

WHITE
 Daniel Basil 23
 John 4
 Capt. John 23
 Lovel 4
 Mary 23
 Polly (Barksdale) 23
 William 62

WHITEHEAD
 Beverley E. 10
 Mary Jane 10

WHITTEN (See Witten)
 Charlotte (Godwin) 31
 Lewis 31

WICKLIFF
Robert   34

WILEY
Benton   24,25,84,85,86
Byron S.   24,84,85
Elvira   24,84
Ferdinand M. 24,84,85
Lucy Ann 24,83,84,85
Oscar   24,84,85
Robert 24,25,83,84,85
Robert May 24,82,83,84
                  85,86
Sally C. (Scott)   86
Sarah Catharine   82
Van Buren   24,84,85

WILKINSON
Sarah   51

WILLIAMS
Benjamin   33
Doctor   24,84
Elizabeth E.   50
Evan   34
Fanny   12
John   67
Nathaniel   3
Robert   3
Samuel G.   20
William   50

WILLIAMSON
Capt. Charles   75

WIL(L)SON
John   61
Robert   1
Robert R.   21

WILLOUGHBY
Joseph   23

WINE
Michael   45

WINN
Martha   18

WINSLOW
Agatha Beverley   24
Beverley   23
Catherine R.   24
Henry   24
Mary   24
Thomas   24
William   24

WINSMITH
Dr. John   70

WITHERS
Richard   56

WITTEN (See Whitten)
Samuel K.   32

WOFFARD
Joseph   15

WOLF
Elizabeth   14
George   14
Jacob   14

WOMBLE
Jordan   79

WOOD
Eleanor H.   48
Joshua   48

WOODFORK
Agatha C.   23
Samuel   23

WOODVILLE
James L.   25,85

WOODWARD
Prudence   52

WOTTEN
William   29

WRIGHT (See Right)
Archibald   11
Gabriel   11
George   11,45
Henry   11
John   22
Richard   1
Susanna   45
William   11

WYATT
Capt. Nicholas   56

WYKE
Peter   62

WYND
Mrs. Frances   68

YATES
   Alice (Jr.)   53

YEARDLEY
   Argall   105
   Francis   105
   Capt. Francis   105
   Sarah (Offley) 105

YOULLE
   Thomas   61

YOUNG
   Hannah   50
   Hercules   50
   James   30
   Sarah   50

720   1153

39